BATTLE FOR THE MARBLE PALACE

ABE FORTAS, EARL WARREN,
LYNDON JOHNSON, RICHARD NIXON
and the FORGING of the
MODERN SUPREME COURT

MICHAEL BOBELIAN

Library of Congress Cataloguing-in-Publication Data.

Names: Bobelian, Michael, author.
Title: Battle for the marble palace : Abe Fortas, Earl Warren, Lyndon
  Johnson, Richard Nixon, and the forging of the modern Supreme Court /
  Michael Bobelian.
Description: Tucson, Arizona : Schaffner Press, Inc., 2019. |
Identifiers: LCCN 2019002222 (print) | LCCN 2019002311 (ebook) | ISBN
  9781943156672 (Pdf) | ISBN 9781943156689 (Epub) | ISBN 9781943156696 (
  Mobi) | ISBN 9781943156665 (hardback)
Subjects: LCSH: United States. Supreme Court--Officials and
  employees—Selection and appointment—History. | Judges—United
  States—Selection and appointment—History. | Fortas, Abe. | United
  States. Supreme Court—History. | Jewish judges—United States—Biography.
  | Warren, Earl, 1891-1974. | Johnson, Lyndon B. (Lyndon Baines),
  1908–1973. | Nixon, Richard M. (Richard Milhous), 1913–1994. | United
  States—Politics and government—History—20th century. | Brown, Oliver,
  1918–1961—Trials, litigation, etc. | Topeka (Kan.). Board of
  Education—Trials, litigation, etc. | BISAC: HISTORY / United States /
  20th Century. | LAW / Government / Federal.
Classification: LCC KF8776 (ebook) | LCC KF8776 .B63 2019 (print) | DDC
  347.73/2634—dc23
LC record available at https://lccn.loc.gov/2019002222

www.schaffnerpress.com

BATTLE FOR THE MARBLE PALACE

Abe Fortas, Earl Warren,
Lyndon Johnson, Richard Nixon
and the Forging of the
Modern Supreme Court

MICHAEL BOBELIAN

schaffner
press

So Long, Earl

Easy on the criminal,
Tough on the cop;

Warren is finally
Going to stop.

Not that it matters.
The damage is done.

Fortas and Thornberry:
On with the fun!

Isn't it curious?
All my dislike

Stems from a Justice
Appointed by Ike.

— by W. H. von Dreele
(*National Review* – July 16, 1968)

To my father, Antranik
Who encouraged me to pursue my dreams

Contents

Author's Preface

My journey in writing this book began seven years ago when I came across a list on the U.S. Senate website of every Supreme Court nomination dating back to 1789. What captivated me about this list was the sudden break in the long and steady succession of uncontroversial nominations beginning in 1968, almost as if a cataclysmic force had revolutionized the confirmation process. Nearly all of the nominees prior to that year, I noticed, were confirmed within days through voice votes, a procedure the Senate employed to vote expeditiously and often unanimously. The most glaring oddity was that in the seven decades leading up to that fateful year, only one nominee failed to get confirmed, a stark contrast to the success rate over the next half century. Attending law school a decade after Robert Bork's abortive nomination in 1987, I was under the widely-held impression that his experience established a new paradigm for Supreme Court nominations, giving birth to the term "Borked" to describe the unorthodox tactics used to defeat him. But looking at the Senate's website made me question this conventional wisdom. It seemed that events in 1968—and not 1987 almost twenty years later—ushered in the modern confirmation process. Fascinated by what I observed, my quest to unearth the origins of this mysterious transformation and its potential repercussions on the present-day Court led to this book.

I later discovered that a series of acrimonious nominations that began during the last days of Lyndon Johnson's presidency in 1968 and continued into Richard Nixon's first term did not take place in a vacuum. They were the culmination of the conflicts surrounding the Court during the 1950s and '60s over civil rights, criminal justice, school prayer, reapportionment, obscenity, and communist subversion. To understand this historic disruption, I therefore had to look deeper into the past and search beyond the confirmation process to find answers.

The 1960s have been a popular subject for countless historians. Likewise, the Supreme Court under Chief Justice Earl Warren's tenure has been well-chronicled by Bernard Schwartz, Lucas Powe Jr., Mark Tushnet, Richard Kluger, and other renowned scholars. Some of the primary characters in this story have also been the subjects of stellar biographies by Robert Caro, Bruce Allen Murphy, and Jim Newton to name a few. *Battle for the Marble Palace* straddles these genres: part biography, part legal analysis, and in large part, a dramatic narrative account of the monumental clashes over the Warren Court that pitted its greatest champions against its most vengeful enemies.

My goal as a chronicler of history is to get my readers to take notice of past events through the power of a dramatic narrative, the discovery of new facts, and the realignment of established ones to forge a new understanding of the cultural and political climate in which these events took place. In that light, this book is neither a legal analysis of the Court's historic cases nor a general history of the 1960s. While some of the episodes that appear in these pages— namely the South's defiance of *Brown v. Board*—have been deeply explored elsewhere, this book examines this era through a different vantage point that spotlights other lesser known—yet equally consequential—battles centered upon the Court. Along with the backlash to *Brown,* these now-forgotten conflicts fueled the Court's politicization, positioning the judicial body at the center of the nation's most divisive debates, and established its status as a pillar of electoral politics, transforming the contest over its future from a mundane, hum-drum selection of justices into a no-holds-barred political brawl that reverberates to this day.

Looking back years later to the origins of this story, I now view the recent tumultuous nominations of Merrick Garland, Neil Gorsuch, and Brett Kavanaugh as telling reminders of what had prompted me to begin this journey in the first place. I hope that you as the reader will find this chapter in our history and its long-term repercussions as intriguing as I did.

MB—Nov. 2018

Prologue

JULY, 1968

When Justice Abe Fortas sat down for his third day of testimony during his nomination hearings on a steaming summer day in the nation's capital, he remained confident of his promotion to Chief Justice. What he did not foresee—what his sharp mind, years of experience, and tireless preparation could not have prepared him for—was that he was about to become an unwitting target in a confrontation that would change the course of history, and find himself in the role of a modern-day version of a hero in a Greek tragedy.

Despite some unexpected resistance to his ascension, he had every reason to feel optimistic. Foes and friends alike recognized Fortas as a brilliant lawyer. Rising from a humble upbringing by immigrant parents in Memphis, he graduated second in his class at Yale Law School. After teaching at his alma mater and stints in various New Deal agencies, he co-founded Arnold, Fortas & Porter, one of the nation's premier law firms. During two decades of guiding corporate clients through Washington's political and regulatory labyrinths, he established a reputation as a fixer. He was a "brain surgeon . . . the guy you call when all else fails," a colleague recalled. But he wasn't just a hired gun for well-heeled clients. Working pro bono, he stood up to Joseph McCarthy and prevailed in *Gideon v. Wainwright*, the groundbreaking case requiring government-funded lawyers for indigent defendants. Fortas and his wife, Carolyn Agger, a prominent tax lawyer, were one of the capital's original power couples. All of these accomplishments came before his arrival on the nation's highest court in 1965.

Aside from these gold-plated credentials, the biggest factor in Fortas's favor was the backing of his patron—President Lyndon Johnson. Other than the Vietnam War, the task of getting Fortas appointed was Johnson's primary obsession in his final months in office. Johnson for years had benefited from Fortas's first-rate legal skills and command of Washington's gamesmanship. Both professionally and personally, their relationship flourished, and by the mid-1960s Fortas had emerged as the president's personal lawyer and political confidant. It was a well-known secret in Washington that no matter the nature of a crisis, the president sought Fortas's counsel: "He's the wisest man I have ever known," the president told his staff.

Eager to secure his dear friend a seat on the Court, Johnson maneuvered Justice Arthur Goldberg into resigning from the bench in 1965 to make room for Fortas. Three years later, the president's desire to promote Fortas to replace the retiring Earl Warren represented far more than a reward to a beloved friend. Johnson sought to perpetuate the liberal dominance of the Court for another generation and safeguard his legacy in the process. At the age of fifty-eight, Fortas could build on Warren's accomplishments for decades to come and shield Johnson's vast legislative achievements from constitutional scrutiny.

Those accomplishments included crushing the South's insurmountable filibusters that had long derailed civil rights legislation. On their own, passage of the 1964 Civil Rights Act and the 1965 Voting Rights Act would have constituted historic feats. The enactment of his brainchild, the nearly two hundred laws dubbed the Great Society, cemented Johnson's status as a legislative genius. Only during the New Deal had Congress been so willing to a follow a president's lead. In the last major congressional showdown of his presidency, Johnson directed all of his acumen and political capital to getting Fortas confirmed.

History also pointed to an easy path for Fortas. Between 1894 and 1967, the Senate had confirmed all but one out of forty-six nominees, typically through voice votes in which senators bellowed out "Yeas" and "Nays" in a chorus instead of a formal roll call. The dearth of testimony accompanying these nominations often made confirmation hearings brief and uncontroversial: one lasted only five minutes. Unhindered by government investigators or inquisitive journalists, and unencumbered by advocacy groups, confirmations proceeded swiftly, many coming to a conclusion within days of a nomination.

Not only did these historic precedents and political factors point to Fortas's inevitable ascension, nothing about Fortas's appointment as an associate justice three years earlier portended any hazards. During his nomination in 1965, Fortas slugged softballs thrown at him by the Judiciary Committee in just three hours of testimony. Despite Fortas's extensive entanglements with the president, neither the Department of Justice nor the Senate conducted any background checks. Special interest groups stayed on the sidelines and the media didn't bother to rummage for scandals. The Senate had hardly bothered to stage a debate before confirming Fortas as an Associate Justice through a voice vote. The entire process took a mere fortnight.

Nothing in Fortas's profile had changed since his swift confirmation in 1965. No one had discovered any black marks on his record and his judicial outlook turned out to be exactly as predicted: a liberal ideologue in the mold of the outgoing chief justice.

Little had changed as well to the Senate's composition during those three years. Democrats still outnumbered Republicans by a two-to-one margin and the same men held leadership posts. Within the Judiciary Committee, fifteen of its seventeen members remained unchanged, including its chairman, James Eastland of Mississippi, whose generous treatment of Fortas in 1965 earned him an invitation to Fortas's celebration party.

Swelling with confidence, Fortas arranged for his clerks to take over some of the administrative tasks typically handled by the Chief Justice's office soon after Johnson announced his nomination on June 26, 1968. He wasn't the only one in Washington to make this presumption: In an editorial endorsing Fortas, *The New York Times* proclaimed that when the "Supreme Court reopens in the fall . . . Fortas will move up . . . to stage center as Chief Justice."

But something was different this time around. Radically different! Unbeknownst to anyone at the time, the Fortas nomination would turn out to be the turning point of a historic transformation that revolutionized the confirmation process and the launching point for the conservative takeover of the Court.

A maverick his entire career, no one was more willing to sabotage Fortas than Strom Thurmond and to buck the capital's pundits and breach the deep-seated customs governing judicial confirmations standing in his way. Enraged by the Democratic Party's turn towards civil rights, Thurmond bolted from the party to become the Republican kingmaker in the South. Unlike some of his peers, however, Thurmond had no qualms over his unapologetic defense of Jim Crow. "We talk about somebody being more Catholic than the Pope," observed a senate aide. "Strom had become more Confederate than Robert E. Lee." The South Carolina Senator reinforced his status as one of the region's leading opponents of integration after the Court issued *Brown v. Board*, the 1954 ruling declaring segregation unconstitutional. Since then, few politicians had spent more time bashing the Warren Court: "Warren has done more harm to the American way of life than any other man holding public office in the history of our country," Thurmond declared weeks earlier, reiterating a theme he had uttered repeatedly since *Brown*.

While *Brown* embodied the Court's original sin in Thurmond's eyes, its other groundbreaking rulings morphed the judicial body into his ultimate bogeyman. "What is wrong" with American society, he asked in his jeremiad, *The Faith We Have Not Kept*, published months before Fortas's nomination. "The trouble began with the attack on the Constitution" and that "assault . . . is being led by the Supreme Court." Under Warren's watch, the Court had indeed upended large segments of American life through a series of far-reaching decisions. It handicapped the government's anti-communist crusade at the height of the Cold War, ended a practice dating back to colonial times in banning prayer in schools, expanded the right to privacy by abolishing restrictions on birth control, invalidated nearly every legislative district in the nation, shielded criminal defendants, and liberated erotica from Victorian-minded censors.

Historically, the Court had taken a back seat in America's culture wars. Under Warren's watch, however, it had evolved into a prominent—and often the preeminent—voice on the most contentious debates of the era. Up until the onset of the Great Society in the mid-1960s, this positioned the Court at the vanguard of American liberalism. In contrast to the liberals extolling this judicial revolution, Thurmond pinned the nation's ills on the justices: "The chief fountain of lawlessness in this country," he declared in *The Faith We Have Not Kept*, is the "United States Supreme Court."

Despite the radical nature of his accusations, when it came to the Court, Thurmond was no outlier. Though he was an unusually vocal segregationist, his antipathy reflected sentiments popular throughout the South. Likewise, his hostility towards the Court's other rulings was consistent with large segments of the populace. Nearly four in five Americans abhorred the Court's school prayer ban and its criminal procedure cases helped turn law and order into the electorate's top concern and a centerpiece of Richard Nixon's 1968 presidential run. As pornography proliferated, three-quarters of the American public found the loosening of its censorship abominable.

From its origins in the South, this enmity spread throughout the nation in the 1950s and '60s, helping to coalesce the voters—evangelicals, blue-collar workers, and southerners—who now constitute the foundation of the modern-day Republican Party. By 1964, these assaults on the Court became fixtures in national elections. While previous presidential candidates had eschewed exploiting the Court's unpopularity—Franklin Roosevelt, for instance, refused to turn the Court into an electoral issue in 1936—attacks upon the Court became central components of the presidential campaigns mounted by Barry Goldwater and Richard Nixon.

What made Thurmond unique among the Warren Court's critics was not his denunciation of its rulings, which were widespread, but his assaults on the institution's standing in the nation's constitutional framework. The 1956 Southern Manifesto he co-authored called upon his fellow southerners to defy the Court. Not one of the Court's detractors through the ages, whether abolitionists fuming over *Dred Scott* or frustrated New Dealers, ever questioned the Court's authority. Masterminding or serving as a wingman for dozens of legislative actions throughout Warren's tenure, Thurmond tried to put the Manifesto's words into law. These efforts included attempts to impose term limits for the justices, grant the Senate the power to overrule the Court, direct federal judges to ignore any rulings breaking with precedent, and require justices with judicial experience. This fervor to profoundly transform the Court's role in a constitutional order nearly two centuries old knew no bounds. Thurmond backed the formation of a new judicial body to supersede the Court. If that wasn't extreme enough, so frustrated by the Court's handiwork, its detractors fell one state short of calling for a Constitutional Convention for the first time since 1787 to undo its rulings! As unpopular as the Court may have been—from 1949 to 1973, the percentage of Americans expressing "great confidence" in the Court plummeted from 83 to 32 percent, the largest drop for any branch of government—and despite carrying significant support within Congress, the unwillingness of many Americans to so dramatically alter the Constitution foiled these attacks.

This litany of failures convinced Thurmond that the best means to control the Court was through its make-up. "In its contest with the Supreme Court," he came to conclude in 1968, "Congress is fighting a losing battle at present. The only power Congress has chosen to exert over the Court is the power of confirmation." Taking this bitter lesson to heart, Thurmond and his allies devised a simple yet blunt strategy now so widely accepted it seems self-evident: keep liberals off the Court and supplant them with conservatives. No matter how outlandish or unprecedented, their willingness to topple the long-established norms Fortas effortlessly navigated just three years earlier transformed the confirmation process from a routine, almost casual, practice that had seen little friction in the past to a no-holds-barred brawl. Thurmond was mindful of the ramifications of his undertaking: "If the Senate refuses to confirm . . . Fortas . . . ," he wrote to his constituents, "it will be a turning point in modern American history."

The harshness that Fortas had endured from Eastland and North Carolina Senator Sam Ervin during the first two days of questioning made it clear to Court observers that this confirmation would not play out uneventfully like those of yesteryear. The prospect of a heavyweight bout between Thurmond and Fortas enticed members of the Washington press corps to show up en masse for the third day of the justice's testimony. To accommodate the overflow of spectators, the Judiciary Committee moved the session from its cramped chamber to the Caucus Room. Capable of holding more than 300 people, it was an ideal—and at a time when these hearings weren't televised, an exclusive—venue for a spectacle. Those in attendance didn't come away disappointed. The highpoint of Thurmond's performance, the moment he delivered the coup de grace marking Fortas's descent from a heroic figure to a scandalized pariah, came during the justice's testimony. Reaching a crescendo after hours of interrogating the witness, Thurmond accused Fortas of encouraging criminals "to commit rapes."

The tirade was just one of the many breaks with well-established customs. Republicans crossed party lines to team up with Southern Democrats to orchestrate the first filibuster for a Court appointment. Just by itself, the willingness to wield the Senate's ultimate parliamentary weapon set the Fortas confirmation apart from its predecessors. But it was only the opening salvo. Warren's enemies accused the Chief Justice of timing his retirement to prevent a Republican president from naming his successor. Claiming Johnson was a lame duck despite ample precedent for successful Court appointments in a president's final year in office, the Court's detractors—much like Mitch McConnell would do in 2016—called for the next president to fill the vacancy. Critics labelled Fortas a crony for his close relationship with the president, exploited questionable earnings from teaching a course to tarnish his reputation, and invited social conservatives to brand Fortas a guardian of criminals and pornographers. Even that last smear failed to satisfy the Court's enemies. Aiming for the jugular, Thurmond aired a series of adult movies to highlight Fortas's lax moral standards. On top of labeling Fortas a greedy crony with a soft-spot for thugs and a penchant for pornography, his adversaries pummeled him with tendentious questions and ad hominem diatribes through eleven days of hearings that stretched over two months. This outlasted the total number of days spent on all of Franklin Roosevelt's nine nominees to the Court. Some of these antics now seem par for the course. But at the time, they were revolutionary and it was during this era that they became fixtures in a process we've lived with to this day.

How has this transformative event been lost to history? The year 1968 burst with enough drama to generate a film festival worth of documentaries. Weeks into the new year, the Tet Offensive demolished the prevailing notion of impending victory in Vietnam. Before the shock had worn off, Johnson did the unthinkable in declining to run for reelection. Less than a week later, on

April 4, Dr. Martin Luther King Jr.'s assassination ignited riots that subsumed a dozen cities in fire and mayhem, which even for a decade of unparalleled turmoil surpassed all previous conflagrations. Another gunman murdered Robert Kennedy two months later and the summer of carnage continued at the Democratic convention in Chicago as thousands of protestors clashed with Mayor Richard Daley's battalion of baton-wielding police. The bombshells continued into the election. As Nixon made one of the unlikeliest comebacks in political history, George Wallace captured the most electoral votes for a third-party candidate in fifty-six years by running on a platform of segregation and economic populism. If that wasn't enough to make 1968 one of the most consequential years in the nation's history, added to these events were Huey Newton's trial, the My Lai massacre, the near downfall of the French republic, the Prague Spring, and the memorable image of Olympic medalists Tommie Smith and John Carlos raising their fists in protest during the award ceremony at the Mexico City Games.

Coming in quick succession, the surfeit of news crowded out this transformative episode taking place in the senate. Yet, just as the Biblical flood marked a clear demarcation of events occurring before and after the deluge, Fortas's nomination fundamentally altered the Court, turning the selection of justices into high-stakes contests over the future of the nation. The noxious confirmation clashes surrounding Clement Haynsworth, G. Harrold Carswell, Robert Bork, Clarence Thomas, Merrick Garland, Neil Gorsuch, and Brett Kavanaugh are a testament to this reality. It's therefore no coincidence that some of the revolutionary tactics deployed in 1968 reemerged in recent confirmation fights over the replacements for Antonin Scalia and Anthony Kennedy. And contrary to conventional wisdom, Bork's nomination in 1986 did not usher in the modern confirmation process. After a peaceful lull, it represented an atavistic return to the cultural, partisan, and ideological wars of this earlier era.

The Fortas nomination also marked the first major step of the conservative crusade to seize control of the Court. Buoyed by originalism and textualism—a pair of judicial philosophies harnessed to promote a conservative agenda—and buttressed by a network of well-financed institutions, like the Federalist Society and the Heritage Foundation, committed to refashioning the federal judiciary, this takeover spanned half a century. Although this movement suffered some setbacks—Harry Blackmun, John Paul Stevens, and David Souter, in particular—it ultimately ushered in the right's domination of the Court and rallied Republican voters, perhaps none more so than Donald Trump's supporters.

But before conservative leaders could put this plan into effect, before they developed the institutions and roster of jurists necessary to restock the Court with proven and reliable ideologues, before they had even devised a workable blueprint for an undertaking that would take decades to come to fruition, they first sought to end the Warren Court's perpetuation under Fortas. Embittered by years of defeat and frustration, they were willing to shatter just about every tradition that had governed the confirmation process since the nation's founding to do just that.

Fast forward fifty years, it is clear that both the tactics deployed against modern nominees as well as the political and ideological considerations that dominate present-day judicial politics hark back to Fortas's confirmation fight. Focused on the immediacy of the battle at hand, none of the adversaries in Fortas's confirmation realized that the episode would, in establishing the template for modern judicial politics, come to serve as a pivotal moment in the nation's history. Instead, as Fortas and Thurmond faced each other down like a pair of rivals out of ancient mythology, they plotted their next moves.

LYNDON JOHNSON AND
ABE FORTAS SHARING A
LAUGH IN THE WHITE
HOUSE, JULY 29, 1965

LBJ Library photo by
Yoichi Okamoto

PART I

CHAPTER I

"This Appointment is Going to be Terribly Unpopular"

The future greatness of America depends upon racial purity and maintenance of Anglo-Saxon institutions, which still flourish in full flower in the South. —James Eastland

We unanimously conclude that, in the field of public education, the doctrine of 'separate but equal' has no place. —Earl Warren (from *Brown v. Board*)

JUNE, 1968

Lyndon Johnson spent the early hours of June 26, 1968 scrambling to lock down the final details of Abe Fortas's nomination. Between eight phone calls and a pair of meetings in the Oval Office, he snuck away for fifteen minutes to the White House's dispensary to follow up with a dermatologist on his skin cancer operation conducted months earlier. With time ticking on the press conference to announce the nomination, it was the only moment he had for himself during the hectic morning. While Johnson was directing his forces from the White House, Attorney General Ramsey Clark received word from Albert Jenner, chairman of the Standing Committee on the Federal Judiciary of the American Bar Association, that the committee had unanimously endorsed Fortas. Validation from the nation's preeminent legal organization wasn't so much a statutory or constitutional requirement but it was one of the many boxes Johnson checked off to inoculate the nomination from the opposition brewing in the Senate. During a phone call with

Clark a little after 9 a.m., Johnson provided last-minute edits to the letters he planned to exchange with Earl Warren formalizing the chief justice's retirement. That Johnson could enlist the attorney general as a scribe was testament to the resources and power at his disposal.

That power was now being tested like never before. Concerned by news of an emerging resistance to Fortas's ascendancy from Southern Democrats and insurgent Republicans, Johnson had spent the past several days fortifying his long-held alliances with the Senate's leadership. Unable to meet in person with Senate Judiciary Committee Chairman James Eastland, Johnson called for a meeting with the senator upon his return from Mississippi to try to shore up the last major holdout. It wasn't going to be easy to coax Eastland, an ardent segregationist who despised Fortas, a jurist who was widely recognized for his commitment to civil rights.

Eastland's roots in southern lore went far deeper than his family's multi-million dollar land holdings, which he administered like a modern-day plantation master, albeit a gentler one who "never whips his niggers and would fire any white worker who did." His maternal grandfather was descended from a local aristocrat, a Civil War cavalry officer who served with one of the eventual founders of the KKK. His paternal line was equally embroiled in the South's fraught racial history. When Eastland's uncle died in a shootout with a former sharecropper, Eastland's father, Woods, took it upon himself to avenge the death. The manhunt proceeded like a Hollywood B movie: Woods's posse killed several innocent bystanders in the pursuit and browbeat a sheriff detaining the purported killer, Luther Holbert. The thousand viewers Woods beckoned to attend Holbert's lynching were not left disappointed by the spectacle. Eastland's father tied Holbert and his girlfriend to a tree. After that, the couple had their fingers cut off while spectators bore into Holbert with a corkscrew. The two were then thrown into a bonfire and burned alive, the victims of one of the region's grizzliest lynchings. Coming at the turn of the century, such race-based cruelty was to be expected in the South. Despite the bountiful evidence against Woods, the judge presiding over his trial dismissed the charges.

Born months after this lynching in 1904 on his family's 5,000-acre cotton farm in the Mississippi Delta, Eastland later developed an interest in politics while attending the University of Mississippi. He spent four years in the state legislature during his twenties and, after a nine-year hiatus practicing law, entered the Senate in 1941. Celebrated for using his pulpit to prop up cotton prices, Eastland was referred to by locals in the Delta as "Our Jim". Fifteen years later, ironically at the behest of Johnson, who was at the time Senate Majority Leader, Eastland became the youngest chairman of the Judiciary Committee, the body responsible for overseeing judicial appointments and civil rights legislation.

Like many of his southern colleagues to come of age in the wake of the Civil War and the demise of the Confederacy, Eastland was a devout segregationist dedicated to white supremacy. Calling African-Americans "an inferior race" on the Senate floor, Eastland believed that the "future greatness of America depends upon racial purity and maintenance of Anglo-Saxon institutions, which still flourish in full flower in the South." *Time* magazine dubbed him the "spiritual leader of Southern resistance" to integration. Unlike some of his peers, Eastland didn't dress up these beliefs with politeness. A civil rights advocate compared Eastland's style with that of Mississippi's other senator, John Stennis:

> The difference between Eastland and Stennis is that Stennis is a segregationist, Northern-style. He uses subtlety. Eastland would say, point blank, "Get the hell out of here, I ain't going to serve you because you're black." Stennis would say, "You don't have a reservation." But either way, you still haven't eaten. One is shrewd and sophisticated in promulgating segregation, the other is blatant—and maybe more honest.

From his post on the Judiciary Committee, Eastland gobbled up 127 civil rights bills like a whale feeding on plankton. The cigar-smoking senator relished the role, boasting of stuffing these bills in his deep pockets.

As influential as he was within the halls of Congress, he was powerless outside of it. To his chagrin, once justices steered their way through his committee they forever lay beyond his reach. This powerlessness added to his enmity towards the Court. A 1965 profile in the *Nation* pointed out that while Eastland lacked his peers' propensity for theatrics, "he has few rivals as an accomplished vilifier of the Supreme Court." Branding the justices a "crowd of parasitic politicians . . . brainwashed by left-wing pressure groups," Eastland vowed to defy the Court's "monstrous proposition" of integration. For fourteen years, he had repeatedly tried and failed to do just that.

Despite Eastland's antagonism towards the Warren Court, his position as the gatekeeper for judicial confirmations meant Johnson had no choice but to turn to him. As chairman of the Judiciary Committee, Eastland "was a power to be reckoned with," remembered Jake Jacobsen, the president's legislative counsel. "If you didn't go along with Jim Eastland on something, he would slaughter you." In what would be a recurring theme in his quest to get Fortas confirmed, the president was repeatedly forced to seek out dubious allies — a skill he had mastered years earlier. Both as Senate Majority Leader in the 1950s and later as president, he never allowed partisan and ideological differences to impede him from reaching out to his adversaries to forge alliances. His relationship with Eastland was no different. Though the chairman persistently tried to obstruct Johnson's agenda, the president had regularly conferred with Eastland since stepping into the White House.

Heading into his meeting with Eastland on the morning of June 26, Johnson had reason to be concerned. Republicans in the Senate, who had never put up much of a fight against the president's legislative agenda, were conjuring up a resistance even before Warren's retirement had been officially announced. The GOP's southern field commander, Strom Thurmond, had vowed to the press that no matter whom Johnson picked, he would "emphatically" and "unalterably" oppose the selection. Though Thurmond was a blowhard whom Johnson could normally dismiss, what made Thurmond's pledge so threatening was the number of Republicans joining him from outside the South. No longer isolated within the Party of Lincoln, Thurmond was now joined by senators from Hawaii, Texas, and Michigan. In recognition of this mounting uproar surrounding the potential vacancy, the June 22 headline by Lyle Denniston, the Supreme Court reporter at the *Washington Star*, the leading city daily alongside the *Washington Post* at the time, announced a "Senate Battle" over Warren's successor. On the same day, *The New York Times* mused over the possibility of an 8-8 tie in the Judiciary Committee should enough of its Republican members team up with the committee's southerners.

A Senate battle? An 8-8 tie? Caught off-guard by the unexpected resistance, Johnson sought Eastland's counsel. He had often relied on Eastland's standing among the Senate's southern contingent to gather information on the twenty or so senators who made up the solidly conservative bloc. Eastland was also, Johnson felt, "one of the best sources of intelligence in the Senate on what the Republicans were doing." The findings Eastland relayed over a series of conversations with Johnson's team over the previous week were disconcerting. On June 24, Eastland told the deputy attorney general, Warren Christopher, "that a fight was building up over the Chief Justiceship." As Johnson's congressional liaisons reported similar findings, Eastland added harrowing details in the early afternoon of June 25. He warned "that a filibuster was already being organized against Fortas" and that it would likely succeed. Southerners were renowned for mounting filibusters, but the parliamentary weapon had never blocked a Court nomination before. Such a move would break with nearly two centuries of precedent.

Eastland wasn't one to exaggerate the magnitude of these threats. As chairman of the Judiciary Committee since 1956, he had seen—and partaken in—an endless stream of southern attacks upon the Warren Court. The group's most notable accomplishment was harassing Dwight Eisenhower's nominee, Potter Stewart, in 1959. Enraged with *Brown*, the southern bloc badgered Stewart with questions—which were more like accusations—about the Court's overreach and managed to delay the confirmation for more than seven months. But they could do little more, garnering a mere seventeen votes against him. They managed to do even less going forward. Byron White, John F. Kennedy's first nominee, waited a mere eight days to get confirmed. Kennedy's second selection, Arthur Goldberg, also breezed to his confirmation in less than a month. On both occasions, the Senate didn't bother to hold a roll call, confirming both men through voice votes, the same procedure used to confirm Fortas as an associate justice in 1965.

If the southern senators had any real bite to their bark, they would have surely blocked Thurgood Marshall's appointment to the Court less than a year earlier. Instead, after a great deal of huffing and puffing that produced plenty of fireworks during Marshall's testimony but little actual results, Marshall was confirmed with a mere eleven votes lodged against him. The failure to defeat *Brown*'s architect was the latest setback in a long list of lost battles by the southern contingent against the Warren Court. While they carped and complained and sometimes delayed the inevitable, the bottom line was that most of their bravado was either a show put on for voters back home or public venting sessions rather than genuine threats to disrupt a succession of new justices throughout the 1950s and '60s who universally supported *Brown*. The fact was that the southern senators who so reviled the Warren Court had not even come close to knocking out a single one of their targets during this series of confirmations.

Things were rapidly changing this time. Having surveyed ten of his colleagues, Eastland noticed that they were "very bitter and outspoken against Fortas." The chairman warned the attorney general that he "had never seen so much feeling against a man as against Fortas."

Others dispatched equally distressing news to the White House. The president's congressional liaison reported that West Virginia's Robert Byrd vowed to do "'everything in . . . his power' to oppose Abe Fortas." Louisiana's Russell Long, according to Johnson's aide, called Fortas "one of the dirty five" for siding "with the criminal against the victims of crime." Long confirmed Eastland's chilling prediction: nominating Fortas would invite a filibuster and pose "real trouble" for the president.

The ABA's endorsement, the finalization of Warren's retirement letter, and other last-minute details were now completed. At 10:37 a.m., less than an hour before reporters were scheduled to squeeze into the Oval Office to hear Johnson's announcement, the president welcomed Eastland at the White House to obtain his blessing. That was a big favor to ask of a man who despised Warren for what he considered to be the chief justice's greatest transgression—the dismantling of a way of life Eastland had spent a lifetime defending.

While historians still debate the causes of the Civil War, the constitutional transformation marshaled in its aftermath paints a far clearer picture. Collectively known as the Civil War Amendments, the Thirteenth, Fourteenth, and Fifteenth Amendments aspired to make manifest the Declaration of Independence's proclamation: "All men are created equal."

Ratified months after Robert E. Lee's surrender in 1865, the Thirteenth Amendment's abolition of slavery corrected the Founding Fathers' greatest sin: the inclusion of bondage in the nation's constitutional fabric. The nation still had to contend with determining just what constitutional rights African-Americans would enjoy. The answer came forth in the Fourteenth Amendment. Enacted three years after the abolition of slavery, it granted citizenship to the freed slaves, bequeathing to them the rights enjoyed by all Americans, and empowered Congress to enforce this new status. In 1870, the Fifteenth Amendment propelled the freed slaves one step closer to full citizenship by granting them the right to vote.

Of the three, the Fourteenth Amendment proved to be the most consequential. Over time, its "due process" and "equal protection" clauses came to apply most of the Bill of Rights to the States and shield not just African-Americans from discrimination but extend its protections to women, gays, and others. By the end of the 20th century, the amendment's reach encompassed concepts as far-ranging as marriage to privacy to criminal procedure. Its original beneficiaries, however, were supposed to be the four million emancipated slaves and their descendants.

Buttressed by federal troops stationed throughout the former Confederacy and a series of statutes enacting the Civil War Amendments, the "Radical Republicans" in control of Congress genuinely resolved to improve the lot of African-Americans. Relying both on the sword and the law, Reconstruction, as it came to be known, represented an unprecedented but ultimately futile attempt to reformulate a way of life centuries in the making. Certainly, conditions for African-Americans improved after the Civil War. They were no longer treated as chattel, could move freely throughout the United States, and enjoyed a modicum of economic prosperity. But though the amendments signified the most far-reaching change to the Constitution since the Bill of Rights, without a systematic effort to restructure the fabric of southern life they would have little bearing for African-Americans. "The law on the side of freedom is of great advantage," renowned African-American abolitionist Frederick Douglass correctly noted, "only when there is power to make that law respected."

No African-American was spared from the debasement of second-class citizenship, not even a congressman. When travelling, "I am treated, not as an American citizen but as a brute," complained Mississippi's first black congressman, John Lynch, on the House floor. "Forced to occupy a filthy smoking car both night and day, with drunkards, gamblers, and criminals; and for what? Not that I am unable or unwilling to pay my way; not that I am obnoxious in my personal appearance or disrespectful in my conduct; but simply because I happen to be of a darker complexion."

Life for the emancipated slaves turned for the worse when federal troops departed from the region in 1877, wiping away most of the modest gains in civil rights made during Reconstruction. Unrepentant for plunging the nation into its bloodiest war, and without remorse for committing one of history's cruelest, longest-running crimes, the Ku Klux Klan's wave of terror characterized the most notorious manifestation of the region's hatred of the 13th Amendment. "The reason of all this is simple and manifest," observed Carl Schurz, a renowned journalist and Civil War general. "The whites esteem the blacks their property by natural right, and however much they admit that the individual relations of masters and slaves have been destroyed . . . they still have an ingrained feeling that the blacks . . . belong to the whites."

Once extricated from federal oversight, southern whites sought to restore blacks to their pre-war status. "They are to be returned to a condition of serfdom," explained Mississippi Governor Adelbert Ames. The dismantling of Reconstruction took place gradually and fitfully. In their first volley, southern whites crushed the fledgling bases of African-American political power. A combination of bullying, electoral fraud, gerrymandering, and the enactment of poll taxes, literacy tests, and other means to rob blacks of suffrage eventually turned the region into a one-party state monopolized by white Democrats.

Next came the exclusion of blacks from the criminal justice system. African-Americans were expelled from police forces and kept off juries. Slowly but surely, the Civil War Amendments and those civil rights bills associated with them lost their potency. A southern newspaper openly declared the region's intent "to make them dead letters on the statute-book."

Stripped of political power, African-Americans had no defense against the economic serfdom that followed. Laws intended to vastly increase African-American incarceration rates supplied the region's white population with cheap labor. Changes to agricultural laws intended to muzzle the growth of free labor pushed nearly all the risk of sharecropping on to black farm workers while granting white landowners most of the economic upside. Deprived of their northern patrons and embattled by white-dominated state governments, African-Americans looked to the judiciary for help. Like every public institution in the South, it too was rigged against them. The courts, critics declared, "are employed to reenslave the colored race."

Though African-Americans never again were subjected to bondage, southern whites had managed to retract most of Reconstruction's gains by the end of the nineteenth century. While it's difficult to accurately gauge the headway made by the freed slaves during Reconstruction, and the subsequent erosion of these advances, one quantifiable measure of African-American progress can be seen in the number of black congressmen elected after the Civil War. Black representation peaked in the 44th Congress (1875-77) with one Senator and seven Representatives. After Reconstruction came to an end in 1877, the number of African-Americans dropped to four and never recovered, hovering between one to three until 1901. With Reconstruction a distant memory by that point, not one of the eleven states of the former Confederacy—Alabama, Arkansas, Florida, Georgia, Louisiana, Mississippi, South Carolina, North Carolina, Tennessee, Texas, and Virginia—would return another African-American to Congress until 1973.

By the turn of the 20th century, liberty and equality—the high-minded concepts extolled in the nation's founding documents—seemed nearly as distant to southern blacks as they had to their forefathers a century earlier. "The most piteous thing amid all the black ruin of war-time," W.E.B. Du Bois wrote of this predicament, "was the black freedman who threw down his hoe because the world called him free. What did such a mockery of freedom mean? Not a cent of money, not an inch of land, not a mouthful of victuals—not even ownership of the rags on his back."

Segregation stood as the bedrock of the apartheid state established throughout the South from the late 1800s through the mid-twentieth century. Nearly every element of public life, from the most essential (like schools) to the most pedestrian (such as bathrooms), remained segregated. Omnipresent "Colored" and "Whites Only" signs exemplified the pervasiveness of the laws and customs known as "Jim Crow". Private institutions mirrored this reality. Just about any commercial, social, or civic institution run by whites excluded African-Americans.

The indignities endured by blacks went beyond the realm of politics and law. A racist social hierarchy dominated the region's interactions. Popular games like "Hit the Coon" and "African Dodger," in which black figurines served as target practice, were popular attractions at festivals. In social interactions, African-Americans were obligated to defer to whites: greetings such as "yes sir" and "no sir" became the refrains used by the black population to address whites. It also meant that black men could not even offer their hand for a handshake as this implication of equality represented too much of an affront to whites. Those straying from these norms suffered intimidation, loss of work, or in extreme cases, death.

Anyone who looked at Jim Crow with an objective eye would have been stunned by how far this condition had strayed from the Constitution's mandates. It was as if, other than ending slavery, the bloodiest war in American history had changed little else.

Widespread lynching was the most diabolic manifestation of Jim Crow. From 1877 to 1950, white southerners lynched more than 4,000 African-Americans. These lynchings came in many forms. In most instances, white mobs hanged black victims. In other instances, they used more barbaric methods. These mobs acted with impunity: only twelve participants were ever convicted. Who after all, would punish them? "The cause of lynching is that we are the only Government on earth that has set up several thousand little-bitty, small, weak, distinctive governments," observed a southerner from the era. "These tiny kingdoms can kill their subjects like dogs if they want to."

The federal response to this horror was anemic. After Reconstruction had come to an end, Congress failed to pass a single piece of civil rights legislation for eighty years. With the federal government unable to intervene and the southern states operating under a one-party system resolved to extend white supremacy indefinitely, African-Americans developed their own institutions to advocate on their behalf. Founded in 1909 by Du Bois and others, the National Association for the Advancement of Colored People (NAACP) branched out across the United States, establishing itself as the nation's preeminent African-American advocacy group by the 1920s. Despite making headway in Congress, its top legislative priority aimed at combatting lynching was perpetually defeated. Of the nearly two hundred anti-lynching measures considered by Congress since the 1890s, the three approved by the House were derailed by Senate filibusters.

The executive branch didn't provide much recourse either. In need of southern allies to pass New Deal legislation, Franklin Roosevelt rejected the NAACP's entreaties to help defeat yet another filibuster in 1935. Though he embraced some civil rights initiatives, Roosevelt's response resembled that of other post-bellum presidents. Some like FDR were sympathetic towards African-Americans but did little on their behalf while others were outright hostile to the minority population. Roosevelt's capitulation provided yet another example of the failure of the political branches to come to the aid of African-Americans. This time around, even the most accomplished president of the twentieth century operating at the peak of his popularity had surrendered to the South.

The Court also deserved blame. It limited the scope of the Civil War Amendments during the late 1800s and early 1900s, preferring to utilize the amendments to shield corporations from economic regulation rather than safeguarding the rights of the emancipated slaves. The fact that the Court's first opportunity to enforce the Fourteenth Amendment in the *Slaughter-House Cases* involved southern butchers—and not African-Americans—symbolized this paradox.

Though the dispute at the center of the case arose from a localized monopoly granted by Louisiana to a single slaughterhouse, it had a far greater impact on the rights of African-Americans. Coming in 1873, just five years after the

Fourteenth Amendment's enactment, the *Slaughter-House Cases* should have been an easy victory for the robust protection of civil rights. This wasn't some ancient edict whose drafters were long gone and their intentions left to the mercy of historical ambiguity. Nor was there any question as to why its backers enacted the amendment. Turning away from these self-evident conclusions, the Court mortally wounded the Fourteenth Amendment and granted southern states immense autonomy over the treatment of their black citizenry.

The justices struck another blow against the southern black populace in an 1875 case involving a poll tax in Kentucky intended to curb African-American suffrage. According to Chief Justice Morrison Waite's opinion, the Fifteenth Amendment did "not confer the right of suffrage upon anyone." It was a befuddling conclusion. Why was the Amendment enacted if not to grant black men the right to vote (women began to vote in 1920)? The ruling wreaked havoc on African-American suffrage, giving a green light to poll taxes and literacy tests denying blacks access to the ballot. On top of these well-known tactics, southern governments placed polling places far away from African-American communities, changed polling locales without notice, and blocked roads on election day. The impact was crystal clear: "The Negro as a political force," observed an owner of the *Atlanta Constitution* in 1889, "has dropped out of serious consideration."

With some exceptions, the Court continued to neuter the Civil War Amendments in the post-bellum era. In 1896, this trajectory of cases culminated in *Plessy v. Ferguson*. The opinion issued by Justice Henry Billings Brown, whom the renowned historian Richard Kluger dubbed "one of the Court's dimmer lights," put the final dagger in the heart of the crowning jewel of the Civil War Amendments—the Fourteenth. *Plessy* endorsed segregation's hypocritical justifications and granted southern legislatures immense leeway in establishing an apartheid state, allowing them to codify into their legal systems the region's racist attitudes and traditions. "Gauged by this standard, we cannot say that a law which . . . requires the separation of the two races . . . is . . . obnoxious to the Fourteenth Amendment." Yet, that's exactly what the Fourteenth Amendment was supposed to do, eliminate a state's ability to treat African-Americans differently than—and deem them subservient to—its white citizens.

Just in case that wasn't enough, the Court further weakened the constitutional provision. In the past, the justices had at least differentiated between government actions and private discrimination, outlawing the former while allowing the latter. In *Plessy*, Louisiana's government instituted segregation. It wasn't the private railroad sued by Homer Plessy that wanted to separate the races and bear the expense of providing separate facilities, it was the state's idea. Applying the logic of its earlier precedents, the Court should have struck down Louisiana's law. Now, the justices scuttled that principle in approving not just state-sanctioned but state-mandated segregation. *Plessy* represented the Court's final capitulation to southern bigotry.

As the sole dissenting voice, John Marshall Harlan forecast the consequences of the Court's ruling. "The present decision . . . will not only stimulate aggressions . . . upon the admitted rights of colored citizens," he predicted, "but will encourage the belief that it is possible, by means of state enactments, to defeat the . . . recent amendments of the Constitution."

Harlan's prognostication soon came to fruition. "Why it is within the limits imposed by the Federal Constitution to establish white supremacy in this state," declared John Knox, the head of Alabama's constitutional convention, five years after *Plessy*. With the Court's blessing, southern governments instituted the final measures of a dystopia in which segregation took on totalitarian dimensions. As if trying to outdo one another, white legislatures found new ways of separating the races. They blocked blacks and whites from comingling in public spaces, outlawed interracial marriage, determined where blacks would live, and ensured that African-Americans received inferior services, education, and economic opportunities. Georgia and Arkansas went so far as to separate prisoners by race. South Carolina's courts ordered different bibles for the oaths administered to black and white witnesses.

For the South's ruling class, Jim Crow represented an all-encompassing political, legal, and social stratification of society. African-Americans deviating from these norms suffered unemployment and harassment, or worse, violent recriminations. As Jim Crow's constitutional foundation, *Plessy* came to dominate the region's popular imagination, serving as the white man's touchstone and the black man's nemesis.

During the 1930s and '40s, the NAACP and the head of its legal team, "Mr. Civil Rights" Thurgood Marshall, chipped away at *Plessy*'s flanks by exposing the farce that, while just about every institution in the South was segregated, African-American institutions were almost never equal to their white counterparts. In cases involving graduate schools, Marshall showed how all-black institutions were underfunded or didn't exist at all. One such victory in 1938 didn't reverse the legal underpinnings of segregation but signified that the justices were no longer willing to tolerate unequal facilities. Occurring the same year that Georgia Senator Richard Russell had decapitated a popular anti-lynching bill, the setback underscored the South's stranglehold over the legislative process. "We couldn't get a damned thing through Congress," Marshall remembered, despite actively lobbying for the provision. "We couldn't even get the anti-lynch bill through." These legislative failures confirmed to him that African-Americans "had to go to the courts."

With Marshall at the helm, other successes followed. During the 1940s, the NAACP relied on the federal judiciary to halt all-white primaries, stop segregation on interstate trains and buses, and quash the use of racially restrictive real estate covenants. For two decades, the NAACP's ability to expose the material and intangible deficiencies of black facilities undercut *Plessy*'s "separate but equal" doctrine. Yet, despite siding with the NAACP, the Court steadfastly declined to reexamine *Plessy*'s underlying logic.

By the 1950s, it was obvious to Marshall that the time had come to attack *Plessy* head on. When several cases questioning the constitutionality of segregated schooling emerged, the Court bundled five of them, collectively referred to as *Brown v. Board of Education of Topeka*. For decades, the campaign to overthrow segregation had rested on the shoulders of Marshall and his associates. Nine decades after the first shots were fired upon Fort Sumter, igniting a conflict ending with promises of liberty and equality to emancipated slaves, the fate of African-Americans was no longer in the hands of civil rights advocates. It was up to the justices to change the course of history.

The justices had first discussed *Brown* on December 13, 1952, a few weeks after oral arguments. Due to its overwhelmingly positive legacy, *Brown* now carries an air of inevitability. But at the time, the case proved to be one of the most vexing in the Court's history. Chief Justice Fred Vinson opened the conference by emphasizing the importance of decades of precedents dating back to *Plessy*. Because of his premature death, no one knows for sure how he would have voted. To those in the room, however, Vinson seemed unprepared to overrule *Plessy*.

Tom Clark also equivocated. Highly deferential to Vinson, the associate justice had voted with the chief justice 90% of the time and had grown up in a then-segregated Dallas. Thurgood Marshall nevertheless had high hopes for the former attorney general. In contrast to the regional mores of the time, Clark's mother ate dinner with her African-American housekeeper. "Now, back in the thirties," Marshall observed, "you didn't do that in Texas." However, sensing that *Plessy* wouldn't last much longer, Clark wasn't ready to bury segregation just yet.

Stanley Reed, like Vinson, hailed from segregated Kentucky, and was the least inclined to overturn *Plessy*. In 1947, he refused to attend a Christmas party because, for the first time, the Court's African-American employees had been invited to the event. When Justice Felix Frankfurter urged him to reconsider, Reed shot back: "this is purely a private matter." Reed's views on race did not change over the years. Just months before *Brown*'s oral arguments, he complained that a ruling barring the capital's restaurants from excluding African-Americans would allow a "nigra [to] walk into the restaurant at the Mayflower Hotel," where the Reeds lived, "and sit down to eat at the table right next to Mrs. Reed!" Unlike Vinson and Clark, he made his views clear: he would uphold *Plessy*.

Hugo Black, on the other hand, believed that the Fourteenth Amendment abolished segregation. It was a bold position for a former member of the KKK. William Douglas also moved to outlaw segregation. Though not as outspoken, both Sherman Minton and Harold Burton were prepared to overturn *Plessy* as well. Consistent with his long-held support of civil rights, Frankfurter, the self-appointed intellectual heavyweight of the group, also wanted to invalidate *Plessy*. He just needed to find a way to do it in a manner consistent with his judicial philosophy. Robert Jackson also abhorred Jim

Crow but struggled with bestowing the judiciary rather than the political branches the power to outlaw segregation.

Though the fractured group declined to take a formal vote, several justices later speculated that four to five of them would have upheld *Plessy*. Aware of the monumental task awaiting them, and desperate to produce a coherent outcome, the fragmented group froze. Frankfurter stepped into this quagmire with a delay tactic. Why not reschedule a new series of oral arguments? Before the justices gathered to witness the rematch, Vinson died suddenly of a heart attack. "This is the first indication I have ever had," Frankfurter told a pair of clerks of Vinson's passing, "that there is a God."

In the *Federalist Papers*, Alexander Hamilton dubbed the Supreme Court the "weakest of the three departments of power." Through much of its history, the Court's home reflected this perception. Changing locations at least a half dozen times, the Court met inside the Capitol building for most of its existence. The move in 1860 from the Capitol's basement to a more majestic chamber previously used by the Senate improved its surroundings but offered no reprieve from the cramped quarters, which forced the justices to work from home. After William Howard Taft became chief justice, he initiated the process of erecting a fortress-like edifice worthy of the Court's stature as a co-equal branch of government. Had he been a stickler for geographical symmetry, he would have insisted on placing the Court somewhere near the Jefferson Memorial to form a triangular configuration with the White House and the Capitol building. The Court instead ended up in a building completed in 1935 adjacent to the Library of Congress, one block behind the Capitol.

Designed by Cass Gilbert, the renowned architect of the Woolworth Tower in Manhattan, the Court's headquarters displayed a neoclassical style. Four outer walls divided by two intersecting wings carved out four courtyards, each adorned by a circular fountain at its center. The western end of the taller of these two wings formed the front entrance to the building. Unlike the Capitol, which could be seen all the way across the National Mall, past the Washington Monument to the Lincoln Memorial some two-and-a-half miles to the west, the plot of land designated for the Court made it impossible to construct a similarly grand visual corridor. To overcome this obstacle, Gilbert installed a series of steps to generate a similar impression. A pair of statues portraying august figures surveyed the Capitol. Named "Authority of Law" and "Contemplation of Justice," they guarded each side of the stairwell to the building's front entrance. A set of bronze doors embossed with friezes depicting historic enactments of the law stood underneath two rows of eight Corinthian columns. The facade resembled an ancient Greek temple, though one dedicated to the law rather than to the temperamental gods. Sandwiched between the columns and a sculpture stood a monograph with the Court's motto in all-capital lettering: "EQUAL JUSTICE UNDER LAW."

Other than a generous amount of oak paneling, marble covered nearly every surface. The floors were marble. The walls were marble. The statues were marble. And, of course, the columns were marble. In search of a variety of colors and tones, the Court's builders quarried marble from Georgia, Vermont, and Alabama within the United States and Spain, Italy, and even Africa. Literally and figuratively, no stone was left unturned. Along with the omnipresence of marble, references to ancient thinkers, ranging from lawmakers to philosophers to religious figures, adorned every corner of the building. Drawn from the Bible as well as Greco-Roman history, they contributed to the neoclassical motif. Alongside these portrayals stood portraits and busts of former justices honoring the Court's legacy.

Upon taking his oath of office inside this marble palace on October 5, 1953, albeit stripped of his customary arsenal, Earl Warren began the task of mending the Court. Ever since he had become the Alameda County District Attorney in 1925, Warren had stood at the top of an institutional hierarchy. As California's governor, he had presided over a ten-figure budget and thousands of employees. The resources available to him at the Court were paltry by comparison. With only two hundred employees at its disposal, the Court offered Warren three law clerks, a secretary, and a handful of messengers and others available for administrative tasks.

Unlike Warren's previous jobs, which positioned him at the head of a chain of command, the justices functioned like a series of small fiefdoms, or what they liked to call, "nine separate law firms." In place of a shared pool of assistants, each justice relied on his own law clerks to conduct legal research and help draft opinions, ensuring that these top law graduates owed their allegiance to the individual justice rather than the Court. This practice also allowed each justice to operate independently of the institution and prevented the chief justice from withholding resources to cajole his brethren. Lifetime tenure shielded the justices from electoral impulses and, unlike the predicament often endured by other government officials, it obviated the need to grovel for favors, campaign donations, or votes. In essence, the autonomy granted to the justices allowed them to operate as sovereigns. And since each justice's vote counted equally, Warren was only the first among equals. His only edge as the highest ranking member of the Court—that being the senior justice in the majority or minority—enabled him to assign the majority or dissenting opinion to a colleague or take it for himself. The ability to address his colleagues first during the Court's conferences also gave him an opportunity to set the tone for a case. Other than these minor advantages, however, the Court's decentralized structure didn't grant its CEO much institutional authority.

The failure of the Vinson Court to reach a consensus on *Brown* was not just a byproduct of the thorny challenges posed by segregation. It reflected a dysfunctional Court, hampered ironically by its four sharpest minds who split the institution into competing factions. In one corner stood Frankfurter and Jackson. Extolled by New Dealers throughout the 1930s, the judicial philosophy they preached called for the Court to defer to the political branches in most instances. Equally supportive of the New Deal, Black and Douglas agreed to grant the government a free hand in the area of economic regulation but insisted on a far more pronounced judicial role when it came to safeguarding individual rights. Black and Douglas came to consider their foes heretics for failing to protect the constitutional rights of Americans. With equal passion, Frankfurter and Jackson beheld their adversaries as legislators masked in judicial robes.

Black, the most senior of the member of the group, became Roosevelt's first appointment to the Court in 1937 largely because of his avid support of the president's New Deal agenda. The embarrassing revelation that he had been a former member of the KKK, compounded by calls for his resignation weeks into his tenure, may have derailed a weaker-willed man. But not Black, who went on to become one of the most influential and longest-serving justices of the 20th century. His resilience came not through his physical prowess—his modest build looked anything but intimidating—but through his stubborn competitiveness. One of his clerks dubbed Black "the most powerful man I've ever met." While his determination appealed to some, this quality also infuriated his rivals. "You can't just disagree with him," Robert Jackson said of Black. "You must go to war with him if you disagree."

Jackson's displeasure with Black stemmed from a long-standing rivalry between the two. In a memo later released to the public, Jackson threatened to resign from the Court when Truman considered promoting Black to chief justice in 1946, a job Jackson coveted. "If war is declared on me," Jackson wrote of his feud with Black in a statement released to the press, "I propose to wage it with weapons of an open warrior, not those of a stealthy assassin."

After stints as solicitor general and attorney general, Jackson left the Court for a year to serve as the nation's chief prosecutor at the Nuremberg Trials. None of the other justices could wield such credentials or his skills in the courtroom. "Jackson should be Solicitor General for life," Justice Louis Brandeis once boasted. Yet, Jackson was twice denied the chief justiceship he felt he deserved. Increasingly exasperated, he directed much of his bitterness towards Black. "I simply give up understanding our colleague and begin to think he is a case for a psychiatrist," Jackson wrote to Frankfurter, his closest ally on the bench.

At first glance, the men made for an odd pairing. Brought up in a poor family in upstate New York, Jackson attended but never graduated from Albany Law School, entering the profession through an apprenticeship instead. His modest educational achievement fomented an inferiority complex when surrounded by lawyers boasting degrees from Harvard, Yale, and other choice universities. It was unexpected then for Jackson to forge an alliance with Frankfurter. Born in Vienna, Frankfurter finished as valedictorian at Harvard Law School before becoming a professor there. With his career taking him back and forth from Washington, D.C. to Cambridge, Massachusetts, he became an unabashed champion of the New Deal. By the time he became a justice, he was already considered a leading expert on the Court.

With wire-rimmed spectacles and neatly trimmed hair, Frankfurter looked the part of an academic. Pompous and erudite, he enjoyed conversing with a diverse group of prominent figures, ranging from Learned Hand to Albert Einstein to Dean Acheson. Many of his letters began with esoteric references to his idol Oliver Wendell Holmes or an obscure British jurist from a bygone age. Possessing encyclopedic knowledge, Frankfurter was a genuine intellectual and liked to play up that role. Regardless of whether he was addressing a group of sycophantic students or peers of equal standing, he didn't know when to silence the professor within. "At the risk of being deemed academic," he began a 1955 memo to the other justices, "a charge to which I unashamedly plead guilty."

No one took more umbrage at Frankfurter's hubris than William Douglas. Born into poverty and plagued by polio as a boy, Douglas became a professor at Columbia Law School, just two years after graduating from there. On the prowl for young, talented New Dealers, Roosevelt appointed Douglas to the chairmanship of the Securities and Exchange Commission in 1936. Douglas's dazzling rise continued three years later, at the age of forty, he became the youngest justice appointed since 1810.

Compared with his heady public persona, Douglas led a lively private life, and kept marrying younger women at a time when no justice had ever been divorced. An avid outdoorsman, he made his home in an arid part of Washington state. Over time, his countenance came to take on the rugged features consistent with his lifestyle, appearing in his official portrait like a less handsome version of the actor Kirk Douglas. William Douglas's me-first attitude made him especially unsuited for an institution requiring its principals to interact constantly with each other and, due to the low turnover among the justices, to do so over a course of many years. "Douglas," explained one clerk, "loved humanity in the abstract, but couldn't stand people in particular." His misanthropic ways turned off just about everyone but Black.

Beyond their philosophical differences, these rivals irritated each other on a personal level. "I thought Felix was going to hit me today, he got so mad," Black said after a heated conference. Frankfurter coined the Douglas-Black alliance "the Axis." Douglas called Frankfurter "Der Fuehrer." A typical exchange from the spring of 1954, in which Douglas took exception to Frankfurter's behavior during a conference, characterized the shattered relationship. "An answer was refused, rather insolently," Douglas wrote to Frankfurter. "This was so far as I recall the first time one member of the Conference refused to answer another member," Douglas vented. Then he threw in a zinger. "We all know what a great burden your long discourses are. So I am not complaining." But, despite these denials, he was indeed complaining. "But I do register a protest at your degradation of the Conference and its deliberations."

This bad blood among the brethren led the legal scholar Noah Feldman to refer to them as "Scorpions".

After the second round of oral arguments, Warren approached the Court's conference on December 12, 1953, determined to break the logjam. Though he was never outspoken about civil rights, segregation nevertheless infuriated him. "Of all the indignities," he recalled, "the most macabre one is that blacks could not even lie in peace and at rest in the same cemetery as whites." On a broader philosophical level, he had come to regard the "individual" as the "all-important, precious object of consideration," during his time as governor. "Civil rights, representative government, and equality of opportunity" came to represent his primary goals.

Outside the conference room, a steady drizzle pierced through the fog. Had the temperature been ten degrees cooler, snow would have covered the Court. The justices entered the meeting in trepidation over the stakes involved. They had already punted on *Brown* once. They could not postpone a ruling a second time. Under these circumstances, Warren's first suggestion provided much needed relief. Sitting at the head of the table, he proposed holding off on any vote. Right off the bat, his brethren embraced the idea. By doing so they would reduce the pressure they faced and prevent opposing positions from hardening right from the case's outset.

His next words were equally shrewd. Unlike his predecessor, Warren believed that the "separate but equal" doctrine "spawned . . . the very essence of inequality." Now, he conveyed this sentiment to his brethren: "I've come to conclude that the basis of segregation . . . rests upon a concept of the inherent inferiority of the colored race," he said. The statement struck at the South's hypocritical justification for segregation. His next words went one step further: "If we are to sustain segregation," Warren concluded, "we also must do it upon that basis."

After exposing the rationalization behind segregation, Warren pinned *Plessy*'s supporters into an uncomfortable corner. "I don't see how in this day and age we can set any group apart from the rest and say they are not entitled to exactly the same treatment as all others. To do so would be contrary to the Thirteenth, Fourteenth, and Fifteenth Amendments," Warren declared. "Personally, I can't see how today we can justify segregation based solely on race."

This opening volley already placed *Plessy*'s backers on the defensive. Now, he sought to sap those supporters of their best argument. Though twenty-four states and the District of Columbia had employed segregated schools when the Fourteenth Amendment was ratified, Warren found the legislative history of the amendment to be inconclusive. From his point of view, the amendment's framers may not have prohibited segregation but they certainly didn't require it. Nor did they prevent future generations from abolishing it at a later time. The inability to glean a definitive interpretation of the Fourteenth Amendment's legislative history—the strongest argument made by the southern school districts in *Brown*—made the issue moot in his eyes.

To keep anyone from straying, the chief justice offered the fence-sitters a reprieve. The Court would not demand immediate desegregation. This brought instant relief to the southerners on the Court. Warren was also careful to avoid an accusatory tone. Over decades of working in government, he had mastered the art of reading people, and he realized that *Plessy*'s patrons on the Court would cringe at such denunciations. He comforted his brethren that the judicial body would rely on its "wisdom . . . to dispose of the matter with a minimum of emotion and strife."

The performance was a masterpiece. One by one, the holdouts from the previous round of arguments began to lean towards Warren's position.

Though still concerned over the eruption of violence throughout the South, Clark began to drop his hesitation to overruling *Plessy*. Unable to find definitive answers in the legislative history, Frankfurter also agreed to strike down segregation. Jackson still preferred congressional action but agreed that as a "political decision, I can go along with it." Once again, Douglas, Black, Burton, and Minton expressed absolute support for overturning *Plessy*. Reed grudgingly acknowledged that *Plessy* "might not be correct now." Ever the sports fanatic, if Warren had been keeping score, his tally would at that point would have been 6-1 with two undecideds—Clark and Jackson—leaning towards striking down segregation.

Warren was aware that the Court's prima donnas couldn't be bossed around like his staff in Sacramento. At 6'1", 205 pounds, Warren's physique could have made him an imposing figure. Yet, Warren didn't employ these features to intimidate others. Instead, he had an easy-going bonhomie, a politician's natural aptitude to mingle with others and move about comfortably in big and small crowds alike. His thinning white hair, broad-faced smile, and Nordic-blue eyes contributed to his guileless, avuncular appearance, and his gravelly voice leavened his otherwise youthful, outgoing demeanor with an air of wisdom.

At some level, it was difficult to pinpoint the reasons for his successful leadership. Surely, his sincerity, forthrightness, and self-confidence helped. Yet, something else was at work. The two great chief justices to precede Warren—John Marshall and Charles Evans Hughes—exuded leadership in part through some ineffable quality, that perhaps Warren might also have possessed. "By some process short of the occult," Fortas noted, "Warren was a great, powerful leader." The chief justice's intellectual prowess certainly mattered but was not the defining source of his success. Though Warren may not have matched Frankfurter's erudition or Douglas's debating skills, such shortcomings did nothing to undermine his confidence. Nor did they damage Warren's reputation among his colleagues. The chief justice "didn't lead by his intellect," explained Justice Potter Stewart. "But he was an instinctive leader whom you respected and for whom you had affection."

Warren spent the next few months trying to secure unanimity. For him, that meant a 9-0 rout overruling *Plessy* as well as the absence of any dissenting or concurring opinions that might dilute the significance of speaking with one voice. It was a difficult task. "Look, these are nine guys, all with some reputation, ability and confidence in themselves," Vinson let loose during a tirade. "If any Chief Justice can knock their heads together and get unanimity he's better than I am." Over a period of months, Warren swayed his colleagues during a series of meetings in which he neither twisted arms nor tried to appeal to their emotions. Instead, he gravely listened to their concerns and slowly brought them to unanimity by chipping away at their worries and disinclinations. On at least five occasions, he took Reed's closest colleagues, Burton and Minton, out to lunch to enlist them to bring Reed around. He made sure to keep Frankfurter and Douglas, both of whom might spoil the mood, from these interactions. If this was diplomacy, then Warren would have earned a medal for building a coalition one justice at a time. Unlike a diplomat, however, he had nothing to offer in a trade. His influence originated from his moral authority and the ability to command respect.

When the justices held their official vote in March, all but Reed favored overturning *Plessy*. Warren's team began writing the majority opinion weeks later. Emphasizing the need for lay people to understand the Court's thinking, he told his clerks to draft a brief opinion free of legal jargon and caustic language. The draft he sent to the other justices may not rank high among the Court's literary works but, what Warren lacked in captivating prose, he made up for in his directness. The other justices quickly acquiesced, offering minor changes to Warren's original text. The score was firmly now 7-2: Jackson and Reed representing the final roadblocks.

Jackson dropped his plans for a concurring opinion after he suffered a heart attack. Warren visited him in the hospital to incorporate his comments on May 13. Sapped of his energy yet enthusiastic over Warren's draft, Jackson offered little resistance, accepting Warren's words nearly wholesale. Eight down—one to go.

By the spring of 1954, Reed stood alone. The about-face required for the Kentucky native to abrogate his life-long beliefs appeared insurmountable. For months, the dissenting opinion he was drafting mirrored the arguments made by the segregated school districts. Fearful that even one dissent would encourage segregationists, Warren visited Reed's office one last time. "Stan," he said in his usual restrained manner, "you're all by yourself in this now. You've got to decide whether it's really the best thing for the country." Ever tactful with his colleagues, Warren expressed sympathy for the South's sentiments yet remained firm on the need for unanimity. Months of understated coaxing and coalition building had brought the two men to this point. It was Reed's last chance to join his brethren. Reed wanted to dissent. Yet, cognizant that he might be blamed for the South's expected intransigence, Reed finally acceded.

The score was now 9-0. "This would have been impossible a year ago," Burton wrote in his diary.

While May 18, 1896, the day the Court issued *Plessy*, represented one of the lowest points in the institution's history, May 17, 1954 could be considered to have been its high point. Traditionally, the Court delivered its opinions orally from the bench, often in an abbreviated form, while releasing a written version to the press. There were no cameras and the justices didn't answer questions. Their opinions spoke for themselves.

"As we Justices marched into the courtroom on that day, there was a tenseness that I have not seen equaled before or since," Warren remembered. Those cognizant of the magnitude of the day made sure to appear. Jackson insisted on attending despite the risk of leaving his hospital bed. Warren's wife Nina, who rarely attended the Court's sessions, also showed up. A phone call to Marshall in Los Angeles convinced him to take the next flight back to Washington. Noticing a large pile of unlabeled opinions, the clerks figured out that something important was about to take place. Clark confirmed their suspicions when he told some of them: "I think you boys ought to be in the courtroom today." Members of the press were not so prescient. The Court's press officer at first told them that it "looked like a quiet day." In fact, nothing of consequence took place for 50 minutes: the Court admitted 118 attorneys to the Supreme Court Bar followed by the reading of three inconsequential opinions. But at 12:52 p.m., the press officer revealed *Brown* was up next, causing a stampede of reporters to bolt up a flight of stairs, just moments after Warren began.

When Warren finally arrived at the opinion's critical juncture, he was more than half-way through the text:

> *We come then to the question presented: Does segregation of children in public schools solely on the basis of race, even though the physical facilities and other 'tangible' factors may be equal, deprive the children of the minority group of equal educational opportunities? We believe that it does.*

That was the first clear signal for *Plessy's* demise. Moments later, Warren struck the final blow. "We conclude unanimously that in the field of public education the doctrine of 'separate but equal' has no place." Speaking in a clear and unemotional tone, that magic word Warren had fought so hard to achieve, "unanimously," sent a bolt of excitement through the crowd. No one screamed in agreement or moaned in disapproval. Yet, it seemed as though some indefinable sensation passed through the room. The 9-0 decision also stunned Marshall, who had remained doubtful of victory, let alone a complete sweep. Marshall felt that Reed, more than anyone else, was likely to dissent. Standing in the lawyers' section, he turned his gaze towards Reed, who acknowledged Marshall's glance with a nod, as a tear ran down his cheek.

It took Warren 28 minutes to finish reading *Brown* and its companion rulings. Bulldozing through more than a thousand pages of briefs and days of oral arguments in ten pages, the ruling's brevity surprised Court observers. Nearly a century after the Civil War, in an astonishingly few words, the sweeping decision finally brought the Court's famous inscription, "EQUAL JUSTICE UNDER LAW," to life

Today, more than six decades later, *Brown* is rightfully remembered as one of the pinnacles of the civil rights movement. From the Court's standpoint, it signified the first step for an institutional revolution. Throughout the nation's history, the Court had been a conservative body persistently operating as a counterweight to the progressive policies of its sister branches. It had also never been a consistent champion of individual rights, as these protections had remained under the purview of the political branches both at the state and federal level. *Brown* served as the opening move in response to the Court's about-face. Instead of continuing to play a reactionary role, the Court under Warren's watch for the first time in its history became a trailblazer for the struggle for civil liberty.

The case launched Warren's career as the most significant chief justice since John Marshall and—along with Lyndon Johnson—the official most responsible for carrying American liberalism to its greatest heights during the post-war era. *Brown* also showcased Warren's willingness to risk a backlash, stand up to strident enemies, and shake up decades of stratified legal and social conventions to thrust the nation a step closer to living up to the Constitution's ideals. Other monumental rulings, far-reaching and controversial in their own ways, were on the horizon, but *Brown* was the lodestar. Symbolically and politically, the ruling confirmed for those inside and outside the Marble Palace that the Supreme Court had officially been christened the "Warren Court."

The Court's willingness to correct the deficiencies of the political branches also turned into a recurring theme during Warren's tenure. Time and again, state and federal officials were unable or unwilling to address long-held legal, political, and constitutional shortcomings. Whether the issue at hand concerned malapportioned legislative districts, or the rights of indigent defendants, or in the case of *Brown*, civil rights, Americans with nowhere else to turn beseeched the Court to resolve problems ideally suited for legislatures. Warren was attuned to this dynamic: "the politicians all stepped out and left it in the Court's lap," he told an interviewer years later. Had they enacted "legislation that should have been there almost a hundred years before . . . the Supreme Court would never have been obliged to make so many civil rights decisions."

Marshall represented the first group of Americans who, finding no success through the political process, turned to the Court for help. His accomplishments turned him into an exemplar for generations of others looking to the judiciary to overcome intractable lawmakers. The Warren Court's willingness to give hope to those left outside the political system opened it up to criticism that it was acting like a judicial legislature. No region harbored more resentment towards the Warren court than the South and no region would come to attack the institution more.

JUNE, 1968

Brown still cast a long shadow over Johnson's meeting with Eastland. For a man convinced that the "Constitution . . . shall be interpreted strictly in accordance with the understanding of the members of the Constitutional Convention who submitted it," *Brown* struck him as an "illegal, immoral and sinful doctrine" that threatened all the ideals he held dear. The fact that Fortas had not joined the Court until well after *Brown* mattered little to Eastland. Believing that Fortas would perpetuate Warren's accomplishments, Eastland treated Fortas's nomination as if Warren himself were up for confirmation. It was one of the many occasions for which Fortas would be punished for his perceived stepping in as Warren's heir-apparent.

When the poker-faced Eastland arrived at 10:37 a.m. on June 26, Johnson greeted him with a handshake and a smirk before sitting him down on a wooden chair adjacent to his desk. The president settled into his leather chair, crossing his long legs while he began to make a case. The seating arrangement reflected Washington's power dynamic. Even when a president was desperate for a congressman's backing, he rarely if ever visited the Capitol to grovel. Instead, congressmen—including the big shots like Eastland—came to the White House to meet with a president, often in the Oval Office, the nation's center of power.

What the room lacked in gaudy displays of authority, it made up for in subtle ways reflected in the office's décor. Adjacent to the entrance, a visitor faced the wooden desk that Johnson had brought with him from the Senate. Topped with green leather and large enough for a grown man to lie down upon, its dimensions reflected Johnson's Texas-sized ambitions. The carpet, throw pillows, and even his phone—which with its rows of buttons resembled an operator's switchboard—were all of varying shades of green. The Stars and Stripes and the presidential flag stood by the windows behind his desk. Five other banners were aligned against a side wall to his right. Three televisions and a bookcase filled the wall to his left. A portrait of Franklin Roosevelt, Johnson's idol, hung above a marble fireplace facing the president's desk. Portraits of George Washington and Andrew Jackson and pictures of Johnson's family also adorned the room. The positioning of Johnson's signature rocking chair allowed him to converse with visitors seated on the two off-white couches in front of the fireplace. The presidential seal of an eagle carrying an olive branch and arrows—Johnson's symbol of power—was embossed eighteen-

and-a-half feet above the center of the room.

Renowned for cajoling and manipulating his adversaries in face-to-face meetings, Johnson made his case for Fortas. Johnson, realizing he had nothing to offer the chairman and, aware that Eastland was too powerful to be bullied and too intelligent to be duped, resorted to reasoning with him instead. To no avail, he pointed to endorsements Fortas had received from influential senators. The chairman dismissed them, arguing that these promises of support would fall by the wayside. Slouching in his chair reading a memo Johnson handed to him, Eastland remained equally unimpressed by the assertions that some southern senators had softened their positions against Fortas.

When Johnson had named Fortas as his favorite to succeed Warren during a half-hour phone call three days earlier, Eastland hadn't objected. But now in the final hour, the chairman interrupted the president to express his dissatisfaction with the choice. Eastland cited a recent speech by Fortas in which he had encouraged Jews to support the civil rights movement, and declared this particularly offensive, interpreting it as a "conspiratorial call for Jews and Negroes to take over America." "Mr. President," Eastland then insisted, "this appointment is going to be terribly unpopular. He's not going to be confirmed by the Senate, and he's going to tear this country up."

Delivered in this late stage, Eastland's dire message must have stung Johnson. He had spent nearly two weeks deliberating his options, devising and implementing a strategy, gathering information from all corners of the capital, shoring up old alliances, and just that morning, putting the finishing touches on what he felt should be Fortas's coronation. With reporters already called upon to expect an imminent announcement from the president, Johnson had no time for a drawn out negotiation. The president already suspected that Eastland had been promised a more favorable nominee by the GOP should a Republican take the White House. Eastland's response confirmed that he wouldn't be able to win the senator's allegiance under the circumstances. Put on the defensive by Eastland's blunt remark, Johnson switched to asking for modest concessions. "I don't want to ask you to do but one thing," the president said, "and that's not to make a statement." Eastland agreed to not bad mouth Fortas in public. "Will you let him out of the Judiciary Committee," Johnson then asked. "Yes,"

Eastland responded but with a caveat—"at my own time."

The outcome wasn't ideal, but so long as Eastland agreed not to bottle up the nomination, Johnson forged ahead, still confident of victory. Less than an hour after the meeting, he welcomed reporters into the Oval Office to commence the press conference announcing Abe Fortas as the next Chief Justice of the United States.

Coming during the waning days of his presidency, the timing of Johnson's nomination of Fortas was both an opportunity and a burden. Among his lesser-known yet distinctly Machiavellian undertakings, Johnson had orchestrated two vacancies on the Court to stock it with ideologically-minded jurists. This latest opening gave him an additional chance to lock in a liberal majority for another generation. Yet, it also came at a tricky time for a teetering presidency. Desperate to find a resolution in Vietnam, the president had planned to focus his attention to bringing an end to the war during his final months in office. Already stricken by widespread riots ignited by Dr. Martin Luther King Jr.'s assassination, his declining popularity among the electorate, and a hostile Congress, Johnson entered this face-off at the weakest point of his presidency. Forced to take on this challenge at this inopportune juncture, he nevertheless enthusiastically welcomed the prospect of securing the Court for decades to come. The possibility that he could appoint Fortas, his close friend and confidant, to lead the Court made the opportunity all the more appealing.

Johnson wasn't the only one contemplating the Court's future. Driven by personal animosity and political calculus, Warren also ruminated over the direction of the judicial body he had molded into a revolutionary force should someone other than Johnson name his successor. Just as he had on so many occasions during his tenure as chief justice, he set in motion a series of events that would change the course of history. This time around, the far-reaching impact of his actions came not from one of his seminal rulings but through his decision to retire.

Chapter 2

"An Abiding Passion"

JUNE, 1968

On June 11, 1968, Chief Justice Earl Warren made one of the most consequential decisions of his career. After nearly a half century in public life—the last fifteen years of which were the most influential for a chief justice since John Marshall—he decided to retire. Not because he disliked his work. Not because the addition of new justices had corroded his command over the Court. Not because he felt his attempts to reshape America were no longer in vogue. Not because he felt compelled to spend more time with his wife Nina, his six children, and grandchildren as he passed his seventy-seventh birthday.

One reason alone explained his decision: Richard Nixon.

Warren so abhorred Nixon, his animosity had reached an intensity typically reserved for political rivals. As former allies within the California Republican party, they had never faced each other in an election. Their rivalry stemmed from a source far deeper and more enduring than a contest for higher office—a vision of America's future. The fact that Nixon's reincarnation in 1968 came in part at Warren's expense certainly antagonized the chief justice. But Warren's scorn reached much farther back in time, simmering slowly during the 1940s before turning white-hot at a critical juncture of his career.

Beginning in 1925, and over a span of 27 years, Warren collected one electoral trophy after another on his way to becoming California's first three-term governor. One position, above all others, stood worthy of his remaining political aspirations—the presidency. His failure to secure the nomination in 1948 left him with one last shot to win the coveted prize. Heading into the 1952 Republican contest, Warren knew he had a narrow path to victory. He needed the balloting to end in a deadlock long enough to break the will of the two front-runners, Ohio Senator Robert Taft and General Dwight Eisenhower. Only then, when victory appeared out of reach, would the delegates search for a compromise candidate.

Eager to recapture the presidency in 1952, after a two-decade drought, the Republicans desperately sought an appealing candidate. The head of the party's liberal establishment, New York Governor Thomas Dewey, remained a powerful force, but there was no way for him to lead the national ticket again after having already lost twice, especially after his stilted performance had botched his big lead over Harry Truman in 1948.

With Dewey no longer the front-man of the party, a two-person contest developed. In his third attempt at the nomination, Taft, the son of the former president, arrived as the standard bearer of the party's conservative wing. Isolationist and rabidly anti-labor, Taft's antagonism towards the New Deal and the Cold War alliances forged after World War II fueled his popularity. *The New York Times* considered him the favorite on the eve of the convention.

Eisenhower, Taft's chief rival, was arguably the nation's most admired war hero since Ulysses S. Grant. Hinging his candidacy on his military record, Eisenhower carried a level of esteem and name recognition that career politicians could only dream about. Compared with the hardened appearance of Douglas MacArthur—another popular war hero—Ike had a soothing grin that softened his countenance. Steering clear of politics after the war had endowed him with a statesman-like aura that lifted him above petty rivalries. Favored by Dewey, Eisenhower's moderate ideology complemented his unequalled popularity.

Capturing more of the sixteen contested primaries than any other candidate, Taft barreled into the convention with momentum. Four decades after the emergence of the primaries, those victories merely represented an opening volley in the contest. Ultimately, the delegates at the convention would determine the party's nominee. And if either Eisenhower or Taft didn't emerge as a clear victor, these delegates would look to another candidate of national stature.

Earl Warren fit the mold of a compromise choice perfectly. In a December, 1951 Gallup Poll, both Taft and Eisenhower appeared on a "Most Admired Man" list alongside Harry Truman, Winston Churchill, and Albert Einstein. Warren, the tenth and last man to make the list, may have lacked their standing, but the poll revealed that he carried far more than regional support heading into the nomination fight. With neither Taft nor Eisenhower entering the July convention as a shoo-in, Warren set himself up to swoop in should neither favorite prevail. Prior to the balloting, the intelligence gathered by Warren's team revealed that three or four ballots would be needed before these delegates would consider switching to him.

Balloting began at 11:49 a.m. on July 11, 1952, in what turned out to be the nation's first televised convention. The mood inside Chicago's International Amphitheatre, already the most feverish Republican convention seen in decades, became ever more frenzied when, in alphabetical order, each state announced its votes. Originally built to house cattle auctions for nearby stockyards, the Amphitheatre lacked the architectural flair of the Chicago Board of Trade, the Blackstone Hotel, or the city's other landmarks. Despite its resemblance to a non-descript warehouse, it went on to serve as a venue for a panoply of events: hosting professional wrestling matches and an annual auto show alongside The Beatles' Chicago debut. The most dramatic moment undoubtedly took place in 1968, when the Democratic Party convened at the boxy arena for an act of self-immolation.

Its use as a storage house for cattle was fitting. Delegates, party insiders, and members of the press crammed inside the three-tiered building. Rather than relying on a stage as in modern-day conventions, organizers positioned a rostrum near the center of the floor, allowing speakers to seemingly levitate above the crowd. Holding up signs of support and energized by brass bands, delegates cheered wildly for their favorite sons like teenage girls at a boy-band concert.

Alabama began the process, giving Taft an early nine-to-five lead over Eisenhower. When California's turn came moments later, it was still an open question to some at the convention whether Warren would maintain his grip over his delegation.

Warren's gubernatorial victories built the foundation of his political strength in the Golden State. Following a fourteen-year stint as the Alameda County District Attorney and one term as California's Attorney General, Warren defeated the incumbent governor Culbert Olson by fifteen points in 1942. Warren's greatest triumph came four years later. He swept both the Republican and Democratic primaries in 1946 on his way to capturing more than 91% of the vote in the general election, ranking it one of the most one-sided electoral victories in American history. These triumphs brought him national acclaim, ultimately placing him on the Republican ticket alongside Dewey in 1948. Dewey's embarrassing loss to Truman did little to erode Warren's appeal: two years later, he defeated Franklin Roosevelt's son, James, by the largest vote margin in California history.

Warren's popularity afforded him an unusual degree of autonomy, giving him the luxury of eschewing the GOP's party machinery in favor of a progressive agenda. For Warren, these progressive ideals—not partisanship or dogged ideology—established the foundation of his governing philosophy. Encouraged by California's cross-filing electoral system, he appeared on the ballot for both the Republican and Democratic primaries. His bipartisan outlook—a Democrat served as his chief policymaker—and a refusal to reward campaign donors or hand out patronage jobs, bestowed Warren with a reputation for integrity, a modern-day version of Plato's philosopher king largely untouched by the ugly vestiges of politics.

In contrast to Warren's progressive sensibilities and statesmanlike demeanor, Richard Nixon was the standard bearer of the party's conservative wing. Having won national acclaim in 1948 through his dogged pursuit of Alger Hiss, Nixon was brash, eager to publicly condemn his enemies, and unlike Warren's appeal to both sides of the aisle, preferred to operate as a partisan attack dog.

Warren was horrified by Nixon's antics in the 1950 senate race—what one historian dubbed "an unequaled low" in California's history—in which Nixon earned the "Tricky Dick" moniker. Nixon's advisor explained the campaign's strategy: "The purpose of an election is not to defeat your opponent, but to destroy him." Applying this principle to his opponent Helen Douglas, the red-baiting Nixon accused her of being "pink right down to her underwear." Desperate for an ally to help him through this trench warfare, Nixon repeatedly looked to the state's leading politico for a lifeline. Angered by Warren's rejection of his entreaties, Nixon told an aide, "Warren might as well be sitting on his butt . . . for all the help he's giving us."

Warren's refusal to share the spotlight with fellow Republicans aggravated those who viewed him as egocentric and aloof. They took to calling him the "Earl of Warren." Perhaps Warren may have been too stingy in sharing the limelight or doling out political favors. Or he may have simply been sticking to his principles. Either way, his unwillingness to partake in some of the obligatory yet distasteful elements of public life endangered his candidacy in 1952.

Days before the Chicago convention, the first group of California's delegates set out from Los Angeles on a chartered Western Pacific train dubbed the "Earl Warren Special". Donning orange baseball caps emblazoned with the letter W, the group of delegates personally vetted by Warren selected William Knowland, a longtime friend and political ally he'd appointed to fill a vacancy in the Senate in 1945, to chair the delegation.

Soon after Nixon boarded the "Warren Special" in Denver, he threw Warren's convention strategy into a maelstrom. Nixon had already undermined Warren through a questionnaire sent to party organizers asking for an appraisal of the Republican field. If that was a bee sting, Nixon's next move was a snake bite. Nixon leaked the results of the hush-hush survey revealing the state's preference for Eisenhower over their own governor. Nixon came to the convention convinced of Eisenhower's inevitable triumph and saw no need to support Warren. Neither political realism nor a fondness for the general could alone explain Nixon's bold decision to sidestep his state's leading politician. Months before the convention, Dewey had told Nixon he could become Eisenhower's running mate, particularly if he managed to shift California's delegation to the general. Nixon couldn't talk about this self-serving possibility out loud. Instead, he discreetly urged members of the delegation to consider backing Eisenhower over Warren.

Political conventions operated like hothouses of rumor and innuendo that make high school cafeteria gossip appear mature by comparison. The confined space of the delegation's train amplified this charged atmosphere. "If you're on the front end of the train," remembered one participant, "you have to run pretty fast before [your] statement gets to the back end of the train." As news of Nixon's proposal traveled through the cars, some delegates warmed to it. Meanwhile, Warren in disbelief watched his grip loosen over his hand-picked delegates. "I just can't understand anybody doing such a thing," he told a colleague. The governor considered it a point of honor for his supporters to remain bound by their pledge to him. Infuriated by the treachery, he coined Nixon the "traitor in our delegation."

Once at the convention, Nixon again urged the delegation to cast its lot with Eisenhower. Since the vast majority of the delegates preferred the general over Taft, some warmed to Nixon's suggestion, leading media observers to speculate whether Warren would hold on to his home state. Yet, whatever momentum Nixon's overture might have gained died when it reached Knowland, who owed his office to Warren, and whose family's kinship with the governor reached back decades. No matter how shrewd he may have seemed, Nixon couldn't overcome the strength of this allegiance. When the Golden State's turn came up, the California delegation cast all 70 votes for Warren.

Half-way through the balloting, the possibility of a deadlock remained viable, with neither front-runner sweeping the most populated states. Illinois gave all but one of its 60 votes to Taft. Massachusetts allotted 16 to Eisenhower and half of that to Taft. Michigan voted 35 to 11 in favor of the general. Warren picked up one vote in Nebraska, Eisenhower got four, and Taft earned thirteen. Greeted with boos from Taft's supporters, Dewey announced New York's delegation: to no one's surprise, 92 of the 96 delegates sided with Eisenhower. Just as predictably, Taft's home state handed him all of its 56 votes. Pennsylvania cast 53 votes for Eisenhower, 15 for Taft, and two for MacArthur.

Knowland's loyalty to Warren barely prevented Eisenhower from clearing a majority on the first ballot. The general tallied 595 votes, just nine short of securing the nomination. Taft came in second with 500 votes. Warren with 81, MacArthur with ten, and Minnesota governor Harold Stassen with 20 votes made up the rest of the field. The threadbare deadlock kept Warren's hopes for a stalemate alive and with it, perhaps his dreams of life in the oval office.

Whatever jubilation he may have felt didn't last long. After the roll call, Minnesota's convention floor manager, Warren Burger (who later would replace Warren as chief justice), asked Warren's delegation to switch its vote to Eisenhower. When the delegation held firm, Minnesota went ahead without the Golden State, announcing its intention to switch its votes from Stassen to Eisenhower. News of the switch triggered another eruption from the crowd, among the loudest of the convention. For Warren, those cheers represented his last hope of reaching the presidency. In less than two hours the voting was over. Within an hour, Eisenhower selected Nixon as his running mate.

Never forgiving Nixon for the perfidy, Warren delivered a modicum of revenge a decade later by privately backing Nixon's opponent, Edmund Brown, for the 1962 California governor's race, telling one reporter that Nixon "has to be stopped." Warren's namesake, Earl Warren Jr., went further, switching parties to become vice-chairman of Brown's campaign. One of his primary tasks was to attack Nixon at Democratic rallies. Just to rub it in further, Warren's son still helped other Republicans on the ticket. Just in case anyone still wondered why the scion of the state's longest serving Republican governor would switch parties became clear during one of Warren Jr.'s press conferences. "Nixon, through backdoor politics and for political gain for himself, pulled the rug out from under us in 1952," Warren's son declared. "He wronged my father."

Warren celebrated Nixon's embarrassing loss to Brown with John Kennedy aboard Air Force One, where the two men were seen "laughing like schoolboys" over Nixon's humiliation.

Time was supposed to soothe old wounds but it didn't leaven Warren's opinion of Nixon any. To his final days, the chief justice considered Nixon an "evil" and "disgraceful character." Warren "felt that Nixon was untrustworthy, a scoundrel, a liar, completely unprincipled, and an exceedingly dangerous person." According to his son, Warren "detested . . . Nixon as an abiding passion." That passion helped explain the timing of the chief justice's decision to resign. After Johnson bowed out of the presidential race in March and Robert

Kennedy was assassinated on June 5, 1968, Warren became convinced that Nixon would become the next president.

Warren knew firsthand how difficult it would be to serve as chief justice with a hostile president in the White House. In 1958, when Congress prepared to strip the Court of its powers and the South brazenly defied the Court's desegregation orders, Eisenhower, who'd appointed Warren to the Court, stood idly on the sidelines, watching the Court's enemies sharpen their knives. Warren, who'd been publicly praised by Truman as "one of the truly great men of our time," felt betrayed by Eisenhower's unwillingness to stand up for the Court. The fraught relationship devolved into a grudge match. "For more than seven years they sat at opposite ends of Pennsylvania Avenue," Eisenhower's speechwriter recalled, "each playing out a noble role, in tragic inevitable estrangement." Warren didn't want to go through that experience again, particularly with Nixon, whose daggers would be longer and sharper than Ike's.

JUNE, 1968

Now, however, Warren's bigger concern was over the question of who would replace him. Doubtful that he'd be able to outlast Nixon's term in office, and cringing at the thought of his nemesis picking his successor, Warren timed his resignation so that Johnson would fill his seat instead. The two leading titans of American liberalism were in harmony on the most important political and social issues of the time. A decade before Johnson pushed the 1964 Civil Rights Act through Congress, Warren fought on the front-lines of the civil rights struggle, hoping Congress and the executive branch would catch up. Frustrated by Eisenhower's refusal to take a stronger stand for *Brown*, the chief justice expressed his frustration in his memoir:

> With his popularity, if Eisenhower had said that black children were still being discriminated against . . . [and] that the Supreme Court . . . now declared it unconstitutional to continue such cruel practices, and that it should be the duty of every good citizen to help rectify more than eighty years of

wrongdoing by honoring that decision . . . we would have been relieved . . . of many of the racial problems which have continued to plague us.

Eisenhower's position irreparably damaged his relationship with Warren. For the chief justice, more than civil rights was at stake. He felt the president's deportment contributed to the onslaught endured by the Court. The men remained respectful in public in later years, but other than pro-forma greetings at official events, rarely spoke with each other. By comparison, Warren so admired Johnson's civil rights record, he credited the president for doing "more to make civil rights a reality . . . than . . . any Administration" since the 1860s.

Together, Warren and Johnson refashioned American society. Johnson's Great Society modernized the welfare state, reformed education, combated urban decay, established housing for the poor, and funded the arts, but its reach, though broad and deep, still had its limits. Warren tackled what lay beyond Johnson's grasp, instituting through judicial decree reforms in criminal justice, reapportionment, school prayer, and free speech. When Johnson's legislative accomplishments were tested in the courts, Warren made sure they passed constitutional muster. Just as importantly for Warren, who received no succor from Eisenhower while the Court faced its most strident critics, Johnson supported Warren's decisions every step of the way. Since Johnson's two appointments to the Court—Abe Fortas and Thurgood Marshall—were reliable liberals, the chief justice had no doubt Johnson would continue Warren's legacy by selecting a replacement in the chief justice's image. Nixon, on the other hand, had vowed on the campaign trail to appoint justices with the specific purpose of undoing that legacy.

In addition to their congruent political views, Warren and Johnson had also grown close since Warren's arrival in Washington. "They liked each other," recalled one of Warren's clerks. "You can sense, when people are together, whether they're genuinely affectionate towards each other." Warren's willingness to put aside his reservations to serve on the commission investigating Kennedy's assassination as a favor to Johnson meant a great deal to the president—turning him into an instant "partisan" for the chief justice. Over the years, each expressed respect for the other. In February 1965, Johnson sent Warren a pair of signed photos calling him "the best Chief Justice." Johnson made sure to invite the Warrens to dinner at the White House, arranged for Warren to use the White House pool, sent birthday and Christmas gifts, and delivered ever-more complimentary encomiums over the years. "You are more than a friend to me," Johnson wrote on Warren's 75th birthday, "you are counsellor and wise companion." To his cousin, Johnson deemed Warren one of the "five... finest men in the United States." Warren, in return, welcomed Johnson's defense of the Warren Court against its many critics.

The two most powerful figures in government didn't limit their exchanges to birthday celebrations and warm receptions however. Both were consummate politicians and trusted each other with sensitive political situations, ranging from Latin American diplomacy to Johnson's displeasure with the Kennedys. Whatever lingering concerns Warren may have had of Johnson's intentions for replacing him on the Court would have been erased by their most recent exchanges in the spring of 1968. Thanking Warren for his "loyalty and friendship," Johnson wrote in April, 1968, "I . . . think of you as the kindest as well as the wisest man I have ever known." But Johnson's actions had more impact than the sentiment expressed in his letters. The president made an unannounced visit to a party celebrating Warren's fifteenth anniversary on the bench. Warren was so "shaken . . . so surprised and so moved" by Johnson's appearance, he talked about it the entire evening and forgot to open Johnson's gift, a pair of silver cups that his wife Nina considered "amongst our most cherished possessions."

After making up his mind, Warren asked Fortas, Johnson's long-time lawyer, confidant, and advisor, to tell the president he would like to meet. On June 13, 1968, the chief justice arrived at the White House to submit his resignation.

Chapter 3

"I Think Abe Would be a Good Chief Justice"

JUNE, 1968

A vacancy on the Court inevitably prompted a barrage of recommendations from senators, political advisors, newspaper columnists, and the Department of Justice, which vetted potential candidates. When rumors of Warren's departure swirled around Washington in mid-June, Senate Majority Leader Mike Mansfield recommended James Rowe, a New Dealer with western roots, to bring geographic balance to the Court. Johnson's aide, Harry McPherson, sent the president a motley list of unlikely candidates. Others pressed Johnson to bring in a conservative jurist. "I am convinced that many of the problems that have plagued America . . . are a direct result of . . . the Court," counseled the evangelical leader Billy Graham. Eyeing Texas Governor John Connally, he urged Johnson to pick a "strong conservative."

Johnson didn't want their advice. He had picked out his man from the moment he met with Warren in the oval office on June 13. Near the end of their fifteen-minute meeting, Johnson asked: "have you got any candidates?" Warren hoped William Brennan, his closest ally on the Court, would succeed him but held his tongue. "No, Mr. President, that's your problem." "What do you think of Abe Fortas," Johnson then inquired. "I think Abe would be a good Chief Justice," Warren replied.

So did Johnson.

This was not a capricious, off-the-cuff decision on the president's part. Johnson had learned from the missteps made by his predecessors, and in doing so, had become far more calculating in selecting justices than previous presidents.

Of the nine justices appointed by Franklin Roosevelt, four in particular—Frankfurter, Douglas, Black, and Jackson—were among the most capable ever sent to the Court. Though Roosevelt appointed them because of their steadfast support for the New Deal, he did not foresee the eventual disunion among them. Soon after they joined the Court, the constitutional debates surrounding the New Deal became moot, giving way to an unforeseen conundrum in which the Court had to balance the rights of individuals against the interests of the government. Throughout the post-war era, the justices repeatedly confronted the challenging task of delineating the contours of these rights on behalf of African-Americans, criminal defendants, pornographers, political dissidents, and others. The four Roosevelt appointees remained staunchly at odds over this unresolved and contentious body of law, so much so that by the late 1940s their feud nearly paralyzed the judicial body.

While Roosevelt couldn't predict the future divisions on the Court, he at least sent to the judicial body some of its keenest minds. Truman, on the other hand, had chosen a handful of mediocre cronies, none of whom turned out to represent his party's increasingly liberal bent.

For his first pick, he disregarded a list of 53 candidates produced by the Justice Department to opt for Senator Harold Burton, a Republican he'd once served with on a committee. This approach typified his thinking. Instead of seeking guidance, he preferred to appoint men he knew well, and Burton filled the mold. Yet in selecting a senator from the opposing party who hadn't practiced law in ten years, Truman showed little concern for Burton's judicial outlook or inexperience. Burton's biographer called him "an average justice" who was "not a bright, witty intellectual." Perhaps Truman should have listened to his advisors.

Truman cherry-picked his second selection, Chief Justice Fred Vinson, from his cabinet. Once again, his association with the nominee—more so than Vinson's qualifications or ideology—colored the president's thinking. He ignored the advice of his confidants, or in this case, that of two retired justices. It too turned out to be a poor selection. A clerk believed the other justices considered Vinson "their intellectual inferior." Frankfurter, the haughtiest of the bunch, thought Vinson was incapable of seeing the "complexities of problems." Vinson's flawed leadership matched his unremarkable judicial skills. Truman picked Vinson to serve as a peacemaker among the warring justices. Yet during his seven-year tenure, Vinson failed to bring any cohesion to the bitterly divided brethren.

The low opinion of this pair of picks didn't change Truman's methodology for his last two selections. He again proceeded unilaterally in picking his close confidant and political ally, Attorney General Tom Clark, as a reward for years of friendship and loyalty. In this case, Truman eventually expressed a measure of regret for the selection. "Tom Clark was my biggest mistake," the president declared years later, not because "he's a bad man. It's just that he's such a dumb son-of-a-bitch."

Clark turned out to be shrewder than Truman maintained, especially when compared with Truman's last pick, Sherman Minton. Like his other selections, Truman had hand-picked Minton without any input from advisors. And like his previous picks, the close friendship forged between them in the Senate seemed to be the key component of Minton's resume. With Minton, Truman had saved the worst for last. Bernard Schwartz, the distinguished chronicler of the Warren Court, graded Minton "the worst of the Truman appointees."

By modern standards, Truman's approach to selecting nominees seemed at best casual, at worst grossly negligent. Whatever one makes of Truman's legacy, from the dropping of the atomic bomb to his come-from-behind victory in 1948, his Court selections were a disaster.

Could Truman really have been so clueless, or were other forces at work? Though he deserves blame for not seeking out the sharpest minds, few people at the time weighed nominees through the strictly partisan and ideological lens that typified the approach decades later. This was partly because the Court at the time was not a theater of the nation's political and culture wars. When the Court expanded the scope of the Constitution's commerce clause during the late 1930s, it removed itself as the target that had culminated in Roosevelt's Court-packing plan. By endorsing the communist witch-hunt in the early 1950s, it continued to maintain a passive role vis-à-vis the president and congress. With few exceptions (most notably, the Court's obstruction of

Truman's seizure of steel mills), the other branches of government saw no reason to pick a fight with the brethren. Within this context, Truman's selections were perhaps not so simpleminded after all.

As misguided as they were, none of Truman's picks backfired from an ideological perspective as much as Eisenhower's selection of Warren. Why did Eisenhower miscalculate so badly? Was he not mindful of the Court's capacity to upend so many areas of American society? Did he not take the time to explore Warren's political philosophy? Or, having made these inquiries, could he not have foreseen the Warren Court's revolution? Eisenhower did have misgivings about appointing Warren to the Court. But those doubts had little to do with Warren's ideology.

In December, 1952, Eisenhower called Warren while the governor was still in bed. "I am back here selecting my cabinet," Eisenhower said, "and I wanted to tell you I won't have a place for you in it." He then explained that after seriously considering naming Warren attorney general, he decided to appoint Herbert Brownell to the post. "But I want you to know that I intend to offer you the first vacancy on the Supreme Court," the president continued. "That is my personal commitment to you."

To beef up Warren's candidacy, Eisenhower offered to make him solicitor general, the government's top lawyer before the Court, until an opening became available. In preparation for his move to Washington, Warren announced on September 3, 1953, his decision not to seek another term as California governor. The plan was set. Warren would serve as solicitor general and join the Court as an associate justice when the next vacancy occurred. Since Frankfurter was the oldest justice and each of his colleagues—including Vinson—was in good health, *Time* surmised that Warren's "best hope" of getting on the Court was contingent on Frankfurter's retirement. But, five days after Warren's announcement, Vinson's unexpected death threw this carefully crafted plan into disarray.

His infectious bonhomie and outgoing personality made Warren ideally suited for a life in politics. However, this public persona masked the fact that he kept few intimate friends. Bartley Cavanaugh was among them. The two had met decades earlier, frequently attending sporting events to relieve them of the stress of their vocations. Their children attended school together, and when Cavanaugh became Sacramento's city manager, the intersection of their professional lives strengthened their friendship. But it was a shared tragedy that ultimately bound the men to one another. In 1950, Warren's youngest daughter, seventeen-year-old Nina "Honey Bear" Warren, was stricken with polio. The timing of the news on the very day of his gubernatorial victory devastated Warren. After seeing her in the hospital, he left the room, found a quiet corner, and wept. "It was the first time that I'd ever seen my father so sad," remembered Honey Bear. Just as she returned home, Cavanaugh's three children became infected with the same disease. The mutual suffering of their children heartened the relationship between Warren and Cavanaugh in a way that no other shared experience could.

Cavanaugh was reluctant to disturb the governor on the morning of September 8, 1953, but the stakes were simply too high to let any more time pass. He called Warren at 5:30 a.m. on the West Coast. "Did you know that the chief justice has just died?" Cavanaugh asked. Just awakened, Warren had not heard the news. "Would you mind if I got my nose into this thing," Cavanaugh pleaded. The governor hesitated. "This is a field that you shouldn't do too much in," Warren replied. Perhaps Cavanaugh was being officious, but knowing how important the Court job was to Warren, he pressed on. "I think there'll be a drive for them," he declared, referring to the likelihood that Eisenhower might placate Catholic calls for a seat on the Court. This wasn't the first time mid-century religious politics had come into play. When Justice Frank Murphy died in 1949, Truman was pressured to replace Murphy with another Catholic. Before Warren could respond, Cavanaugh crafted a strategy to contact Cardinal James McIntyre in Los Angeles. McIntyre "will get in touch with Cardinal Spellman in New York," Cavanaugh explained, referring to the nation's pre-eminent Catholic cleric, "who in turn will get in touch with the cardinal in Washington" to vouch for Warren.

Warren vacillated. Yes, he wanted the job and wanted it badly. But he couldn't openly lobby for it. To do so would be particularly unseemly right after Vinson's death. Cavanaugh persisted in the face of this reluctance: "Well," he insisted, "just let me do that and let it go from there." Warren consented, and hours after Cavanaugh started a transcontinental chain reaction of phone calls, Catholic leaders blessed Warren's nomination.

As news of Vinson's death spread, political pundits also placed Warren at the top of a short list of replacements. "Gov. Earl Warren," wrote James Reston, an influential, Pulitzer Prize-winning journalist, "was being prominently mentioned as a likely successor."

One roadblock stood in Warren's way. While Vinson's sudden death provided an opportunity for Warren to join the Court earlier than planned, Eisenhower's failure to anticipate such a scenario threatened his chances. Expecting one of the older justices to retire well before Vinson, Eisenhower had also predicated his offer to Warren under that premise. When Vinson's death upended this expectation, the president vacillated. He had few qualms about appointing Warren as an associate justice, but he did not feel bound to making Warren chief justice. Reluctant to name Warren to the Court's top job, the president ordered the attorney general to begin a widespread search for candidates within the judiciary.

Eisenhower's fixation with judicial experience was unusual at the time. While the Court would eventually become the exclusive province of judges (of the eighteen justices appointed since 1976, only one lacked judicial experience), for much of the twentieth century, presidents routinely picked cabinet members, senators, governors, and private lawyers who traversed the political and judicial worlds. President William Howard Taft went on to become chief justice. Charles Evans Hughes jumped from New York's governorship to the Court in 1910, left the judicial body six years later to seek the presidency, served as secretary of state during the 1920s, and returned to the Court in 1930. Black ended his decade in the Senate to join the Court and throughout the 1950s held presidential aspirations. James Byrnes, on the other hand, ditched his lifetime seat on the Court to become Roosevelt's Director of Economic Stabilization. It's difficult to envision any current justice leaving the Court for a short-term administrative position, even an important wartime posting. Douglas moved from the Securities and Exchange Commission to the Court and both Roosevelt and Truman flirted with naming him their running mate. Vinson spent far more time as a congressman, a department head in

Roosevelt's White House, and treasury secretary than he did as an appellate judge before joining the Court. Truman later offered to help Vinson succeed him in the White House. Having served as the mayor of Detroit, governor of Michigan, the head of the Philippines (which was still under American rule in the 1930s), and attorney general, Frank Murphy brought a similarly diverse resume to the job. In fact, of the Court's remaining eight justices at the time of Vinson's death, only Minton had joined with prior judicial experience. Under these circumstances, despite Eisenhower's trepidation, Warren's background unquestionably fit the mold of a typical justice in the 1950s.

Warren sensed from the start that Eisenhower might skip over him. Soon after his conversation with Cavanaugh, he contacted advisors throughout California to further his cause. It didn't help that Knowland, then the Senate Majority Leader, was overseas when Warren needed an influential ally to lobby the president. "Earl is pacing up and down," Knowland's father told a colleague. "Because Bill is over in Chungking, and isn't back yet, and he wants that chief justiceship if he can possibility get it."

Events inside the White House also began to conspire against Warren. Brownell's search turned up six candidates: associate justices Jackson and Burton, circuit court judges Orie Phillips and John Parker, and New Jersey's Chief Justice Arthur Vanderbilt. The press briefly anointed Jackson the favorite with Warren taking over as an associate justice. Jackson carried a black mark for supporting Roosevelt's 1937 Court-packing plan, however, and selecting him would amp up his quarrel with Black, further handicapping an already dysfunctional Court. Burton, the other sitting justice, lacked the gravitas to lead his brethren. Brownell also crossed out Phillips and Parker for surpassing Eisenhower's age limit of sixty-three, and Vanderbilt lacked the temperament to tame the divisive justices.

Initially a threat, these strike-outs eventually strengthened Warren's standing, as did the exclusion of well-positioned candidates outside the judiciary. Preferring to remain in charge of the nation's foreign policy, Secretary of State John Foster Dulles turned down Eisenhower's offer and the media's fixation with Dewey proved to be conjecture. The removal of these potential rivals from Brownell's short list made Warren the front runner. No one better fulfilled the president's requirements for the job: Warren carried a national stature, was younger than sixty-three, possessed the executive skills needed to oversee both the Court and the federal judiciary, and was a centrist Republican. Despite Warren's advancement to the head of the line, Eisenhower still hesitated, wondering as he had for some time whether the Court suited Warren's temperament. "Do you think that he would really want to be an associate justice," Eisenhower had asked Warren's secretary at a White House breakfast months earlier. "Wouldn't it be pretty rarified for him?"

Eisenhower's continued silence two weeks after Vinson's death encouraged a parlor game of media speculation.

On September 27, 1953, Brownell and Warren finally met at the VIP lounge of McClellan Air Field outside Sacramento to put an end to the speculation. Brownell didn't arrive simply to anoint Warren. He came with the task of feeling out the governor. Was Warren prepared to join the Court right away, Brownell asked, or did he prefer to spend some time as solicitor general first? Reaffirming his "lifelong ambition" to join the Court, Warren jumped at the immediate opening. Were Warren's political views consistent with that of the president? Without going into detail, Warren reiterated his support for Eisenhower's policies. Did the president's offer to Warren include the chief justice's job? This is where Eisenhower's reservations boiled to the surface. Perhaps Brownell was hoping Warren would latch on to the president's apprehension and voluntarily bow out. He dangled a cabinet position to sweeten the offer. Though Eisenhower's promise had rested on a faulty assumption, Warren wasn't about to let the honor-bound general renege. He told Brownell that the president's pledge to him was for the first vacancy on the Court. With that bit of unpleasantness behind them, Brownell returned to Washington.

A day later, Brownell reviewed Warren's record with the president one last time. Though he had rarely spoken directly to Warren about his political beliefs, Eisenhower concluded that Warren was "a man whose philosophy of government was somewhat along the lines of my own" in a letter to an army colleague. The only cause of consternation that remained was Warren's lack of judicial experience. "Sure, we wanted a Charles Evans Hughes," a White House insider told *Time*. "But where the hell do you find one?" To assuage these concerns, Brownell asked Warren's close associates whether the governor had enough trial experience to sit on the Court. As a former district attorney with twenty-five appearances before the Court, Warren had far more than most justices. A positive review of Warren's performance as California's attorney general and his work as chairman of the criminal law committee of the American Bar Association eventually placated Brownell. At the end, even with some lingering doubts, no other candidate better fulfilled Eisenhower's requirements and no one else received the same degree of consideration. After this final review, nothing stood in Warren's way.

The announcement of a new justice did not proceed as a major media event at the time. Presidents didn't slate the occasion for primetime television and nominees—now accompanied by their families for photo-ops—did not deliver speeches on their own behalf. It was a far more casual affair. With Warren still in Sacramento, Eisenhower stepped into the Indian Treaty Room of the Executive Office Building on September 30 for a 24-minute press conference. Naming Warren was just one of the topics on his agenda, which included the proliferation of nuclear arms, political events in Poland, the federal debt limit, a proposal for a federal sales tax, and potential revisions to the Taft-Hartley law. Dubbed the "Cupid Room" by reporters for the four ornate busts of cherubs positioned in the corners, the nautical-themed space with inlaid Minton floor tiles was an arrangement of geometric shapes in blue, white, and brown. It first doubled as a library and reception area for the Navy before being repurposed for press conferences. The president opened the session for the 239 in attendance with a reference to the first game of the World Series between the Yankees and the Dodgers. "I could start off . . . by confirming something that is certainly by no means news anymore," he joked, before formally naming Warren. Eisenhower went on to espouse the governor's "reputation for integrity, honesty" and ironically, "middle-of-the-road philosophy. . . . [H]e is a man who will make a great Chief Justice," Eisenhower assured the audience.

Since the Senate was not in session and the justices had urged the president to fill the vacancy quickly to ensure the smooth operation of the Court, Eisenhower made Warren a recess appointment. It meant that Warren would sit in on cases and vote on rulings without first obtaining Senate confirmation. The question as to whether these circumstances would undermine his independence by pressuring him to make decisions favored by the very senators who would vote on his appointment at a later date didn't come up during the press conference. And if the Senate later rejected his nomination, it could have created a constitutional crisis. Today, a recess appointment would ignite a political war. But at the time, few in Congress or in the press showed any concern.

Considering Eisenhower's regret in selecting Warren, the big mystery is why the president and attorney general failed to foresee Warren's jurisprudence. They weren't alone. William Stringer in the *Christian Science Monitor* characterized Warren as a "man whose political philosophy approximates that of President Eisenhower." A survey of legal experts by the Associated Press also predicted that Warren would do little to alter the Court's direction.

These viewpoints shed far more light about the Court's standing in American life in the 1950s than expose gross failures on the part of the White House. Few if any Court observers viewed the Court as a central battleground in American politics, in part because they failed to foresee the Court's eventual role in the political and social conflicts that came to dominate Warren's tenure. The rights revolution Warren launched had not yet erupted. The culture wars that plunged the nation into endless strife had not yet emerged. And the Court as an institution had historically shied away from divisive conflicts. These factors provided little incentives for presidents to closely scrutinize a nominee's ideology, particularly in relation to constitutional issues that were just beginning to appear on the horizon.

Besides, if anyone had bothered to carefully inspect Warren's political philosophy they would have found a progressive, largely non-partisan Republican, focused more on problem-solving than ideology. "There wasn't really a right wing and there wasn't really a left wing when my dad was active in the governorship," remembered Warren's son, Robert. "There was a Democratic party and a Republican party, and in a lot of respects they were the same." Just how did this play out from an ideological standpoint? Consistent with the GOP's widespread displeasure with the New Deal, Warren criticized Roosevelt during a 1952 television interview for subverting "state and local government" by "centralizing all administrative power in Washington." Yet,

Warren didn't clamor for a smaller government: he called for a constructive one, making him difficult to classify using modern day political labels. This dichotomy was on display in a number of ways. As governor, Warren reduced sales taxes while raising pensions; expanded unemployment insurance while supporting the anti-labor Taft-Hartley Act; and preached balanced budgets while supporting rent control. Statewide universal healthcare was his most ambitious social program—hardly at the top of the Republican wish list either then or now.

It is also easy to see why Warren's public record would have generated false assumptions about his judicial philosophy. As a long-time, and what Brownell and his own son dubbed "a very tough prosecutor" who favored the death penalty, Warren should have sided with law enforcement over the rights of criminals. A key proponent of Japanese internment during WWII, Warren should have embraced the government's anti-subversion measures aimed at combating the Soviet menace at the height of the Cold War. An enemy of vice throughout his years as a prosecutor, he should have fervently censored pornography. As an opponent of legislative reapportionment during his governorship, Warren should have granted other states the freedom to formulate their own legislative bodies. And as a champion of states' rights, Warren should have kept the judiciary out of the historically state-controlled arena of education.

Yet, in each instance, Warren's rulings shocked his critics. Was he a closet liberal or would a more extensive review on Eisenhower's part have unearthed his true colors? The attorney general, at least, felt that his analysis revealed no hint of Warren's eventual jurisprudence. "His liberal views," Brownell surmised years later, "came really after he went on the court." Had Brownell bothered to scrutinize Warren's upbringing, it would have also been difficult to draw definitive conclusions as to his ideology.

Methias, his Norwegian immigrant father, had lived through a type of Dickensian tragedy common in the late nineteenth century. His younger brother died in infancy, his mother died when Methias was four years old, and lastly his older brother succumbed to tuberculosis on Christmas Day. After marrying Warren's Swedish mother, the couple moved to California. Destitution followed Methias's every footstep. When Warren asked his father why he, Earl, didn't have a middle name, he responded: "My boy, when you were born I was too poor to give you a middle name."

Warren, the younger of two children, was born in Los Angeles in 1891 and grew up in the San Joaquin valley, the vast agricultural heartland of the state. Like many residents of Bakersfield, Methias worked for the Southern Pacific Railroad, the predominant employer in the dusty pit-stop one hundred miles north of Los Angeles. It was a barren existence, with no theater, library or recreational activities of any kind.

A frugal, serious, and stable family life ingrained in Warren many of the characteristics that helped catapult him to greatness. Deprived of an education, Methias emphasized its importance throughout his son's life, helping Warren attain a college degree. Alongside this focus, Methias instilled in his son a strong work ethic. At nine years old, Warren delivered ice in 100+ degree temperatures. Subsequent employment included delivering baked goods, driving a mule-powered grocery wagon, working as a bookkeeper, delivering newspapers, tutoring, and operating in various positions for Southern Pacific. Methias also ingrained in Warren a strong ethical code that embraced morality over religion.

Living in this largely classless yet diverse society populated by Mexicans, Chinese, and Jews, Warren saw up close the challenges faced by the nation's poor. The railroad's exploitation of its workers left an indelible mark, engendering in him a lifelong compassion for the underdog. "I saw every man on the railroad not essential for the operations of the trains laid off without pay and without warning," Warren recalled. "I saw minority groups brought into the country for cheap labor. . . . I helped carry men to the . . . emergency hospital for amputation of an arm or leg that had been crushed because there were no safety appliances . . . to prevent such injuries. . . . There was no compensation for them, and they went through life as cripples."

In 1908, Warren left for UC Berkeley, the state's premier public university. His academic prowess there would seem pedestrian in comparison to modern day justices. He was an above average student and captured no leadership posts. He acknowledged viewing the university more "as a community of lively, stimulating people than as a community of scholars." Not much had changed when Warren enrolled at Berkeley's Boalt Law School, where he graduated with "reasonably good" grades. The lack of academic success never hurt him professionally and, in a way, allowed his other talents to bloom. Jim Newton described this phenomenon in his exemplary biography of the chief justice: "Warren's love of practical learning and reliance on his personal experience over academic diligence . . . grounded his ideology in real life and infused his politics and jurisprudence with a common, practical touch."

After eighteen months at a law firm, Warren ended up at an Army camp in Virginia where he witnessed Jim Crow in action for the first time. "I remember how shocked we . . . were because the city was bedecked with Confederate flags," Warren recalled in describing a Memorial Day trip to Richmond. "They were everywhere, and not an American flag was to be seen."

Until Honey Bear's struggles with polio, the greatest tragedy in Warren's life took place in 1938. While home alone in Bakersfield, the 71-year-old Methias was beaten to death with an iron pipe by an unknown assailant. The news devastated Warren, who uncharacteristically wept in front of the press. The anguish of the crime compounded by a failure to capture the killer didn't turn Warren into a vendetta-fueled prosecutor, however. Nor did it undermine his belief in upholding an individual's constitutional rights no matter the stakes. "I believe the preservation of our civil liberties to be the most fundamental and important of all our government problems," he wrote to a colleague months after his father's death. "They constitute the soul of democracy."

Years later, a California Republican identified Warren's "championing of rights of the little fellows . . . to his thinking as a boy who has come up from his father's railroad worker's position." Neither Brownell nor Eisenhower made that connection. The consequences of misjudging Warren's judicial ideology, and that of other justices of the era, explain in part the types of nominees selected in recent years. Not only do modern nominees endure far greater scrutiny, they are also compelled to present a reliable and proven track record.

Considering the information available at the time, including Warren's gubernatorial record and the way the nation viewed the Court's role, no one could have predicted his impending judicial revolution. "Actually, there was little in the Chief Justice's career to suggest that he would ever cast himself in the role of a social revolutionist," a right-wing critic admitted years later. In fact, the conventional wisdom painted Warren in exactly opposite terms. "Examination of Earl Warren's 25-year record in public office fails to reveal much promise that he is a potential giant in U.S. history," *Time* declared. "The Warren utterances and speeches have never risen above the level of safe, dull political prose. He has rarely tried anything which had not been tried before. A calm man . . . slow to anger, he has stuck close to the middle of the road."

Unhappy with nominating Warren—he called it "the biggest damn fool thing I ever did"—Eisenhower nevertheless eschewed any ideological litmus tests for future justices. He did insist, however, that his four remaining appointments possess prior judicial experience. If history is our scorekeeper, however, these picks still left Eisenhower with a losing record. Two of his appointees, John Marshall Harlan II in 1955 and Potter Stewart in 1959, turned out to be center-right justices. His two other picks, Charles Whittaker and William Brennan, completely failed to push forth a conservative agenda.

On his first day on the Court, Whittaker told a pair of clerks: "Boys, I've never felt so inadequate in my entire life." His already shaky self-confidence deteriorated over time. "Mr. Attorney General, make me a district judge again," he pleaded later in his tenure. "I understood being a district judge. I don't understand this stuff. I can't deal with Felix Frankfurter and Hugo Black. I'm not that kind of a mind." The lack of strong convictions turned Whittaker into easy prey for the lions on the Court. In some of the testiest cases, he ping-ponged back and forth, sometimes leaving the Court's conferences in tears. Suffering from untreated depression and unable to tolerate the stress of the job, Whittaker had one of the shortest stints on the Court, a far cry from the long tenures modern presidents aim for in sorting through potential nominees. Just as importantly, Whittaker's resignation in 1962 opened the door for Kennedy to pick a far more liberal replacement, further tipping the institution into a Democratic stronghold.

Also confirmed in 1957, Brennan may have been Eisenhower's worst pick from the standpoint of a modern scorekeeper. Catering to Catholic voters leading up to the 1956 election, and convinced, incorrectly again, that Brennan was a judicial moderate despite being a Democrat, Eisenhower appointed the New Jersey Supreme Court Justice to the bench. Quickly establishing himself as Warren's chief lieutenant, Brennan remained a target of conservative derision three decades past Ike's retirement.

Court appointments give presidents the opportunity to influence public policy far past their time in office. For some presidents, it becomes their most enduring legacy. Gerald Ford, for one, believed his appointment of John Paul Stevens represented his greatest accomplishment during his brief presidency. The most famous example of the long-lasting impact of a Court appointment was John Marshall, who, in serving for 34 years past John Adams's presidency, established the constitutional framework of an infant nation. From this vantage point, Eisenhower failed miserably. Only two of his five picks turned out to be reliable conservatives while Warren and Brennan became the liberal tag team refashioning American society. Years later, Eisenhower confessed his regret to CBS News producer Fred Friendly. "Those two are very important jobs," he said, referring to the Warren and Brennan appointments, "and I didn't do a very good job with them."

Kennedy's judicial record was only moderately better. In his 31 years on the bench, Byron White, Kennedy's first selection, was difficult to characterize. On a court dominated by liberals in the 1960s, he tended to side with conservatives. The Court's lurch to the right in the 1970s and '80s placed him at its center. Though Kennedy also avoided ideological litmus tests, his second appointment, Arthur Goldberg, was far more representative of the Democratic Party but he served only three terms before resigning. Taken together, Kennedy's selections fared no better than Truman and Eisenhower.

JUNE, 1968

Acutely aware of these missteps, Johnson was the first president to fully grasp the importance of selecting the type of justice who would continue a president's agenda far past his reign and shield his legislative accomplishments from constitutional scrutiny. The president was so keenly aware of the importance of selecting a suitable justice, he machinated two openings just to be able to place men of his choosing.

Johnson's desire to land Fortas a spot on the Court was a no-brainer for the president. "He had a high, high regard for Abe Fortas," remembered one of the president's aides. "They were just so close." Fortas was a longtime friend and advisor, a political fixer who'd dug out Johnson from many a fox hole. His greatest rescue came in Johnson's 1948 Senate primary. Turning aside accusations of fraud, Fortas's legal wizardry secured Johnson the dubious election by a mere 87 votes. Without that victory, Johnson's career may have stalled. Their relationship encompassed every aspect of Johnson's life. Fortas managed Johnson's lucrative financial holdings. When Johnson needed help filling government positions, Fortas provided recommendations. When Johnson needed a fresh look at any problem ranging from a legal issue to foreign policy, he sought Fortas's counsel. "The best way to describe" their relationship, Larry O'Brien, Johnson's campaign manager and later the commissioner of the NBA recalled, "is when Abe spoke, the President listened." When scandal threatened Johnson's aides, Fortas was brought in for damage control. When Johnson took the oath of office minutes after Kennedy's assassination, he called Fortas first: "Abe," he said on the phone, "Stand by. I need you." Fortas suggested the formation of the Warren Commission and drafted a good portion of Johnson's inaugural speech as president. "He's the wisest man I have ever known," Johnson told his staff. The two remained so close Fortas described himself as a "presidential adviser" in the *Who's Who* guide and listed his business address as "c/o White House."

Their bond was undoubtedly strengthened by their shared personal experiences. Both grew up poor. Both were from the South. And both held a soft spot for liberal causes.

Born in 1910 in a Jewish enclave in Memphis, Fortas grew up in a home he described as "poor as you can imagine." The only extravagances allowed Fortas by his Orthodox father were violin lessons. Like many immigrant families, Fortas looked to education to rise out of destitution. "With Abe, it was study, study, study," Fortas's brother recalled. "He had a goal to attain." At fifteen, Fortas finished high school, where he had captained the debate team and formed a jazz ensemble centered around his violin performances. "Fiddlin' Abe" began to enter the upper strata of Memphis's social circles, a good training ground for his time in Washington decades later.

An undergraduate degree from Southwestern College was Fortas's last pit stop outside America's elite corridors. In 1933, he graduated salutatorian from Yale Law School where he held the most prestigious post available to a student: editor-in-chief of the law review. While serving as a law professor at his alma mater, he plunged into the heart of the New Deal, finding work at several of the alphabet soup agencies forged in the 1930s, the most prominent of which was the Securities and Exchange Commission. His promotion to Undersecretary of the Interior Department during the Second World War capped off his years of government service. After the war, he joined two partners to form a firm renowned for navigating clients through Washington's treacherous rapids: Arnold, Fortas & Porter. A brilliant attorney was often referred to as a "lawyer's lawyer" in legal circles. A professor at Yale Law School called Fortas a "lawyer's lawyer's lawyer." Fortas was the driving force behind the firm, and his clients included foreign governments, Washington power brokers like Johnson and Douglas, and a bevy of corporations such as Coca Cola, Pan Am, and Philip Morris. "The recognition of Abe Fortas as . . . a legal giant was pretty widespread," remembered O'Brien. He never formally reentered public life again but regularly served on government oversight panels and bar association committees. He also sat on the boards of five companies, including Federated Department Stores, a leading retailer, and was a trustee of Carnegie Hall, the Kennedy Center, and other Brahmin cultural institutions. Deeply philosophical, an accomplished amateur violinist, and a benefactor of the arts, Fortas was a modern incarnation of a Renaissance man: "I wouldn't be surprised," one of his clerks told *Time*, "if tomorrow I were to find out that Abe Fortas leads a secret life as a published poet in South America."

Fortas established a reputation for championing underdogs. During the height of McCarthyism, his firm spent $30,000, a small fortune at the time, defending a professor caught in McCarthy's crosshairs. His role in one of the seminal criminal law cases of the twentieth century introduced him to a broader audience. Appointed by the justices as a special counsel, Fortas was the winning lawyer in *Gideon v. Wainwright*, the 1963 case requiring the states to provide legal counsel to indigent clients in criminal cases. Douglas called Fortas's appearance "the best single argument" he had witnessed.

Fortas's biography played out like the quintessential American story: a child of poor immigrants overcoming the pervasive anti-Semitism of the era to climb to the top of America's meritocracy. The trajectory paralleled Johnson's own rags-to-riches story.

Born two years before Fortas in a modest farmhouse, Johnson grew up in Johnson City, Texas, a desolate hamlet about fifty miles west of Austin that was named after his ancestors. The twentieth century came late to the area, that was stricken by pervasive poverty and lacked electricity and indoor plumbing.

Despite these humble origins, Johnson's grandfather ran out to tell the neighbors: "A United States Senator's been born today." Yet, like a European aristocrat at the turn of century, what privileges Johnson carried in his title—his father served as a populist Democrat in the state government—he lacked in wealth and power. Johnson's father Samuel blew one potential fortune after another betting on cotton prices in a stubbornly barren soil. "My daddy," Johnson recalled of the man he idolized, "went busted waiting for cotton to go up." His father's failure as a speculator left the family in a state of destitution. At times, when the Johnsons lacked enough firewood on the coldest of days, the family huddled together to make it through the night. "We were poor, but we always had enough to eat," recalled a neighbor. "But once I ate over at the Johnsons', and there was bread and a little bit of bacon, and the bacon was rancid, too." Others derided the Johnsons' "filthy, dirty . . . house." Even more demeaning than the humiliation of receiving handouts, Samuel's misfortune made the family a target of ridicule. "Sam Johnson's a smart man," the townsfolk tended to say, "but the fool's got no sense."

The family's dire position sent Johnson to Southwest Texas State Teacher's College—what a colleague called a "little half-assed" school—rather than a university fitting for the state's elite. Johnson's experience while attending the modest institution along with a stint teaching at a school near the Mexican border ingrained in him a life-long passion to help minorities and the underprivileged. At the Mexican-American school, Johnson cared for a group neglected by others, making sure that his students mastered English. He went to every means to care for them. He asked his mother to send 200 packages of toothpaste for his students. He visited the corrugated shacks these migrant families lived in to make sure their kids would attend a debate or baseball game. He even taught English to the janitor after school. This passion to help those in need would not reveal itself until his presidency. "You never forget what poverty and hatred can do when you see its scars in the face of a young child," he recalled years later of his time teaching.

Johnson's prospects grew brighter when he started a legislative job in Washington in 1932 and, a year later, was elected speaker of the "Little Congress," an association of House workers. He married Claudia Alta Taylor two years later and she helped him set his sights ever higher. In 1937, he entered the House for what turned out to be an uneventful tenure. Barely showing any interest in the position, he rarely spoke on the floor or sponsored legislation. Anyone looking at him would have never suspected his aptitude for power or discerned his ideology: his capacity to mask his views convinced liberals and conservatives alike that he sat firmly in their camp.

With Fortas's help, Johnson entered the Senate in 1949 after winning the primary by a razor-thin margin of 87 votes, earning him the sarcastic nickname, "Landslide Lyndon." No longer bogged down by a desultory attitude, he quickly gained prominence under Richard Russell's stewardship. After he became Majority Whip in 1951, Minority Leader in 1953, and Majority Leader in 1955, he possessed unrivalled power inside the Capitol.

Kennedy's tragic assassination in 1963 made Johnson an accidental president and a punching bag for Kennedy loyalists who viewed him as an unprincipled interloper. Less than a year later, he trounced Barry Goldwater to become president in his own right. As his esteemed biographer Robert Caro pointed out, power reveals. And once in power, Johnson shed any semblance of his former self. Long distrusted by liberals for his southern connections, Johnson pushed through Congress the most ambitious civil rights agenda since Reconstruction, and only the New Deal surpassed his Great Society's ambitions for addressing the nation's social failings.

Coming off his landslide election, Johnson reached the apex of his power and was ready to wield it to enact his ambitious agenda: "what the hell's the presidency for?" he asked. From the White House, he commanded the awesome machinery of the federal government like a generalissimo leading an invasion force. Nothing stood in his way. Once the holdouts in the South retreated, Congress offered little resistance, bending to Johnson's will by enacting not dozens but hundreds of items of legislation affecting civil rights, education, healthcare, the environment, consumer protection, immigration, housing, and the arts. Only one branch remained beyond his reach—the Supreme Court. To safeguard his accomplishments, and to keep the judicial branch in harmony with the rest of a government willing to do his bidding, he sought to fill the Court with amenable jurists.

Fortas checked off all of Johnson's boxes. The president longed for a dependable liberal in his 50s who could both get along with Black and Douglas and enjoy a stellar reputation among legal circles. These were certainly worthy barometers for a Democratic president in the mid-1960s. Less noble was Johnson's other motive. He wanted to place a spy of sorts to inform him of the Court's inner workings. But it wasn't just about politics even for Johnson, among the most cunning men to set foot in the White House. He was eager to reward and honor his close friend with a position at the pinnacle of the legal profession. "To Abe Fortas," Johnson wrote on a presidential photo sent to his friend, "whom there is no better, with love, Lyndon B. Johnson."

Requiring top-notch qualifications, a president's backing, the Senate's blessing, and—with so few openings, fortuitous timing—a job on the Court was among the scarcest in American politics. Because of these imposing hurdles, some of the nation's finest jurists never joined the exclusive club. Perhaps no one exemplified this fate more than Learned Hand, whose career as a trial and appellate court judge spanned nearly the entire first half of the twentieth century. Though countless lawyers and judges backed his candidacy, presidents repeatedly passed over him. Other potential nominees, such as mid-century favorites Edward Levi and Henry Friendly, appeared on numerous presidential short-lists only to plummet like a rocket running out of fuel before reaching the cosmos. Or in the case of Robert Bork, another perennial contender, one that exploded in mid-flight.

Ever-impatient, Johnson wasn't going to wait for a vacancy. To make room for Fortas, he planned to remove one of the sitting justices. It was as audacious as it was quintessentially Johnson. The Court, however, was the most insulated branch of the government: a president had no sway over a sitting justice.

In the summer of 1965, Harvard economist John Kenneth Galbraith handed the president an opening to exert some influence. The convoluted chain of events began with the untimely death of Adlai Stevenson, the U.S. Ambassador to the United Nations, on July 14, 1965. Afraid that Johnson would coerce him to take the position, Galbraith told the president that Goldberg "was a little bored on the Court" two days after Stevenson's death. Yes, Goldberg had mentioned that the Court's pace couldn't match the rush he felt as a union lawyer and labor secretary. Satisfied nonetheless, Goldberg had no desire to leave. Like a man seeking the last lifeboat on a sinking ship, Galbraith embellished out of desperation and, with no idea that Johnson coveted a slot on the Court for Fortas, he couldn't have suspected what was to come next.

Unyielding to the end, Johnson chipped away at anyone's defenses until they crumbled. It's what helped him become a legislative puppet master. It's also what drove his subordinates to tears and his colleagues into submission. A notorious manipulator, Johnson fluffed one man's ego while crushing another's to get his way. If all else failed, he typically resorted to an in-your-face style. The "Johnson Treatment" often began with him grabbing someone by the lapels or arms, and while his 6-foot 4-inch frame towered over a shorter man, Johnson poked his target with his hands or jabbed his head in a rooster-like motion, invading the man's personal space like a boxer cornering an opponent in the ring. Out of his mouth spewed the most convincing arguments: a slew of policy justifications, statistics, moral persuasions—whatever was needed. Johnson wasn't a fast talker and he was an unexceptional public orator. But in these private sessions, he spoke almost without pausing, preventing any interjections. And when his interlocutors did fire back, his trigger-ready mind unleashed a rebuttal like a litigator prepared for cross-examination. For the most recalcitrant targets who couldn't be convinced, for those who couldn't be bullied or bribed, Johnson did not point to any political calculation or attempt to trade favors but instead pulled on their sense of patriotic duty. They had to obey his wishes, not for his sake but for their country's well-being. The Treatment broke down the strongest of wills and nothing personified the intoxicating allure of Johnson's words more than his ability to persuade Warren to chair the Warren Commission over the chief justice's strenuous objections. "You were a soldier in World War I," Johnson told Warren soon after the Kennedy assassination, "but there was nothing you could do in that uniform comparable to what you can do for your country in this hour of trouble." "Oh, when he puts on the heat," Warren remembered, "and pictures it the way he can, it's pretty tough to say no." Hubert Humphrey described being on the receiving end of the Treatment in blunter terms: it was "an almost hypnotic experience. I came out of that session covered with blood, sweat, tears, spit— and sperm."

Johnson unleashed the same tactics on Goldberg. At first, the justice turned down an offer to lead the Department of Health and Human Services. Over a series of meetings, including one on Air Force One, the president lured Goldberg to the U.N. job with promises to have him serve as a "principal adviser" in Vietnam. "While he likes the Court," Johnson told Galbraith after speaking with the justice, "he loves peace more, and he thinks he has a better chance to do something about it here." To sweeten the offer, Johnson suggested the possibility of something more alluring on the horizon. "You're over there on that Court, isolated from the action," he told the justice, "and you can't get to the Vice Presidency from the Court." These kinds of grand promises were par for the course for Johnson. "You'll be involved in everything," the president told Goldberg according to Joseph Califano, Johnson's domestic advisor. "You're my second secretary of state." Goldberg didn't last long. Only four days after Galbraith's suggestion, the justice agreed to switch jobs.

Goldberg's resignation from the Court shocked Washington's establishment. The tag team chroniclers of the capital's inner workings, Rowland Evans and Robert Novak, called it "the most surprising rabbit" of Johnson's presidency. Why would a justice with lifetime tenure in one of the highest positions in the U.S. government give up that throne for a temporary posting? Why indeed? Goldberg, the son of an immigrant, the first in his family to go

beyond elementary school, felt he "owed the country a great deal." Johnson catered to Goldberg's innate patriotism. On top of this "compelling call to duty,"
Goldberg's high self-regard did the rest. Mistakenly believing that he would
be granted the authority at the U.N. to "play a key role" in Vietnam, Goldberg
convinced himself that he, a masterful negotiator, could resolve the quagmire
in Asia. He never became a principle adviser on Vietnam, and bitterness and
disappointment marred his time at the U.N.

The next phase of Johnson's plan turned out to be surprisingly difficult.
Fortas had already rejected Johnson's overtures to become attorney general
in 1964 and he had more reasons to resist a position on the Court a year later.
Fortas enjoyed his $200,000 annual salary which, along with his wife's hefty
income, financed a Rolls-Royce, a summer home in Westport, Connecticut, an
art collection, and three French poodles. A $100,000 mortgage for a new home
in Georgetown hung over him. A justice, by comparison, earned only $39,500
a year. He didn't want to abandon his firm in the midst of a major growth
spurt and his wife Carolyn Agger, also a partner at the firm and a leading tax
lawyer, was vehemently opposed to the idea of him leaving. Finally, Fortas
feared that his nomination would open up the presidency to accusations of
"government-by-crony."

"Resistance is futile," say the Borg, the villainous extraterrestrial species
from the iconic sc-fi TV and movie series *Star Trek*. It could have been Johnson's motto as well. After "painful searching," Fortas declined the offer in a
handwritten letter dated July 19. On July 21, he again rebuffed the president.
Johnson sent Goldberg and William Douglas, Fortas's old mentor, to do some
recruiting on his behalf. That also failed. On July 27, Fortas again rejected the
offer, this time during a meeting with the president.

Resistance was futile! Having seen the irresistible force first-hand, Goldberg told his clerks: "He's going to wear him down. He'll wait until the end
of time." Johnson phoned Fortas on July 28 to discuss his press conference
announcing a major troop increase in Vietnam. "How's your blood pressure,"
Johnson asked. "A little worried," Fortas chuckled in response. "Come on
over," Johnson said, inviting Fortas to review his speech. "I don't know what
will happen . . . but don't be surprised."

"Look, you don't suppose he is going to lean on me some more about this," Fortas asked his partner, Paul Porter, as he prepared to leave his office for the White House. "I think you are off the hook," Porter said reassuringly.

Minutes later, Fortas again refused Johnson's offer as they walked from the Oval Office to the East Room. "Now look, Abe," Johnson fired back, "they need you on the court. You may never have the opportunity again. Take this job." Fortas held firm. Just moments away from going on stage to address the nation, Johnson pounced again: "I'm sending fifty thousand boys to Vietnam today and I'm sending you to the Supreme Court. You can watch the announcement here on television or you can come over with me to the press conference." Fortas had repelled his friend admirably. He had withstood the Treatment better and longer than most. His powers of resistance finally dissolved. Without ever giving his assent—"to the best of my knowledge . . . I never said yes" Fortas declared years later—he followed the president to the East Room and took a seat in the front row alongside the press corps.

Twenty-two minutes into a speech on Vietnam followed by a desultory list of subjects, including the appointment of John Chancellor to the Voice of America, Johnson finally announced Fortas's nomination. Fortas sat quietly through the pronouncement, evincing a fleeting grin when Johnson finished. The calm appearance masked his anxiety: he returned to his office visibly shaken, his shirt soaked with sweat.

The nonchalant nature of the nomination process would shock a modern observer. The president announced Fortas's nomination at the tail end of a speech largely devoted to other subjects. As if partaking in this conspiracy of indifference, none of the reporters asked about the nomination. The Senate acted just as cavalierly. Two weeks after the nomination, with less than three hours of hearings and no background checks or investigations of any consequence, the Senate confirmed Fortas by a voice vote.

Despite his initial reluctance, Fortas confessed to Douglas his excitement "at the prospect" of joining the Court after his confirmation on August 11, 1965. The overwhelming response he received mirrored his excitement. Hundreds of congratulatory letters and telegrams from cabinet members, agency heads, law school deans, titans of industry, cultural leaders, and judges poured in. "I just want to shout my gratification," wrote USC's law school dean, in a typical missive to Fortas. Expressing no regrets, Goldberg wrote in a telegram: "BRAVO OUR HEARTS GO WITH YOU." But one of those felicitations contained within it an ominous message. "I am happy for my Country," Bobby Baker, Johnson's former Senate gopher wrote, "but sad for you personally."

With Fortas ensconced in the Court, Johnson eyed his next target. Eager to appoint the first African-American justice, Johnson had the ideal candidate in mind: Thurgood Marshall, the nation's most renowned black lawyer. To make room for Fortas, the president only had to move Goldberg. That was like playing checkers. This time around, his machinations looked more like chess.

To spruce up Marshall's resume, Johnson plucked him from a post on a federal appellate court to have him made solicitor general. A stint at the position had catapulted the careers of justices Stanley Reed and Robert Jackson. That was the easy part. The hard part was to create another vacancy.

For his next move, Johnson moved Attorney General Nicholas Katzenbach from his top post at the Justice Department to take the number two job at the State Department. It was a clear demotion for a man most remembered for his courageous standoffs at southern universities resisting integration. It was also a job for which Katzenbach, who had no foreign policy experience to speak of, wasn't ideally suited, yet nonetheless coveted.

The checkmate was now only a couple of moves away. Johnson had mixed feelings about giving Ramsey Clark—the son of Justice Tom Clark—the top job at the Justice Department, but was willing to do so for the opportunity to fill another seat on the Court. Weeks after Katzenbach's departure, he decided to put his plan into action. Johnson was aware that placing a father-son duo in these posts would generate an ethical quandary with no easy work-around since the government played a role in about half the Court's cases. Even if Ramsey had nothing to do with a case, the public might think that father and son were conspiring. Though an advisor explained to Johnson that Clark would only have to recuse himself on the rare occasions his son appeared before the Court, Johnson knew that his old friend would sacrifice his post to make way for his son to become attorney general.

Clark's son, however, still had hopes of keeping his father in the Marble

Palace. During a phone call with Ramsey on January 25, 1967, the president asked him straight out: "You think you could be Attorney General with your daddy on the Court?" "Well, I think," Ramsey paused, searching for words. "I guess I think other people ought to judge that. . . . I know that as far as I'm personally concerned that that would not affect my judgment. I don't think it would affect dad's judgment. I'd hate to see dad get off the Court." He paused for a longer moment this time around, clearly searching for a way to keep his father on as a justice. Ramsey rambled a bit, preaching how his father's conservative views on law enforcement would strengthen Johnson politically. It was a worthy but futile appeal. "My judgment is that if you became Attorney General, he'd have to leave the Court," Johnson insisted.

A month after this conversation with Ramsey, Johnson nominated him to lead the Justice Department. Within two hours of his son's nomination, Clark submitted his resignation, effective at the end of the Court's term. Days later, former Attorney General William Rogers offered to make the case to keep Clark on the Court. The very notion that Rogers genuinely believed that Johnson would welcome such assistance revealed the president's mendacity. Having orchestrated Clark's departure, it would have been comical for Johnson to now look for a way to undo his own handiwork.

Weeks after Clark's departure, Thurgood Marshall, another reliable liberal in his 50s who could solidify the Democratic hold over the Court for many years, took his place.

When it came to replacing Warren, the president had one more thing in mind. He recognized that his historic civil rights bills and Great Society programs had so radically changed the fabric of American life, they would inevitably face repeated challenges in the courts. Obsessed with his standing among American presidents, he wanted the next chief justice to protect his greatest achievements and prevent a lurch to the right. "I feared . . . a conservative Court," Johnson acknowledged in his memoirs, "a reversal of the philosophy of the Warren Court, and a dissipation of the forward legislative momentum we had achieved." No one would do more to shield his legacy than Fortas.

CHAPTER 4

RECRUITING THE "THE WIZARD OF OOZE"

JUNE, 1968

Johnson spent the days after his meeting with the chief justice putting out feelers. He expected the southern senators to put up the biggest roadblocks to getting Fortas confirmed. What discouraged him was the intel pouring into the Oval Office. Regardless of the source of the information, it pointed to an opposition far more intense than he had expected. The president also recognized that election-year politics would embolden Republican senators to obstruct Fortas's elevation. It was no surprise that Strom Thurmond had already launched a media blitz against the nomination. He had made a living bashing the Warren Court and didn't need an election to issue a clarion call. What was more disconcerting for Johnson was the uprising from rank and file Republicans who had never mounted any kind of real opposition during past confirmations. The math was simple. Alone, neither group could defeat Fortas. But together, they could prevail.

Johnson understood the Senate's power structure better than anyone to have stepped into the White House since WWII. The Constitution made no distinctions among senators but the political reality was that seniority ruled the institution. To squash these brewing revolts, the president reached out to his old allies within the leadership of both factions, starting with Minority Leader Everett Dirksen.

Born in 1896 in Pekin, a tiny hamlet in the agrarian flatlands of central Illinois that was named after Peking due to its shared longitude with the Chinese capital, Dirksen lived out a Horatio Alger story. Pressed into financial hardship by their father's early death, Dirksen and his two brothers worked the family farm in the morning, delivered produce on the way to school, and returned to the land in the afternoon. Years later, Dirksen dropped out of the University of Minnesota to hover above the trenches of WWI in a scout balloon. Upon his return, he led an eclectic life, selling medications, building washing machines, and working in a bakery, all while aspiring to become an actor and writer. The failure to publish dozens of novels and short stories snuffed out those literary ambitions but introduced him to his wife, whom he met during a rehearsal for one of his plays.

It was a good thing, too. Dirksen was better suited for politics than literature. After a stint as Pekin's commissioner of finance, he spent sixteen years in the House before jumping to the Senate in 1951. Eight years later, he took over the Republican caucus as Minority Leader.

A career in public life allowed him to apply the lessons he learned as an amateur thespian to his new profession. Dirksen was an articulate, energetic, and over-the-top orator. "He was a ham but a loveable ham," recalled a senate aide. In a single speech, he could be sincere and ironic, solemn and melodramatic: A 1959 *Harper's* profile described him as "grandiloquent, sanctimonious, priggish, and earnestly earnest." *The New York Times* was less kind, ascribing to Dirksen a "reputation for ridiculous rhetoric, political opportunism and blatant reaction." He amassed monikers like a professional wrestler: "Irksome Dirksen," "the Wizard of Ooze," "the Liberace of the Senate," and "Oleaginous Ev."

His unkempt hair flared from the top of his head like a rooster's, making him appear—as Bob Hope put it—"like a man who had been electrocuted, but lived." Dirksen's flamboyance revealed itself through his diction, along with an uncanny ability to raise his voice to a crescendo or soften it to a whisper as the moment called for. He never slurred or elided his words, enunciating every syllable with such care it was as if they had been sent to him from the heavens. "When you listened to Dirksen talk you'd say 'God, this is magnificent,'" recalled a senate staffer. "It was beautiful and melodious. . . . He should have been a Shakespearean actor." Waving his index finger through the air like a conductor wielding a baton, Dirksen enhanced his oratory through gesticulations. Typical of his performances, the Minority Leader was on the Senate floor when a group of elderly women advocating for Social Security showed up in the gallery. "Ladies, I was on the floor, defending the Republic against the onslaughts of the opposition," Dirksen told them, "when I was informed that forty lovely girls wished to see me. I immediately removed the armor of the warrior and put on the cloak of the poet."

Over the years, liters of bourbon and an overindulgent smoking habit—coming out of surgery for lung cancer, he reflexively reached for his breast pocket to snatch a cigarette—thickened his voice into a hoarse baritone. By the late 1960s, his broad nose and long ears slouched from his fleshy face, with large pouches under his pale blue eyes masked by wide, black-framed glasses. His hair shifted to a silvery-white mix. Ulcers, kidney ailments, and emphysema conspired with long hours to accelerate the aging process, corroding the theatrics of his youth but never diminishing his daylight-to-midnight work ethic.

Though he considered himself a conservative, Dirksen was never an ideologue. His willingness to make deals with Democrats generated disgust and admiration in equal portions. Illinois liberals deemed him a "snake-oil salesman" for backing Joseph McCarthy. Conservatives denounced him as an unprincipled flip-flopper willing to cross partisan lines. A Chicago newspaper counted Dirksen changing his positions 163 times during his sixteen years in the House alone. "He is a delightful companion," a southern senator once remarked, "but he changes too often for me. I never know where he is." Was he a wily opportunist or, as Dirksen offered in his own defense, a thoughtful statesman willing to adapt to "new circumstances and new conditions"? Definitely a bit of both. In the most consequential moment of his career, at least, he emerged as the latter, playing a key role in passing the historic 1964 civil rights bill.

Dirksen would fall short of reaching the Senate's pantheon but, alongside Robert Dole, he was the most significant Republican senate leader of the postwar era. Though in charge of only 30-odd senators during his tenure, he was able to direct a motley crew ranging from New York's Jacob Javits on the left to Barry Goldwater on the right to form a formidable minority far surpassing its numerical inferiority. Since Dirksen's shortage of foot-soldiers confined him to forming ad hoc coalitions with liberal or conservative Democrats to maximize his influence, he infrequently pushed his own agenda. Forced to be selective under these circumstances, he nevertheless spent a great deal of political capital challenging one of the Warren Court's most disruptive rulings for much of the 1960s.

For all of Warren's accomplishments as chief justice, few now mark the establishment of the one-person, one-vote principle as his greatest achievement. When he had a chance to reflect on his legacy, however, Warren considered the seminal ruling on reapportionment, the 1962 case *Baker v. Carr*, as the "most important case of my tenure." He wasn't alone. Many politicians in the 1960s considered the battle over reapportionment the "great issue" of their era.

By 1960, malapportioned—or unequally populated—legislative districts had metastasized into a national cancer. Every state had at least one instance of a two-to-one ratio between its most and least populated legislative districts. In many cases, the disparity amounted to a wholesale perversion of democracy. With a population of 791, Colebrook, Connecticut, had the same number of state representatives as Hartford's population of 162,178. Thirty-eight people in one Vermont town elected the same number of representatives as Burlington's 33,000 residents. Los Angeles County, with a population of 6,038,771, had the same number of state senators as a California district with 14,294 residents. Legislative districts ranged from 13,050 to 556,326 in Georgia; 915 to 93,460 in Idaho; and 3,868 to 331,755 in Arizona. Besides being patently unfair, such imbalances practically invited unbridled gerrymandering. Michigan was perhaps the most notorious practitioner of these dark arts: in the 1954 election, Republicans earned less than half of the votes in the state's senate races but captured two-thirds of its seats.

Congressional districts were equally warped. In 1960, the largest House seats were double the size of their smallest districts across nineteen states. Several states had ratios that were far worse: Michigan again stuck out with congressional seats ranging from 177,431 to 802,994 people. The fact that so many congressmen owed their positions to these distortions led one observer to call the body the "House of Un-Representatives."

Compounding the problem, most states refused to follow their own mandates by regularly readjusting their districts to reflect changing population figures. A mere twenty states redrew their legislative districts between 1940 and 1960: Alabama last recalibrated its districts in 1906, Connecticut in 1903, and Maryland in 1867.

Rural areas were the primary beneficiaries of this corrupt system. A University of Virginia report published in 1961 concluded that "big city voters have less than one-half the representation of people in open-country areas." Another study determined rural areas were overrepresented by 25 to 30 seats in Congress. In other instances, malapportioned districts favored no special interests or geographic regions. They were simply random and arbitrary, the work of negligent stewards. The Founding Fathers considered the states the bastions of liberty. When it came to the simple arithmetic of establishing equitable legislative representation, however, state governments failed to live up to the responsibility assigned to them, making a mockery of American democracy.

As one of the worst offenders, Tennessee made for a ripe target for reform. Since 1901, the legislature had ignored Tennessee's constitutional mandate to reapportion districts, allowing 37% of voters to elect two-thirds of the state's senators. Voters in Memphis, Tennessee's largest metropolitan area, had their votes diluted by more than 50%. Its tiniest counties, on the other hand, were over-represented by 600%. "The pigs and chickens in our smaller counties have better representation in the Tennessee legislature than the people of Nashville," its mayor complained. These were more than abstract statistical formulations. The malapportioned legislature funneled resources needed by growing metropolitan areas to depopulating rural locales. "I believe in collecting the taxes where the money is—in the cities—and spending it where it's needed—in the country," quipped an influential rural legislator.

Unable to institute reforms through the political process, the state judiciary, or Congress, Tennessee's disgruntled voters looked to the Court as a last resort in *Baker v. Carr*. In Warren, they found a sympathetic patron. Described as a modern-day "Platonic Guardian" by Anthony Lewis, Warren saw the Court as a tool to help the disenfranchised and underprivileged. Filing a petition to the Court required following rigid guidelines down to the minutia of using precisely sized paper. Unable to hire attorneys and incapable of navigating the complexities of an appeal, many indigent petitioners sent messy, often indecipherable appeals to the Court. A highbrow judge would have brushed off these entreaties. Instructing his clerks to effectively serve as the petitioners' advocates in these cases, Warren did the opposite. This was not a cosmetic directive intended to depict the Court as an egalitarian institution. Several of the Court's iconic cases—including *Miranda* and *Gideon*—came before the justices through this process.

Mindful of the failures of the other branches of government, Warren also viewed the Court as the institution most capable of achieving the ideals enunciated in the nation's founding documents. If "all men are created equal" as the Declaration of Independence had boldly asserted, then why was the reality of American life so far removed from this ideal? Warren longed for a nation that lived up to the lofty standards etched into the Constitution. In pursuing this goal, he had little patience for criticism of an over-reaching judiciary. Instead, able to place himself in the shoes of the disadvantaged litigants, Warren felt that judicial restraint had long been used as an excuse to leave "many problems basic to American life" unresolved. "We have failed to face up to them, and they have piled up on us," he wrote in his memoirs. With malapportionment, in particular, he blamed a timid Court for making "change hopeless" by refusing to tackle an issue previous generations of justices considered a "political issue" beyond the reach of the judiciary.

On the surface, *Brown* and *Baker* seemed to have little in common. But within Warren's worldview, both cases rectified important social ills overlooked by the political branches. His willingness to have the judiciary fix these shortfalls put him on a collision course with a new group of enemies— state officials.

Much like *Brown*, the fact that *Baker* upended one of the nation's most deeply entrenched practices—by forcing the reformulation of nearly every legislative district in the nation—rather than its legal rationale marked its historic significance. And just like *Brown*, *Baker* spawned an assault on the justices that far surpassed Warren's expectations.

The first steps took place in Biloxi, Mississippi on July, 1962, at a regional conference of the Council of State Governments, a non-partisan organization focused on professionalizing state governments and preaching states' rights. Coming months after the *Baker* ruling, the delegates at Biloxi adopted a resolution calling for a constitutional amendment to block the federal judiciary from reviewing apportionment cases. From these southern roots, the campaign's next phase spread to various, interlocking associations. Two months after the Biloxi meeting, 750 state officials gathered in Phoenix. "As a group," one observer of the conference noted, "they certainly felt changes were going to affect them personally. . . . There had been . . . a large amount of underlying criticism of Supreme Court decisions, but it was *Baker* . . . that crystallized resentment into action." What contributed to the shock was the Court's dismissal of practices dating back to the founding of the republic. "In an instant," the *National Review* grumbled, "the law of the land was overturned; right became wrong, and wrong right." Though most of the state officials were obscure figures barely known in their own districts, they were the masters within their select fiefdoms. Now the Warren Court threatened their modest domains. Building on the work started in Mississippi, the delegates charged a nine-person committee to come up with a plan to subvert *Baker*.

By the end of the year, the committee conjured up a plan. It is "impossible to believe" that the Founding Fathers "envisaged such potency for the pronouncements of nine judges," the committee's chairman Lloyd Lowrey told the crowd at the annual conference hosted by the Council of State Governments in December, 1962. Based out of a rural area north of Sacramento, and the record-holder for winning the most unopposed elections in California history, Lowrey made it his mission to curtail Warren's powers.

Despite the immense hurdles to altering the Constitution, Lowrey laid out the committee's recommendations for three amendments, which together constituted some of the most "fundamental and far-reaching" changes to the Constitution ever contemplated. The first proposal sought to excise Congress out of the amendment process. This modification to Article V of the Constitution could have been titled "The States Strike Back." Seeking to strip the federal courts of their jurisdiction over apportionment cases, the second proposal mirrored the suggestions made in Biloxi. The final proposal, an attack on the Court so radical it would have made Thurmond blush, called for a new "Court of the Union" administered by state chief justices to review Supreme Court rulings involving federal-state issues. Angered that the Tenth Amendment, which preserved for the states all powers not prescribed to the federal government, had been "raped twice a day for 10 years" by the Warren Court, Illinois representative Warren Wood pushed the last proposal to a crowd driven into hysteria. Terrified of *Baker*'s sweeping reach, the state delegations at the conference passed the first proposal 37-4, the second 26-10, and the Court of the Union proposal 21-20. Taken together, they amounted to what *The New York Times* editorial board later called a "states' rights counterrevolution of dismaying dimensions."

Progressing stealthily and unnoticed by Washington insiders, the amendments quickly gained traction. Eighteen states approved the first proposal, fifteen backed the second one, and five approved the Court of the Union over a period of months. The torrid pace bode well for their backers: only nine states had approved the Sixteenth Amendment (legalizing income taxes) and thirteen states had approved the Eighteenth Amendment (prohibition) during the first six months after their submission to the states. Tipped off by Arthur Freund, a lawyer based in St. Louis, Warren watched in dismay: "I was astounded by the number of States which have seriously considered the proposals," he wrote to Freund.

Since justices refrained from openly campaigning on political matters, Warren was reluctant to speak out. Without the legal profession's backing, however, Warren feared "there is no telling how far" the proposals "might go." The chief justice finally spoke up at Duke Law School, which had invited him to deliver the keynote address at the inauguration of its new building on April 27, 1963. (Ironically, the school didn't invite Nixon, its most famous alumnus, to the ceremony.) Careful to avoid political issues, Warren tended to focus on abstract legal theories and historic observations during these speaking engagements. True to form, he reviewed the foundations of the Constitution during his address at Duke. Yet, he was so distraught at the momentum of the States' Rights Amendments, that he decided to break with protocol. "It must be apparent to all that these proposed Constitutional Amendments," he said after describing the three proposals, "would radically change the character of our institutions" and undermine the "stability of the . . . Constitution." Then he sounded the alarm. "I suppose there are... many in this audience who have never heard of these proposals. . . . Yet . . . twenty-four States . . . have adopted one or two or even all three of these proposals." He ended the speech with a call to action: "If lawyers are not to be the watchmen for the Constitution, on whom are we to rely?"

Dozens of bar associations and prominent attorneys answered his call, none more so than Walter Mondale, the head of the National Association of Attorneys General who spearheaded a nationwide campaign. Labor and civil rights groups as well as media outlets also jumped into the fray. In a *Newsweek* editorial titled "The Assault on the Union," the influential political commentator Walter Lippmann called the proposed amendments "sinister and radical." The *Wall Street Journal* editorial board, a persistent critic of the Warren Court, nonetheless warned against tampering with the Constitution. Blaming right-wing groups for doing the "devil's work far better than Communists could do," President John F. Kennedy also spoke out against the amendments. Weeks after Warren's speech, the proposals sputtered. Now under a national spotlight and pressured by local bar associations, three states rejected the amendments and New Jersey rescinded its support in quick succession. Declaring victory, *Time* proclaimed: "it appears that . . . the U.S. Constitution is in no danger of burning down."

A conflagration may have missed the Constitution but it certainly spread to the legislative houses across the nation. *Baker* unleashed a restructuring of American government not seen since the 1860s. State and federal judges did most of the groundwork recalibrating legislative districts while the justices issued a series of decisions in 1963 and 1964, laying down the contours of the one-person, one-vote principle. The final blow to malapportionment came in *Reynolds v. Sims*, a ruling requiring equal-sized legislative districts in both houses of bicameral legislatures, which like Congress often had one population-based legislative chamber and one devised according to geographic features. "Legislators represent people, not trees or acres," were Warren's enduring words from the 1964 decision. "Legislators are elected by voters, not farms or cities or economic interests." For Warren, the Constitution's primary purpose was to protect individuals—not farmers or industrialists, municipalities or counties, or upstate or downstate populations. Any justification to the contrary, no matter how deeply rooted in tradition, stood in conflict with this underlying principle.

Reynolds served as a defining moment for Warren. Admitting to having acted out of "political expediency" as governor, he defeated a proposal in 1948 to fairly reapportion California's legislature. "Many California counties are far more important in the life of the State than their population bears," he proclaimed in a speech at the time, essentially arguing to protect the very interests he denounced in *Reynolds*. Years later, the "Platonic Warren" acknowledged that facing "the question from a judicial viewpoint" led him to a more sagacious conclusion. To his supporters, this marked his evolution. To his critics, it reeked of hypocrisy.

Dirksen was no ideologue but, from his perspective, these lines of cases represented "one of the greatest threats to the system of government that we have had in one hundred and seventy-five years of our national existence." In hindsight, Dirksen sounded melodramatic. But hailing as he had from a rural area, the terror of urban domination was all too real for him. If each legislative chamber was based on population in his home state, then the single mega-metropolis of Chicago could "do pretty much as they please with respect to the other 101 counties," Dirksen cautioned in an interview published by *U.S. News & World Report*. "There's no end to what might be done." Dirksen spent his remaining years toiling over what he considered to be "the most important Constitutional issue" of his generation.

Weeks after the Court handed down in *Reynolds* on June 15, 1964, the Minority Leader reached a deal with Johnson and the Justice Department to suspend the ruling for two years. This grand bargain convinced the *Washington Post* that passage of Dirksen's measure "seemed assured." Ironically, the primary opposition came from Dirksen's fellow senator from Illinois. Paul Douglas felt equally impassioned about the issue, calling it "the most important . . . legislative fight in decades." Both in substance and form, Illinois's two senators could not have been more dissimilar. Douglas was a Democrat—Dirksen a Republican. Douglas was from Chicago—Dirksen from the state's rural center. Douglas had a doctorate—Dirksen was a dropout. Douglas reviled horse-trading—Dirksen reveled in it. Douglas was a rebel—Dirksen a consummate insider.

As loathsome as liberals found the filibuster, Douglas stymied Dirksen with one extended over six weeks. This was Dirksen's first setback.

When Congress reconvened in 1965, Dirksen redoubled his efforts. Using the federal congressional model as a template, he proposed a constitutional amendment allowing a state to have one chamber based on factors other than population. Through the support from 30 of the 32 Republicans in his caucus alongside 21 southern Democrats, he was sixteen shy of the magic number needed to pass a constitutional amendment. With early estimates showing no more than one to two dozen senators in the opposing camp, Dirksen began the second round against Douglas with a formidable lead.

Throughout the spring of 1965, Dirksen's amendment along with a handful of less popular alternatives received a full hearing by Senator Birch Bayh's Subcommittee on Constitutional Amendments. The bevy of witnesses recruited by both sides stretched the testimony over a span of ten weeks, during which mayors from big cities butted heads with politicians from sparsely populated regions. Chicago's Mayor Richard Daley provided one of the strongest justifications for reapportionment. "The primary reason why many of our general assemblies have failed to observe the principle of majority rule is that it is too much to ask men of both political parties to vote themselves out of office. . . . It was necessary for the Supreme Court," he told Bayh's committee, echoing Warren's philosophy, "to reestablish the fundamental concept of democratic government which the States have refused for so long to carry out themselves." The president of the American Farm Bureau fired back, warning that only Dirksen's amendment could safeguard "minority interests" and ensure that "local views and concerns will not be buried and lost before the power of majorities."

Though publicized as a fight between urban and rural interests, the contest over Dirksen's amendment largely took place behind the scenes in what turned out to be an old-fashioned tug of war between big business and big labor. Already a favorite of corporate America for preaching fiscal responsibility and combating organized labor, Dirksen found a natural ally in a community terrified of reapportionment. The U.S. Chamber of Commerce's national magazine communicated these fears to its readers in a 1964 article, "How Reapportionment Threatens Business," listing issues—the minimum wage, industrial regulation, corporate taxes, unemployment insurance, and workers compensation—that would be relinquished to big labor should urban legislators dominate state governments. As states began to comply with *Reynolds* in 1965, the Chamber bemoaned the transfer of "considerable voting power to blue-collar workers and the unemployed" as if it was witnessing the siege of the castle walls by barbarians.

One of the Chamber's most avid spokesmen turned out to be Robert Moses, New York's infamous master builder. "The Supreme Court now legislates," Moses complained in a 1964 editorial published by the Chamber. "Until we change the Constitution, any five judges out of nine . . . are ruling the country." With each passing paragraph, Moses grew more hyperbolic, unleashing his harshest screeds against majoritarian rule. "Is there any answer to . . . proportional representation, which has failed dismally everywhere, which helped Hitler to rise, brought communism into East Germany, encourages splinter parties, intrigue, mob rule and irresponsibility, and negates all genuine leadership? . . . Be wary," he warned, "of one man-one vote slogans as the essence of democracy and of any system that promotes mob rule."

Douglas's allies were equally passionate. George Meany, the head of the AFL-CIO, so feared Dirksen's amendment he made defeating the measure a higher priority than his union's long desire to repeal the dreaded "right to work" provision of the Taft-Hartley law. To counteract the Chamber's lobbying, the AFL-CIO and a host of other unions joined forces with the NAACP, ACLU, and other civil rights groups in March, 1965. They made for natural allies: civil rights groups feared malapportioned legislatures would disenfranchise African-Americans and big labor saw an opportunity to advance a number of economic objectives at the state level.

Finally, on August 4, 1965, after eight hours of debate led by the pair of Illinois senators, Dirksen earned 57 votes, leaving him short of the two-thirds majority needed to pass a constitutional amendment. The extensive hearings combined with delay tactics by senate liberals allowed the AFL-CIO to corral more than two dozen senators originally thought to be siding with Dirksen. The defeat constituted his second setback.

Though urged by his friends to quit the "lost cause" after these consecutive defeats in 1964 and 1965, Dirksen pressed ahead. Publically, he continued to rest his case on the will of voters. "Why don't you confess the fact that you don't trust the people; you don't believe in the people," he lashed out at an opposing senator during a televised debate. "I do." It was a compelling but mendacious argument. Nothing laid bare that duplicity more than Dirksen's secret partnership with the nation's leading political consultant—Whitaker & Baxter.

Founded in 1933 by a pair of newspaper reporters, Clem Whitaker and Leone Baxter, the nation's first political consulting firm established instant credibility by helping to defeat Upton Sinclair, a gubernatorial candidate who petrified California's business community. Over the next two decades, the pair went on to win 70 out of their 75 campaigns ranging from statewide races to local ordinances.

Operating largely out of California before its move to Chicago, the firm was bound to brush up against Warren. Their first major interaction came when Warren reluctantly hired Whitaker & Baxter for the 1942 governor's race. Warren's wife, Nina, bristled at the firm's insistence on highlighting Warren's picturesque family to curry votes. The relationship remained fraught and when Whitaker & Baxter issued an unauthorized press release on the eve of the election, Warren fired the firm. The duo never forgave him and helped bring about Warren's most stinging setback as governor—his initiative for universal health care. Ironically, the warring parties found themselves on the same side of the 1948 contest to fairly apportion the California legislature.

After Whitaker's namesake, Clem Whitaker Jr., took over the firm in 1958, he maintained its vast corporate contacts, making it an ideal partner for Dirksen heading into another round against Douglas. Yet, teaming up with a corporate lobbying shop for what Dirksen advertised as a democratic movement made any potential partnership unseemly. "There is one point I should like to correct," Dirksen uttered on the Senate floor on August 4, 1965, "that I had hired . . . Whitaker & Baxter . . . I did not know that such a firm ever existed. I could not accumulate enough money in a lifetime ever to be able to afford hiring a firm of that kind."

A week later, he signed up with the firm.

Whitaker proposed a campaign relying on pamphlets, thought leaders, and grass roots efforts in every state to sway "public sentiment." To finance the ambitious operation, he looked to corporate executives and placed Bryce Harlow, a pioneer in corporate lobbying who later became a domestic advisor to Nixon, as the Acting Finance Chairman. Using Orwellian terminology—more typical of modern-day advocacy groups—Whitaker named the group "The Committee for Government of the People."

To launch the campaign, Whitaker invited 85 business leaders in September, 1965—just weeks after Dirksen's second loss to Douglas—to a dinner party at the posh Madison Hotel in Washington to "discuss the gravest constitutional question facing the country in our lifetime. . . . We are confident that victory can be achieved," the invite professed, "but it will require the combined support of leaders like yourself." The invitation list included executives from Monsanto, Kaiser, Dow Chemical, DuPont, Hewlett-Packard, Bank of America, Chase Manhattan, Proctor & Gamble, GM, Ford, Chrysler, Wells Fargo, Alcoa, AT&T, Goodyear, Gulf Oil, Standard Oil, Westinghouse, GE, Sears, U.S. Steel, PG&E, and Texas Instruments.

In the next phase of the campaign, Whitaker & Baxter reached out to sympathetic executives, asking them to each recruit up to a dozen colleagues. While networking among business leaders had long existed, Whitaker's systematic and meticulous approach amplified the power of his vast network. He made sure to cross-reference and regularly update the recruitment lists to optimize outreach efforts and where feasible, Whitaker selected individuals with industry-specific connections: tapping J. Ed Warren of the Cities Service Company (the predecessor to CITGO) to take charge of the oil industry, for instance.

Whitaker oversaw every facet of the process, preparing sample letters for executives, expanding the list of potential recruits, ghost-writing correspondence for Dirksen, and coordinating with the senator's staff. Speeches and pamphlets prepared for the campaign overly dramatized reapportionment's dangers. "It should thus be abundantly clear that the opposition consists of a coalition of big city bosses and labor leaders who expect to control every State legislature," one such pamphlet read. Another "Fact Sheet" warned: "With control over state legislatures, big city political bosses will have life-and-death control over legislation." Some of the warnings—like a 32-hour workweek— bordering on fantasy nevertheless seeped into the recruiting materials.

Backed by assurances from a D.C. law firm that federal lobbying laws wouldn't apply to the committee's work, allowing it to keep its finances concealed, Whitaker produced a list of monetary quotas for companies starting at $5,000 and reaching up to $30,000 at the top end. AT&T, GE, and Gulf Oil each pitched in $30,000; Pacific Gas & Electric, $25,000; Union Pacific, $2,000. Various divisions of Standard Oil contributed $33,000. In a matter of weeks, Whitaker had built a $350,000 war chest. Individual executives from Proctor & Gamble, Manufacturers Hanover Trust, DuPont, and other top companies also added thousands of dollars. To circumvent in-house policies prohibiting donations to political causes, some companies sent funds through individual executives. In other instances, donors sought anonymity. Karl Bendetsen, a former military officer involved with Japanese internment during WWII, asked that any public disclosure of a donation be listed under his wife's name.

To prepare for the public phase of the campaign, Whitaker hired dozens of full-time staffers split between a national organization and regional committees. Dirksen primarily contributed by recruiting high-profile executives from U.S. Steel, GE, DuPont, Ford, and AT&T to finance the operation and government officials for leadership positions. Eventually, he settled on a bipartisan group of ten congressmen from every region of the country—including Nebraska's Roman Hruska, Ohio's Frank Lausche, and New York's Carleton King—to serve as the public face of the national committee. Hundreds of local officials and business leaders manned the state-wide groups. New York's Robert Moses and Lloyd Bentsen, a Texas insurance executive who went on to become a senator and vice presidential candidate, were among the more notable participants.

Brandishing Whitaker's clever catchphrase for the campaign—"Let the

People Decide"—Dirksen introduced the Committee for Government of the People to the public on January 19, 1966. Months of groundwork paid dividends. More than four hundred media outlets covered Dirksen's media blitz. "The Committee recognizes," Dirksen announced at the launch, masking the true nature of his patrons, "that its financial resources are limited in comparison with the tremendous wealth and manpower of the big city labor leaders who are engaged in an all-out effort to attempt to thwart the will of the people on this issue. Our strength is in the essential justice of our cause."

In subsequent months, the committee orchestrated a massive grass roots campaign. The national organization and its local affiliates disseminated more than two million pamphlets, assembled 24 letter-writing campaigns targeting business and community leaders, placed 90-second spots in more than a hundred television stations, and reached out to nearly five thousand newspapers. The full-court press succeeded: 70 percent of the editorials tracked by the committee favored Dirksen's amendment, including the *Los Angeles Times*, *San Francisco Chronicle*, *Washington Star*, *Chicago Tribune*, and *New York Daily News*.

In this rematch, Dirksen came close to succeeding—at one point finding himself just three senators short—but Douglas and the AFL-CIO held on to enough vacillating senators to prevail on April 20, 1966. This time, the 55 to 38 margin put Dirksen seven votes shy of reaching the two-thirds threshold. That was his third setback.

The loss should have marked Dirksen's last stand. He had lost three times and his corporate sponsors considered reapportionment "a dead issue." Instead of quitting, Dirksen moved ahead on a parallel track to bring forth his desired amendment, this time through an unprecedented and potentially revolutionary mechanism: a constitutional convention.

Article V of the Constitution allowed the states to impel Congress to call a convention to propose amendments. The convoluted path requiring two rounds of approvals—two-thirds of states to call a convention followed by three-quarters of states to approve any proposed amendments—explained why none of the 206 previous attempts to a call a convention had succeeded. Was it a longshot? Yes. Bordering on the outlandish? Absolutely. Yet the mere threat of holding one had worked before. In 1912, only after 31 states had called for a convention did the Senate capitulate to decades of pressure and approve the Seventeenth Amendment requiring the direct election of senators.

Unlike his public battles with Douglas, Dirksen cloaked this program in secrecy, working in conjunction with the American Farm Bureau and the Council of State Governments—the same group behind the States' Rights Amendments in 1963—to lobby state legislatures. It was a wily strategy. Since Congress didn't keep track of the state-by-state petitions as they came in, few people outside of Dirksen's inner circle maintained a running tally, allowing the petition drive to go unnoticed. When Illinois and Colorado filed petitions in March of 1967, the total reached 32. Days later, Dirksen predicted he would soon reach the 34-state threshold.

As Dirksen inched towards the finish line, the press exposed his covert operation. "Most of official Washington has been caught by surprise" by the headway made by Dirksen, the Supreme Court reporter Fred Graham wrote in *The New York Times* on March 18, 1967. Just as Warren had sounded the alarm on the States' Rights Amendments in 1963, Graham's article sparked an immediate reaction from liberals. Echoing his colleagues on the Senate floor, New York Senator Jacob Javits warned of a "broad-scale attack on the Bill of Rights." In the pages of the *Saturday Review*, John Kennedy's former speechwriter, Theodore Sorensen, feared the coming of a "constitutional nightmare." Even the *National Review* worried the nation would plunge into "a period of profound constitutional crisis."

Though Dirksen made assurances that any potential convention would limit itself to apportionment, critics remained frightened by the prospect of a "runaway" convention instituting broad changes to the Constitution. There was ample precedent for this anxiety. When the Founding Fathers convened in Philadelphia in 1787, they initially intended to fix the shortcomings of the Articles of Confederation. Instead of tinkering with the Articles as planned, they scrapped it altogether for an entirely new government. A plethora of unanswered questions made this prospect all the more harrowing. Did all of the petitions have to be identical? Were the ones submitted by malapportioned (26 of 32) legislatures valid? Could Congress limit the scope of a convention to just reapportionment? Practically overnight, this obscure provision of the

Constitution became a hot topic among scholars and the subject of congressional hearings.

Despite the uncertainty looming over the process and accusations that many of the petitions were invalid, Dirksen dove into the legislative trenches to reach the 34-state benchmark. In Ohio, Pennsylvania, Vermont, and Iowa, his aides identified legislators who needed cajoling, prodding, or a dose of ingratiation from the minority leader. Dirksen's team considered every alternative to sway legislators. In Delaware, his aides tried to recruit DuPont to persuade the Assembly's majority leader, who worked for the company. In some states, Dirksen served as a mediator between competing factions. In others, he testified before legislative committees.

To add gravitas to his cause, Dirksen tried to recruit Eisenhower to join him in a public forum to discuss his crusade and considered holding the impending convention in Philadelphia "in order to highlight the relationship of this issue to the wisdom of our Founding Fathers." The search for a fitting venue turned out to be a bit premature. The glare of the national press turned state legislators into petrified turtles. Only Iowa petitioned Congress after Graham's article, leaving Dirksen just one state short of his goal.

Dirksen's quixotic campaign has largely been forgotten to history. Yet, it personified the widespread resentment directed at the Warren Court far beyond *Brown, Miranda*, and a handful of other cases that continue to dominate the popular imagination.

JUNE, 1968

Throughout his political life, Johnson relied upon his personal connections to overcome partisan and ideological barriers. Few relationships exemplified this approach more than Johnson's bond with Dirksen. Their roles as Majority and Minority Leader in the late 1950s should have pitted them as rivals. Instead, Johnson made Dirksen a "full partner" of his legislative agenda. "They thoroughly understood . . . and . . . greatly admired each other," remembered Senator George Smathers. Passage of a modest civil rights measure in 1960 reflected both their teamwork and mutual admiration. "It took no courage on my part" to get the measure enacted, Dirksen confessed on the Senate floor. "But for the Majority Leader . . . it is a remarkable tribute." They also got along personally, sparring with one another on the Senate floor as if partaking in a friendly sporting contest. "They would speak against each other, and then pretty soon in Johnson's office here would come Dirksen and we'd all sit around and have a drink," Smathers recalled. "They were . . . two of a kind." The needling between the legislative heavyweights reflected their genuine friendship. During the late 1950s, Dirksen became enamored of Johnson's car phone—space age technology at the time. The next day, he had one installed in his car and called Johnson to boast about it. "Yes, but excuse me Ev," Johnson replied from his car, "I've got to answer the other phone!" When Johnson moved on to the White House, Dirksen established an effective working relationship with Michael Mansfield, the Senate Majority Leader who served as the president's floor leader, while remaining on good terms with the president. The two sages frequently sought each other's counsel over drinks—Johnson preferred scotch, Dirksen went with bourbon—and when Dirksen was hospitalized, Johnson called him every day.

Though Senate Democrats vastly outnumbered Republicans throughout Johnson's presidency, the clash between its conservative and liberal camps forced Johnson to seek out Republicans for help. Dirksen had delivered the key votes to break the 60-day southern filibuster to pass the historic 1964 Civil Rights Bill and proved essential to enacting the Voting Rights Act a year later. Now, eager to fend off any potential threats to getting Fortas confirmed, Johnson relied on their friendship to ask Dirksen to make good one last time.

Dirksen visited the White House on the evening of June 24 for a tête-à-tête with the president. When he was Senate Majority Leader, Johnson had usurped space throughout the Capitol to carve out a seven-room suite. Painted in shades of green and gold, his office in the Capitol building turned into a baronial space replete with his favorite portraits, frescoed ceilings, and a marble fireplace on top of which stood a life-size portrait of himself. Reporters called it the "Taj Mahal."

As president, he had an entire building dedicated to his needs, and, it should be mentioned, his giant ego, which the president advertised in not so subtle ways. "LBJ" appeared on shirts, handkerchiefs, and jewelry. Mono-grams weren't unique to Johnson, but applying his initials to those of his wife (Lady Bird Johnson), daughters (Lynda Bird and Lucy Baines Johnson), and dog (Little Beagle Johnson) reflected an overblown ego. Even his Texas ranch included three flags: the Stars and Stripes, the Texas Lone Star, and a blue standard with five stars and his initials.

Johnson conducted most of his meetings in the Oval Office. For more inti-mate conversations, he sometimes turned to his "little office" a few steps away. Furnished with a couch, two lounge chairs, two side tables, and two lamps, the tiny chamber felt crammed. Thick curtains covered the windows and a shelf with three televisions decorated the wall closest to the door. A frame holding photos of his five predecessors hung on the opposite wall. In the Oval Office, he liked to sit on a rocking chair. In the study, Johnson preferred a leather chair with high arm-rests he could swivel in any direction. Dirksen sat facing him no more than five feet away on an overstuffed couch.

The president made his case for Fortas. His credentials were unimpeach-able. And as the first Jew to be nominated for chief justice, he thought it would be foolish for senators with sizeable Jewish supporters to contest the nominee.

Despite his disagreements with the Warren Court, Dirksen agreed to help. It's difficult to appreciate his position from a modern-day vantage point, es-pecially when considering that, in addition to his efforts to overturn *Baker*, he also spent most of the decade proposing a constitutional amendment to reverse the Court's ban on school prayer. The fact is that Dirksen and Johnson were friends and colleagues. To the displeasure of critics within Dirksen's caucus, this relationship—more than partisan rivalries or ideological differences—carried the day between the two men. Dirksen also relished the role of playing the savior of Johnson's legislative initiatives, making this his last chance to help a friend. The Minority Leader only made a couple of demands in return. Fearful of facing Adlai Stevenson III in the coming election, he asked for a weaker opponent. The president promised to contact Chicago Mayor Rich-ard Daley to coax Stevenson against running in the coming election. Next on the Minority Leader's wish list was the Subversive Activities Control Board (SACB), a holdover from the McCarthy era that had become superannuated.

Reviving the SACB would boost Dirksen's credentials among conservatives who cast a wary eye on him for associating with Democrats. For the board to remain alive, it needed referrals from the Justice Department, which had stopped sending it work. Johnson was happy to oblige. He called in Larry Temple and issued an order: "Larry, I want you to get in touch with Ramsey Clark and tell him to refer some cases to the SACB." Weeks later, Dirksen would feign outrage at the hint of a trade with the president. But for now, less than an hour after his arrival, he departed satisfied.

There was one more factor motivating Dirksen. Peeved by the threat to his leadership the Republican uprising represented, he promised to shut down the growing rebellion. A muscular show of strength would help Johnson but also reaffirm his authority within the Senate. "There will be a little ruckus but," he assured Johnson, Fortas will "be confirmed, period."

Confident that Dirksen would tame his caucus, Johnson next targeted the one man capable of subduing the Warren Court's brashest enemies in the South—Georgia's Richard Russell.

CHAPTER 5

"I AM DOING EVERYTHING WITHIN MY POWER TO CURB THIS WILD COURT"

The Supreme Court will rule the country — RICHARD RUSSELL

In William Faulkner's *Absalom, Absalom!*, the past persistently imposes itself on the present, a prevalent theme for the South's great novelist who coined the phrase: "The past is never dead. It's not even past." That adage applied to many of Jim Crow's defenders—perhaps none more so than Richard Brevard Russell, Jr.

Having grown up with the ghosts of the Civil War, Russell was a product of the South's troubled history. His family, prominent plantation owners in Georgia and South Carolina since colonial times, had descended from the South's upper caste, what a Georgian publication deemed "the oldest and choicest American stock."

The fortunes of that stock plunged with the arrival of General William Sherman's Union forces in 1864. They burned down the cotton mill established by Russell's grandfather and emancipated the family's slaves, forcing his grandmother to flee in a carriage. Laid destitute through the loss of their material possessions and social standing, the Russell family yearned to revive its antebellum glory.

Born in 1897 in a small town in Georgia about 50 miles northeast of Atlanta, Richard Russell frequented the Civil War fortresses and the Confederate soldiers still manning them, avidly listening to their tales of heroism. During long hours of solitude in a field near his family's farm, he replayed these battles, reenacting the courageous charges of Confederate legend. Inspired by his father's lectures on the family's loss, Russell became obsessed with the war, devouring every title he could dig up on the subject. It was as if the Civil War had never ended for him. Yes, the soldiers put down their arms. Yes, the slaves were set free, serving as persistent reminders to their former masters of their lost patrimony. And yes, the Confederate states rejoined the Union, unrepentant of their crimes and unapologetic for the carnage they caused. For Russell, the South had never regained its rightful place in the nation, and was still at war—not with artillery shells and cavalry charges, but through a political, economic, and social tug-of-war with a nation resolved to dismantling a sacred way of life.

The past's hold over Russell didn't end there. His father, a gifted lawyer who went on to become Georgia's chief justice, had nearly returned the Russells back to their rightful place among the state's upper crust. But his feats fell dreadfully short. Nothing symbolized the unfinished business left for his son than his five electoral defeats. Desperate to redeem the family name, his father doggedly reminded Russell of his responsibility: "You can have—and you must have—a future of . . . distinction," the judge implored, "or it will break my heart. . . . My son—my namesake—never let this thought leave your mind."

Russell didn't disappoint his father. Attendance at the Gordon Military Institute and the University of Georgia Law School placed him among the state's elite. At twenty-three, he became a state legislator; six years later, he became the leader of the Georgia House. In 1931, he eclipsed his father by winning the governor's seat by the largest margin in the state's history. He also happened to be the state's youngest governor, and two years later, the nation's youngest sitting senator. Playing out like a biblical fable of a family's rise, fall, and resurrection, six decades after their demise, Russell's meteoric elevation fully restored his ancestry's legacy.

At over six feet, Russell's erect posture, combined with his regal countenance—his angular nose, deeply socketed eyes, and receding hairline that amplified the curvature of his forehead—endowed him with a sense of purpose that was immediately clear to anyone around him. Reporters described him as an "Olympian" carrying a "Roman presence." "He was smiling, intelligent, and easy, at home with . . . the people of Winder, Georgia," Harry McPherson, wrote admiringly in his insider's account of the Capitol, "to whom he was leader and judge and perhaps a manifestation of God Himself."

For Russell, an introverted, lifelong bachelor who eschewed social outings, the Senate became his mistress. He mastered its parliamentary tactics—memorizing its 22 rules and reviewing the 1,326-page guide to parliamentary precedents. "I don't know how many times . . . Paul Douglas and others," recalled a senate staffer, referring to the chamber's liberals who regularly dueled against the Georgian, "would think they'd found an answer in the rules and they'd come forward and try to hit Russell head on, and then all of a sudden they'd find themselves flat on the legislative ground."

His willingness to study the chamber went beyond its rules. He took care to evaluate all sorts of legislation to better appreciate his colleagues' concerns. By reviewing local newspapers from around the country, he developed an understanding of national affairs at the local level. The time he spent monitoring the Senate's every action didn't end there: almost nightly, with a cigarette and glass of Jack Daniel's, Russell read the *Congressional Record*. "The Senate is my life," Russell once told a reporter. "I don't have any family or home life."

Over time, all of this accumulated knowledge established Russell as a legislative wizard. "Senator Russell had the best qualifications for the Senate of any man I knew," Johnson said years later. When peers ran into roadblocks, Russell offered compromises. When he found a more precise way to write legislation or drafted an amendment to better harmonize a bill with its sponsor's purpose, he offered these improvements quietly so as not to attract media attention. His discretion, combined with a courteous light touch to those he could have bullied compounded the impact of his assistance, allowing him to build a reputation as a problem solver willing to grant credit to others. In the "politics of Congress," observed a legislative aide, "he had no peer." Russell "knew the Senate, its traditions and rules as none other did."

Postings on the Armed Services Committee and to an agricultural subcommittee propelled Russell to prominence in both areas. Among the coldest of Cold Warriors, he played a central role in the military's budget after WWII. No matter the magnitude of his accomplishments in these areas, however, history ultimately would record these endeavors as sideshows. Historians would instead remember him for his greatest passion. From the moment he stepped into the Senate in 1933, Russell dedicated his life to preserving the southern way of life.

Through most of the twentieth century, the South's command over Congress resembled that of an anchor, not quite capable of directing a ship but stout enough to impede its movement. The key for the region lay in its control over leadership positions. From 1911 to 1961, seven of the twelve Speakers of the House came from a former slave state. Its power in the Senate was even greater by comparison.

After successively striking down anti-lynching legislation in 1938 and neutering Roosevelt's Fair Employment Practice Committee, an organization intended to curb workplace discrimination, Russell became the undisputed head of the "Southern Caucus," a group of twenty or so senators from the former Confederate states. The chief congressional correspondent for *The New York Times* considered Russell the "most influential man on the inner life of the Senate," one who "could actually command the votes of others." The *Philadelphia Tribune* called him the "20th Century president of the Confederacy." His associates within the Southern Caucus heartily agreed. In their eyes, Russell was a hero: "I do not think that even Robert E. Lee had a more coordinated army or a more loyal following," observed one of its members.

Assiduously avoiding racist comments in public, the mannerly Russell frowned upon the uncultured tactics employed by some of the Caucus. This restraint was essential to his strategy. Outnumbered in the Senate, Russell exploited his carefully crafted persona as a racial moderate to recruit allies from other regions. Those senators became more inclined to succumb to Russell's arguments because they rested on anodyne concepts like states' rights and were dressed in heartening assertions of racial progress from the South's composed leader.

While he may not have matched his colleagues' propensity for launching racial epithets, he too was an ardent segregationist. In an interview with *The National Review*, he warned that the "experience of other countries . . . has demonstrated that the separation of the races . . . is highly preferable to amalgamation. I know nothing in human history that would lead us to conclude that miscegenation is desirable." In a private letter, he was even more deliberate. "Any southern white man worth a pinch of salt would give his all to maintain white supremacy." He later suggested repopulating the nation's African-Americans "over all sections of the nation" to ease "racial tensions" and arrive at "a permanent solution." Though the idea got no traction, social engineering on such a scale had ominous overtones.

Article I § 7 of the Constitution established a straightforward legislative process. "Every Bill which shall have passed the House of Representatives and the Senate, shall, before it become a Law, be presented to the President of the United States; If he approve he shall sign it." If the president vetoed the proposed bill, then both houses of Congress could together override that veto with a two-thirds majority. In comparison to the kingdoms then in existence, where legislative bodies acted largely as rubber stamps for a monarch's will, the American model made it difficult to rapidly and effortlessly promulgate legislation.

What the Founding Fathers did not foresee was just how many other obstacles future generations would add to the lawmaking process. One-hundred-seventy-five years after the Constitution went into effect, Congress had installed a series of roadblocks. Nearly all bills first went through congressional committees, giving their chairmen the power to singlehandedly slow down or derail legislation. "A Senate committee is an imperious force," wrote William White in 1956, "its chairman . . . is emperor." Once an emperor was seated, he held his post as long as his party remained in power, making it dangerous to cross him. The mechanisms by which committees wielded their power were often as simple as they were effective. For those bills that the chairmen found distasteful, emperors delayed hearings or refused to hold them altogether. On other occasions, they prevented a bill's progress to the Senate floor by withholding a committee report or refusing to schedule a vote by its members. It was a slow death by starvation. The bills they favored, on the other hand, were quickly scheduled. The delays didn't need to last long. The commencement of a new congressional session every two years reset all the work of the previous one. Combined with all of the recesses built into the congressional calendar, it didn't take much effort to postpone a bill. Delaying a measure indefinitely by employing means that were inscrutable to the media and the public was nearly as lethal as voting it down. Committees also did most of the work of writing legislation before sending it out to the full chamber. With all this leverage, the bills approved by these committees had a good chance of becoming law. Those rejected by the emperors rarely had a chance. "It is said that in ordinary life one cannot rid himself of unpleasant things simply by willing them to go away," White explained, "but a powerful Senate committee chairman very often can do just that."

Russell amplified the South's strength through the chairmanship of key committees. Operating as Russell's field commanders, they swallowed up civil rights legislation like black holes. Eastland happened to be the most notorious of the bunch.

If a civil rights bill did manage to escape their grasp, the region's leaders resorted to their ultimate weapon—the filibuster, a parliamentary barricade set so high that it required two-thirds of the Senate to overcome the obstacle. Nearly universally, the South's 22 members supported these filibusters, allowing Russell to corral only a dozen additional senators from other regions to prevail. Bonded by a common cause, unity and discipline multiplied the caucus's power well beyond its actual numbers. "So marked and so constant is this high degree of Southern dominion," White noted, "that the Senate might be described without too much violence to fact as the South's unending revenge upon the North."

Suspicious of any civil rights legislation, Russell feared that even modest changes to Jim Crow threatened to unravel the South's apartheid state. "There can be no such thing as token integration," he said in response to those willing to make concessions. "This is merely a device of the race mixers to obtain total and complete integration." Like a military leader preventing a breach of his line, Russell fended off wave after wave of offensives. Nothing got past Russell's legion of knights. Not legislation abolishing poll taxes; nor legislation proscribing all-white primaries; nor legislation ending government-sponsored discrimination; nor even legislation outlawing lynching. And certainly not legislation questioning the bedrock of southern racism—segregation.

Brown didn't so much as overrun Russell's impregnable defenses as circumvent them, undoing decades of vigilance by the Georgian senator and his legion of segregationists. Terrified by the prospect that *Brown* signified the "long insidious step toward" the mixing of the races—exactly the complete downfall of Jim Crow he had long dreaded—the Court's ability to sidestep Russell's congressional stranglehold plunged him into the kind of hyperbole that was atypical for him. Infuriated by Warren's coup, Russell dropped any pretense of moderation that had long enhanced his reputation among his peers. On the day of the ruling, he accused the justices of a "flagrant abuse of judicial power" on the Senate floor and beseeched his colleagues to help him find "ways . . . to check the tendency of the court to disregard the Constitution." If that didn't sound like the type of vitriol one would expect from a hothead like Thurmond, then his later declarations certainly did. "But now we find the Supreme Court is writing more law than the Congress," he declared in 1957. If the three branches of government didn't return to their traditional roles, he complained, "the Supreme Court will rule the country." Russell blamed the Court's "radical members" for the South's "greatest crisis since Appomattox." Convinced that the justices, under the NAACP's spell, held an "unwarranted prejudice against the South and her white people," he carried a particular animus towards Warren. The senator bemoaned the chief's leadership over an "assortment of political hacks" and "weak men" on the bench to fulfill his "messianic" vision "to put the Court in the legislative field" and amass "powers that no one had . . . thought the Court possessed." And why did Warren malign so many to get his way? In order "to set up a judicial tyranny." Throughout his tenure, Warren's critics had used many expletives to demean him. Being called a tyrant was perhaps a first. Unlike most of his peers who were powerless to do much more than spew venom, however, Russell vowed to retaliate. "I am doing everything within my power to curb this wild Court," he wrote to a friend, the "worst that was ever assembled."

JUNE, 1968

Heading into their meeting on June 25, 1968, Johnson was fully aware of Russell's hatred for Warren. He also knew that Russell found Fortas equally abhorrent. Confident of his ability to secure the allegiance of even his most recalcitrant adversaries, the president felt that he could convince his onetime mentor to endorse Fortas's candidacy. Just as he had with Dirksen the evening before, Johnson counted on the strength of his friendship with Russell to outweigh whatever reluctance the senator might have had to backing the nomination. Russell, after all, was practically Johnson's surrogate father in a relationship dating back decades.

In his never-ending quest for power, Johnson attached his fortunes to Russell when he entered the Senate in 1949. Desperate to be something more than an acquaintance, Johnson knew that the only "way to see Russell every day" was to sit alongside him on the Armed Services Committee. He finagled a seat on the desired committee and once he caught Russell's attention, Johnson made sure to impress Russell at every turn. "Lyndon was always quick to identify whoever were the major figures on the stage," Lady Bird Johnson observed years later. He had cozied up to Speaker Sam Rayburn while serving in the House by taking advantage of Rayburn's burning desire to serve as a father figure. Russell was also a childless bachelor and through flattery, Johnson courted him in a similar fashion. Because Russell was a fan, Johnson took a sudden liking to baseball and began to show interest in Russell's greatest passion, the Civil War. He arrived at the Capitol early and left late, allowing him to join Russell for breakfast and dinner on a regular basis. "There was no one that worked as . . . many hours . . . as Senator Russell," recalled his aide, "unless it was . . . Johnson." He toiled alongside Russell on Saturdays, and realizing Sundays were a difficult time for the lonely bachelor, Johnson invited Russell to his home and prompted his daughters to call him "Uncle Dick". Russell made annual pilgrimages to Johnson's Texas ranch and the two men frequented sporting events together. Johnson's assistant quipped that the Texan "would have married" Russell if the latter had been a woman. It wasn't much of an exaggeration: Johnson hung a photo of Russell on his office wall.

Somehow, their incongrous temperaments never hindered their relationship. Johnson was a bronco marauding in a stable full of show ponies. Putting it euphemistically, a Senate staffer described him as a "shouter." Vulgar and thunderous, he spat out expletives like a machine gun. An early riser who worked late into the night, he expected the same devotion from his subordinates, whom he also expected to be accessible at all times. When he called Joseph Califano's office and found him using the lavatory, he had a phone installed in the bathroom the same day to ensure the aide's constant availability. According to Smathers, one of Johnson's lieutenant's in the 1950s, Johnson could be a "real tyrannical, tough, disagreeable, dictatorial fellow." Unconcerned with decorum, Johnson publicly showed off a surgical scar and issued orders from his bed, shower, or even while on the toilet. When he lifted his beagle by its ears at an event in the White House, he never contemplated that the gesture might offend dog lovers across the country. As uncouth and unrefined as he may have been, Johnson was also vain, insisting that photographers capture the left side of his face. If Johnson was the village brute, Russell was its patrician. Withdrawn and averse to small talk, he carried himself like a statesman. "Richard Russell was everybody's ideal," recalled Smathers. "He was the most polite, thoughtful fellow that you ever saw. . . . Smart, knew how to get along with everybody." Compared to Johnson's meandering monologues and profanity-laced outbursts, Russell spoke in a deliberate manner, answering questions comprehensively as if he had spent hours perfecting his response. A Senate staffer described Russell as "dignified" and "gentlemanly"—antonyms of the adjectives used to portray Johnson. A loner, Russell was drawn to history and literature while Johnson preferred social interactions over intellectual pursuits. Ever a genteel practitioner of the fine arts of politics, Russell brandished his authority with a light touch compared to Johnson's in-your-face style. But that's where the men converged. Despite being polar opposites, their masterful understanding, accretion, and use of power bound them together.

In their years in the Senate, Johnson's flattery and mutual infatuation with power could only take the master manipulator so far with the Georgian. What mattered most to Russell was Johnson's commitment to Jim Crow. Johnson's voting record during his twelve years in the House established him as a "good southerner." Soon after his arrival in the Senate, Johnson burnished these credentials by helping to maintain the filibuster's potency in a parliamentary showdown with liberals out to debilitate the tactic. In his maiden speech on the Senate floor in 1949, he defended the South's positions on civil rights. Both his public declarations and willingness to preserve the South's power within the Senate established his bona fides with Russell: "Our political philosophy was very closely parallel," he said of Johnson. The NAACP thought so as well, reprimanding Johnson for helping to deny African-Americans "the rights of first-class citizenship."

Russell and the NAACP both had Johnson pegged incorrectly. He was a chameleon and when it came to civil rights, he spoke with a forked tongue. In a speech delivered on the Senate floor the day after *Brown* was issued, Johnson urged his fellow senators to accept the "accomplished fact. However we may question the judgment of the men who made this ruling, it has been made." The grudging acceptance was as moderate a reaction one could expect from a Texas politician. In a letter sent to a Texas judge ten days later, he wore a different mask. "Like you," the letter began, "the Supreme Court decision left me shocked and dismayed. . . . I am no lawyer, but I have had sufficient experience in the field of government to agree with you that it is hard to find a legal basis for the reasoning." As president, Johnson displayed his true colors but during his years in the Senate, he convincingly positioned himself as Russell's ally on racial matters.

The fact that their relationship worked on both the personal and political level bound the men to each other ever tighter. Sure, Russell could have used another reliable southerner to defend Jim Crow. To the Georgian, however, Johnson represented far more than an adept lieutenant. Johnson became the apotheosis of Russell's ambitions, the vessel through which he could vicariously live out his own ambitions. While Russell may have resurrected his family's name in Georgia, he was unable to return the South to a national power. No southerner had been elected president since Zachary Taylor in 1848. Russell was convinced that capturing the White House was the key to integrating the region into the country's cultural fabric, and his failure to clinch the Democratic nomination in the 1948 and 1952 elections due to his defense of Jim Crow had left him shattered.

Johnson was another matter. As long as he walked the tightrope on civil rights, he had a chance at the White House. For Russell, such an achievement would be his triumph as much as his protégé's. Johnson successfully achieved this feat in passing the 1957 Civil Rights bill. Coming nearly a century after Reconstruction, the bill was a milestone for civil rights supporters. At the same time, the watered-down version eventually enacted into law did little to change the realities of the South's apartheid state. By giving northern liberals a symbolic victory while shielding Jim Crow, the bill was a political tour de force for Johnson. The same could be said of Russell. He helped shoot down the most potent elements of the bill yet was willing to allow some ineffectual legislation to become law to boost Johnson's national appeal. "The victory would help Johnson in his 1960 bid . . . to win the Democratic Presidential nomination," he assured southern leaders.

For Russell, no sacrifice was too big to promote Johnson. His recommendation of Johnson, then only a first-term senator, to serve as the party's official leader over his own candidacy personified his willingness to catapult Johnson's career at his own expense. Just as importantly, Johnson's success relied upon Russell's ability to prevent the Southern Caucus from harassing the Majority Leader for making concessions on civil rights. He did so by helping Johnson avoid publicly siding with one faction of the party over the other. The Southern Manifesto, a declaration signed by more than one hundred southern congressmen in 1956 urging the region to defy the Court, typified Russell's thinking. "There was no question whatsoever," explained Johnson's aide, that anyone signing the fiery decree "could never become president." Russell understood this as well. He allowed Johnson to publicly maintain his distance from the Southern Manifesto by not asking him to sign the document even when the Majority Leader's imprimatur would have boosted the southern cause: "of course we wanted him to sign it," recalled Stennis, one of the Manifesto's authors. By keeping his flank protected from the southern contingent, Russell allowed Johnson to portray himself as a centrist who would be palatable to both factions within the Democrat Party, and with that, a formidable candidate for the White House. Despite suspicions by liberal Democrats of Johnson's true motives, the plan worked for the most part. "Every so often he'd drop that little atom bomb," Hubert Humphrey, one of the chamber's leading liberals, recalled, "that when it was all said and done," Johnson would remind them, "'I wasn't there when they signed that Southern Manifesto. I said no.'"

JUNE, 1968

Russell arrived at 6:39pm on June 25 for a meeting in the president's study where Johnson had met with Dirksen the night before. Ever the willing student, Johnson had learned how to wield power under Russell's tutelage but his authority never extended over Russell. When they came to "loggerheads about something," Smathers recalled, the "only guy that ever would make Johnson back off was Dick Russell." An iconic photo of them taken in 1963 exemplified this dynamic. The two men stood face-to-face just inches apart in a stare down like a pair of heavyweights at the opening of a championship bout. Looking up into Johnson's stone-cold visage, and feeling the presence of his oversized body hovering ever closer like a bird of prey, most men would have crumbled under the circumstances. But Russell stood his ground.

Johnson didn't try to bully or sucker Russell at their meeting. "One could not persuade Senator Russell by sweet talk, hard talk, or any kind of talk," Johnson recounted in his memoirs. Instead, the president offered him something far more appealing and honorable than a political trade or a threat: a seat on the Court for Homer Thornberry. Thornberry was the president's longtime friend and colleague who had taken Johnson's vacated House seat when Johnson moved to the Senate. He helped Johnson weather the greatest crisis the nation had seen in decades, standing by Johnson's side on Air Force One when he took the oath of office after Kennedy's assassination. Appointed by Johnson to an appellate judgeship, Thornberry established a strong reputation on the bench.

Johnson's staff wasn't as enthusiastic about the selection. When Temple warned that Thornberry would be ripe for charges of cronyism, the president fired back: "What political office did you ever get elected to?" Concerned about a pushback from Senate Republicans, Defense Secretary Clark Clifford suggested packaging Fortas with a respected Republican jurist. Lying in bed in his pajamas, he fired back, "I don't intend to put some damned Republican on the Court." As Clifford, accompanied by Fortas, walked out of the bedroom, Fortas told the Defense Secretary, "I understand exactly what you were trying to do . . . but I couldn't very well sit there and disagree with him when he wants to make me Chief Justice." Johnson wasn't blind to the potential for criticism: "of course, they'll say I'm a crony," the president admitted to Dirksen just hours before meeting with Russell. He just didn't give much weight to the charges. "But am I supposed to nominate somebody the *St. Louis Post-Dispatch* says is a great man that I don't know?"

When it came to political matters, Johnson was his own best counsel. He felt Thornberry could sweeten the bitter pill of accepting Fortas for Southern Democrats, who looked favorably upon Thornberry despite his center-left record. Russell in particular, who was Thornberry's hunting companion, put him at the top of his wish list for the opening. "When you sit in a duck blind all day with a man," Russell told Johnson at their meeting, "you really get to know him." The pairing worked as hoped. "I will support the nomination of Mr. Fortas," Russell told Johnson, "but I will enthusiastically support Homer Thornberry."

The two decided to celebrate their understanding together. Johnson called Thornberry in Austin and when he told the Texas judge of the unexpected news, Russell picked up the phone to congratulate Thornberry: "I'm for you all the way."

Even more than Dirksen, it's difficult to appreciate Russell's decision. Yes, Thornberry's inclusion made the prospect of seeing Fortas in Warren's chair more palatable. But at the end, it wasn't Thornberry but the strength of the bond between Russell and Johnson that convinced Russell to accept Fortas. This wasn't the first time Russell had cast aside his deeply held beliefs to help Johnson. Disgusted by the Democratic Party's adoption of a strong civil rights platform at the 1960 convention, he declined to campaign for the Kennedy-Johnson ticket. Twice rebuffed by Russell, Johnson asked his mentor to reconsider: "Come for my sake, Dick" he pleaded on his third try. Unable to turn him down, Russell acquiesced.

After the meeting, the two men spent dinner reminiscing with Johnson's wife and daughters about Russell's regular visits to the Johnson home during their years in the Senate. Russell would want to play with the children while Johnson tried to discuss the Senate's business. For a few moments, they re-lived a bit of their glory days when Johnson's oldest daughter, Lynda, induced smiles among the dinner guests with her patty-cake rendition.

One day after securing Dirksen's pledge to squash the Republican revolt, Johnson allied himself with the leader of his other potential challengers. No one was more capable of smothering southern opposition than Russell. The time had come for Johnson to make his announcement.

PART II

Chapter 6

"We Will . . . Vote Against Confirming Any Supreme Court Nominations of the Incumbent President"

JUNE, 1968

The morning after he dined with Russell, Johnson made final preparations for the press conference scheduled to announce the Fortas-Thornberry ticket. One remaining item on his to-do list was the exchange of letters with Warren. Following their initial conversation, Warren had sent Johnson a letter of resignation. "I hereby advise you of my intention to retire as Chief Justice of the United States effective at your pleasure," Warren wrote in the two-paragraph letter. At the behest of the justices, Eisenhower had made Warren a recess appointment in order to prevent a disruption in the Court's operations. Applying the same logic, Warren wanted to ensure a successor was in place before formally stepping down. Johnson's response should have been a mere footnote in the annals of history. His inveterate instinct for craftiness took over, however, mucking up what should have been an afterthought. Instead of accepting Warren's resignation at some set date, he instructed the Department of Justice to draft the following provision: "I will accept your decision to retire effective at such time as a successor is qualified." This was not the work of a careless scribe. Confident that Warren would stay on "until hell froze over" if necessary, Johnson wanted to preserve the option of keeping Warren should Fortas's candidacy falter. It was an unlikely scenario but in the back of his mind, Johnson wanted the letter to serve as an insurance policy should the unthinkable happen.

After editing the letter with Clark, reviewing the details of the nominations one last time with several associates and advisors, and a last-minute meeting with Eastland who delivered a dismal prognosis, Johnson welcomed reporters for an 11:30 a.m. press conference inside the Oval Office.

Holding notepads and pens, the White House press corps huddled attentively around Johnson's desk like players waiting to hear a pep talk from their coach. Johnson began by reading the exchange of letters with the chief justice and then named Fortas as Warren's replacement and Thornberry for the spot that would become available upon Fortas's elevation. Other than three questions about the nominations, the reporters spent the bulk of the press conference on other matters. At this early stage of the process, the press corps—the reporters most attuned to the political winds in Washington—showed no qualms about the president's selections.

Despite the unanticipated rumblings he had heard from Eastland and others, Johnson remained confident of victory on the day of the announcement. The pledges he had received from Dirksen and Russell in the previous two days all but guaranteed victory. The votes under their command combined with more than the 40 liberals who formed the backbone of Johnson's base in the Senate made the president an insurmountable frontrunner. Tallying 73 senators in favor of the nomination, enough to overcome a filibuster if necessary, a head count conducted by the White House staff confirmed his rosy assessment.

Fortas's ability to sail through his initial confirmation in 1965 also gave Johnson confidence. The usual southern malcontents who had jousted with Justices Stewart and Marshall during their hearings hadn't pestered Fortas during his testimony before the Judiciary Committee. No one else of consequence within the government bothered to closely scrutinize Fortas at the time either. Endorsements from leading advocacy organizations and the media's most influential voices—*Time, The New York Times*, and the *Washington Post*—turned out to be overkill. There simply was no need to orchestrate a grass roots campaign or hit the airwaves to make a case on Fortas's behalf. With almost no debate, all but three senators confirmed Fortas as an associate justice. The entire process, from Johnson's announcement to Fortas's confirmation, took just two weeks with no hiccups.

Nothing in Fortas's background had changed since his swift confirmation three years earlier. His personal life remained free of scandal and his liberal jurisprudence in the mold of the outgoing chief justice surprised no one in the capital. His opinions earned praise for their acumen and prose style, confirming the broad perception of him as one of the nation's brightest legal minds.

The composition of the Senate provided Johnson additional comfort. Just as they had in 1965, Democrats held a two-to-one advantage and the same senators manned the major leadership posts. Within the Judiciary Committee, fifteen of its seventeen members remained unchanged, including its chairman, Eastland, who had escorted Fortas through the confirmation process as if the nominee were on a VIP tour back in 1965.

In fact, if history was any guide, there was no reason to think the Senate would go through with a filibuster let alone offer any significant resistance. Dating back to the nation's origins, Congress' upper house had historically deferred to the president in the selection of justices. A 97% confirmation rate since 1894 had pushed this level of deference to historic highs.

Members of Johnson's White House team were more optimistic than their boss. To a man, they saw no storm clouds on the horizon in what they expected to be a repeat performance of the swift and uneventful confirmation Fortas had glided through three years earlier.

Fortas also had reason to be overjoyed. The circumstances surrounding his initial nomination in 1965—in which Johnson tore down Fortas's resistance to accepting the position by hijacking him at the last minute—had caused Fortas great distress and upset his wife. This time around, he approached the opportunity with alacrity, working closely with Johnson to secure himself the Court's top job. Fortas's social circle had already begun to celebrate. A stream of letters from fellow justices, former business associates, and some new acquaintances—such as Israel's Ambassador Yitzhak Rabin—pouring into his office congratulated Fortas for reaching the pinnacle of his career. In their eyes, his confirmation was a mere formality. "I am just as happy as you must be," Marshall wrote on the day of Johnson's announcement. "A great day for the USA."

Not everyone in Washington was so sanguine to hear the news.

Michigan Senator Robert Griffin was flying into Washington on June 14 when he noticed an intriguing headline on the front-page of the *Wall Street Journal*: "WARREN RESIGNATION?" Coming one day after Warren's meeting with Johnson, the piece provided an insider's account of what had transpired in the Oval Office. Warren, the article expounded, "hopes to have a voice in selection of successor, doubts Nixon would heed him." The piece made Griffin uneasy. He thought Warren was meddling in the affairs of the other branches. "This is the business of the President and the Senate," he uttered to himself.

When he reached his office later in the day, Griffin asked his legislative assistant to draft a speech castigating the chief justice for trying to manipulate his succession. Distracted by other matters, Griffin left the speech unfinished, and it may have stayed permanently dormant had fate not intervened. A week later, while driving to work on Constitution Avenue, he heard a newscast conveying a similar message. When he slowed down on First Street, he caught a glimpse of the Supreme Court building. The juxtaposition of the radio broadcast with the appearance of the Marble Palace led him to a fateful decision. Suspecting a "political maneuver" between Warren and Johnson to prevent Nixon—the likely GOP candidate—from naming the next chief justice, the emotions he had felt on the day he had seen the *Wall Street Journal* headline resurfaced. "This is one Senator," he swore to himself, "who will not go along with such a maneuver. Maybe nothing can be done about it, but now I must speak out." Even as his assistants told him the idea of opposing the president "would be like beating" his head "against a wall," he vowed to take a public stand that day.

Griffin wasn't a wide-eyed optimist. He had first-hand knowledge of Johnson's grip over Congress and resented how Johnson used his pull with Dirksen to manipulate the Republican Caucus. No other president he had dealt with during his years in Washington "exceeded" Johnson's "legendary . . . ability to deal with Congress." The first-term senator was also cognizant of his own meager status. His seat on the back row of the Senate chamber, a section called "Boystown" for housing the Senate's junior members, meant his colleagues expected him "to be seen and not heard."

Though soft-spoken, Griffin was not one to back down from a seemingly unwinnable fight—an attitude he developed at a young age. Born in Detroit in 1923, Griffin was told in high school that, weighing in at a measly 145 pounds, he could never play guard. He overcame the naysayers, going on to become a star offensive lineman. At about the same time, he became the first in his family to attend college, and in order to pay his tuition, he washed dishes and worked on an assembly line. After earning two battle stars in WWII, he graduated from the University of Michigan Law School, then turned to a career in politics.

Despite being repeatedly told that "he had no chance" of defeating a House incumbent in 1956, Griffin prevailed. Three years later, he co-authored the Landrum-Griffin bill, a sweeping reform of the nation's labor laws over the opposition of rank-and-file Democrats. For his next big move, he helped engineer the ouster of Charles Halleck—Dirksen's co-star in the "Ev and Charlie" show—from the House Republican leadership in 1964. In 1966, Michigan's governor appointed Griffin to a vacant seat in the Senate. Months later, he burnished his reputation as the capitol's David by trouncing the next Goliath in his path, the state's popular former governor Soapy Williams.

Griffin's friends described him as the "mild-mannered . . . Clark Kent"— *Newsweek* went with the more dismissive epithet, "mild-mannered actuary"—who transformed into a "Super-Senator" during a crisis. That transformation was underway on June 21, 1968. Later that day, Griffin cleared his calendar and got to work finishing the speech he'd begun a week earlier. "I want to indicate emphatically . . . " he declared on the Senate floor, "that I shall not vote to confirm an appointment of the next Chief Justice by a 'lame duck' President." The decision "should be made by the next President . . . after the people have [had] an opportunity to speak." The idea that a president's authority expired well before the constitutionally mandated date was, Griffin admitted, made "tongue-in-cheek."

Griffin's characterization masked his disingenuousness. Based on research reports he received from the Library of Congress, Griffin knew that, while historically nine nominees made in a president's final year in office did not receive the Senate's imprimatur, eight were confirmed, including the universally revered Chief Justice John Marshall, appointed by John Adams just weeks before his term ended. The research also revealed that with no recent precedents—the last nomination made under these circumstances had taken place in 1893—Griffin was entering uncharted territory. In fact he was motivated as much by political ambition as he was suspicious of a plot orchestrated by Warren and Johnson. Unsure whether anyone else would latch on to the notion that Johnson's "lame duck" status constituted grounds for rejecting Fortas, Griffin plowed ahead with what he felt was his best argument nonetheless.

Griffin made for an unlikely candidate to lead an assault against Fortas's nomination. As a moderate Republican, he had rarely targeted the justices in the past. Yet, he was far more partisan than Dirksen and, with no one within the GOP taking the initiative, he became the leader of the anti-Fortas movement by default. Soon, Texas's John Tower and South Carolina's Strom Thurmond joined Griffin's growing rebellion. If that was the first shoe to fall for Dirksen, the next one was much louder. Hours after meeting with the president on June 24, Dirksen dined with his son-in-law, Tennessee Senator Howard Baker. "Mr. D.," Baker said, "I can't go along with you. I'll fight the confirmation until we . . . install a new administration."

Dirksen arrived at the weekly conference of Republican senators on June 25 prepared to squash what he considered an insolent challenge to his authority. But Griffin was no pushover. "Don't underestimate the power of this young man," Halleck warned Dirksen. Ambitious and eager to rise up the ranks, Griffin was willing to risk Dirksen's ire with his insubordination. Having abetted in Halleck's coup while serving in the House, he was not afraid to challenge Dirksen, whom he felt handicapped the Republican Caucus. "There was sometimes the feeling that Dirksen and Johnson would get together and then make some sort of agreement," the Michigan senator complained years later. "There was some dissatisfaction with the lack of consultation." Griffin's attitude reflected Dirksen's waning control over his caucus. Seven other senators sided with Griffin at the conference while only two "voiced reservations" about opposing a potential nomination. The meeting, observed one participant, "was just awful" for Dirksen.

Realizing that he might lose the vote at the meeting, Dirksen postponed taking a formal tally by the caucus for a week in order to buy time to recruit enough of its members to his side in that duration. Refusing to wait a week, Griffin huddled around Senator George Murphy's desk in the Senate chamber—adjacent to Griffin's in Boystown in the back of the chamber—minutes after the GOP conference. "If we're not going to take a stand right away," Griffin told his colleagues, "the issue can be lost." "To hell with waiting for a week for the next Policy luncheon," Murphy added. Best known for acting in a series of musicals, Murphy symbolized the increasing conservativism within California that brought Ronald Reagan to power. "Let's get up a statement declaring our opposition and get some of our colleagues to sign it."

While Johnson and Fortas were still basking in the afterglow of the president's announcement, Griffin and Murphy spent the day gathering signatures for the letter that Griffin drafted. Aiming to splash water on Johnson's announcement, Griffin released the document hours after the president's press conference:

> It is the strongly held view of the undersigned that the next Chief Justice . . . should be selected by the newly-elected President. . . . We will, therefore, because of the above principle, and with absolutely no reflection on any individuals involved, vote against confirming any Supreme Court nominations of the incumbent President.

The nineteen signatures Griffin collected constituted more than half the Republican caucus. The appearance of Thurmond on the list was predictable. The inclusion of Hiram Fong and other moderates was far more startling. Such widespread resistance to the party's leadership meant that Dirksen, one of the two pillars Johnson was relying on to carry the nomination, would face an uphill struggle to fulfill his promise to the president.

Curious to learn more about the freshman senator who dared to openly take on the president, the press asked to meet with Griffin in person. It would be the first time anyone outside of the Republican Caucus took notice of him. Eager to make a good impression, he was restless the entire night trying to figure out how to commence his press conference the next day—June

27. Wearing dark-framed glasses and sporting short, conservative sideburns, the Michigan senator spoke in his office surrounded by reporters and camera crews in his standard, Midwestern accent that could have belonged on the evening news. Standing at 5'7", and delivering his words with none of the theatrics routinely employed by Dirksen, he was not a captivating figure. It didn't matter on this day. The meaning of his words—not their method of delivery—was the source of his strength.

The biggest takeaway from the press conference came during the question-and-answer session. When asked if he would stage a filibuster, Griffin demurred. Exploited by southern Democrats to thwart civil rights legislation, filibusters had a notorious reputation at the time. A year earlier, Griffin had joined those trying to reduce the threshold to defeating a filibuster from 67 to 60 senators for this very reason. "I don't believe any small interest group or regional bloc should have a hammer-lock on our procedures," he explained at the time. A reporter asked a follow-up question: "Senator, you said you are ready to speak at length if necessary to block these nominations. Is there any difference between that and a filibuster?" Worthy of an able lawyer's cross-examination, the question trapped Griffin into a corner. He tried but couldn't prevaricate any longer. "Well," Griffin responded, "I don't know that there is a difference." That's all they needed to hear: the reporters raced out of Griffin's office to report the news. His response to that query meant that those murmurs and rumors swirling around Washington of a potential filibuster were no longer merely conjecture. For the first time in American history, the Senate prepared to stage a filibuster to block a nomination to the Court.

While Griffin was publicly declaring war against the nominations to the press, the Senate Judiciary Committee was meeting in a closed-door session on June 27. Looking at Johnson's open-ended response to Warren's resignation, North Carolina's Sam Ervin, another long-time enemy of the Warren Court, questioned whether a vacancy existed at all. "There is no vacancy until the President accepts it," Thurmond added. "He has to retire and the President has to accept it, . . . and then you have got . . . a vacancy." Intended to be an insurance policy, Johnson's letter to Warren handed his enemies an opportunity to put up another barricade. The letter may have been constructed awkwardly but no reasonable person could have assumed that no vacancy existed. Why else did Johnson hold a press conference to publicly announce Fortas and Thornberry?

Although Johnson had feared he might face some opposition, he found himself blindsided by the mounting resistance. How could the president have underestimated the opposition? He may deserve blame for not realizing how tenuous Dirksen's hold over the Republican Caucus had become; but it would also have been completely reasonable for the president to dismiss Griffin. A senate aide from the era put the first-term senator's standing in context: "Young guys just don't filibuster. . . . If they are foolish enough to try it, they'll find that it doesn't work."

He wasn't the only one to write off Griffin. The media joined the prevailing wisdom in Washington downplaying the senator's insurgency. The influential columnist James Reston decried Griffin's "Nineteenth Century politics" of resorting to "old and discredited" appeals to "partisan political grounds." Assuming a smooth confirmation, *The New York Times* editorial board expressed "optimism that Mr. Fortas will" serve a "lustrous" tenure in Warren's footsteps. Despite expressing some reservations about the Warren Court's legacy, the *Washington Star* also concluded that Fortas "seems unlikely" to face "a formidable barrier to his promotion." The television newscasts echoed these sentiments. On the CBS evening news, Roger Mudd reported no signs of opposition within the Senate and predicted, as Johnson surmised, that Thornberry's inclusion would make Fortas more palatable to the South. Congressional correspondents reporting to Bill Small, the head of CBS's Washington bureau, "came back with word that there were . . . some complainers, but they aren't going to get anywhere." Finding the notion of a lame duck preposterous, ABC's Frank Reynolds relegated Griffin's antics to the "silly season" induced by the election. A newspaper in Michigan aptly summed up the media's consensus in a headline: "Opposition to Fortas Not Great But Pesky."

Griffin's wife also considered his gambit a longshot. "Do you realize that you are fighting the Supreme Court, . . . the Democratic leadership and the Republican leadership as well as the President? . . . Just who do you think you are?"

Regardless of what his skeptics thought, Griffin's audacious ploy represented the first real crack in Johnson's plans. What came next widened that fissure.

JULY, 1968

Marriages are unpredictable. Unable to withstand the tiniest speedbumps, some dissolve rapidly. Others thrive under the most trying circumstances. Typically formed out of expediency, political marriages are especially vulnerable to coming apart. Ad hoc coalitions fashioned to tackle a crisis end up crumbling during more temperate times. Ideological cracks develop into chasms over time. Politicians sometimes veer so far from their roots they switch parties, a change of allegiance so unfathomable it would be like a Yankee fan rooting for the Red Sox. Yet the marriage between Johnson and Russell endured despite the giant obstacle standing between them—civil rights.

Russell had always seen Johnson's rise to the presidency as a means to an end. Desperate to see a southerner become president, his former apprentice's arrival in the White House should have been a cause for celebration. Johnson instead disillusioned Russell at every turn, passing sweeping civil rights legislation not seen since Reconstruction. Even more odiously for the president's mentor, Johnson vanquished Russell's marathon filibuster in the process, handing the senator the biggest setback of his career and bringing to an inglorious end his decades of vigilance against the swelling tide of civil rights.

The political bludgeoning he endured at the hands of his former disciple considerably cooled Russell's feelings towards Johnson in the mid-1960s. He'd tell constituents in Georgia: "I had a very close relationship with the President when he was in the Senate . . . but I don't have that same relationship now." Their disagreements grew larger throughout Johnson's Great Society initiatives and the Vietnam War, both of which Russell opposed. Though the philosophical breach could not have been bigger, Russell continued to function as a sounding board for the president during frequent meals at the White House. Forever indebted to Russell's patronage during his years in the Senate, the president reminded his aides that Russell remained his "dearest friend" for whom he had great affection. "LBJ loved Richard Russell," remembered a Johnson aide particularly close to both men. Buoyed by this mutual admiration, their relationship thrived in spite of the divergent political beliefs that would have torn apart most other political marriages.

While presidents maintained a tight grip over the selection of justices, they deferred to senators from their party to recommend candidates for district court positions. When a vacancy occurred in a federal court in Georgia in February, 1968, Russell banked on this prerogative to recommend Alexander Lawrence, a longtime political ally with strong qualifications for the opening. Senators typically sent a list of preferred candidates on such occasions. Unwilling to consider anyone else, Russell broke with this practice and sent only Lawrence's name.

Lawrence was a respected legal scholar and political operator with a stint as the president of the State Bar of Georgia. Few in the state's legal community could point to a more experienced and talented person for the job than Lawrence. Sponsored by one of the Senate's powerbrokers and brandishing stellar credentials, Lawrence's appointment awaited only the formality of a background check. The ABA quickly gave him high marks. The hitch arose during the Justice Department's review. Pointing to a 1958 speech in which Lawrence scolded the Warren Court for its "judicial arrogance," civil rights groups opposed Lawrence's candidacy. As a simple way to establish an official's segregationist bona fides, such declarations had become staples of the South's political class in the years after *Brown*. A decade later, the liberals in control of the Democratic Party used *Brown* as a litmus test, disqualifying anyone who made such utterances from higher office. The attorney general in particular was loath to give his consent to anyone who had embraced segregation no matter how politically expedient it was in the 1950s. Clark's disapproval of Lawrence's appointment transformed what should have been a mundane request by Russell into a source of contention.

When the press picked up on the brewing tension, it raised the stakes for Russell. Having publically tied his name to Lawrence's nomination, the senator had to prevail to save face. Failure on such an inconsequential issue would undermine his standing among peers on far more substantive matters. Fully aware of the potential repercussions, Clark nevertheless rebuffed Russell's attempts to overrule him. "Mr. President," Clark told Johnson at a meeting in the White House, "I know that this is important to Senator Russell . . . but we're receiving a lot of opposition from minority groups." The attorney general emphasized how the appointment of a segregationist would hamper the enforcement of the president's various civil rights initiatives and serve as yet another impediment to integration.

Johnson was torn. He genuinely wanted to keep segregationists off the courts and applied civil rights as a litmus test for judicial appointments. Yet, he was desperate to preserve his intimate rapport with Russell: "If we come to the final conclusion that we can't appoint him," Johnson told Clark, "then we'll come to that conclusion. . . . But if there's any way at all that . . . he can be appointed . . . without doing anything to undermine the judiciary, I want to do it. I want to appoint this man." Johnson was unwilling to issue a direct order—despite his reputation for bossing around underlings, he didn't have that kind of authority over the attorney general—but it was close to being one.

When Clark continued to defer, Russell made another direct plea to Johnson in early May. Trying to find a way out of the predicament, Johnson explained that Clark would resign if the president overruled him. This was no bluff on Johnson's part. Clark's forceful stance on civil rights made him a favorite of Johnson's liberal critics, which made it all the more difficult for Johnson to expel him from his administration. Russell dismissed these concerns. Regardless of the dynamics of Johnson's relationship with Clark, Russell felt justified in demanding that his request be honored. A senator of his standing had an ironclad right to select a federal district court judge and none of his personal appeals to the president had ever been turned down before. "Are you President or is Ramsey Clark?" he asked Johnson cynically. Johnson's position became more untenable when new reports of Lawrence's checkered past ossified Clark's position. On May 11, three months after Russell's initial recommendation, the attorney general told Russell that he would never support the appointment.

Each of Russell's requests followed by Clark's refusals upped the ante. Their tussle was no longer centered on an obscure judicial vacancy. It now entered into far more dangerous territory, turning into a contest over competing principles and the most important measuring stick in Washington—power. On May 20, Russell wrote a four-page letter again urging Johnson to act. "I have never made a personal appeal to you for a Presidential appointment. . . . In this instance, however, where only a local appointment is concerned and a man of great competence and high character has been suggested, I feel justified in insisting most respectfully that you send Mr. Lawrence's nomination to the Senate." Increasingly cranky over the rebuttals, Russell complained to Johnson's aide two days later: "Ramsey Clark is no great asset to the President."

When Johnson met with Russell in the White House on June 25 to gain the senator's blessing for Fortas and Thornberry, the president tried to reassure Russell of Lawrence's pending appointment. He was fibbing. The reality was that the president and the attorney general were working at cross purposes. No matter how deeply the president valued his friendship with Russell, Clark refused to cave in. Johnson had erroneously assumed that Clark, like his father, the former justice, would turn out to be more of a pragmatist than a purist. Though pressed again by Johnson to take action, Clark continued to withhold his approval in the hope that more damning information would trickle in about Lawrence that could definitively torpedo the appointment.

The broad view of history pits politicians as ideological and partisan rivals. But politics is often a deeply personal enterprise. Grudges and betrayals can fuel rivalries while seemingly inconsequential slights can destroy relationships.

Irate at Clark for acting "like a child" and frustrated by Johnson's inability to secure Lawrence's seat, Russell travelled with his secretary to his Georgia residence in late June where he dictated a letter expressing his grievances. Upon his return to the capital, he met with Johnson's aides on July 1. Sensing the growing tension, Johnson instructed Temple to "take Harry McPherson with you. . . . Russell is as fond of Harry as a son, and that'll be your entrée." The admiration was mutual. "Often I found myself offering counsel to him," McPherson wrote in a memoir, "seeking to forward his purposes, because his character and professionalism were magnetic to me."

Johnson made the right call. Years of smoking had squeezed the air out of Russell's lungs. Relying on oxygen tanks to help him get through the day, the former workhorse had been reduced to a part-time schedule. Barely able to stand up when Johnson's team arrived, Russell nevertheless forced his sickly body up from his office couch to hug McPherson. In a wheezing voice, the senator asked McPherson about his family before the men turned to the topic of the Court nominations. When Russell inquired about Lawrence, Temple assured him that the president and attorney general were "still working on it." "Well, you tell the President that I said that I'm still very, very interested," Russell told the president's emissaries. Temple left the "pleasant" interaction believing the senator remained committed to the Fortas-Thornberry ticket.

The letter Russell had drafted in Georgia arrived at the White House the next day. A page-and-a-half in, he revealed his sense of betrayal:

> To be perfectly frank, even after so many years in the Senate, I was so naïve I had not even suspected that this man's nomination was being withheld . . . due to the changes you expected on the Supreme Court . . . until after you sent in the nominations of Fortas and Thornberry while still holding the . . . nomination of Mr. Lawrence. . . . Whether it is intended or not, this places me in the position where, if I support your nominees for the Supreme Court, it will appear that I have done so out of my fears that you would not nominate Mr. Lawrence.

Johnson was stunned. Regardless of the rift that had formed between them in recent years, he and Russell had always been forthright with each other. Now, his mentor thought the president was exploiting Lawrence's candidacy to keep Russell in line. Russell was flatly wrong. Johnson was crafty. Johnson was manipulative. And Johnson would do just about anything to get Fortas confirmed. But the president never intended to link Lawrence's posting to the senator's support for Fortas. If anything, the selection of Thornberry—not Lawrence's appointment—was supposed to appease Russell. Angry and humiliated, Russell did not see it that way. Perhaps his waning health had dulled his political antennae or, unable to appreciate the dynamic between Johnson and Clark, Russell misconstrued why the president didn't simply dictate orders to his chief law enforcement officer. Either way, the endless delays had frustrated Russell past his breaking point.

Wounded and belittled, Russell lashed out at his former apprentice in the next passage:

> I still dislike being treated as a child or a patronage-seeking ward heeler. When I came to the . . . Senate some thirty-odd years ago, I did not possess much except my self-respect. When I leave . . . I still intend to carry my self-respect back to Georgia.

Some marriages survive the toughest traumas, but this breach cut too deeply—even more deeply than the rupture over civil rights. After all they had endured, their marriage fell apart due to a messy cocktail of misconceptions and bruised egos.

Putting aside their severed personal bond, the political consequences became clear to Johnson as he made his way through the letter:

> This is, therefore, to advise you that, in view of the long delay in handling and the juggling of this nomination, I consider myself released from any statements that I may have made to you with respect to your nominations.

Johnson was "bullshit" with Clark, recalled Califano. Why the president was unwilling "to pay the price of a Lawrence nomination for the Fortas nomination is a real puzzle. . . . All he had to say was, 'Ramsey, send it over here or quit. Stop fucking around.'" The president, finally, did just that. "Ramsey," he said on the phone minutes after reading the letter, "I'm very unhappy. I think your foot-dragging on this has destroyed one of the great friendships I've had." Clark wasn't the only one at fault. Wrongly assuming that his bond with Russell would persevere no matter the circumstances, the president miscalculated as badly as his attorney general.

Going through several drafts, the White House staff scrambled to write a response to make amends. "I think . . . a little salute to Senator Russell's justifiable pride in his integrity might be helpful" suggested McPherson. After denying any link between the Lawrence and Fortas-Thornberry nominations, Johnson ended his two-page apology:

I am frankly surprised and deeply disappointed that a contrary inference would be suggested. Both my own standards of
public administration, and my knowledge of your character,
would deny such an inference.

Delivered in person by Johnson's aide, it did not sway Russell. Neither Johnson's intermediaries, nor his own personal appeal days later could assuage the
aggrieved senator. The attorney general finally pitched in, rushing Lawrence's
nomination to the Senate for a hasty confirmation. Clark's concession did not
appease Russell either. (Ironically, everyone had Lawrence wrongly pegged:
he turned out to be a champion of integration.) Russell and Johnson—the
teacher and student, the father-figure and the son he longed to make president—had remained close for two decades despite their differences over civil
rights. After the Lawrence fiasco, they never met again as friends.

Only days after Johnson had joined forces with Dirksen and Russell, the former struggled to keep his caucus in line and the latter abandoned his long-time
friend. Without Russell, Califano predicted, "we didn't really have a prayer."
Russell's next move brought Califano's prediction a step closer to reality.

Griffin's commitment to a filibuster during his June 27 press conference
earned him credibility among the southern senators who had been skeptical
about his willingness to use a tactic the GOP had long condemned. On his
way to Michigan for the Independence Day recess, Griffin stopped at his
mother's home in Pontiac, a suburb of Detroit. She told him that Russell had
called from Georgia.

Since the late 1930s, southern Democrats had regularly aligned themselves
with Republicans from the Midwest and Plains states. This "conservative coalition" lacked a formal leader, functioned without a caucus, and operated on
an ad hoc basis with no comprehensive legislative agenda. Despite these deficiencies, when the coalition came together, it was a potent force, and one that
Russell relied upon to help him defeat civil rights bills and uphold the sanctity
of the filibuster. The coalition went dormant during Johnson's wave of Great
Society legislation in the middle of the decade. Riding a conservative backlash

in 1968, it came back strong to win a string of legislative victories.

Even amid this resurgence, contacting Griffin was still an unconventional move for the Senate sage. In an institution ruled by seniority, Russell wouldn't deign to reach out to a first-term senator, particularly a member from the other party who voted for every civil rights measure Russell held in contempt. Russell's recognition of Griffin's growing clout convinced him to break with the Senate's well-established mores. But that alone didn't fully explain his motives. It was one thing to drop his commitment to Fortas due to a personal slight. It was another thing altogether to join forces with the opposing party to actively sabotage the nomination. Perhaps it was his waning health. Perhaps he had grown frustrated by Johnson after all of these years. Or perhaps, it was his deep-rooted enmity for Warren that explained his willingness to take this extra step of vengeance. A decade earlier, Russell had written to a friend: "I am doing everything within my power to curb this wild Court." His views had not changed one iota. "I can assure you," he wrote to a constituent in the midst of the Fortas confirmation, "that my efforts to return the Judiciary to its proper role . . . will continue."

Eager to gauge the number of senators Griffin could rely on in a filibuster vote, Russell asked Griffin when they spoke in early July, "Bob . . . how many votes have you got against cloture?"

"Well, Dick, I think I now have twenty to twenty-two votes on my side of the aisle," Griffin answered. The number had grown in the week since Griffin surprised the capitol with his insurrection. "And I guess I can always count on some Western votes because those fellows just don't believe in cloture."

"Are you serious about this thing?" Russell asked. "Are you going to stick with it?"

"Yes, Dick," Griffin answered back confidently. "I'm dead serious about it."

So was the Georgia senator. "I'll be with you," Russell said.

CHAPTER 7

REMATCH OF THE WARREN WARS

We will resist this judgment of the court. — JAMES KILPATRICK

JULY, 1968

U p to 1968, confirmation hearings had followed a familiar pattern. They usually began with a senator from the nominee's home state delivering an encomium on his behalf. Then, other than an accommodation for a witness with a scheduling conflict, the nominee testified followed by others championing or opposing his nomination. That was the template Eastland followed for each of the seven previous confirmation hearings he oversaw since becoming chairman of the Judiciary Committee in 1956.

But, not this time. Instead of beginning with Fortas's sponsor, Tennessee Senator Albert Gore, as originally planned, the committee asked the attorney general to open the hearings on July 11, 1968. The break with tradition was an ominous sign for the Fortas camp. The fact that the committee had asked Clark to comment on whether the exchange of letters between Warren and Johnson created a vacancy was even more foreboding.

Wasting no time with pleasantries and skipping the typical tributes of admiration and gratitude made to an attorney general for appearing before the committee, Eastland opened the overcrowded session by asking Clark: "Now what are your views?"

Going into the hearings, Clark knew his job was to defuse any suggestion that Warren was scheming with Johnson to rig his succession. Pointing to recent confirmations of ambassadors, generals, and lower court judges whose replacements were confirmed prior to their official retirement date, Clark emphasized that the committee could proceed under the circumstances. Clark's deputy at the Justice Department, Warren Christopher, had uncovered a similar exchange of letters between Justice Horace Gray and Theodore Roosevelt. It wasn't a recent example but as the closest one they could find on point, Clark relied on the analogous circumstances surrounding Gray's retirement in 1902 to legitimize the interchange between Warren and Johnson.

Sam Ervin, the former justice of the North Carolina Supreme Court regarded as the leading constitutional expert within the Judiciary Committee, wasn't buying any of it. Like many of his southern peers, Ervin traced his lineage back to the Confederacy: his grandfather had been a veteran of the war. Born in 1896 just months after *Plessy*, Ervin went on to excel at Harvard Law School. After serving in WWI and working in private practice, the "ol' country lawyer" whose library housed some 35,000 books (most of them on the law) earned an appointment to fill an empty Senate seat by reassuring voters of his antipathy towards *Brown*. "I love the South," he declared when asked about the case. "Many persons whose blood runs in my veins died for a cause they believed to be right. I honestly believe that if usurpation by the court continues, the Constitution of the United States will be destroyed."

For several minutes, the senator moonlighting as a constitutional scholar and the young but self-assured attorney general dueled with one another as though they were still in a law-school debating contest. "It is apparent here that the present Chief Justice has not retired," Ervin exclaimed several minutes into their joust. Each time Ervin pressed Clark to concede that Warren's letter didn't constitute an intention to retire, the attorney general circled back to his list of precedents. "I am not impressed by precedents, the nature of those you stated," Ervin scolded Clark at the end of his interrogation. "Murder has been committed in all generations . . . but the commission of murder has not made murder meritorious. . . . The same thing about precedents which are in conflict with the law."

After Hruska and Fong continued in the same line, Thurmond began his onslaught. Unlike the other senators who challenged Clark with hypotheticals—what would happen if Warren changed his mind or stayed on should the Senate reject Fortas—Thurmond openly accused the chief justice of trying to plant his "friend and protégé" on his throne.

Such bravado, combined with a willingness to trample on the Senate's mores, was emblematic of a career spent as a firebrand. Thurmond bolted from the Democratic Party in 1948 to run as a third-party candidate after Truman insisted on a strong civil rights platform. He returned as a prodigal son, but against the wishes of the party's elders, he ran under the Democratic banner as a write-in candidate in 1954, handily taking the senate seat—the only time the feat has been accomplished. A decade later, he abandoned the party for good to become the Republican powerbroker in the South. None of these acts of mutiny or his questionable romantic liaisons with significantly younger women derailed his electoral fortunes. "Strom is like a cat with nine lives," explained his longtime assistant, Harry Dent. "You could throw him off the Empire State Building and he'd land on his feet every time."

His personal habits were equally unconventional. Thurmond's dedication to a healthy lifestyle—he lived to be 100—set him apart from his hard-drinking, chain-smoking colleagues. He preferred prune juice over scotch, consumed whole wheat bread well before it became a fad, and carried around a tooth brush and dental floss to cleanse his teeth after every meal. He had high-protein cereal flown in from Switzerland and dates trucked in from California. At Clemson University, he ran long distance track, and his daily exercise regimen well into his golden years included morning calisthenics, a three-mile run, and weightlifting in his office between meetings. "The South," McPherson pointed out, "was curiously tolerant of extravagant personalities." Thurmond was among the most extravagant the region had ever produced. "If he were a fictional character," a reporter wrote of Thurmond in 1968, "he would not be believable." Disposed to playing the quirky showman, Thurmond relished entertaining the press corps with spontaneous outbursts of push-ups and knee-bends. *Life* magazine ran a picture of him at 44 doing a head-stand with his 21-year-old bride Jean Crouch looking on. The story behind their engagement matched Thurmond's propensity for the quixotic. Thurmond dictated his proposal to Crouch, who was then his secretary: "My darling Jean, Loving you as I do, I want you to be my wife without too much delay." Crouch accepted through a typed letter. The nuptial to a younger bride—his second wife was 44 years his junior—established Thurmond's reputation as a lothario in the male-dominated capital. "When he dies," Texas's Tower purportedly said, "they'll have to beat his pecker down with a baseball bat in order to close the coffin lid."

These droll attributes may have softened Thurmond's persona as a combative legislator but never mitigated his fanatical devotion to segregation. Thurmond was a scion of Jim Crow. His grandfather fought at the battle of Appomattox; his father, John, served as a campaign manager for Thurmond's boyhood hero, "Pitchfork" Ben Tillman, who was responsible for instilling Jim Crow into the state's constitution. "South Carolina has disenfranchised all of the colored race," Tillman boasted to the Senate at the turn of the century. "We have done our level best, we have scratched our heads to find out how we could eliminate the last one of them. . . . We stuffed ballot boxes. We shot them. We are not ashamed of it." John's loyalty to Tillman knew no bounds: he once killed a man over a dispute involving his patron. Born in 1902, Thurmond accompanied his father to Tillman's farm throughout his childhood where he came to idolize the state's greatest advocate of white supremacy.

During stints as a local superintendent of education, a state senator, a judge, governor, and senator, Thurmond had established himself as a champion of segregation. Other than George Wallace, no one seemed to better encapsulate the unbending southerner determined to fight for Jim Crow until his last breath. No institution threatened that vision more than the Warren Court. "Let us make it grimly clear to the court," Thurmond professed after *Brown*, "that we reject" its course of action. Confederate flags were ubiquitous in certain quarters of the South and Thurmond's office was no exception. But few of Dixie's devotees decorated their office with a cannonball fired at the Battle of Fort Sumter.

Thurmond's propensity for hyperbole made him sound so off-kilter it would have been reasonable to occasionally question his sanity. "Centralized control of education has historically been the escalator to absolute power for dictators," he bellowed in one of his many apocalyptic pronouncements. That inclination resurfaced when Thurmond got the last crack at Clark. Ignoring the attorney general's testy exchange with Ervin, Thurmond asked Clark:

"Either there is a vacancy or there is not a vacancy. Now, why not face up to it." Thurmond was trying to bait Clark into an outburst. "I have nothing else for the Attorney General, unless he would care to answer that." Two hours into this barrage of questions, Clark maintained his composure: "I have answered it several times," he responded, careful to avoid a snarky comeback.

Sensitive to the optics of having a pack of segregationists launch another assault against the Warren Court, Russell and Griffin had agreed to allow the Republicans to take the lead. Breaking with this script, the southerners on the committee couldn't help but take this opportunity to pounce on a nomination that they had turned into a referendum on Warren's legacy. Through their aggressive, brusque, and disrespectful cross-examination of Clark, they tried to manhandle the attorney general and he wasn't even their primary target.

Taking pot shots at the Court and its defenders was nothing new for this cohort. It wasn't as if Thurmond, Ervin, Eastland and their associates had stood in silence all those years only to spontaneously explode in 1968 like a long-dormant volcano unexpectedly erupting. The fact was that they had used every means possible to prevent *Brown*'s implementation and undercut the Court's authority over a period of fourteen years. And they certainly weren't alone. Thousands of local southern officials helped implement what came to be known as "massive resistance." Orval Faubus, Bull Connor, George Wallace, and many other admirers of Jim Crow became national figures by playing bit roles in this drama. What changed during Fortas's nomination were the power dynamics at work. Griffin's ability to corral close to twenty Republicans—combined with Johnson's flagging presidency—allowed Warren's enemies to do more than harass nominees and stage dramatic but ultimately futile campaigns to demoralize the Warren Court. They finally had the chance to notch a victory against the justices that had long eluded their grasp.

Southern senators weren't the only ones planning their revenge against the Warren Court. By 1968, James Kilpatrick, already the leading conservative media personality of the era, was on the cusp of achieving the stardom that would make him the most influential political columnist of the 1970s, catapulting him to become a regular fixture on *60 Minutes*. From his base in

Richmond, he had expanded his brand nationally with a newfangled message predating modern-day conservatism: "before there was a Ronald Reagan or Rush Limbaugh," a veteran Republican explained decades later, "there was . . . Kilpatrick explaining public-policy issues from a conservative perspective."

Just like Eastland, Ervin, and Thurmond, Kilpatrick was a veteran of the "Warren Wars"—the political and cultural battles surrounding the Warren Court. But unlike those senators, he participated not by sponsoring legislation or delivering fiery speeches but by formulating the intellectual foundation underpinning the region's widespread defiance.

Born in Oklahoma in 1920, Kilpatrick had grown up and come of age in a family environment indoctrinated in southern racial customs. Kilpatrick's grandfather had served as a captain in the Confederate army, and during Reconstruction he fought to oust officials in New Orleans trying to institute a multi-racial government. Named after the Confederate general Thomas "Stonewall" Jackson, Kilpatrick's father moved to Oklahoma, bringing with him a fondness for Jim Crow.

Kilpatrick's parents wanted their second of three children to pursue a literary career far removed from his father's timber trade. Encouraged by his mother Alma, the precocious Kilpatrick devoured books, tackling *One Thousand and One Nights* at the age of five. Alma also cultivated his appreciation of writing by teaching him the rhyming patterns of poetry and poetic structure while he sat cross-legged on his bed. The local library served as a second home for him; there he immersed himself in Rudyard Kipling, T.S. Eliot, and other literary giants. Kilpatrick published his first piece in a children's magazine, an essay on Charles Lindbergh's transatlantic flight, at age six. In the fifth grade, he started a newspaper.

Whereas his mother nurtured his literary ambitions, Kilpatrick absorbed much of his worldview from his father Thomas, a conservative who wholeheartedly embraced the laissez-faire ideology popular during the Gilded Age. His father's views of the Constitution, encompassing the southern focus on states rights and limited federal power, also colored Kilpatrick's emerging political philosophy. Growing up in Jim Crow's heyday had led Kilpatrick to view segregation as a natural facet of the social order.

The primary hardship Kilpatrick endured during childhood arose from a series of family traumas in the late 1930s. His father's timber business collapsed during the Depression. At about the same time, Kilpatrick forever severed his relations with him when his father left for California with his secretary, abandoning Alma to support a bankrupt family on her own.

These setbacks never slowed down Kilpatrick's determination for a life in letters, however. By thirteen, Kilpatrick began working as a copy boy at the *Oklahoma City Times*, his first posting in a seven-decade career in journalism. Eager to reach his goal, he finished high school two years early to enroll at the University of Missouri's journalism school, among the best in the nation. In search of a job in 1941, his cover letter claimed that "he knew the streets of Paris as well as he knew the streets of Philadelphia." He heard back from Virginia's leading political newspaper, the *Richmond News Leader*, asking him to consider $37 a week salary. Only twenty-one years old, Kilpatrick didn't bother to answer the question. "Will arrive Monday," he responded in a telegram, turning his hiring into a fait accompli.

Compared with Oklahoma, that achieved statehood in 1907, Virginia proudly dated its ancestry back to the nation's colonies. Prancing around like modern-day aristocrats, the tight-knit group in control of the state's political class—the "First Families of Virginia"—anointed Harry Byrd, a descendant of Richmond's founder, to serve as their feudal steward. Byrd became governor in 1926 before switching over to the Senate in 1933 where he went on to serve for more than three decades. Described by one senator as a "little antediluvian in his social and political views," Byrd firmly believed that the laws should "be enforced by the white people of this country."

Kilpatrick's penetrating coverage of the judiciary and state politics for the *News Leader* helped him enter Byrd's inner circle, an oddity for someone outside Virginia's First Families, and earned him the moniker, "the terror of Richmond." His beat also fueled Kilpatrick's growing fascination with the law. Years later, he declared that he would have studied law instead of journalism if he "had to do it all over." Often conversing with lawyers and judges, Kilpatrick became an avid reader of the Court and its fabled jurists. Inevitably, these two subjects led him to the biggest issue of the era—civil rights.

Just as civil rights was becoming an increasingly divisive issue, Kilpatrick took over the newspaper's top job in 1950. He injected a combative tone into the *News Leader*'s editorials, and in one he proudly proclaimed that he shunned "wishy-washy or fence-straddly" positions in favor of a "provocative, . . . outspoken, sometimes outrageous page, calculated to stir up the animals and keep the adrenals flowing"—the mid-century version of a modern-day shock jock. The new responsibilities at the paper never slowed down his output or his uncanny ability to tackle a multitude of subjects. He averaged a half million words annually, the equivalent of a 3-4 inch book. Of the many topics he covered, nothing matched his infatuation with *Brown*.

This fixation with *Brown* was unavoidable. The ruling represented the biggest blow to white supremacy in a century. The last time the South's white population felt this threatened, it abandoned the Union. This time around, Kilpatrick and a group of like-minded editors at the *News Leader* rejected secession as an option. "We will resist this judgment of the court," Kilpatrick assured readers instead, "we will resist it quietly, honorably, lawfully, but we will resist it with the strength of a tradition that has resisted tyranny before."

For the region to categorically avoid integration, its resistance to *Brown* required more than an endless stream of outrage and vitriol. The South needed a plausible theory to pull off an unprecedented attempt to defy a direct order from the nation's highest judicial body. Desperate to concoct such a legal justification, Kilpatrick stumbled upon a defunct theory—interposition.

Fashioned by Thomas Jefferson and James Madison, interposition claimed the States possessed the power to reject federal directives. On its face, the theory stood in direct contradiction to the Constitution's unequivocal establishment of federal supremacy over the States. Despite this fatal flaw, Kilpatrick wasn't the first person to embrace interposition out of expediency. When the Federalists found their party in decline in the early 1800s, they turned to the concept to beef up their last stronghold in New England. It was a disingenuous about-face for the political party. Having spurned the concept while in power during the Washington and Adams administrations, they looked to it to fend off their own extinction.

Every attempt to employ the theory proved equally self-serving and futile. In 1809, the Court explicitly rejected the application of the concept to federal judicial rulings. "If the legislatures of the several States may, at will, annul the judgments of the courts of the United States . . . the Constitution itself becomes a solemn mockery . . ." John Marshall wrote for a unanimous Court.

Decades later, John Calhoun's abortive resurrection of interposition led to the nullification crisis. In vanquishing Calhoun, then-president Andrew Jackson offered a resounding defense of federal supremacy. "I consider, then, the power to annul a law of the United States, assumed by one State, incompatible with the existence of the Union, contradicted expressly by the letter of the Constitution, unauthorized by its spirit, inconsistent with every principle on which it was founded, and destructive of the great object for which it was formed." It would be hard to find a more cogent and affirmative rejection of interposition. Yet, that didn't stop northern abolitionists from calling upon the theory two decades later to circumvent federal mandates to return runaway slaves. The Confederacy's reliance upon interposition to secede marked the theory's last major revival. (In recent years, some of the legal arguments against the Affordable Care Act relied upon interposition as well).

This inglorious track record did nothing to smother Kilpatrick's enthusiasm. Cultivating arcane speeches and dormant legislation unearthed at the Richmond Library, he resurrected the concept. On November 21, 1955, just two weeks after interposition struck him "like a bolt of lightning," Kilpatrick unleashed his findings in the *News Leader*'s pages. Through an editorial titled "Fundamental Principles," he laid out the historical basis for interposition: "Jefferson and Madison," he wrote, "did prophesy a time when the Federal government might usurp powers not granted it." In such instances, he continued, the States could interpose—or negate—the federal action. For the next four months, the tens of thousands of words Kilpatrick pounded out on his typewriter turned this obscure theory into a household word in Virginia.

Despite his budding recognition, Kilpatrick had no interest in directing angry mobs or delivering combative speeches. His methodical delivery and hyper-analytical speaking style made him ill-suited for public rallies compared with theatrical orators like George Wallace. Kilpatrick's arsenal consisted primarily of the written word, a weapon he wielded as effectively as anyone in the South. Ever the wordsmith, his portrayals of the Court relied upon vitriolic descriptions. In one instance, he blamed the Court for the "rape of the Constitution"; in another, he characterized *Brown* as "a revolutionary act by a judicial junta". Though the message remained the same, he applied a more restrained tone when writing for national publications. The justices have "created . . . the right to attend a non-segregated public school," he wrote for the *National Review*. "The Court . . . simply created the right; and in doing so, the Court had to do a lawless thing. It seized from the states a power plainly reserved to the states." These attacks on the justices often ended with an assertion southern detractors repeated throughout Warren's tenure: "The Court undertook not to interpret the Constitution but to amend it." In this worldview, it was the Court, and not the South, which was depicted as the outlaw. "These nine men repudiated the Constitution, spit upon the tenth amendment, and rewrote the fundamental law of this land. . . . If it be said now that the South is flouting the law," Kilpatrick exclaimed, "let it be said to the high court, *You taught us how*."

Spearheading the region's fight against *Brown* placed Kilpatrick firmly near the top of the long list of Warren's detractors. Yet, in relying on interposition to execute his attacks, his entire enterprise rested on a sham. Kilpatrick realized from the outset that, though clothed in scholarly robes, interposition was a farce. Prominent lawyers from the region, including future justice Lewis Powell, berated Kilpatrick for touting "legal nonsense." Peddling interposition under these conditions was like misleading a terminal cancer patient with promises of a new elixir. It may have provided a short-term boost to morale but was ultimately doomed. Despite these false pretenses, the concept provided a valuable purpose to Kilpatrick even as it would come to cause long-term harm to the region by building false hope. On a big-picture level, Kilpatrick hoped "that if six or seven . . . Southern States should unite in a common front, all of them undertaking to nullify the Court's mandate . . . the Supreme Court would be faced with a truly formidable problem in enforcing its orders."

The first half of his strategy worked better than he could have anticipated. From his office at the *News Leader*, interposition spread like a wildfire in a drought-stricken forest, or as Kilpatrick wrote, "an idea that grew like dandelions and crab grass." Just one month after Kilpatrick introduced audiences to interposition, he sold 13,000 pamphlets summarizing his findings.

In short order, the Virginia legislature came under pressure to scrap its inchoate plans for gradual desegregation. Using interposition as their cudgel, Kilpatrick and Byrd smothered any voices within the legislature leaning towards an accommodation with *Brown*. In January, 1956, Kilpatrick warned "that the hour has come to stand up and be counted. . . . We resist now, or we resist never. We surrender to the court . . . or we make a stand." Overwhelmed by pro-segregationist forces, the Virginia legislature enacted an interposition bill authored by Kilpatrick pledging to "take all appropriate measures . . . to check this . . . encroachment by the Supreme Court." Kilpatrick's brainchild won by a landslide: 36 to 2 in the state Senate, 88 to 5 in the House.

Interposition proved to be immensely valuable to segregationists. By serving as a legal reproach to the Court, it draped *Brown*'s opponents with a layer of legitimacy. "In interposition," declared Byrd, "the South has a perfectly legal means of appeal from the Supreme Court." "I only wish we could have gotten started on this sooner," the senator wrote to the editor. Russell also saw Kilpatrick's creation as a "lawful means . . . to bring about a reversal of this illegal and unconstitutional decision of the Supreme Court."

Interposition's allure also arose from its originality. Many of the Court's critics simply re-litigated *Brown* in their denouncements. Writing in the *U.S. News & World Report*, the former justice James Byrnes delved deeply into the Fourteenth Amendment's legislative history in an editorial that, at times, read like a law review article. The fact that the Court had thoroughly reviewed the same material, receiving extensive submissions from the southern school districts, the NAACP, and the solicitor general, didn't stop these unending regurgitations of *Brown*'s merits. Bypassing these stale arguments made interposition's fresh approach more appealing.

The persona of its chief spokesman also boosted the theory's popularity. The restraint Kilpatrick employed in discussing racial issues made him more welcoming to a national audience compared with some of the provincial cranks gleefully bellowing out racist epithets. Soon after Kilpatrick became famous throughout the South, William Buckley of the *National Review* and David Lawrence of the *U.S. News & World Report* tapped him to write about civil rights.

His avoidance of the verbiage used by hard-core segregationists masked his true feelings, however. In his 1957 screed railing against *Brown*, he blamed the blight of broken marriages and venereal disease on African-Americans, and feared that, like a virus, they would infect white students in integrated schools. In private, he argued that the African-American race had "debased every society in which its blood has been heavily mixed." Responding to Martin Luther King Jr.'s "I Have a Dream" speech, Kilpatrick dismissed African-Americans as "an inferior race" in an article slated for the *Saturday Evening Post* (and subsequently canceled) titled "The Hell He is Equal".

The reason a concept as obscure, unorthodox, and fanciful as interposition could catch on was that since the vast majority of white southerners so abhorred integration, they were willing to embrace any far-fetched doctrine. The region's initial disapproval of *Brown*—which stood at 71% a week after the Court's decision—hovered in that range for years while the rest of the nation grew more accepting of the ruling. Nor did the region's white population become inured to the idea of integration over time. Two years after *Brown*, only 5% of white southerners favored immediate integration. Even fifteen years after *Brown*, when only a small fraction of African-American students attended integrated schools, 58% of southern whites still felt that integration had moved along too quickly. These sentiments naturally colored the region's views of the Warren Court: while most of the nation held "greater respect" for the Court over Congress, the South favored the latter by a nearly two-to-one margin.

Interposition's popularity caught many outside the South off-guard. "I'm afraid we assumed that after a short period of time of one to five years, the states would give in," Thurgood Marshall explained. "We did not, however, give enough credence to the . . . Richmond papers . . . who were determined that they would build up the type of opposition that would prevent the states from voluntarily going along." Marshall wasn't the only one surprised. "The Court expected some resistance from the South," Warren explained years later, "but I doubt if any of us expected as much as we got."

Inspired by interposition, Thurmond started to prepare a written declaration in 1956 to take a united stand against the Court. The timing of Thurmond's action a few months before the election alarmed Adlai Stevenson, who feared that the proposition would undermine his presidential bid by tearing apart the fragile Democratic coalition, and thus pitting northern liberals against the party's southern bulwark. Stevenson's emissary whom he dispatched to quell Thurmond made no headway. "It's no use trying to talk to Strom," an official told Stevenson's envoy. "He believes that shit." Thurmond's penchant for treachery and his brash attitude in challenging the Senate's customs turned the South Carolina senator into a renegade within the tight-knit Southern Caucus. Wary of Thurmond's potential to botch the region's retort, the Caucus turned to Russell to take over the drafting process.

When a team led by Russell presented a finalized draft on March 8, 1956, 101 of the South's 128 congressmen signed what came to be called the Southern Manifesto. Every representative from seven states—Alabama, Arkansas, Georgia, Louisiana, Mississippi, South Carolina, and Virginia—penned their name to the document. The Manifesto's uncompromising language turned it into a litmus test for the region's politicians. Those who signed it stood with the South. Those who resisted paid the price in the polls.

Four days later, Georgia's Walter George unveiled the South's declaration on the Senate floor. "The unwarranted decision of the Supreme Court in the public school cases is now bearing the fruit always produced when men substitute naked power for established law," he said, reading from the Manifesto's opening. "We regard the decision of the Supreme Court in the school cases as a clear abuse of judicial power." The document then rehashed the arguments put forth in *Brown* by the segregated school districts before turning back to the Court's power-grab. "Though there has been no constitutional amendment or act of Congress changing this established legal principle almost a century old, the Supreme Court . . . with no legal basis for such action, undertook to exercise their naked judicial power and substituted their personal political and social ideas for the established law of the land." In a backhanded endorsement of interposition, the Manifesto next praised "the motives of those States which have declared the intention to resist forced integration by any lawful means." The last line promised endless resistance: "We pledge ourselves to use all lawful means to bring about a reversal of this decision which is contrary to the Constitution and to prevent the use of force in its implementation."

It was an astonishingly bold document. Not one of the Court's former critics, from Thomas Jefferson to Andrew Jackson to Abraham Lincoln to Franklin Roosevelt, had gone so far. The Manifesto's brashness, its willingness to go to new extremes, signaled to the world the South's muscular and united stand against the Court.

The Manifesto succeeded in serving as a rallying cry in the region, what one historian described as the "South's resistance to *Brown* turned into something close to a political counterrevolution." Armed with interposition and encouraged by the Manifesto, Virginia promulgated thirteen bills barring integration by the end of 1956. The deep-seated racism of the region revealed itself through the legislation's punitive nature. More tempered measures would have allowed—but not required—school districts to flout *Brown*. Instead, Virginia authorized the governor to shut down any school district with plans to integrate. Any deviations from the rigid racial code set forth by the state's political elite had to be crushed.

By the summer of 1957, Florida, Alabama, Georgia, Louisiana, Mississippi, South Carolina, and Arkansas also enacted interpositions bills. The legislation coming out of Alabama and Georgia considered *Brown* "null, void, and of no effect." Mississippi's version deemed *Brown* "unconstitutional, invalid and of no lawful effect within the confines of . . . Mississippi." These states also promulgated 106 bills aimed at thwarting any attempt to implement *Brown*, ranging from a refusal to integrate, to the closure of public schools, to subsidies for white-only private schools. The accretion of these measures forged a fortress-like wall of "massive resistance" in much of the former Confederacy with interposition serving as this wall's barbican. "There is a feeling that knits together the Georgian, the Virginian, the Carolinian, the Louisianan," Kilpatrick believed. "All of us stand figuratively on the ramparts together, facing a common foe."

Segregationists received widespread grassroots support at every turn. White Citizens' Councils—known as the "country club clan" or "white-collar

Klansmen" because their members came from reputable local businesses and civic associations—served as "shock troops" at the local level. Established just months after *Brown*, their membership rolls swelled to 250,000 by the end of the decade. The Councils' emphasis on non-violence didn't diminish their potency. They bullied African-Americans into capitulation through threats of job losses and other forms of economic distress. Encouraged by Eastland, whom *Time* dubbed their "patron saint," the Councils pressured whites sympathetic to integration through public shaming or business boycotts. "Social ostracism, economic sanctions, and political punishment were the weapons," wrote Tennessee's Gore (the father of the future Vice President), a moderate on racial matters who refused to sign the Manifesto when Thurmond ostentatiously presented it to him on the Senate floor.

One factor in particular made it easier to resist the Court's edict. *Brown* did not outlaw an unconstitutional governmental practice, such as a limitation on a specific type of speech or law enforcement practice or a ban on abortions. It would have been fairly straightforward to halt such practices. Instead, the ruling required active and complex government action through changes to the funding, administrative structure, and attendance policies of countless school districts. These administrative elements made its enforcement particularly cumbersome, something Kilpatrick exploited from the outset. "Let us pledge ourselves to litigate this thing for 50 years," the editor urged. "If one remedial law is ruled invalid, let us try another; and if the second is ruled invalid, then let us enact a third. . . . When the court proposes that its social revolution be imposed upon the South 'as soon as practicable,' there are those of us who would respond that 'as soon as practicable' means never at all."

State after state followed his advice, with school districts resorting to intimidation tactics, legal delays, and cat-and-mouse games. To avoid sending their children to integrated schools, many Virginians flocked to all-white "segregation academies." North Carolina offered free tuition to private schools catering to white students. Tennessee allowed white students to transfer out of desegregated schools. Mississippi and Louisiana made it a crime to attend an integrated school. Alabama vowed to abolish the entire public school system rather than integrate.

With southern leaders lashing out at the justices at every turn, it was no surprise that some of their unhinged admirers would take this venom to heart. On the night of July 13, 1956, two men burned a pair of crosses on the grounds of Warren's apartment complex. "I was just trying to make people aware of something they already know," one of the perpetrators said in his defense, "that the Supreme Court really was out of order."

What was astonishing about the South's defiance was not the region's antagonism towards the Court, which had been a target of ire in various epochs. It was the degree to which the region brazenly, and in such significant numbers, attempted to subvert its directives that made the reaction so exceptional. It was one thing to cry foul. It was another thing altogether to question the Court's authority. This resistance eventually set the region on a collision course with the justices: "Mr. Warren sowed the wind," Kilpatrick prognosticated. "[H]e has not yet reaped the whirlwind." One didn't need the prescience of a Greek oracle to foresee that years of hateful rhetoric and unabashed defiance would plunge the region into an epic clash with the Court. The collision finally occurred on the afternoon of August 28, 1958.

Little Rock was an unlikely setting for the South's inevitable showdown with the Court. Other than the Border States, Arkansas was one of the few places in the South open to accommodating *Brown*, albeit through token integration. The Little Rock crisis could have been averted had not the voices of moderation succumbed to the segregationist frenzy taking over the region. Orval Faubus started out as one of those moderates, cultivating black voters in his gubernatorial triumph in 1954. Brought up in rural poverty, given a middle name honoring his father's socialist hero, Eugene Debs, and instilled with an education in labor and social activism, Faubus held views on *Brown* that typified his worldview: he told a private group, "If I had been on the court, I would have voted that way myself." His moderation collapsed in the face of segregationists disposed to exploiting *Brown*. Months after Faubus's inauguration in 1955, James Johnson, the director of the White Citizens Council in Arkansas, led the forces accusing Faubus of failing to stand up to the judicial marauders. To shield his flank, Faubus ran as an unabashed segregationist when challenged by Johnson in the 1956 primary. This crass strategy worked flawlessly: Faubus won the Democratic primary, trounced his Republican opponent in the general election, and pushed through a referendum on interposition. Whether he was a Machiavellian villain willing to betray his principles for political gain, or a devout believer in Jim Crow, Faubus set the stage for the standoff in Little Rock.

In a city of 107,000 where whites outnumbered blacks by three to one, the Little Rock school board's desegregation plan called for starting at the high school level and gradually working down to the lower grades. Like the many games of subterfuge orchestrated by southern school districts, it was designed to do the minimum required to fend off full-scale integration.

After several rounds of court battles between the NAACP and local officials over the scope of the proposal, the school board moved to admit nine African-American students to Little Rock Central high school for the 1957-58 school year. Calling it modest would have been an overstatement. But for a population obsessed with maintaining Jim Crow, any integration, no matter how numerically inconsequential, spurred a violent reaction. Faubus poured fuel over this volatile situation by shedding all semblance of his former progressivism. His statements became ever more explicit over time: at one point, he warned that "blood will run in the streets" should integration proceed. He was not the only voice preaching defiance. The presence of segregationists from outside the state preaching resistance turned Little Rock into the front line of the battle against the justices for the entire region. And in turn, this explosive cocktail turned the case—*Cooper v. Aaron*—over efforts to desegregate Little Rock into more than a dispute over how *Brown* should be implemented, a question easily mired in legal minutiae. It transformed *Cooper* into a symbolic contest between the Court and its most brazen critics across the South.

Faubus's next move sharpened the stakes for the justices. When he commanded the National Guard not to enforce *Brown* but to block a federal court order for integration, he set the stage for the unforgettable scene on September 23, 1957, of an angry white mob jeering at the quietly dignified black students trying to make their way into school. Immortalized by newspaper photographers, the indelible images of this event came to symbolize the integration struggle at that time. It also marked the moment when Eisenhower could no longer maintain his apathetic approach to the issue. Exasperated by Faubus's antics and pinned into a corner, Eisenhower reluctantly stepped into the imbroglio.

Well before the Little Rock crisis, Eisenhower blamed *Brown* for instigating the "most important problem facing the government domestically." Throughout his presidency, he struggled to tackle an issue that, in his eyes, brought him only misery. "I think that no other single event has so disturbed the domestic scene in many years as did the Supreme Court's decision . . . in the school segregation case," he wrote to a friend.

The difficulties *Brown* posed for Eisenhower began while the case was still in progress. Based in the Department of Justice, the solicitor general was the federal government's top representative before the Court. Because the justices often asked for the solicitor general's input in cases in which the government was not a party, Court watchers dubbed the position the "tenth justice." When the Court asked the solicitor general to weigh in on *Brown*, Attorney General Brownell's decision to side with the NAACP caused a rift with Eisenhower. During his childhood in Kansas and later as a West Point cadet, Ike grew up in a world where African-Americans were non-existent. His years in the army saw him stationed largely in the South and the Philippines, where racism also thrived. He did not speak out against the nation's segregated armed forces and during his many visits to Augusta National Golf Club, he listened to racist jokes from his southern pals and sometimes repeated them. At the same time, his vow to end segregation in Washington, D.C. indicated that he was not an ossified racist. Over time, he pushed for the watered down civil rights bill that was enacted in 1957. It's therefore difficult to assess Eisenhower's mixed record on civil rights. What is clear is that, discomfited by the topic, he hoped the problem would go away.

When Brownell offered his support for the NAACP's position, Eisenhower disassociated himself from his own administration's policy. Privately, he hoped the Court would uphold *Plessy*, telling Brownell, "I think . . . that the best interests of the United States demand an answer in keeping with past decisions." (It should be noted that in his memoirs, Eisenhower declared unequivocal enthusiasm for *Brown*.) At about the same time he conveyed his displeasure to Brownell, the president hosted a stag dinner in the White House. When the dinner came to an end, Eisenhower pulled Warren aside on the way to another room where coffee and after-dinner drinks were being served. "These are not bad people," he said, referring to southern whites. "All they are concerned about is to see that their sweet little girls are not required to sit in school alongside some big over-grown Negroes."

The apprehension he exhibited during the lead up to *Brown* continued into its aftermath. His first chance to publicly discuss the case laid bare this discomfort. Asked whether he had any advice for the South, he responded: "Not in the slightest." The best he came up were bromides urging the region to remain "calm and . . . reasonable." What was the most telling was not what he said but what he declined to say. He refused to applaud the ruling or condemn segregation and grew irritated when dispelling the notion that his administration deserved credit for *Brown*.

Having long lived in surroundings ruled by Jim Crow's strictures, Eisenhower's sympathies remained unchanged despite the growing importance of civil rights during his presidency. In a 1957 letter to Byrnes, he assured the governor that, having "spent a not inconsiderable part of my life in the South," many of his "dearest friends are in that region." His affinity for the region colored his view of *Brown*: echoing the opinion espoused by Court critics, Eisenhower believed the ruling harmed rather than improved racial relations. To overcome "the passionate and inbred attitudes . . . developed over generations," he preferred a gradual approach to desegregation.

Though Eisenhower didn't deliberately fan the flames of southern intransigence, he didn't bother to put out the region's fires either. Hard-core segregationists looked to his half-hearted approach as a sign of his tacit approval. "Much of the tension in the South . . . could have been avoided if . . . Eisenhower had taken a strong, positive stand on the question of civil rights and the Supreme Court's decision as soon as it was rendered," Martin Luther King observed. "If President Eisenhower had used his good offices to say that 'This is the law and it should be obeyed,' that would have accomplished much,"

Thurgood Marshall explained years later. "We hoped for it. And we found out too late that indeed, President Eisenhower was opposed to it." Warren felt the same way, blaming Eisenhower for the heightened racial animus of the era. The president's unwillingness to publicly support the ruling and defend the Court played a key role a decade later in Warren's decision to retire.

Eisenhower's public stance was not his only action hindering integration. Preventing the Justice Department from enforcing *Brown* placed the onus of overseeing desegregation on the federal courts, a task for which they were ill-suited. His failure was far more striking when it came to addressing the South's outrageous concoctions. He refused to discredit interposition, and couldn't muster a reproach to the Manifesto, the most toxic decree issued by the South. "Now let us remember this one thing," he said in a press conference on March 14, 1956, the "people who have this deep emotional reaction . . . were not acting over these past three generations in defiance of law." Urging patience, he reminded reporters that *Brown* "completely reversed" the legal landscape. He then framed the Manifesto as a tempered pronouncement in consideration of its avowal to "to use every legal means" to subvert the Court.

This position placed the president at odds with his own party, which zealously sought to take credit for *Brown*. Leading up the 1956 Republican convention, he ordered Brownell to delete any mention of the "Eisenhower Administration" in the initial draft of the GOP's platform on integration. He threatened to avoid the convention should those in charge of the party's platform insist on inserting a stronger link between the White House and desegregation. After some pushback, the president agreed to the following provision: "The Republican Party accepts"—instead of "concurs," another substitution Eisenhower insisted upon—"the decision of the U.S. Supreme Court that racial discrimination in publicly supported schools must be progressively eliminated."

Though unwilling to praise *Brown*, Eisenhower refused to stand idly by while Faubus brazenly flouted a federal court order. "We cannot possibly imagine a successful form of government in which every individual citizen would have the right to interpret the Constitution according to his own convictions, beliefs, and prejudices. Chaos would develop. This I believe with all my heart," he wrote to a colleague, "and shall always act accordingly." On

September 24, 1957, the president dispatched the 101st Airborne Division to enforce the court's directive.

In the popular retelling of the episode, the Little Rock crisis ended with Eisenhower's deployment of troops in the fall of 1957. But for the justices, a series of convoluted legal maneuvers turned the events in Little Rock into a standoff with their adversaries. Unwilling to stand up to the forces lined up against it, the city's school board abandoned its modest plan for integration and requested a 30-month delay. On June 21, 1958, a federal judge endorsed the school board's request. On August 18, the Eighth Circuit Court of Appeals overruled this decision. A week later, for only the third time in its history, the Court scheduled an emergency session to determine the legality of the board's request to postpone integration.

Regarded as a first-rate trial lawyer, Richard Butler was a WWII veteran routinely representing Arkansas' public utilities and various corporations. On August 28, 1958, the tall, courtly attorney made a straightforward appeal to the justices relying on the untenable position faced by the school board. While he largely stuck to this line of argument, Butler veered from his script more than half-way through his presentation:

> As long as . . . popular editorialists in our community were say-
> ing that this was not the law of the land and . . . there were ways
> to get around it . . . and there where laws on the state statute
> books of Arkansas as well as other states throughout the South
> diametrically opposed . . . with . . . Brown . . . left the people
> of our community as well as people of many communities in
> actual doubt as to what the law was and . . . people in our part
> of the country wanted to believe that this thing could . . . be
> circumvented entirely.

Kilpatrick's brainchild had finally made its way to the Court. "Regardless of whether or not the people of Arkansas should recognize the United States Supreme Court decisions as the law of the land," Butler continued in a slow delivery. "The plain fact is that they have not and it is most difficult for them to do so, if not impossible when the Governor of the State says, that that is not the law of the land." It was one of the most impudent statements ever made to the justices, and the fact that Butler issued the proclamation inside the Court's hallowed space made it all the more insulting.

Just a shade over 7,400 square feet, the courtroom within the Marble Palace was a fitting venue for the nation's highest judicial body. In front of a backdrop of four ionic columns separated by red hanging curtains, the nine justices—with Warren in the middle—sat at a straight bench hovering above the rest of the room. A lectern for the lawyers stood in front of the chief justice. Desks and chairs for opposing counsel were situated on either side of this podium. Seating for about 160 onlookers filled out the rest of the room. Like much of the rest of the building, marble was omnipresent: an ivory-colored variety from Spain on the walls, an Italian light-sienna variety for the 24 columns dispersed throughout the room. A who's who of ancient sages such as Solomon, Justinian, and Muhammed decorated the four friezes floating above the mortals on the floor. With 44-foot tall ceilings, it was an august and austere space ruled by protocol. Unlike the floor of the House or Senate, where congressmen regularly held sidebars, the Court's chamber prohibited such chatter, limiting conversations to the lawyer standing at the podium and the justices. It goes without saying that the justices also frowned upon those openly questioning their authority.

Compared with Frankfurter—who swiveled his chair as if trying to relieve a nervous tic, asked clerks to fetch him materials, and barraged lawyers with questions—Warren typically maintained his poise during oral arguments, handling advocates with a gentle touch. The chief justice shed his usual equanimity, however, when Butler, seeking to extract some sympathy from Warren for Arkansas's plight, referred to similar difficulties the chief justice must have encountered as governor. The comparison Butler attempted to make between Warren and Faubus pushed the chief justice over the precipice. "But I never tried—I never tried to resolve any legal problem with this kind as Governor of my State," he cut in.

"We realize that," Butler answered back. Careful to avoid uttering the word "interposition," Butler nevertheless returned to the concept. "The point I'm making is this," he said. "That if the Governor of any State says that a

United States Supreme Court decision is not the law of the land, the people of that state until it is really resolved have a doubt in their mind and a right to have a doubt." Furious with Butler's declaration, Warren interjected a second time. "But I have never heard such an argument made in the Court of Justice before and I've tried many a case over many years."

Though never directly referenced by the Arkansas lawyer, the meaning of his statement was clear: Kilpatrick's interposition legitimized the South's defiance. Faubus's next move gave the justices little choice but to meet this challenge.

After the oral arguments on August 28, 1958, Faubus summoned the legislature to a special session to pass fifteen bills authorizing him to close down any schools targeted for integration and channel public funds to private, segregated institutions. These latest gestures were not the actions of a humble litigant praying for the Court's mercy. Nor was the timing a coincidence. Faubus raised the stakes by withholding his signature from the bills, vowing to sign them only if the Court refused to capitulate.

The governor's latest salvo changed the nature of the case. From a purely legal standpoint, the Court in *Cooper* was asked to determine whether the school board's request for a delay was justified under the circumstances. From a broader perspective, Little Rock had developed into a proxy for an entire region's insolence. And now, Faubus's latest barefaced challenge to the Court's authority "created an atmosphere of historic crisis" among the justices. It was now up to the justices to determine whether they would issue a ruling limiting their discussion to the specifics of the board's request or a wider ranging opinion meeting the challenge set down by their adversaries.

On September 29, 1958, the justices filed into the courtroom to announce their ruling in a chamber full of anxious spectators. Other than Douglas, who was traveling, Warren looked at each justice individually when announcing each of them as co-authors. The unanimity the justices found so critical during *Brown* remained paramount during *Cooper*'s deliberations. To make it clear to naysayers that *Brown* was not the handiwork of a handful of radicals, John Marshall Harlan suggested that every justice—and not just Brennan, the opinion's true author—sign the ruling, a practice never undertaken before.

"As this case reaches us," the chief justice began to read from the text of the decision, "it raises questions of the highest importance." Unlike *Brown*, where the Court didn't reveal its conclusion until well into the ruling, the justices arrived at the heart of the decision in the first paragraph. The case "involves a claim by the Governor and Legislature . . . that there is no duty on state officials to obey federal court orders" and "that they are not bound by our holding in *Brown*." The justices issued a blunt response: "We reject these contentions."

While the justices sympathized with the school board's predicament, they could not countenance sacrificing the rights of the African-American students "to . . . violence and disorder." "In short, the constitutional rights of children . . . declared by this Court in the *Brown* case can neither be nullified openly and directly . . . nor nullified indirectly by them through evasive schemes for segregation whether attempted 'ingeniously or ingenuously.'"

Applying easy-to-follow and unimpeachable logic in what turned out to be a straightforward case from a legal perspective, the justices could have stopped there. But they chose to reaffirm the Court's authority and, after four-and-a-half years of silence, struck back at their detractors. The Court reiterated that *Brown* was now "the supreme law of the land. . . . No state legislator or executive or judicial officer" could challenge this reality without violating the Constitution. After positioning the Court at the top of the nation's constitutional hierarchy in general terms, the justices turned to Faubus in particular: "A Governor who asserts a power to nullify a federal court order is similarly restrained."

This was the second opportunity for the justices to stop. They had dismissed interposition on a conceptual level and gave Faubus a spanking. But they elected to go one step further by responding to critics accusing a handful of judicial extremists of social engineering. "The basic decision in *Brown* was unanimously reached" they declared in *Cooper*'s final paragraph. "Since the first *Brown* opinion, three new Justices have come to the Court. They are at one with the Justices still on the Court who participated in that basic decision as to its correctness, and that decision is now unanimously reaffirmed."

JULY, 1968

For a short while after *Cooper*, Kilpatrick kept up the fight, forming the Virginia Commission on Constitutional Government to support "racial separation." Able to read the tea leaves before many other segregationists, however, Kilpatrick conceded defeat far earlier than the rest of the region. "As a creature of law," he wrote in 1962, "racial segregation in the United States is dead. Many staunch Southerners, declaring themselves unwilling to surrender, do not realize that as a matter of law, the war is over." For the next stage of his career, Kilpatrick signed up with Long Island's *Newsday* in 1964, putting him on a track to reach a national audience. To burnish his reputation outside the South, Kilpatrick eschewed the sectional rants that had made him a household name in Dixie. "From my own professional point of view," he wrote to an editor in 1966 in response to a proposal to print an unpublished piece, "the problem is quite simply that I do not want—and could not possibly afford— to be publicly associated with these views. . . . My syndicate tells me that the biggest single obstacle to further sale of the column is my reputation as an old-fashioned Southern racist and segregationist." Concerned with the threat of his past sabotaging his new-found popularity, he tried to buy back the unpublished article. Elevated by his syndicated column, "A Conservative View," Kilpatrick's notoriety next took him to the *Washington Star*, that syndicated his column in almost a hundred newspapers. Kilpatrick had earned such a high-standing within Washington's conservative circles that, in 1968, a bureau chief from the *Chicago Daily News* said it was "almost as if he's a congressman from some huge district."

Savoring the chance to finally strike his nemesis, Kilpatrick wasn't about to let Warren depart on his own terms. As a parting gift to the chief justice in his national column, he called Warren's tenure a "disaster in the field of jurisprudence."

When Eastland, Thurmond, Ervin, and Kilpatrick ardently lined up against Fortas in the summer of 1968, it was as if they were putting the band together for a rematch of the Warren Wars. For these veterans of the fourteen-year conflict, this latest skirmish wasn't really about Fortas or Thornberry at all: it was a continuation of the many battles that they had fought and lost against the Court's liberal bloc. The primary difference was that unlike their past offensives, which were fought on the Court's home turf, this struggle would play out in the Senate, where they—not Warren—came armed with the most potent weapons. Warren and his judicial allies may have cast aside decades of precedent in *Brown* and belittled interposition and the Manifesto in *Cooper*, but now, in the last political melee of his career, a struggle over his very legacy, Warren was forced to face his most strident critics on their terms.

These veterans of the Warren Wars approached this latest slugfest with a new strategy. Ervin, for one, came to the realization that one thing and one thing alone could impede the Warren Court. "I have long felt that the most important means of returning the Supreme Court to the role the Constitution has given it," he wrote to a constituent, "would be to appoint men to the court who have the proper attitude towards its function."

Unable to find enough partners outside the South during most of Warren's tenure, they watched Eisenhower, Kennedy, and Johnson stack the Court with justices predisposed to supporting civil rights. Griffin was the difference-maker this time around. If his coalition held firm, the Warren Court's biggest rivals could pick up enough allies from outside the region to finally prevail.

Emboldened by his secret alliance with Russell, Griffin took on a more aggressive tone by mid-July. Out went his tentative search for some charge that might stick, and replaced now by a new sense of confidence. That confidence was on full display on the second day of the hearings. Appearing before the Judiciary Committee on July 12, Griffin doubled down on his contention about Johnson's lame duck status. What had started as a flippant rationalization back in June had now hardened into a stout justification for his objection to Fortas. The senator's commitment to it didn't make the argument any less specious, however. The president's powers under the Constitution never diminished as he approached the end of his term. They remained the same from the day he took office to the moment they expired at noon on January 20 (March 4 until the Twentieth Amendment was adopted in 1933) and not a minute earlier. If the United States was attacked days before this date, surely

Griffin wouldn't inhibit Johnson from defending the country simply because time was running out on his presidency.

Even when it came to judicial nominations, the idea of a lame duck had no standing. Since the 1780s, more than half a dozen presidents had nominated sixteen justices during an election year, often after it was clear that they would not continue in the White House. John Adams and Benjamin Harrison successfully nominated justices weeks before their terms expired; Andrew Jackson and Martin Van Buren just days before. More recently, Eisenhower appointed Brennan in 1956 weeks before election day. The timing of this selection could have opened a Pandora's Box. As a recess appointment, Brennan took a seat on the Court prior to obtaining Senate approval, which came months later. Had Eisenhower lost the election, Brennan would have been the lamest of ducks.

The circumstances surrounding Warren's retirement played into Griffin's hands. Griffin had no way to expose Warren's true motives so he did the next best thing—insinuate them. Uninterrupted by the committee's members during his opening remarks, he no longer cast his objection to the nomination as a prudent measure allowing the next president to select Warren's successor. Nearly a month into the brewing confirmation fight, he recast his opposition in bolder terms: "never before has there been such obvious political maneuvering to create a vacancy," he exclaimed, "so that an outgoing President can fill it and thereby deny the opportunity to a new President." Growing more insensate over time, Griffin even accused the president and chief justice of conspiring to undermine the Republic.

During his eighteen-minute statement, Griffin turned his sights to yet another charge—cronyism. Just as Johnson had predicted, his close association with Fortas and Thornberry gave critics an easy mark: "It is highly unusual for a President to subject himself to the charge of 'cronyism' in connection with a nomination to the Supreme Court," Griffin explained. "And never before in history has any president been so bold as to subject himself to the charge of 'cronyism' with respect to two such nominations at the same time."

Intended as the sweetener for the South, Thornberry was now depicted as a liability. But he was ultimately the undercard for the main event. Because

Fortas—not Thornberry—embodied the Court's liberal bloc, it was Fortas who would remain the primary target of the judicial body's enemies. "Mr. Chairman," Griffin told the Committee after disclosing a list of favors Fortas had conducted on behalf of the president since becoming an associate justice, "I do raise the question whether Mr. Fortas should be rewarded with the position of Chief Justice . . . because he performed such services as a friend of Lyndon Johnson." While the delivery may have lacked a flair for the dramatic, the impact of his words opened a new theater of war against Fortas.

Griffin's charges of cronyism were tailor-made to oppose the nomination. In that sense, they were politically convenient for the time. But they had an afterlife far beyond this confirmation fight. Though no one could have foreseen it at the time, Griffin helped change the ground rules for future appointments. No president would again select a confidant until George W. Bush's botched nomination of Harriet Miers, who as his White House Counsel was denounced for her close ties to the president.

Griffin also wanted to drive home a larger point about the Senate's historical role in the confirmation process. Few remember his words now but they were among the most prescient spoken in the summer of 1968:

> A good deal of the current controversy revolves around the appropriate functions of the President and of the Senate in the circumstances which confront us. There are some who suggest that the Senate's role is limited to merely ascertaining whether a nominee . . . possesses some minimum measure of academic background or experience. I should like to emphasize at the very outset that any such view of the Senate's function . . . is wrong. It does not square . . . with the intention of those who conferred the advice and consent power upon the Senate.

Griffin may have been motivated by short-term political goals, but he was on to something profound in urging his colleagues to alter this dynamic. "To assure the independence of the judiciary . . . , it is vitally important then to recognize that the . . . power of the Senate. . . is not only real, it is at least as important as the power of the President to nominate," Griffin exclaimed near the end of his prepared statement. At least as important as the power of the president? That had never been the case. Not with any president during Griffin's lifetime. And certainly not with Johnson. Speaking as if he was oblivious to the powers aligned against him, the freshman senator pressed on anyway: "There are times in the course of history when the . . . Senate . . . must draw a line and stand up. This is such a time."

Immediately after Griffin finished his prepared remarks, Dirksen, the senior Republican on the Committee, unleashed his wrath. Brimming with confidence after flipping four of the 19 senators in Griffin's camp, Dirksen poured "eloquent and polysyllabic scorn" over Griffin's arguments. "First," the Minority Leader began, "I find that term 'lame duck' . . . as entirely improper and a very offensive term." Still peeved at Griffin for opposing his leadership, Dirksen addressed only the other committee members, willfully ignoring the Michigan senator a few feet away as if Griffin weren't even in the room.

Dirksen then responded to Griffin's charge of cronyism by pointing to Truman's four nominations. In listing the number of connections between Truman and his selections, Dirksen grew more incensed: "if ever anybody was a crony . . . it was Fred Vinson. . . . I do not know that anybody got up on his hind legs and shouted cronyism."

Re-energized by his performance, Dirksen referred to a number of close relationships between presidents and justices: Frankfurter was FDR's advisor and Douglas a regular at his poker games; Kennedy appointed a campaign manager and cabinet secretary to the Court; Abraham Lincoln, Dirksen added, as he slipped into one of his theatrical orations, "renowned all over the world, and whom you can only explain as having been ordained by God Almighty" also appointed his campaign manager. "I would hate to think that history is going to rise up to say that Lincoln was guilty of cronyism." Now on a roll, the "spellbinding... Dirksen... stole the show with some virtuoso verbiage," a *Newsweek* reporter observed. "That is why I say this is a frivolous, diaphanous—you know what that means, don't you—" the Minority Leader said as Griffin's complexion turned white at the volley of insults, "argument that that just does not hold water."

Griffin responded to Dirksen's insults by finally shedding his unassuming

"Clark Kent" persona. "He has only half the power," Griffin shouted back, referring to the president. "And it is about time the Senate realized that," he continued, pounding the table as his voice grew louder. "He only has half the power and we have the other half, and we ought to assert ourselves."

CHAPTER 8

RED MONDAY

Our society must deal with the Court as it deals with many other transgressors of law and order. ——L. BRENT BOZELL,
NATIONAL REVIEW EDITOR, MARCH 6, 1958

JUNE, 1968

I t was a cruel irony that just as Fortas was on the verge of reaching the pinnacle of his life, forces beyond his control would dictate his destiny. Unable to take center-stage in his own story, it was as if he were a guest at his own wedding. His adversaries were willing to shatter every deep-seated custom to sabotage his ascension, forcing him to navigate a rapidly shifting landscape he had effortlessly traversed three years earlier. But there was one other malevolent force looming over him. Fed up with *Brown, Miranda,* et al., Warren's detractors looked to settle their scores not with the outgoing chief justice, who remained beyond their reach, but the heir to his throne hand-picked by Warren's collaborator in the Oval Office, Lyndon Johnson. Confined by the opposition to playing the role of Warren's proxy and Johnson's protégé, Fortas made for a natural target, giving conservatives one last chance to chasten the twin titans of American liberalism. By the start of the hearings, Fortas's nomination had evolved into a rematch to avenge these past losses. And no loss showcased how close the Court's foes had come to subduing the Warren Court more than a legislative battle in 1958 in which Johnson emerged as Warren's savior. That confrontation wasn't over segregation or criminal procedure or any of the other memorable decisions attached to

Warren's legacy, but over McCarthyism.

After Griffin's testimony, four witnesses accusing Fortas of having ties to communism appeared before the Judiciary Committee. When Fortas had been the target of similar allegations during his confirmation hearings three years before in 1965, Eastland of all people came to his defense, dismissing one accuser's point-by-point indictment with a single line: "What has that got to do with the nominee?" This time around, the cigar-chomping chairman gave these witnesses wide leeway to paint the justice as, at best, a naïf duped by communists, and at worst, a traitor. If one had to pick which version of Eastland reflected his true nature, the 1968 edition was far more genuine. That's because the only thing that infuriated the Mississippi senator as much as *Brown* were the Court's rulings reining in McCarthyism.

The same could have been said of Kent Courtney, the chairman of the Conservative Society of America, one of the fear-mongering organizations omnipresent throughout the Cold War. A former Pan Am pilot, Courtney entered politics as an organizer for the John Birch Society, the preeminent right-wing group of the era. Infatuated with wide-eyed conspiracies, he co-authored a book with his wife, *America's Unelected Rulers*, in which he described Henry Kissinger as an "extreme-Left Democrat" and accused Eisenhower of utilizing international institutions to undermine America's sovereignty. Just as Courtney reached the peak of his influence in 1968, Fortas became his latest fixation. "In summary, in these seven cases, Justice Fortas ruled with the Communists," he told the Committee, reiterating the allegations made by the other right-wing witnesses. "I believe that Abe Fortas should be impeached."

Were Fortas's enemies on the committee using these witnesses to smear the justice? Absolutely. But that alone didn't fully explain their presence. In between *Brown* in 1954 and the height of the Court's liberal revolution in the mid-1960s, the Court decapitated the government's far-reaching anti-communist program. This is where Courtney and company fit in. Among the most despised during Warren's term in office, these rulings broadened the attacks against the justices from an exclusively southern pastime to a national enterprise that, in 1958, culminated in one of the gravest threats ever faced by the judicial body. What is telling about this episode is how it foreshadowed

BATTLE FOR THE MARBLE PALACE

what transpired a decade later. In both instances, congressional conservatives mounted an unprecedented attack against the Court and the combatants in 1958—Johnson, Thurmond, Russell, McClellan, and Eastland—reprised their roles for a rematch that would profoundly impact the Court, and its putative crown prince Fortas.

By the time eleven leaders of the American Communist party were put on trial in downtown Manhattan in 1949, America's second Red Scare was well into fourth gear. Unable to uncover any concrete steps taken by the defendants, prosecutors based their case on statements made by party members. At the end of the longest criminal trial in the nation's history, America's communist leadership was found guilty of violating the 1940 Smith Act, a law proscribing the advocacy of the violent overthrow of the government. Ten of the defendants, including Eugene Dennis, the General Secretary of the American Communist Party, received five-year sentences. One defendant, a recipient of the Distinguished Service Cross during WWII, was sentenced to two years less because of his valor.

Dennis and his co-defendants found little relief on appeal. Writing for the U.S. Court of Appeals for the Second Circuit, the legendary jurist Learned Hand brushed aside the Smith Act's restrictions on free speech to uphold the convictions. Months later in June 1951, the Supreme Court confirmed Hand's decision. *Dennis* meant that no major governmental institution—not Congress, not the president, not the state governments, and not the Court—stood in the way of an anti-communist crusade about to go into overdrive.

Granted a free hand by the Court, the Justice Department ramped up its dragnet of left-wing sympathizers, Congress enacted a series of laws to bolster the framework of investigations, loyalty oaths, and immigration controls utilized in the pursuit of "pinkos," and state and local governments piled on with their own initiatives.

The communist witch-hunt ruined the lives of countless Americans. Elia Kazan and others who turned on their associates lived with the stain of their betrayal. Arthur Miller and those electing to stay silent faced imprisonment. The House Un-American Activities Committee (HUAC)—the forum Nixon employed to take down Alger Hiss—along with various Senate panels slandered civil servants and military personnel. Scholars were ostracized for defending academic freedom. Former members of left-wing groups or those who were simply friends with a bygone communist—the so-called "fellow travelers"—were individually branded with the modern-day equivalent of a scarlet letter. The HUAC blacklist wrecked the careers of 10,000 people by some estimates. Some of those who lost their vocation included the "Hollywood Ten" while others who suffered no permanent wounds, such as renowned composers Leonard Bernstein and Aaron Copland, still had to endure the glare of government investigations.

Though the Red Scare turned up few actual Soviet spies, several high-profile incidents in the early stages of the Cold War, most notably Alger Hiss's perjury conviction and Ethel and Julius Rosenberg's disclosure of atomic secrets to the Soviet Union, convinced the American public of the omnipresence of fifth columnists. The 20-20 view accorded by history exposed these incidents as anomalies and revealed the truth about the era's overblown fears. But such rationality rarely prevailed during times of hysteria: the same cauldron of fear and paranoia led to the Palmer Raids following WWI, Japanese internment during WWII, and as a more ancient example, the Salem witch trials.

On April 2, 1956, the Court became the first major governmental body to reverse course and put a brake on McCarthyism's excesses. *Pennsylvania v. Nelson*, which struck down the sedition laws of 42 states, was the first crack in the dam. A week later in *Slochower*, the Court rebuked the brutish tactics used by investigators to intimidate witnesses relying upon the Fifth Amendment right against self-incrimination. In the last of this trifecta, on June 11, 1956 the Court held that the security program for federal employees established by Congress applied only to "sensitive" positions. The symbolism of these rulings carried far more weight than the underlying legal issues. Though careful to couch their decisions in legal maxims, the justices delivered a clear message that the judiciary, at least, which Justice Douglas feared had been "transformed into agents of intolerance," would no longer tolerate these witch-hunts.

Politically handicapped after his censure in 1954, Wisconsin Senator Joseph

McCarthy, the Red hunter after which the period came to be named, was desperate to recapture the limelight. Civil rights and communism being Eastland's twin obsessions, made him the ideal person to give McCarthy a new forum. Johnson illuminated how these two disparate concepts somehow melded gracefully with the senator's worldview: "Jim Eastland could be standing right in the middle of the worst Mississippi flood ever known, and he'd say the niggers caused it, helped out by the Communists." I.F. Stone, a leading journalist of the era, fittingly named Eastland the "Mississippi McCarthy."

McCarthy played his part with relish when invited to testify before Eastland's subcommittee responsible for overseeing the nation's internal security program on June 26, 1956. "Discussing the latest outrage perpetrated by the Supreme Court is becoming a regular habit," he opened. "I thought that when the *Nelson* decision . . . was handed down that the Supreme Court then had reached a rock bottom low in judicial irresponsibility." Though neutered, the Senate's biggest bully wasn't muzzled. He barked out his signature refrains, this time directing them at the justices: "The problem is no longer one of Communist infiltration," he warned. "The Supreme Court has opened the flood gates, and invited the Communists to walk right in." The name-calling came next. "Now, the Supreme Court, which is for the most part manned by incompetent, irresponsible left-wing judges who conceive themselves as a super-Congress, has moved in to nullify the anti-Communist program of the Congress and the Executive Branch."

Along with their rabid anti-communism, Eastland and McCarthy had one other thing in common. In stark contrast to the radicalism of their assertions, both men spoke in a matter-of-fact monotone, as if they were ordering a pizza instead of accusing the nation's highest court of treachery. Often holding a pen or a pair of glasses while speaking, the Wisconsin senator—with skin "like the pale pulpy underside of a mushroom"—rarely deviated from a flat delivery. Likewise, Eastland also maintained an even-keeled posture. Speaking in a stern style, he seldom dialed up the volume. He was no Thurmond, who did not hesitate to break into a tirade. Eastland was just as cantankerous but delivered his diatribes in bullet points rather than outbursts. Wearing black-rimmed glasses, only Eastland's meaty cheeks and round face softened his cold demeanor.

Eastland jumped into McCarthy's monologue, like a lion arriving midway into a kill to help tear apart a carcass.

Eastland: There is just one pro-Communist decision after another from this court, is there not?

McCarthy: You are so right.

Eastland: What explanation could there be except that a majority of that court is being influenced by some secret, but very powerful Communist or pro-Communist influence?

McCarthy declined Eastland's invitation to label Warren a Communist. "But there is something radically wrong with him," the senator exclaimed, blaming the chief justice for sinking the Court to a "new low." "I cannot understand why a man with practically no legal background," he added, echoing the criticism made by Southerners, "was ever selected as a Supreme Court Justice." He ended his testimony with an apocalyptic warning: "Our constitutional form of government is in grave jeopardy. . . . Mr. Chairman, it is the duty of the Congress to face up to this fact, and to take steps to prevent the Supreme Court from usurping the powers of other branches of our Government."

Legislation sponsored by the pair added to the more than 70 Court-curbing measures introduced in the 84th Congress (in session during 1955-56). Surpassing Roosevelt's doomed Court-packing scheme, many of the bills sought to fundamentally alter the Court's composition and its standing in America's constitutional structure. Alabama Congressman George Huddleston Jr. proposed a bill requiring lower courts to ignore the Court whenever it broke with precedent. A proposal from the Peach State sought to ban the Court from overturning precedents older than fifty years old. Conveniently, such a rule would have placed *Plessy* beyond Warren's grasp. Blatantly targeting Black, Douglas, and Warren, one bill sought to bar any members of Congress, heads of federal agencies, and governors from joining the Court up to five years after leaving office. Senator John Butler of Maryland tried to mandate a 75-year-old retirement age for the justices. Louisiana Senator Russell Long proposed twelve-year term limits on future justices and required nominees to have six years of judicial experience prior to joining the Court. The obsession with Warren's lack of judicial experience led other senators to submit similar measures.

If these critics had examined the Court's history, they would have realized the folly of their suggestions. Only three prominent former justices—Oliver Wendell Holmes, William Howard Taft, and Benjamin Cardozo—joined the Court with more than a decade of judicial experience. That figure paled in comparison to the number of exceptional justices with no prior judicial experience, including Joseph Story, Charles Evans Hughes, Louis Brandeis, William Douglas, Robert Jackson, Felix Frankfurter, and Hugo Black, as well as the Court's most revered jurist—John Marshall.

Of the anti-Court measures proposed by the 84th Congress, House Resolution 3 (or HR 3) was the most far-reaching. Introduced by the author of the 1940 Smith Act, Virginia Congressman Howard Smith, and backed by the association of state governors, the National Association of Manufacturers (NAM), the U.S. Chamber of Commerce, the American Bar Association, and the National Association of Attorneys General, HR 3 sought to overturn *Nelson*.

Three of the 70 anti-Court bills introduced by the 84th Congress were reported to a committee but none—including HR 3—made it to the floor of either chamber. Similarly, with only three others in attendance, McCarthy's testimony before Eastland's subcommittee turned into an echo chamber with few outside the hearing room taking notice. But the testimony would prove to be momentous, the tremor foretelling an oncoming earthquake. It would take a few more rulings for that earthquake to strike.

In the ensuing months, other cases impairing the nation's various anti-communist initiatives trickled in. A pair of them issued just four days after McCarthy's death in May, 1957 put an end to the guilt-by-association tactics used to ruin the lives of countless Americans. The applicant's "past membership in the Communist Party does not justify an inference that he presently has bad moral character," Black wrote in one of the cases, adding that "it cannot automatically be inferred that all members shared their evil purposes or participated in their illegal conduct."

That membership in the Communist Party wasn't a sign of a person's moral character or that all communists did not embrace an evil purpose was news to most Americans in the 1950s. "While the Senate last week was burying McCarthy," wrote I.F. Stone, "the . . . Supreme Court buried McCarthyism." Stone's observation was a bit premature, however, as the Court's major strike against McCarthyism did not occur until a month later.

On June 3, 1957, the justices found themselves in the thorny area of balancing an individual's constitutional rights against the nation's security interests. Up to the 1950s, that balance firmly tilted in the government's favor. In *Jencks v. U.S.*, the Court upended this script by refuting the FBI's refusal to divulge the names of witnesses and sources of evidence used to prosecute defendants associated with communism—a common practice sanctioned by previous judges.

Two weeks later on June 17, 1957, the judicial body issued four more communist-related rulings on a day its critics dubbed "Red Monday." For Warren, the common bond among the rulings lay in his displeasure with the "sadistic attacks" launched by McCarthy and his ilk, although these were sentiments that the chief justice kept private until after his retirement. In his memoir, he cited one case in particular in which an individual had received a year-long sentence for refusing to name his college peers. "I mention this example to show the extent of overzealousness that was rife in those days," Warren wrote, "and something of the human suffering it could cause." On Red Monday, the Warren Court made its most significant attempt to combat this suffering.

In the opening paragraph of *Watkins v. U.S.*, the most noteworthy of the cases, Warren highlighted the Court's appreciation for the task it was about to undertake. "The controversy thus rests upon fundamental principles of the power of the Congress and the limitations upon that power," Warren wrote. "We approach the questions presented with conscious awareness of the far-reaching ramifications that can follow from a decision of this nature."

Anxious "to remove needless targets for criticism," no one on the Court was more concerned by the potential backlash than Frankfurter. "As a matter of prudence," Frankfurter wrote to Warren days before the Court issued *Watkins*, "the stiffer our condemnation of . . . Congress the less provocative should be the expression of it." Making the Court's first limitation on Congress' investigatory powers—a power *The New York Times* described "as all but limitless"—this was not going to be easy during an epoch in which congressmen regularly slandered witnesses. There was more than anecdotal evidence to highlight this abuse. From 1792 to 1942, Congress issued 108 contempt citations. HUAC alone issued 135 between 1945 and 1957.

Warren's opinion railed against this abuse. "The power of the Congress to conduct investigations is inherent in the legislative process," his opinion in *Watkins* acknowledged. "That power is broad. . . . But, broad as is this power of inquiry, it is not unlimited." And here, the justices took a shot at Congress' excesses. "There is no general authority to expose the private affairs of individuals without justification. . . . Investigations conducted solely for the personal aggrandizement of the investigators or to 'punish' those investigated are indefensible."

Now that the justices had rebuked Congress, they turned to its favorite cudgel. In *Yates v. U.S.*, the Court threw out the guilty verdicts of fourteen communist leaders by narrowly construing the Smith Act, the very law used to crush the American Communist Party in *Dennis* six years earlier. A third case imposed the limitations established in *Watkins* upon state legislatures. The least consequential case issued on Red Monday limited the discretionary powers of the Secretary of State to discharge allegedly disloyal employees. Through the four Red Monday rulings, the Court did not confine itself to any one facet of the nation's broad anti-communist program. Nor did it limit itself to any one area of law. The cases instead upended a diverse set of institutional practices, and in doing so, the Court managed in a single day to constrain Congress, the executive branch, and every state in the Union. Coming at the height of the Cold War, it was an audacious move.

Red Monday triggered a vicious reaction, and once again, the South served as the first wave of a beachhead landing with Thurmond taking on the role of platoon leader. Appearing on ABC days after Red Monday, he called the Court a "great menace to this country" for endangering the nation more than "any other branch of the Government in the history of the country." That was a bold allegation. But he didn't stop there. His comments on the Senate floor tied into the latest geopolitical developments. "While we are thinking of the tyranny in Hungary," he said, referring to the Soviet invasion of its eastern

European satellite, "I wish to take a few minutes to discuss . . . the tyranny of the judiciary." Tired of simply ranting against the justices, Thurmond called for their impeachment.

Among the many reprimands issued by Eastland, the other half of the dynamic duo, the principal one accused the Court of "attempting to consolidate all government power in its own hands." Former justice James Byrnes, a titan of southern politics, went further, insisting that the "Supreme Court must be curbed." The region's lesser lights chimed in with similar condemnations. "It seems that if there is one thing that is well settled," Georgia Congressman James Davis uttered on the House floor, "it is that a Communist cannot lose a case in the . . . Supreme Court." "Members of the House," Alabama's George Andrews told his colleagues, "let me appeal to you to take action before the Supreme Court destroys this nation." "They are a greater threat to this Union than the entire confines of Soviet Russia," bemoaned South Carolina Congressman Lucius Rivers.

Georgia took these recriminations to their logical conclusion. Adopted by the Georgia General Assembly, a resolution enacted in 1957 claimed the Court's liberals "unlawfully usurped the powers of the people to amend the Constitution and have exercised legislative powers vested solely in Congress" to give "aid and comfort to the enemies of the United States" and sponsor a "pro-communist racial integration policy." Just through these assertions alone, the twelve-page resolution represented an astonishing depiction of the Court. Georgia's solution to dealing with these brigands pushed the resolution further into the stratosphere of extremism—wholesale impeachment of two-thirds of the justices.

Unlike the response to *Brown*, southerners were no longer isolated. In the coming days and weeks after Red Monday, a broad array of detractors lined up against the justices. The future chief justice Warren Burger typified the expansion of the anti-Court coalition. At that point serving as an appellate court judge on the D.C. Circuit, he bemoaned the "unfortunate trend of judicial decisions" that granted the guilty "vastly more protection than the law-abiding citizen." Speaking at a conference of state attorneys general in late June, New Hampshire Attorney General Louis Wyman lamented that the sacred text of the Constitution was left "tortured out of all rational historical proportion." Testifying before the House, the nation's leading law enforcement officer—FBI director J. Edgar Hoover—recounted a communist's characterization of the rulings as the "greatest victory the Communist Party in America has ever received." From the justices' perspective, it was difficult to imagine a more damning endorsement.

Criticism also emanated from more moderate quarters. House Minority Leader Joseph Martin, Jr. of Massachusetts was neither a McCarthy acolyte nor a segregationist. Yet, he too declared on national television that the Court "crippled the investigating committees" within Congress and was "very inimical to the country." On the left coast, California's Donald Jackson bemoaned the Court's attempts "to completely nullify and vitiate the efforts of the Congress . . . to seek out American agents of the conspiracy." From the Great Plains, North Dakota Senator Karl Mundt urged Congress to repeal the "decisions which stultify the power of Government . . . to defend itself." A colleague from the Keystone State recommended adding a tenth justice to the bench, ideally one who is a psychiatrist.

Southern leaders relished this widespread criticism. It gave them cover, making it easier to counter the perception of their antagonism as one built purely on racial animus. "The recent decisions regarding Communism were not cases that originated in the South," Georgia's Russell expounded in a Q&A published by the *National Review*. "Not only the South but the entire country today is menaced by the constant attack on our . . . system of government."

Prominent media outlets echoed this outcry of dread and disdain. "The boys in the Kremlin may wonder why they need a fifth column in the United States," the *Chicago Tribune* maintained, "so long as the Supreme Court is determined to be so helpful." New York's *Daily Mirror* deemed Red Monday "a moment for weeping" as Cleveland's leading newspaper, *The Plain Dealer*, conceded defeat to the Soviets: "Well, Comrades, you've finally got what you wanted. The Supreme Court has handed it to you on a platter." "Maybe the United States needs an American Supreme Court," South Carolina's *News & Courier* sarcastically declared. One of the Court's biggest media critics, David Lawrence of *U.S. News & World Report*, condemned the rulings as "Treason's Biggest Victory".

Led by Buckley's *National Review*, the budding conservative press picked up from its recriminations over *Brown*. "The Court . . . is sitting no longer as a judicial bench but as the nation's supreme legislature," the magazine's editorial screamed on June 29, 1957. "Even more frighteningly," Forrest Davis wrote a week later, "the Court . . . confirmed . . . that in all cases dealing with Communism it hastens to the side of those guilty . . . of bearing a part in the Great Conspiracy fathered in Moscow." Davis blamed the justices' lack of judicial experience for the "[i]ntellectually inadequate . . . dumb core" of jurists hobbled by "commonplace minds."

All of this negative publicity fed the public's rage. "Numerically," *The New York Times* observed, "the judgments of this term lighted more fires" than the outcry borne from *Brown*. "If a movement should start in Congress to impeach one or more of the learned justices," the *New York Daily News* predicted, "it might have much popular support."

The justices were sensitive to the storm clouds looming over them. Black and Douglas, long used to criticism, nevertheless worried about the Court's negative perception. So did Brennan. "I may have been the instrument (in my first year!) for decreasing the standing of the Court," he wrote to Frankfurter in August, 1957. For the first and only time in his judicial career, his mother questioned his judgment. "I never had any difficulty being proud of your opinions on the New Jersey Supreme Court," she told him. "But how could you do this?"

Equally cognizant of the tide turning in their favor, the Court's enemies moved beyond issuing angry declarations. This time, they wanted action.

Historically, attempts to curb the Court have nearly universally foundered. One early effort allowing Congress to vote the justices out of office failed four times from 1805 to 1816. Angered by various rulings during the early 1800s, seven states passed resolutions questioning the Court's review of state actions. None of these measures put a dent in the Court's standing. In 1821, Senator Richard Johnson—a future Vice President—unsuccessfully endorsed a constitutional amendment to transfer appellate review of certain cases to the Senate. Another plan contemplated in those years required five of seven justices (the Court moved to nine justices in 1837) to strike down state laws. Six attempts to enact the measure in the 1820s ended disastrously. Ever resentful of Chief Justice Marshall's stranglehold over the judicial body, Thomas Jefferson's wish-list included less demanding impeachment procedures to remove distasteful justices. Founding Father or not—he too had no luck.

Dred Scott inspired a new generation of Court-curbing proposals. Though Congress fundamentally transformed the Constitution through the Civil War amendments, it declined to alter the Court's standing. The Court's propensity to strike down progressive legislation during the Gilded Age ushered in the next era of recriminations followed—as usual—by congressional inaction. Roosevelt's Court-packing plan exemplified just how difficult it was to refashion the Court. Sponsored by a president with a clear mandate and a pliable Congress that routinely did his bidding, the scheme only garnered 22 votes in the Senate, making it the biggest defeat of his presidency.

This record of futility didn't stop the Court's enemies from trying again. Congressional desire to strike at the Court had been percolating since *Brown*. Yet none of the Court-curbing measures introduced in the 84th Congress made it to the floor of either house. There simply wasn't enough animosity towards the Court outside of the South to buttress them. Red Monday tilted that calculus in the other direction. The dozens of anti-Court measures sponsored by the conservative coalition introduced in the 85th Congress (in session from 1957-58) sought to overturn individual rulings, strip the Court of its powers or added new qualifications to future appointments.

Of the fourteen Court decisions under fire, *Jencks* became Congress' first target. After continued negotiations between Congress and the Justice Department, the fifth version of the *Jencks* bill—that required the FBI to disclose certain information under the review of a trial judge—passed both houses on August 29, 1957. Only two senators voted against the measure; not a single member of the House did. It was not quite a resounding victory, however. Watered down by rounds of negotiations, it ended up not so much a rebuke but a tepid warning to the Court to slow down—similar to a child receiving a "time out".

Brimming with confidence, the Court's detractors were in search of a bigger trophy. This new assault originated not from one of the South's stalwarts but from McCarthy's former wingman, William Jenner. Growing up in Indiana's rural communities near the Kentucky border, Jenner had become enamored with a nineteenth century vision of America far removed from the global complexities of the post-war world. He practiced law in a small town and spent eight years in Indiana's state senate until voters sent him to Washington at the cusp of the Cold War. His desire to preserve the bucolic, utopian charm of his childhood fueled his ardent isolationism. Enraged by the nation's snowballing internationalism, he lashed out at those responsible for America's post-war global alliances. Typical of his hyperbolic style, Jenner labeled George Marshall, one of the most renowned war heroes and diplomats of the era, a "living lie" posing as a "front man for traitors."

On July 26, 1957, Jenner walked out of McCarthy's shadow to issue his rebuttal to the justices. During the debate on a historic civil rights bill, he accused the Court of becoming "a legislative arm of the Government" that "has dealt a succession of blows" to the nation's security. Far broader in scope than the Jencks bill, Senate Resolution 2646 (S 2646) set out to bar the Court from hearing appeals in five different categories of cases involving: (1) the powers of congressional committees; (2) the federal loyalty program; (3) state subversion laws; (4) subversive activities of educators; and (5) state regulations regarding admissions to the bar. While each proscription addressed one or more of the Court's communist-related rulings, S 2646—unlike the Jencks Bill—had no pretenses of clarifying a gray area of the law. This was a full-scale effort to strip the Court of its historic powers of oversight over the other branches of government.

Other than this narrow group of cases listed in Article III § 2 of the Constitution, the Court served as an appellate body whose jurisdiction was determined by Congress. The Judiciary Act of 1789 had established much of the machinery of the federal court system and laid out the Court's jurisdictional reach. Despite the power bequeathed to it by the Constitution, Congress infrequently tampered with the judiciary's jurisdictional reach. Outside of one instance in 1868, it unsuccessfully considered more than ten bills limiting the Court's jurisdiction from the 1820s to the 1880s. Angered by the Court's rejection of the Child Labor Act in 1923, senators William Borah and Robert La

Follette also failed to pass bills empowering Congress to override the Court's rulings. In addition to the Court-packing plan, Congress in 1937 proposed 33 measures weakening the Court's ability to review federal laws. None of them ever became law.

That history of futility didn't slow down the Court's adversaries. When Eastland and Jenner launched hearings on S 2646 in early 1958, 53 witnesses testified before Eastland's subcommittee. While there was plenty of fiery rhetoric, no one could match the point-by-point take-down of the Court offered by William F. Buckley's brother-in-law, L. Brent Bozell, the *National Review* editor whose Yale Law degree made him ideally suited for the role. Doggedly ideological in an era far less divisive than ours, Buckley and Bozell brandished words to spread their gospel and moonlighted as political consultants. Having served as McCarthy's speechwriter, Bozell co-authored with Buckley a book deplored in *The New York Times* for its "bald, dedicated apologia for 'McCarthyism.'" Bozell managed to walk away from his relationship with the discredited senator unscathed to ghost-write the bible of modern conservatism, Barry Goldwater's *The Conscience of a Conservative*.

The justices needed "to be disciplined," Bozell insisted to the subcommittee. "Our society must deal with the Court as it deals with many other transgressors of law and order." During his systematic critique of the Court's rulings, phrases like "national disgrace," "inexcusable," and "gratuitous abuse" spewed from his mouth. Uninterrupted by the members of the subcommittee, the editor urged Congress to "chasten the Supreme Court and make it behave." His ire reflected the fact that well before law and order, the counter-culture, the Vietnam War, obscenity, and civil rights would dominate the culture wars of the 1960s, the Court had developed into the leading bogeyman for America's conservative vanguard.

The Council of the Defenders of the American Constitution and other right wing groups piled on the hateful rhetoric. But this time, these anti-communist groups were joined by mainstream institutions such as the National Economic Council and the Veterans of Foreign Wars. The primary heavyweights on the other side of the ring included the AFL-CIO, ACLU, and the NAACP. This attentiveness from some of the nation's most powerful special interest groups signaled an important evolution in the Court's standing. Historically, special interests had taken a modicum of interest in the Court. The battle over the Jenner bill began to transform this dynamic. For the next decade, the NAACP and the AFL-CIO went on to join forces repeatedly to defend the Warren Court while leading business organizations lined up on the opposing side.

Though Jenner's concoction breezed through Eastland's subcommittee, the full Judiciary Committee was another matter. The multitude of liberals and moderates on the committee bottled up S 2646. The bill was simply too radical, and its backers—a collection of isolationists and segregationists—too small in number to mount a serious threat to the Court. On March 10, 1958, CBS News relayed the widely-held belief that the bill was unlikely to get past the Judiciary Committee. Even if it had, reported George Herman—who went on to become the longest serving moderator on *Face the Nation*—"there is little doubt that on the floor of the Senate the leadership of both parties will quickly pigeonhole it for good."

To save Jenner's bill, Maryland's John Butler suggested changes to make S 2646 "more palatable to the opposition." Also a McCarthy acolyte—Harry McPherson called Butler, Jenner, and McCarthy "peas in a bad pod"—Butler owed his seat to the Wisconsin senator, who barged into Maryland's 1950 senate race to retaliate against Butler's opponent—Millard Tydings. Entering the election as an unknown Baltimore lawyer, Butler nevertheless upset the incumbent with McCarthy's help, prompting a Senate investigation exposing oversized campaign spending, unusual amounts of out-of-state contributions, and the use of tabloids and other dubious means to disseminate falsehoods (the 1950s equivalent of a "Fake News" campaign) orchestrated by McCarthy's forces. The highlight of the misinformation campaign was a doctored photo of Tydings meeting with a prominent communist. Despite concluding that Butler approved of the antics, the Senate allowed Butler to keep his seat largely out of deference to McCarthy, who had reached the apex of his influence at that point.

Butler's modified bill on March 24, 1958 preserved only Jenner's call to prohibit the Court's review of bar admission policies. Otherwise, Butler's version sought to overturn the Red Monday rulings by amending various statutes rather than restricting the Court's jurisdiction. His modifications got the watered-down bill past the Judiciary Committee.

Matters were far more serious for the justices in the House. One year after failing to get HR 3 to the House floor, the House passed it 241-155. Originally intended to overturn *Nelson*, HR 3 had a far broader application, which is what made it more threatening than its weaker counterparts. Unless Congress specified, a federal law would not bar state legislation on the same issue. On the surface, it seemed like a harmless and obscure provision of interest primarily for legal scholars but from a practical perspective, the "legislation seeks to nullify much of the protection that the Federal courts have granted to colored citizens," the NAACP warned in a 1958 memo. The "pending bills are of grave concern." In fact, many of HR 3's backers hoped these fears would come to fruition.

Just as momentum was starting to build, the Court's enemies received a boost from an unlikely quarter.

If political memoirs provide an opportunity to settle scores, then Warren's targets were both predictable and unexpected. Repeated jabs in his autobiography at his arch-nemesis Nixon and disappointment with Eisenhower were foreseeable. Surprisingly, Warren heaped his greatest indignation on the American Bar Association, the premier legal group in the nation. "Throughout the years of the McCarthy era," Warren wrote, "the American Bar Association almost never had a kind word to say for the Court. On the contrary, it did much to discredit us." It wasn't just the recriminations that stung Warren but the fact that it came from the "one organization from which the Court had a right to expect an enlightened appraisal of its work and a public defense of it."

In 1957, at the invitation of two English organizations, the ABA decided to hold its annual meetings in London. To celebrate the magnanimity of the event, organizers invited Warren and two other justices to attend and slated Winston Churchill to address the conference. In contrast to the high praise that his British hosts lavished upon Warren—Churchill regaled the Court as the "guardian and upholder of American liberty"—the ABA's Committee on

Communist Strategy and Tactics released a report blaming the Court for encouraging "Communist activity". If "the courts lean too far backward in the maintenance of theoretical, individual rights," the report declared, "it may be that we have tied the hands of our country and have rendered it incapable of carrying out the first law of mankind—the right of self-preservation." Going one step further, the report endorsed the very legislative measures put forth by congressional Court bashers.

Forbidden by protocol to publicly defend the Court, Warren stood silently in the face of the damning report. No one in the bar association stood up for the justices as the ABA assembly accepted the report without objection. "After that," Warren observed, "I was more or less a pariah." Infuriated by the affront, Warren resigned from the ABA weeks later. The ABA's report, Warren wrote in his resignation letter, "was the most widely publicized action of the Convention. It conveyed the thought to the world that in the unanimous opinion of the American Bar, the Supreme Court . . . is advancing the cause of Communism."

Coming just days after Jenner proposed S 2646, the London report supplied the Court's enemies with new ammunition. Congressional critics repeated the ABA's findings, twice printing the entire report in the *Congressional Record*. To his final days, Warren remained convinced that the ABA's posture undermined the judicial body. "If the Court had been given credit by the ABA for integrity when it was accused of being dishonest in its efforts to insure equal rights for minority groups," the chief justice wrote, "or when it was accused of subversion . . . then I am sure that the opinions of a sizable proportion of the people would have been more tolerant."

Others within the legal community didn't help Warren's cause either.

Over a period of three days in February, 1958, Learned Hand, the oracle of the federal judiciary, delivered the Holmes Lecture, the most prestigious talk hosted by Harvard Law School. The atmosphere surrounding Hand's lectures was electrifying. Nearby parking lots filled up quickly, and, to accommodate the overflow of visitors organizers set up loudspeakers in two other classrooms. One participant said the charged atmosphere felt like "the entrance to a big theater where a hit was playing." The highlight of the event took place during the second day when Hand admonished the Court for assuming "the role of a third legislative chamber." For outsiders, the declaration was shocking, but for those who knew Hand well, however, the sentiment reflected his displeasure with the Warren Court. Writing to Frankfurter two years earlier, he bemoaned Warren's lack of distinction. "The more I get of your present Chief, the less do I admire him." Hand passed on a derogatory nickname he had heard from a mutual friend who referred to Warren as a "Dumb Swede". Such name calling—"Pontifex Maximus" for Warren, "Hillbilly Hugo" for Black, and the "Jesus Quartet" for the Court's liberal bloc—became the norm for Hand, who was disillusioned with the justices' willingness "to impose their own solutions upon others." Nothing revealed the gravity of Hand's disillusionment more than the concession he made in a letter to Frankfurter, that despite his unfulfilled "ambition to be on the Court," he openly questioned "whether I should have enjoyed myself."

Hand refrained from such name-calling during his presentation at Harvard. But the end-result resembled that of many others accusing the Court of over-reaching: "For myself it would be most irksome to be ruled by a bevy of Platonic Guardians. . . . If they were in charge, I should miss the stimulus of living in a society where I have . . . some part in the direction of public affairs."

Suspicious of the justices' ability to resolve the nation's biggest problems by suppressing "social experiments which it does not approve," he pointed to *Brown* as an example of the Court's willingness to place its own opinions over that of the democratically elected branches.

Hand had delivered an early Christmas gift to the Court's enemies. "As you know, your name and prestige have been asserted in aid of the proposition that the Supreme Court is 'legislating,'" New York Senator Jacob Javits wrote to Hand, "and your Harvard lectures . . . have been given both by proponents in the Senate and newspapers columnists as justification for legislation to curb the Court."

The Court's congressional foes in fact repackaged Hand's words for their own hearings and speeches. Georgia's Herman Talmadge typified the approach: "when the voice of one of the Nation's most eminent and erudite jurists is raised in protest against the calculated efforts of the Justices . . . to set themselves up as a super legislature," he stated in a speech on the Senate floor in March, 1958, "its significance cannot be ignored." Southern newspapers excitedly broadcasted Hand's critique as did other conservative voices within the media. Citing Hand's recriminations, an editorial in the *Wall Street Journal* asked: are the justices simply "Lawmakers in Black?" Lawrence of the *U.S. News & World Report* found new ways to censure the court. "Judge Hand issues a warning as to what the American citizen faces," Lawrence wrote soon after the lectures, "whenever the Supreme Court not only restricts the right of legislative bodies to legislate but itself assumes a legislative function."

Hand's rebuke encouraged other prominent legal voices to speak out against the Court. "There can be no doubt," Edward Corwin, the Princeton professor considered the nation's leading constitutional historian, declared in a *New York Times* editorial in March, 1958, that "the court went on a virtual binge and thrust its nose into matters beyond its competence, with the result that . . . it should have aforesaid nose well tweaked."

One after another, large numbers of lawyers piled on. Though the nation's fraternity of judges rarely rebuked one another in public, the Conference of State Chief Justices continued the streak of condemnations from the legal community. The Court "too often has tended to adopt the role of policy maker without proper judicial restraint," its 1958 report concluded before turning spiteful. "It has long been an American boast that we have a government of laws and not of men. We believe that any study of recent decisions of the Supreme Court will raise at least considerable doubt as to the validity of that boast."

Buoyed by the Court's unpopular opinions, encouraged by Eisenhower's unwillingness to defend the Court, and legitimized by Hand et al., the anti-Court forces in the House won a clean sweep by the summer of 1958. In addition to HR 3, the lower chamber passed bills expanding the government's security program, overturning *Yates*, granting the State Department authority over the issuance of passports, and resurrecting the anti-subversion laws torpedoed by *Nelson* through a series of one-sided votes. Heading into the summer of 1958, it was up to the Senate to determine the Court's fate. It was eerily telling that most of the participants and the battle-lines that they drew over Red Monday were resurrected a decade later in determining Fortas's fate. And in both instances, Johnson was to rely upon his acumen as a legislative genius to emerge as the Warren Court's champion.

Chapter 9

Rematch with LBJ

To make a run at the White House, Johnson needed to be tolerated by liberals who could veto the selection of any presidential candidate. Yet, the foundation of his political strength remained in the South. The primary challenge to this balancing act arose from the diametrically opposed views on civil rights maintained by the party's factions. In 1957, he managed to corral enough concessions from both wings to push through a historic civil rights bill without wrecking the party, an accomplishment Hubert Humphrey deemed "a near miracle". It didn't take Johnson's political acumen to recognize the potential for the Court bills to broaden this fissure. When he realized, in August, 1958, that HR 3 and the Jenner-Butler bill were more than a passing fancy, he stepped in to derail them. To succeed, he would need every tool at his disposal.

Johnson was called the "Master of the Senate" long before his acclaimed biographer Robert Caro used the term to describe him. "He just had unusual power," recalled Thurmond decades later, "more than any leader has ever had while I have been in the Senate." "Johnson ran the Senate," recalled Florida Senator George Smathers. "For several years, he ran the United States government. . . . Johnson was the single most powerful person, even more so than Eisenhower."

Up until the development of formal leadership positions in the early twentieth century, senators amassed power through their reputation and personal influence. At first, the Majority and Minority leadership posts were administrative in nature and did the bidding of their party's leadership. When Johnson became Majority Leader in 1955, he recalibrated the position to propel himself to become the most powerful senator of the twentieth century.

Johnson's mastery was all the more striking in a body considered unmanageable. Shielded far more than their peers in the House from electoral headwinds, Senators operated like independent sovereigns. The ability to single-handedly block legislation through a filibuster and the constitutional privileges accorded exclusively to the Senate—namely the confirmation of presidential appointments and affirmation of treaties—amplified the power of each senator. Their comparatively lower numbers also elevated their status: the House contained 435 members; the Senate a mere 96 in 1958 (one hundred in 1968). While most voters recognized their senators, far fewer Americans could identify their Representatives. That gave senators greater name recognition, and when combined with their longevity, a national following.

To accrue power under these circumstances, Johnson focused on the thing that mattered most to his colleagues—their electoral fortunes. Setting committee assignments was one of the initial steps Johnson took to aggrandize his standing. In the past, a combination of seniority and a party caucus determined committee assignments. When Johnson became Majority Leader, he wrestled control of much of the process. By breaking with tradition to distribute some of the plum assignments to junior senators, he won control over the newly minted crop of senators while also appropriating some of the decision-making historically left to committee chairs. To further advance his leverage over his colleagues, Johnson doled out campaign funds collected from oil and gas interests in Texas to loyal senators. Much of the rest he did through his sheer talent as a legislator. He wasn't alone in partaking in the myriad negotiations needed to produce legislation. What set Johnson apart was his aptitude for these tasks. Johnson's "skill within the Senate," according to one of his legislative aides, "implied a knowledge of wheeling and dealing, intricate trade-offs, elaborate posturing—all the black political arts."

These darks arts regularly involved Johnson's talent for sizing up and manipulating his fellow senators. "Johnson had different approaches," Florida Senator George Smathers explained. "He had a whole arsenal of shots that he would use. One of them was sweet talking, the next one was doing a favor for you, the next one was talking rough to you, the next one was appointing him to a committee. . . . But whatever was needed, that's what he would use on that particular fellow." Whatever was needed. These words so personified Johnson's governing philosophy, they could have been used as his epitaph.

Johnson's grasp of the Senate's centers of power turned him into a chameleon and a con man. "He was as strong as steel and, when he wanted to be, as pliant as a sapling," recalled Javits. With those he couldn't bully, such as Russell, he was deferential, even sycophantic. Johnson drove the more pliable senators like galley slaves on a Roman trireme. When a new round of senators came in after an election, Johnson called daily meetings to discuss his agenda. Unable to look for housing or tend to other matters, one of them asked a veteran senator: "Why does he hold these meetings? Does he work this way all the time? Doesn't he realize Rome wasn't built in a day?" One of them quipped in return: "Yes, but Johnson wasn't the foreman of that job!"

Nothing was too inconsequential or too outlandish for Johnson to get his way. At one point, he tried to persuade a college to grant a senator an honorary degree. On other occasions, he made sure the chamber was full for a senator seeking the limelight. When William Proxmire was appointed to fill the seat left open by McCarthy's death, Johnson had Proxmire picked up from the airport and quickly sworn in to be available for a vote in the evening. Whatever was needed.

Ever the tactician, Johnson never held a grudge if he could turn an opponent into an ally. But if he couldn't turn a senator to his side, the Majority Leader shunned a colleague for months on end until the man capitulated. "I don't know that . . . Johnson ever frightened anybody. . . by saying 'I'll cut you off.'" Smathers recalled. "He wasn't that crude. . . . He was a consummate artist. . . . He was the Andrew Wyeth of the Senate. . . . If you . . . saw him do this, you just kind of amazed yourself."

Whatever was needed, including something as straightforward as manipulating the legislative calendar. "Johnson used to clutter the calendar," remembered a senate staff member. "He used to keep bills from being voted on so you had to come and ask." In other instances, if a vote on a pending bill was going to be close, Johnson scheduled the vote when certain senators were out of town to tip the balance in his favor.

And if all of these methods of persuasion failed, if Johnson had no other levers he could wield over a colleague, he would personally lobby an intractable senator. When he did so, the Majority Leader typically resorted to the Treatment to coax his colleagues. "When Johnson wanted to persuade you of something," according to Ben Bradlee, the executive editor of the *Washington Post*, "you felt as if a St. Bernard had licked your face for an hour." Mastery of all of these levers gave Johnson unequaled power. "Johnson elevated the majority leadership to a much more powerful position than it ever had been before," Smathers observed.

To defeat the anti-Court measures, Johnson sought to prevent the House bills from reaching the floor so that they would expire at the end of the term in late August. It was a simple delay tactic long used to quietly extinguish bills. This strategy came under strain when Eastland pushed the bills through the Judiciary Committee in early August, preparing them for the Senate's consideration. Russell made the next move. Knowing exactly how to circumvent his apprentice's roadblock, the teacher threatened to hold hostage a series of appropriations bills that Johnson needed to pass before the end of the session in order to avoid a government shutdown. The crafty maneuver worked perfectly: "I think we're going to have to give them their day on these Court bills," Johnson conceded. To get the appropriations bills through, Johnson brokered a deal scheduling votes on two modest anti-Court measures. Even with the concession, Johnson was still in the lead: neither of the two biggest threats to the Court—the Jenner-Butler bill (S 2646) or HR 3—was among them.

Russell's maneuver revealed the limitations of Johnson's mastery. Russell and a few of the Southern committee chairs maintained enough clout to withstand Johnson's bullying. There were also the loners and rebels who simply couldn't be domesticated. In a tight-knit caucus of Southern senators, Thurmond always stuck out as a nonconformist. His willingness to defy Johnson began months into his first term. In exchange for a coveted assignment on the Armed Services Committee, Johnson asked Thurmond to vote his way on a military budget matter. Thurmond refused. When the Majority Leader saw Thurmond in a hallway after the vote, Johnson tightly squeezed Thurmond's arm and growled at him to follow orders. To hit home his point, Johnson kept the rebellious senator off the Armed Service Committee for three years.

The South Carolina senator never learned his lesson.

On August 20, 1958, Thurmond sabotaged Johnson's compromise with Russell by threatening to offer HR 3 as an amendment to every bill still on the Senate's schedule unless there was a vote on the Jenner-Butler bill. With just about any other senator, Johnson could have dismissed the threat as a bluff. But coming months after Thurmond's record breaking 24-hour filibuster during the 1957 Civil Rights bill, before which Thurmond dehydrated himself through a series of steam baths to avoid trips to the bathroom, the firebrand's capacity for audacious behavior could not be underestimated. To avoid a government shutdown, Johnson capitulated to a vote on S 2646. Though that decision would leave the pro-Court forces in a vulnerable position, Johnson, having surveyed the senate, was confident he would prevail on a straight-up vote anyway.

After nearly a year of plodding, the Court's foes finally arrived at the long-awaited, hoped-for moment. "The result of this line of Supreme Court decisions had been to bring about a crisis," Jenner said on the Senate floor hours before the vote on S 2646. Forced into a corner, the only recourse for Congress was to "withdraw appellate jurisdiction from the Supreme Court." Jenner handed the torch over to Butler, who started his speech with a list of grievances. The "people of this country," he said, "are greatly troubled and widely dissatisfied with the results of a series of decisions . . . which have gone beyond the Court's proper sphere; which have involved judicial legislation; which have amounted to unwarranted invasion of . . . other . . . branches of the Government; which have invaded the rights of the States . . . ; which have . . . sought to substitute the Court's judgment for the . . . judgment of the Congress."

After regurgitating the condemnations made by the ABA and Hand, Butler systematically critiqued several of the communist rulings. "The fact is that the Court has given Communists a better break than any other class of litigants."

The final speaker before the vote returned to the message conveyed by the Court's guardians throughout the past year. "This provision is contrary to our historic principle" and "once we begin to whittle at the jurisdiction of the

Supreme Court," Missouri Senator Thomas Hennings warned, "the flood-gates will open. Then heaven help the United States." The nation didn't need divine intervention just yet. As Johnson expected, though Jenner and Butler could huff and puff on the Senate floor, S 2646 fell short by a 49-41 vote.

The Jenner-Butler bill was finally dead. The Court was saved, and with it, Johnson's political aspirations. It was time to finish up the session and return home for the election season.

Immediately after the vote, Hennings, Paul Douglas of Illinois, and Johnson jockeyed for recognition from the Senate's presiding officer, Nevada's Alan Bible. Situated directly in front of Bible and accorded the privileges of being the Majority Leader, Johnson had the right to speak first.

Much more than the House, tradition dominated the Senate with many of its rules and customs dating to 1789. Those traditions arose not just from its formal rules and informal practices but the very architecture in which it was housed. Construction on the Capitol began in 1793, and after a major expansion of the building to accommodate the growing membership in both houses of Congress, the Senate moved into its modern space on the north wing of the Capitol in 1859. Just a shade over 9,000 square feet, the chamber was a rectangular-shaped room with a platform at the center of one end with the presiding officer situated in the middle. Positioned to the front and sides of the presiding officer's raised dais, various staff members administered the body's daily operations along with the Senate pages flanking the marble rostrum. Renovations in the 1940s removed many of the ornate characteristics of the chamber's mid-nineteenth century roots. Red Levanto marble laced with gray and green lines replaced the cast-iron pilasters, and a steel and plaster ceiling took the spot of the iron ceiling and skylight. Twenty busts of vice presidents guarded the seating gallery, including ones of John Adams and Thomas Jefferson placed behind the press gallery just above the central dais.

Senators sat facing the central rostrum in four concentric semi-circles stretched from one end of the room to the other. Like rows in a theatre, which incline from front to back to give the more distant spectators a clear view of the stage, the space's five tiers rose from the dais to the back of the chamber.

Historically, Republicans sat to the left of the presiding officer and Democrats sat to the right, with the center aisle marking a line of demarcation. Each senator received a desk and, starting in 1927 for the Democrats and 1937 for the Republicans, their leaders sat in the two centrally located desks on the first row of seats regardless of whether they were in the majority or minority. Johnson's spot in particular, Desk X, had been previously occupied by Joseph Robinson, Alben Barkley, Scott Lucas, and Ernest McFarland, all of whom had signed the inside drawer.

The advent of the leadership positions along with the central seating granted to them endowed the Majority and Minority Leaders with prerogatives foreign to past generations. In 1937, Vice President John Nance Garner added to this growing clout by giving priority to the Majority Leader—followed by the Minority Leader—to be recognized first when multiple senators vied for the presiding officer's attention.

Alan Bible, however, broke with Garner's precedent in bypassing Johnson for Douglas, who was screaming from the third row. "I offer an amendment," Douglas said. After a year on the defensive, the pro-Court forces were about to launch their first offensive.

Having overcome a tragic childhood, Douglas developed into a champion of progressive causes. His mother died when he was four and his father, an abusive drinker, caused his stepmother to take him and his brother away to rural Maine. Douglas graduated from Bowdoin College, where he was a campus radical, and earned a Ph.D. in economics from Columbia University. At the age of fifty, he temporarily left his teaching post at the University of Chicago to join the Marines in WWII. He got out of his assigned desk job to fight in Okinawa where a bullet largely rendered his left arm useless, and he was awarded both a Bronze Star and a Purple Heart. In 1949, he entered the Senate.

Surprisingly, Douglas's propensity for shabby suits and devotion to facts and piercing logic managed to charm voters. "That guy's no politician," observed a steelworker during Douglas's first senate campaign. "He doesn't try to con you." Yet his tendency to browbeat his colleagues with an evangelical streak of do-goodism made him seem a curmudgeon. While serving as a Chicago alderman, he was often outvoted 49-1.

Douglas's uncompromising purity frustrated the über-pragmatic Johnson, who had a deep aversion for lost causes. "All they do is fight, fight, fight," Johnson said of Senate crusaders like Douglas "and get fifteen . . . votes. . . . I would rather win a convert than an argument." Douglas, in turn, reviled Johnson's overbearing leadership: "To Johnson," Douglas believed, "the Senate was a circus and he was the ringmaster." Along with Oregon Senator Wayne Morse, another loner unwilling to bend to Johnson's will, Douglas repeatedly tried to sabotage the Majority Leader's plans. And for that, Johnson punished Douglas by keeping him off key committees. The one jewel in Douglas's position on the Joint Economic Committee was its regal offices, plush with an expansive view stretching all the way to the Lincoln Memorial. In search of a bigger space for his budding empire, Johnson seized the committee's space for his own use. The mockery continued in subtle ways. The Majority Leader ignored Douglas while addressing the senator's aides and urged senators to remain in the cloakroom while Douglas was delivering a speech to ensure his words were uttered to an empty chamber.

Coming moments after the defeat of the Jenner-Butler bill, Douglas's proposal to have Congress express "its full support and approval of the . . . historic decisions of the Supreme Court . . . holding racial integration unlawful" constituted a declaration of war against the South. It wasn't just his message that caused a stir but the timing. Instead of quietly savoring the triumph of a year-long struggle, Douglas's attempt to pull off a victory lap reopened the battlefield. Douglas didn't seem to care but with this win in his grasp, Johnson saw no need to risk it. The Majority Leader unsuccessfully tried to shut down Douglas's proposal by submitting one of the mild anti-Court measures he had negotiated with Russell days earlier.

Douglas was easy to admire for his pure-minded resolve, and his sentiments conceivably might have heartened the justices. But in the middle of this legislative warfare, the Court needed a field general, not a preacher. Unable to draw support from moderates, Douglas's amendment flopped. And while he and Morse were winning debating points, their unnecessary provocations rallied the Court's foes within minutes after their disheartening defeat. Immediately after the Senate had dispatched Douglas's amendment, the Court's newly invigorated enemies completely broke with Johnson's script. Instead of voting on the moderate anti-sedition measure scheduled by Johnson days earlier, Arkansas Senator John McClellan substituted the language of HR 3 in its place.

Johnson hated to ad-lib on the Senate floor. "Under Johnson," remembered Douglas's aide, the legislative body functioned "like a Greek tragedy. Nothing went on in the Senate that hadn't happened off the floor beforehand." Now for the second time on that day, the Senate was reeling out of the Majority Leader's control.

Lobbyists and advocates had spent weeks preparing for this moment. While the Court's backers—the NAACP, ACLU, and AFL-CIO—were unable to make inroads, the Chamber of Commerce and NAM put together a potent grass roots campaign. Of all the Warren Court's monumental rulings, its decisions affecting the business community have received the least attention. America's corporations feared the Court would threaten to unwind well-established areas of the law. Concerned with the consequences of the *Nelson* decision on labor laws and a series of rulings impacting various industries, the Chamber took particular umbrage with an antitrust case involving DuPont and General Motors, characterizing it as "another instance of the continued trend in the Court to disregard precedent." Working through its local chapters, the Chamber's members urged their congressmen to support HR 3.

NAM's lobbyists took a more D.C.-centric approach. Encouraging local businesses to reach out to their elected officials, NAM relayed the names of any senators who responded positively to Thurmond and McClellan to secure his vote. The daily count maintained by NAM and Thurmond counted forty-eight favorable votes in mid-August.

"'Vote-counting,'" wrote Caro, "is one of the most vital of the political arts, but it is an art that few can master, for it is peculiarly subject to the distortions of sentiment and romantic preconceptions." The best vote-counters vacuumed information from all corners. The outspoken supporters and opponents of a bill were easy to identify. It was the inconspicuous senators one had to pinpoint. A senator might have revealed his intentions first-hand or through a legislative aide. Sometimes, intelligence arrived serendipitously, by overhearing a senator in the cloakroom or after several rounds of drinks at a cocktail party. Sometimes, a thorough understanding of the senator's principles or constituent interests could point to a good estimation of his intentions.

Most vote-counters employed similar mechanisms to keep track of each senator's vote. A typical tally sheet was a narrow, rectangular shaped page with three columns: the left and right columns were titled "Yeas" and "Nays" respectively and the middle column included an alphabetical list of senators. A date and a spot to fill in the bill number appeared on the bottom of the page. The other conventional tally sheet filled up a standard 8.5" x 11" page. A "Date" and "Issue" line stood at the top. This time, three sets of columns with the "Yeas," an alphabetical list of names, and "Nays" running from left to right, filled up each set. When these sheets were unavailable, senators drew up hand-written score sheets, typed up lists, or simply ripped out a page from the congressional directory as a makeshift scorekeeper's guide. Whether prognosticating a vote while legislation was pending or tracking a roll call during an actual vote, each vote-counter employed his own note-taking methodology. Some simply checked the Yeas or Nays column next to each senator's name to count the votes. Others wrote "X"s or drew circles in the columns, depending on whether a vote was expected or not.

Johnson preferred to use the long, rectangular tally sheet, and as he ran his thumb down the list of names, he only filled in a column when he was absolutely sure of a colleague's vote. When a staff member once offered his conjectures rather than concrete conclusions, "What the fuck good is thinking to me," Johnson shot back. "Thinking isn't good enough. Thinking is never good enough. I need to know!" Johnson would proceed with a vote only when he was certain of its outcome. He primarily gathered intel on his own and through Bobby Baker, his jack-of-all-trades assistant. Baker's role as a gopher for Senate Democrats gave him unbridled access to its members. Combined with his uncanny ability to function like a human sponge, Baker scouted the Democratic cloakroom where senators spoke freely. It was there, in the inner confines of the Senate where much of its business was conducted, that Baker often learned a senator's vote. "Baker did the vote-catching," recalled a senate staffer, "and he went out with his butterfly net to catch whatever he could." When he wasn't eavesdropping, Baker reached out directly to senators as Johnson's emissary. Johnson also drafted Smathers, Humphrey, and other lieutenants for the task of counting and cultivating votes. It was their job to see where a senator stood on a bill, what problems troubled him the most, and what changes might sway the senator to Johnson's position. Senate staffers also fed Johnson information. One aide kept an up-to-date list of every piece of legislation under consideration, keeping abreast of its sponsors, whether it was mentioned in a speech, and its status at the committee level.

The shrewd deployment of these resources made Johnson "a great counter," explained Jim Rowe, his 1960 campaign manager. "Someone would say, we've got so many votes, and Johnson would say, 'Hell, you're three off. You're counting these three guys, and they're going to vote against you.'"

Humphrey, one of the chamber's liberal titans, was also an expert vote-counter. He assured Johnson that the amendment proposed by Arkansas Senator John McClellan substituting HR 3, the harsh anti-Court measure approved by the House, for the modest measure Johnson had intended to place before the Senate, would never pass. Johnson saw no need to extend the debate after receiving Humphrey's assurances. At 11 p.m. that night, the roll call began. Under the Senate's rules, the chamber's clerk called out each senator in alphabetical order. If someone failed to respond when called, he could still cast a vote as long as he did so before the expiration of the allotted time. Half an hour later, it was over. And to everyone's surprise, McClellan's amendment prevailed, 46-39.

The unexpected outcome plunged the Senate into bedlam. McClellan, Jenner, and Butler began screaming—"Vote! Vote! Vote!" Coming off the procedural victory, they wanted to lock in their advantage with a final, substantive vote.

Shocked and angry, Johnson sat paralyzed.

When Russell had catapulted Johnson to the leadership post, Johnson insisted that Russell sit directly behind him to provide his counsel at all times. Now sitting at that desk, Russell realized the full consequences of what was about to transpire. Hurling insults at the Court was one thing. Actually throwing the legal system into disarray was too radical a solution, even for Russell. He leaned over and whispered to Johnson, "Lyndon, you'd better adjourn this place. They're going to pass that Goddamned bill." When Johnson shot up from his seat, it was impossible to miss his agitated demeanor. For a man obsessed with controlling every element of the legislative process, this proved to be one of the few surprises of his tenure.

While Senate liberals gathered in the back of the chamber to plan their next move and the "press went berserk" in the galleries, Johnson followed his mentor's advice. "I should like to have the Senator yield to me for the purpose of making a motion to adjourn until 12 o'clock tomorrow," Johnson told Vice President Nixon, who was then presiding over the chamber. "It is 11:30 in the evening. I think Members are ready to go home." The delay tactic was a blatant attempt to thwart the momentum of the anti-Court forces just when they were on the verge of victory. When those forces yelled for Nixon's attention, Johnson slammed them down with the institutional prerogatives accorded to him as Majority Leader. "The motion is not debatable," Johnson declared. "I move the Senate adjourn."

Nixon concurred: "The motion is not debatable," he repeated.

Jenner and McClellan were furious. "Mr. President, I asked for recognition before the motion was made," Jenner said. "I was yelling at the Chair." McClellan told Nixon: "I was trying to obtain recognition." Jenner then asked Johnson to withdraw his motion. "No; I will not withdraw the motion," Johnson struck back. Standing at his desk with a clipboard during the roll call over his motion to adjourn, Johnson ostentatiously recorded every senator's vote. The intimidation tactic worked. Johnson prevailed 70-18. The triumph gave Johnson a temporary reprieve but he still needed a handful of senators to change their positions and do so in less than twenty-four hours when the Senate would reconvene to vote on HR 3.

After the adjournment, Johnson went over to the distressed Humphrey in the back of the chamber. "You boys screwed up," he said furiously. "I don't know what you did, but you screwed up. You told me wrong. . . . If you want to beat this thing," he continued, "there's still a way."

Johnson led Humphrey, Anthony Lewis of *The New York Times*, and a member of his staff to his office. Interrupted only by his secretary's delivery of a new round of Cutty Sark whiskey and soda every twenty minutes, Johnson delivered a moving two-hour monologue on the need to block the bill and the maneuvers it would take to do so. The chameleon whose ideology no one could pin down revealed his passionate dedication to the Court that night. He wasn't out to simply advance his presidential ambitions. He genuinely wanted to protect the Court's liberal achievements, so much so that he asked Humphrey to do the unthinkable. Knowing that Humphrey despised the filibuster and had repeatedly railed against its exploitation to block his cherished civil rights measures, Johnson nevertheless urged him to put one on. "Hubert, they're really gonna lambaste you for filibustering."

Every bit of Johnson's mastery was on display the next morning. It began with an attempt to shift the field of battle. Instead of an up-and-down vote on HR 3, he moved to have the Senate vote on a motion to send the bill back to the Judiciary Committee for further study. This way, some of the more modest Court antagonists could vote for the motion without looking like they were voting against the bill on the merits. Johnson then delayed the noon adjournment by nearly five hours to give him more time to coax his colleagues in the Democratic cloakroom. Adorned with a marble fireplace, spring water from around the country, and soft leather couches lining the walls, the cloakroom allowed the senators to rest, talk in private or practice their speeches without having to return to their offices in the other Senate buildings. Manning the L-shaped cloakroom behind the swinging doors of the Senate chamber, pages answered calls for the senators at the old-fashioned wooden phone booths like the ones "Superman would change his outfit in." Once caught by Johnson on one of the room's cushy couches, his favorite spot to deliver the "Treatment," trying to extricate oneself from his tirade was like trying to escape from quicksand.

Johnson had grown accustomed to changing a senator's vote, sometimes right on the floor. When he walked up and grasped a senator in the middle of a roll call, "You would see votes changed right in front of your eyes," a Senate aide remembered. Once, he didn't bother to leave his spot, yelling "Change your vote" at Delaware's J. Allen Frear.

Johnson also knew that while some senators couldn't vote for his motion, either out of their personal beliefs or pressure from constituents, they didn't have to vote against it. Simple absenteeism would be just as helpful in some instances. "We have the votes to recommit if you don't vote" he told Democrats Bob Kerr and Frear in their offices. "If you vote, it will be a tie. That will permit Vice President Nixon to break the tie and get a lot of political advertising and publicity out of it." Frear agreed to remain off the senate floor while a colleague announced that he was "absent on official business." The Majority Leader also convinced North Dakota's Milton Young, who had voted for the McClellan amendment the night before, to stay away.

When Johnson spotted Ohio Senator Frank Lausche on the chamber floor, he warned him that the pro-Court forces would bring the Senate to a standstill should HR 3 prevail. The possibility would prevent the Senate from passing critical appropriations measures. That was enough to convince Lausche to change his vote.

Johnson nullified two more anti-Court votes by exploiting the Senate custom of pairing. An absent senator who still wanted to make it look like he voted could be "paired" with another absent senator who was on the other side of the same issue. A "live pair" occurred when an absent senator asked a senator in attendance who would have voted the other way to abstain from voting. In either instance, the phantom yea and nay votes cancelled each other out, and therefore would have had no impact on the outcome of a vote. Historically, senators arranged for these pairs out of courtesy to one another. Johnson distorted the practice into another weapon in his arsenal. By pairing two senators who opposed HR 3 but were unable to attend the session with two in attendance who were in favor of McClellan's amendment, he wiped out two votes for the anti-Court forces. Outfoxed by the master yet again, no one in the opposition managed to prevent Johnson from turning an innocuous practice into a manipulative tool.

At the start of the session on August 21, 1958, Johnson's headcount showed a 40 to 42 deficit. Of all the targets on Johnson's tally sheet, Utah Republican Wallace Bennett who gained his seat in 1950 by accusing his opponent of associating with communist organizations, was the toughest potential convert on his list. The fact that Bennett was the former chairman of NAM made him especially unreceptive to Johnson's overtures.

Johnson found Bennett's weakness and it happened to be his soft spot for Nixon. The Founding Fathers made the Vice President the presiding officer of the Senate, allowing him to chair the legislative body, and more critically, cast tie-breaking votes when necessary.

Due to the importance of the Court-curbing measures, Nixon was compelled to attend the session the night before. He reappeared the next day just in case he had to break a tie on HR 3. Aware that Bennett was desperate for Nixon to be president, Johnson conveyed to Bennett that his vote would lead to a 41-41 tie, forcing Nixon to cast the deciding vote. Here is where Johnson's machinations came through when they were most needed. "Change your vote and save Dick Nixon from being put on the spot," he told Bennett. If Nixon voted against the Court, Johnson explained, then he would anger Republican moderates. If he voted the other way, he would upset the Party's conservatives. Either position, Johnson argued, would damage Nixon's presidential prospects in 1960. It was exactly the opposite of what Johnson had told Kerr and Frear just hours earlier.

Bennett was caught in a cross-fire. Should he betray NAM and forego his support for HR 3, which he had co-sponsored? Or should he stick to his principles and support his allies? Hoping his vote wouldn't be the deciding one, Bennett tried to stall. When the roll call began for McClellan's amendment, Johnson began to circle the chamber floor like a hen protecting its nest. Bennett was nowhere to be found when the clerk called his name. When Kerr stepped in from the cloakroom, Johnson and Baker grabbed him by the arms and pushed him back inside pleading with him one last time not to vote. Kerr finally acquiesced. When Thurmond's wife realized Kerr and Frear had switched sides, she called them "darn cowards" from her seat in the gallery.

The vote proceeded as Johnson expected until the clerk called out George Malone's name. The Nevada Republican had voted for HR 3 the night before. Swayed by a call from the AFL-CIO, he switched his vote. Johnson had done enough to get to a 40-40 tie. Now it was up to Bennett, who had returned to the floor, to break the tie. When he responded "Aye" in a steady voice to strike down HR 3, the gallery gasped. The announcement of the final tally by the Senate clerk turned McClellan white with anger, sweat soaking from his brow. One observer felt the senator might collapse from exhaustion. McClellan had good reason to be distraught. Less than twenty-four hours earlier, the anti-Court forces maintained a seven-vote advantage. "When all the black magic had wrought its wonders," reported Rowland Evans, McClellan's amendment was defeated 41-40.

Anthony Lewis of *The New York Times* labeled the victory one of Johnson's "great triumphs." Thurmond was not so complimentary. "We tried to get that bill passed and we got it passed that night," he recalled. "But the next day he switched it around." Nearly ten years to the day, Thurmond and his allies plotted their revenge. It was yet another example of Fortas's misfortune that he was being punished for another's man's sins—this time those of his patron. At least Fortas had Johnson, still the "Master of the Senate," in his corner for the rematch against the Court's foes.

JUNE-JULY, 1968

Johnson's reign over the Senate continued into his presidency. He succeeded in dismantling the Southern bloc's impregnable defenses to enact a series of historic civil rights bills, and in his pursuit of a Great Society, inundated Congress with every item on a liberal's wish list. The establishment of Medicare alone would have exceeded the legislative accomplishments of most administrations but it was simply one of the crown jewels of his overstuffed trophy case. Head Start, Food Stamps, and Medicaid were the battalions in the vanguard of the president's "War on Poverty." Environmental bills included the Clean Air and Water acts. The Great Society gave birth to such non-profit media organizations as PBS and NPR and reopened America's doors to immigrants. More than a dozen bills boosted primary and secondary education, and established departments for housing and transportation. Nothing escaped Johnson's wide-ranging agenda, from regulation of the speed limit to the formation of the NEA. Congress enacted nearly all of these bills in rapid succession. The 89th Congress alone, in session from 1965 to 1966, promulgated

181 out of Johnson's two hundred proposed measures for, what the president boasted was, a .905 "batting average."

This mastery stemmed from Johnson's keen understanding of the Senate. As president, Johnson built upon his experience as Majority Leader to develop a team of advisors whose primary task was to gather intelligence on each congressman. Mere communication with a congressman's office wouldn't suffice. The president demanded that they know how a congressman would vote. What he wanted. What he was willing to trade. The team primarily responsible for Fortas's nomination included Joseph Califano (Johnson's head of domestic staff), Marvin Watson (assistant for political affairs), Jim Jones (Watson's assistant), Mike Manatos (congressional liaison), Ernie Goldstein (domestic advisor), Barefoot Sanders (legislative counsel), Harry McPherson (special counsel), and Larry Temple (special counsel responsible for coordinating with the Justice Department). Paul Porter, Fortas's former law partner, worked closely with this group. Ramsey Clark and Warren Christopher oversaw the efforts at the Justice Department. Beyond this core group, cabinet officials, congressional allies, special interest groups, business leaders, influential friends, and a bevy of assistants throughout the federal government did the field work of preparing speeches, reaching out to the press, and lobbying senators.

Vote counting remained one of the crucial tasks that Johnson's aides conducted on nearly a daily basis. One of their earliest tallies on June 27 counted four southerners leaning towards confirmation with six against and the rest unknown. Reports pouring into the White House revealed just how challenging it would be to woo some of these holdouts. Infuriated at the president for seeking counsel from others, Arkansas's John McClellan—the same senator who proposed the Court-curbing amendment a decade earlier—might come around, Johnson's staff learned, only "if someone begs him to." Those pleas took various forms: Johnson's aides asked a dairy trade group, a lawyer from McClellan's law firm, and August Busch of the beer empire to implore McClellan to switch sides. McClellan may have been prickly, perhaps even shallow, but at least he was pliable. So was Louisiana's Russell Long, who despite labelling Fortas "one of the dirty five" for his criminal procedure rulings, was open to negotiating with the White House. For a growing number of southerners, however, no amount of begging, cajoling or horse-trading could budge them.

Troubled by this growing insurgency, Johnson took direct control of the confirmation process at the end of June. "We've got to get this thing through, and we've got to get it through early because if it drags out we're going to get beat," he warned his staff, which was far more optimistic than the president. Under Johnson's command, the immense machinery of the presidency went into overdrive. Counting on a vast network of contacts within the business world, unions, special interest groups, and the media, Johnson's formula for victory was simple: aid Fortas's backers in the Senate, flip over as many adversaries as possible, and weaken the opposition. A diagram of the campaign would have looked like a series of concentric circles emanating from the Oval Office and expanding outward.

Though NAM and the Chamber of Commerce had repeatedly railed against the Warren Court, Johnson looked to corporate leaders for assistance. Fortas's experience as a corporate lawyer combined with his pro-business rulings made him more appealing than the chief justice to the business community. And, similar to his approach with Russell and Dirksen, Johnson relied on personal relationships and the power of the presidency far more than any ideological associations to conscript allies. Earlier in the decade, Johnson had tapped Henry Ford II and J. Paul Austin of Coca-Cola to serve on the board of the National Alliance of Businessmen, a jobs-forming organization, and had relied upon business leaders to lobby for an urban renewal bill. Now, the White House returned to those same executives for help.

Undermining Griffin, in particular, became a major focal point of their campaign. The White House asked Ford to speak with Griffin and to convince Michigan Governor George Romney (Mitt's father) to undercut Griffin's efforts. UAW president Walter Reuther also rounded up executives within Michigan to dissuade Griffin. On this point, at least, labor and management were in agreement. The initiative paid immediate dividends. "I am concerned that opposing the Supreme Court nominations may be hurtful," a utility executive wrote to the Michigan senator at Reuther's behest on July 8.

While Ford was the point-man on Griffin, other executives lobbied their contacts within the Senate. Austin assured the White House that he could "deliver" a handful of southern senators "'deeply indebted to [me] in one way or another.'" The CEO of Aloha Airlines offered to speak to Hawaii's Hiram Fong over lunch. The lobbyist for American Airlines also reached out to Republican senators. Defense Secretary Clifford was convinced the DuPonts could sway the senators in Delaware, where the company was headquartered. Nearly a dozen executives were assembled to reach out to Senator John Tower in Texas. The general counsel of General Motors offered his "wholehearted support" for Fortas to Eastland.

Looking beyond the nation's executive suites, the White House searched far and wide for influential voices. Manatos, Johnson's congressional aide, asked his friend, Fred Goodstein, to "apply a great deal of pressure" on Wyoming's Clifford Hansen. Clarence Mitchell, the NAACP's chief lobbyist, made headway with "doubtful Republicans." The AFL-CIO and UAW, the nation's two most powerful unions, contacted dozens of senators. Prominent D.C. lawyers signed on to the White House's campaign and one from New York urged the media mogul Sam Newhouse to put out favorable editorials. The president ordered an aide to contact Leon Higginbotham, an African-American federal judge, to urge Pennsylvania's black legal community to petition Senator Hugh Scott and asked William Coleman, a black attorney based in Massachusetts, to reach out to the African-American senator Edward Brooke. He also wanted the ABA to speak out on Fortas's behalf. For its Senate allies, the administration ghost-wrote speeches and sent research materials rebutting Griffin.

Eager for positive media coverage, McPherson, the special counsel, urged a *Washington Post* editor to "keep the heat on" the opposition. On the west coast, the *Los Angeles Times* promised to oppose a filibuster in its editorial pages. "By in large," observed a White House staffer, "the press is in our side." In fact, the Washington press corps had largely downplayed Griffin's insurgency without the need for the White House's solicitations.

It wasn't a complete sweep for Johnson's forces, however. The Court's traditional media critics continued their harangues. Lamenting Johnson's choice of a crony, the *Wall Street Journal* expected strong resistance and David Lawrence, the conservative columnist whose columns now appeared in three hundred publications, urged voters to punish any senators supporting Fortas. The amount of paper the *National Review* had spent condemning the chief justice over the years could have consumed a handful of forests. Warren's pending retirement didn't soften its stance. The *Review* catalogued Warren's legacy as "RECKLESS, DISLOCATIVE, MALADROIT, ARBITRARY, ECCENTRIC, PRESUMPTUOUS, ILLOGICAL, SUBVERSIVE, USURPATORY," and "IRRESPONSIBLE." Setting aside the issues of cronyism and Johnson's lame duck status, the publication narrowed in on the "real reason that" Fortas and Thornberry "are objectionable: because these two men are statist liberals."

The rest of the White House's strategy also produced mixed results. Coca-Cola managed to get Virginia's Harry Byrd to shift his position. Of the ten senators contacted by Eastern Airlines president Floyd Hall, however, three were "absolutely" or "vehemently opposed" to Fortas. Dubious of Fortas, the rest remained undecided or were leaning against confirmation. Disappointed with Johnson, the textile industry didn't suit up its "first team" for the lobbying campaign.

McPherson's visit to Robert Byrd of West Virginia (not related to Virginia's Byrd) exemplified the limitations faced by the White House. At the meeting, the senator railed "against 'forced integration and leniency toward Communists, atheists, and other immoral people.'" Regardless of his respect for Fortas's legal acumen, Byrd stood against the nominee "because he opposed today's Court itself." Such obduracy posed a nearly insurmountable hurdle. "These are my views," Byrd told McPherson, "and it doesn't matter how many people the President sends up here to see me about them; they won't change."

To overcome these holdouts, Johnson resorted to his time-honored method of doing whatever it took. "[W]e would have traded damn near everything except the Grand Coulee Dam" to get Fortas confirmed, Califano recalled. That mindset led Johnson to seek help from America's Jewish community. Though Fortas was not a particularly devout Jew, his nomination aroused anti-Semitism. Besides a fanatical belief in the justice's alleged role in an international communist conspiracy, letters to the Judiciary Committee were sprinkled with anti-Semitic remarks. "Johnson has turned the whole Federal Executive Department over to JEWS," warned an "American Christian" in a typical tirade. Blaming Kennedy's assassination on a Jewish conspiracy, he urged the Judiciary Committee to not "betray [sic] USA into the hands of JEWS." A letter originating from upstate New York feared that Fortas worked for a Jewish cabal out to "destroy Christian culture." A hand-written note from a federal prison urged Eastland to "INITIATE IMPEACHMENT PROCEEDINGS AGAINST THAT ANTI-AMERICAN JEW." Some of these sentiments were also purported to exist within the Judiciary Committee. Eastland apparently asked another senator: "You're not going to vote for that Jew to be Chief Justice, are you?"

Johnson exploited this ugly fact to recruit prominent Jewish individuals and groups to campaign on Fortas's behalf. It was a delicate task. Avoiding direct accusations of anti-Semitism, the administration resorted to innuendo and guilt by association. McPherson told an editor, for instance, "that those who have more acceptable purposes in opposing Fortas might find themselves in bed with anti-Semites."

The White House enlisted Harry Cohen, Hruska's former campaign manager, to lobby the Nebraska senator. It tapped Bob Gutwillig, an editor at the New American Library, to contact Bennett—the same senator Johnson had coerced a decade earlier during the vote on HR 3. The Anti-Defamation League tried to contact Louisiana's Russell Long. Abe Ribicoff, a former congressman and Connecticut governor, agreed to speak to several senators. Abe Goldstein, a Jewish businessman based in Atlanta, persuaded Georgia Senator Herman Talmadge to back down from his support of a filibuster. B'nai B'rith sent a notice to its officers to "counteract possible mischief" aimed at Fortas and the American Israel Public Affairs Committee conveyed its concerns to 150 prominent Jewish leaders. The American Jewish Committee warned its followers of "extremists" who were "exploiting and aggravating" anti-Semitic sentiments. Gene Wyman, a major Democratic fundraiser based in California, attended a meeting with 75 Jewish leaders intended to pressure Murphy—Griffin's co-conspirator in the GOP's resistance movement—to back off from a filibuster. "We have gotten the Jews wound up," Wyman reported back to the White House.

Once again, Griffin remained the primary target. The *Jewish News*, a Detroit newspaper, didn't accuse Griffin of bigotry but bemoaned that the senator's "drive to keep Fortas from becoming the first Jew in American history to occupy the nation's third highest post has been gleefully welcomed by the lowest dregs of anti-Semitism."

Despite making some inroads, these efforts also ran into roadblocks. The feelers put out by the American Jewish Committee returned a mixed bag of responses. Since all of the potential Jewish contacts in Texas opposed Fortas's nomination, none agreed to contact Tower. Some of the moves coming out of the White House also bordered on the amateurish. When McPherson found a photo of Fortas and a Jewish philanthropist wearing yarmulkes at a benefit concert, he told the president: "I'll circulate it and try to get the Jewish groups behind us." Johnson had his secretary send the photo back with a message: "This doesn't mean a god damn thing. I've had on more of those things than Abe has."

Even with the misfires, the White House's campaign pressured the opposition. "Since I've been here," Senator Murphy told reporters, "I've never seen an arm-twisting effort as well-organized or as broad as this." Johnson's tactics also aggravated Griffin. "The White House is pulling out all the stops," he grumbled to reporters in early July. But the freshman senator proved he wasn't a pushover. "The politics that has been injected by President Johnson" in the confirmation process, Griffin told a reporter, "has been met by politics on the other side. . . . I think we will win this battle." Dismissed by the press, underestimated by the administration, and repeatedly mocked by Dirksen, he persevered. He turned down Ford's overtures, telling the automobile scion that he "takes exception to anybody being appointed" by a lame duck president. He was particularly defensive about being labelled an anti-Semite. "The fears expressed" by critics about the unleashing of a "Pandora's box of anti-Semitism," the senator believed, "were more fancied than real." To deflect these accusations, he told the press in late June that he would support returning Arthur Goldberg—who was Jewish—to the Court. Ultimately, these charges fizzled away when New York's Senator Javits, a Jewish Republican who had long championed the Warren Court, vouched for Griffin and dismissed lazy allegations of anti-Semitism. "I do not know whether or not anti-Semitism is a factor in respect to anyone who opposes the Fortas nomination," Javits declared in a statement. "But it is certainly not a charge to be made . . . recklessly unless it is based on solid evidence."

These uneven results exposed the truth of Johnson's diminishing influence over Congress. When pondering whether to run again a few months earlier, he had told his aides: "The Congress and I are like an old married couple. We've lived together so long and . . . we've asked so much of each other over the years we're tired of each other." Some of the erosion was a matter of arithmetic. Republicans gained three senate seats in the 1966 midterms and one more in 1968 when Charles Goodell (father of the NFL commissioner) took the spot left open by Robert Kennedy's assassination to bring their total to thirty-seven. Some of it was political. Griffin typified how an election year would make Republicans more inclined to resist the president. Much of it was due to Johnson's dwindling political capital. The tools available to him as Majority Leader were no longer at his disposal. He could no longer dangle committee assignments, hand out campaign funds from Texas oil barons, or launch his parliamentary machinations from the White House. And with only months left in his presidency, he couldn't dole out favors and dispense punishments with the same potency. Even worse, his deep unpopularity with congressional liberals over the Vietnam War had undermined his relationship with the very senators he most needed to back Fortas. These senators had repeatedly defended the Warren Court. Asked to assist an unpopular president with an election approaching, they didn't have the heart for yet another fight. His unpopularity with the public also undermined his standing. After a long, steady decline from its highs in 1964, his approval rating reached its lowest point during the confirmation. Johnson's advisors also let him down. They failed to foresee Griffin's insurgency and were ignorant of Griffin's secret alliance with Russell. Like a boxer who had fought one too many fights, Johnson entered the rematch with the Court's foes well past his prime.

The administration's waning influence appeared in the head counts conducted in early July. About 65 senators—down a handful from the tallies taken in late June—remained in support of the nomination with about a dozen undecideds. Recognizing these shortfalls, Manatos, the president's congressional liaison, pondered asking Eisenhower to make a public statement on the president's behalf.

Fortas had plenty of insights as well, and in past years, he would've been the point-man on such a campaign. Now, the glare of the nomination prevented him from publicly coming to his own defense and, out of fear of appearing too cozy with the White House, he was prevented from the types of activities where he would normally wield his magic. Working within these restrictions, Fortas relied on Porter, his former law firm partner, to implement his ideas. Together, they sought help from Fred Lazarus, the president of Federated Department Stores, and Fortas asked Max Fisher, a Jewish oil mogul based in Michigan, to call upon Griffin during his vacation on Capri. It must have been frustrating to be relegated to the sidelines for the most important political battle of his life. What made the experience all the more excruciating was how his role as the president's loyal advisor was now backfiring. Throughout the years, Fortas's close relationship with Johnson had raised his standing in Washington. Now, his critics had turned this into a liability.

Though still favored to prevail, Fortas's faltering candidacy raised the stakes of his appearance before the Judiciary Committee on July 16. It would be his most public—and best—opportunity to do what he'd been prevented from doing for some weeks—take center-stage in his own drama.

Justice Abe Fortas voices his opinion during a White House Cabinet meeting, March 20, 1968

LBJ Library photo by Yoichi Okamoto

PART III

Chapter 10

Going the Distance with the "President's Fixer"

JULY, 1968

O n the morning of July 16, accompanied by his sponsor, Tennessee's Senator Albert Gore, Fortas walked into Room 2228 of the Senate office building dressed in a tailored blue suit and gray tie. An energized crowd welcomed his arrival in the same venue that had hosted his uncontentious testimony three years earlier. Arriving six minutes before the scheduled start time, Fortas greeted a friend and delivered a hefty smile for the photographers. Forbidden to take any footage once the hearings began, cameramen jockeyed to get in their shots before the show started while reporters elbowed each other for the ideal vantage point to watch the expected fireworks. Griffin took a seat among the audience, but the spectators who couldn't jam into the room were forced to wait in the marble hallway outside. Thirteen of the Judiciary Committee's members entered from an adjacent conference room and filled their positions on the raised, semi-circular platform. Fiddling with a cigar, Eastland situated himself in the middle. Republicans sat to his left, Democrats to his right.

The fact that Fortas was compelled to appear at all came as a bad omen, and it gave his adversaries the opportunity to use him as target practice. No sitting justice and no nominee for chief justice had ever testified before Congress. When Warren turned down a request to testify during his confirmation in 1954, Deputy Attorney General William Rogers advised the Senate that his appearance would set "an unfortunate precedent". Applying the same logic, the safe move would have been for Fortas to decline the committee's invitation. The Senate had accepted such refusals from Minton and Warren with little pushback, but the hostility surrounding Fortas eliminated that option this time around. Eastland warned the Justice Department that Fortas would have to testify to "have any chance" of success. Clark and Christopher at the Justice Department concurred that the committee would be "severely offended" if Fortas refused its invitation. Considering that Fortas "had done superbly well" before the same committee three years earlier, they counseled him to appear.

One other element factored into Fortas's decision—his ego. His past experience jousting with hostile congressional committees infused him with a sense of bravado. "I am not a novice in Washington," Fortas boasted. "I am not a novice in Senate hearings." Buoyed by a dossier of research materials sent to him from the Justice Department as well as a list of subjects that the Republican senators were going to broach leaked to him from his old law firm, Fortas was confident of winning a duel against any senator. Unable to defend himself in public, he reasoned that this might be his only chance to take on his accusers.

Sitting alongside the nominee, Gore opened the proceedings with a workmanlike summary of Fortas's accomplishments. Leading up to the hearings, he had attempted to defuse the controversy surrounding Warren's retirement status by urging the president to "have another exchange of letters and remove all doubts" about the situation. In an attempt to neutralize the brunt of the questioning Fortas was about to undergo, he made a similar move. "I am sure," he told the committee, "that there are severe limitations upon the kind of questioning that a legislative committee . . . may properly submit to a sitting Justice." No one knew exactly to what extent the separation of powers built into the Constitution's fabric shielded the justices from their sister branches. Gore made a case for that barrier to be as large, thick, and impenetrable as possible. "Also," he added, "a judge is under the greatest . . . necessity to avoid . . . explaining opinions of the Court lest he may appear to be adding to or subtracting from what has been decided, or may perchance be prejudging future cases."

Playing the role of a behind-the-scenes advisor for most of his life, Fortas lacked a politician's innate sociability: the justice, an acquaintance explained, doesn't go "around kissing babies". In private consultations, Fortas spoke so softly he was sometimes barely audible to anyone more than an arm's reach away. He didn't embellish his discourse with war stories, and by the 1960s, he had shed any remnants of his Memphis drawl. Methodical and deliberate, he measured every word as if it was being transcribed in a court of law. Rarely bombastic or combative in public settings, he exuded a witty, clever, and sometimes biting but measured disposition. Whether discussing heady subjects like poverty or civil disobedience, or delivering a wisecrack, he rarely departed from his deadpan delivery. Combined with his sartorial refinement, slender build, and a receding hairline, these attributes radiated professionalism—but little charisma. What Fortas couldn't match in Warren's magnetism in a crowded room or Johnson's manic hold over a captive audience he made up for with an analytical mind as sharp as a samurai's sword.

For the interrogators relishing the opportunity to have a member of Warren's posse in their sights, extracting concessions from Fortas was going to be like squeezing water from a rock. Notorious for bullying witnesses, Eastland was the first senator to learn this lesson when he peppered Fortas with questions about his role as Johnson's counselor. Fortas conceded that the president occasionally asked him to sum up the points made at meetings—a facilitator of sorts, nothing more. Even under the most generous interpretation, this was a dishonest portrayal and the White House knew it. Those in the administration familiar with Fortas's role were "really queasy" with the justice's answers to the committee. "If he didn't lie," Califano believed, "he came as close to lying as you can come."

"Abe," former justice Arthur Goldberg warned Fortas back in 1965, "according to present reactions, people do not like a Supreme Court justice being too close to a president." Neither Fortas nor Johnson bothered to listen. To them, it was as if Fortas's ascension to the Court hadn't changed the attorney-client relationship between the two men. Soon after settling in the Court, Fortas sent the president the number to his "private direct line" and continued to refer to Johnson as his "Boss".

Just about every response Fortas made to Eastland's queries on this subject masked this truth, starting with the frequency of his interactions with the president. "It occurs very seldom," Fortas pledged to the committee. In fact, from August 11, 1965, when Fortas was sworn in as a justice, to Johnson's announcement of his nomination on June 26, 1968, the two men met with each other over eighty times. Some of these engagements took place in the White House at cabinet meetings, dinners with foreign dignitaries, or consultations in the Oval Office. Fortas even attended more cabinet meetings than Goldberg, the U.N. Ambassador. At other times, they met over meals at the Fortas residence or boat cruises or other unofficial venues. On top of these face-to-face meetings were the innumerable phone calls, memorandums, and letters they sent to one another as well as the occasions Fortas dispatched his advice through intermediaries.

The president asked for Fortas's counsel on just about any subject. The Vietnam War? Yes. Civil rights? Certainly. Labor strife? Yes, again. Antitrust enforcement? That, too. Comprising both mundane and cerebral tasks, the services Fortas provided included speechwriting, reviewing legislation, and crisis management. In 1966, Johnson asked Fortas to "write . . . a directive to the Cabinet" regarding the copper markets and provide input on the State of the Union message. In 1967, Fortas edited a speech on civil rights. "Fortas has several problems with it," Johnson's top domestic advisor Joseph Califano relayed to the president. "I have modified it" to address the passages the justice deemed "corny and trite . . . but it may not be enough for Abe." A month before Fortas's nomination to replace Warren, the White House asked for the justice's views on the "ten most significant problems facing this Nation" in preparation of the federal budget and the president's final State of the Union address. Less than a week before the nomination, Fortas drafted a letter on behalf of the president for the national broadcasters. It was one thing for Johnson to have a sounding board for some of the thorniest issues of his presidency. It was something altogether to have Fortas serve alongside the White House staff like a member of the executive branch. Senator Thruston Morton once called the Oval Office on pending legislation and was told: "Well, the President is away, but Mr. Justice Fortas is here and he's managing the bill for the White House."

Surely legal matters must have been off-limits. "Let me . . . make this absolutely clear," Fortas assured the Judiciary Committee, "that since I have been a Justice, the President . . . has never . . . talked to me about anything before the Court or that might come before the Court. I want to make that absolutely clear." In addition to his other prevarications about the services he had rendered for Johnson, this too was a lie. Johnson had the Justice Department at his disposal but still felt no compunction in calling upon the "best lawyer" he knew as if Fortas were merely moonlighting as a justice. Fortas handled a variety of legal matters. On one occasion, he authored a memo on the rights of protestors picketing near the White House and what measures police should take to "further . . . reduce the numbers involved." In another instance, the White House asked for his guidance on "election reform" and whether to lower the voting age to eighteen.

Unable to restrain themselves from reprising their long-held roles, Johnson and Fortas inevitably breached the one taboo they should have never broken. Johnson appointed Fortas in 1965 in part to provide intelligence on the Court's inner workings. The justice certainly didn't disappoint once in office. Fortas offered a prediction on how the Court would rule on the president's authority to institute price controls. He gave advice on what to include in a brief that the government was preparing to file with the Court. Counseling Johnson on the constitutionality of an anti-crime bill, Fortas co-authored the message accompanying the president's veto. On another occasion, the justice discussed the constitutionality of a proposed congressional limitation on the president's role as commander in chief. "Relatively fresh from Harvard Law School," Califano recalled, "where professors left the impression that Supreme Court justices lived and worked in ivory towers, I was surprised to see Fortas discussing a constitutional question that might come before the Court and even speculating on the Court's likely action." After a 1967 meeting in the White House to discuss Johnson's reelection campaign, Fortas told another participant, "I shouldn't be at these meetings." Yet, he continued his role, perhaps out of a combination of loyalty and sense of duty. In a private letter to Justice Harlan, Fortas justified his moonlighting: "I felt that I had no alternative to complying with the President's request for participation in the matters where he sought my help."

Fortas kept all of these dealings hidden from the Judiciary Committee, and when asked about specific events he couldn't obfuscate, he chose to mislead its members. In response to a query from Eastland, Fortas replied that he scanned Johnson's statement on the 1967 Detroit Riots "before it was delivered." That's it. Nothing more. The reality was starkly different. During a marathon session at the White House lasting sixteen hours, Fortas served as Johnson's right-hand man during the crisis. Over the objections of his staff, Johnson released a proclamation drafted by Fortas: "I had the best damn constitutional lawyer in the country write that statement," the president boasted. "The statement was a product of Abe Fortas *presidential consiglieri*," Califano bemoaned, "not Abe Fortas *presidential counselor*."

Unknown to anyone on the committee, the misrepresentations by the man referred to as "the President's fixer" kept piling up. "To the best of my knowledge," Fortas testified, "I have never, since I have been a Justice, recommended anybody for a judgeship." But just two months earlier, while Johnson, Clark, and Russell were wrangling over Alexander Lawrence's appointment to a federal judgeship in Georgia, Fortas had advised the president to go ahead with the appointment. Despite Clark's legitimate reservations, it was a "reasonable price to pay for the essential good will of Senator Russell," he wrote to the White House. There was no need, Fortas reiterated, to destroy "the good relationship between Russell and the President." On June 24, the day before Johnson met with Russell, Fortas again told the White House: "I think we should go ahead on this now for sure." Here was one of Johnson's closest advisors exhorting him to appoint Lawrence and it was one of the few occasions the president didn't listen.

Unable to make any inroads, Eastland gave up. McClellan's follow up questions couldn't crack Fortas's fortress of obfuscation either.

Now it was Ervin's turn to take a swing at the elusive piñata. The North Carolina senator typically employed a folksy persona by spinning yarns of his adventures as a lawyer intermixed in with biblical anecdotes. Ervin discarded those amiable qualities for one of a prosecutor. While Fortas had been invited before Congress to answer questions, Ervin didn't seem interested in the answers the justice had parried with thus far.

The pink-faced senator with jowls hanging from his cheeks and "eyebrows twitching like a rabbit's nose," hogged the limelight, barely allowing Fortas to get in a few words edgewise as he used his pulpit to repeatedly bash the Warren Court. "I would like to say," Ervin lectured, "there are a great many people in the United States who do not feel that the Supreme Court during recent years . . . has manifested a willingness, and an ability to interpret the Constitution according to its true intent." The timing of the Court's rulings— whether they came before or after Fortas's arrival—didn't matter to Ervin. In his eyes, Fortas was a proxy for Warren and since Ervin couldn't take on the chief justice directly, he did the next best thing in belittling the heir apparent.

"Well, don't you agree with me that law would be destitute of social value . . . if the Supreme Court is going to indulge habitually in overruling prior decisions?" he asked in one of the few breaks from his monologue. Having passively listened to Ervin besmirch his judicial record, Fortas relished the opening for a counter-attack.

Fortas: Senator, we should not overrule prior decisions lightly, except in the clearest kind of case. I came across a statement that you made, when you were on the North Carolina Supreme Court.

The justice referred to an opinion that Ervin had authored, overturning a ten-year-old precedent. For a man wedded to *stare decisis*, the legal doctrine emphasizing the importance of precedents, Ervin's departure from that sacred principle gave Fortas an opening.

Fortas: And here are some of the things you said about the problem of *stare decisis*. . . . "Besides, the doctrine of *stare decisis* will not be applied in any event to preserve and perpetuate error and grievous wrongs."

. . . I cite it here because it so illustrates our problem—your problem as a judge. . . . I am sure what you tried to do is interpret and apply the due process clause of your constitution . . . and that I assure you is what I do and what I will always do.

As Ervin's face turned to a deeper shade of pink, the press in the hearing room reacted gleefully to Fortas's retort. Rattled by the exchange, the senator grew defensive about his decision-making in the case.

Ervin: Applied it in accordance, with the exception of the previous decision of the Supreme Court of North Carolina, with every case I could find on the subject in the United States.

Ervin's response sounded eerily like something a member of the Warren Court might say. The logical implication of Fortas's argument was clear to anyone in the room: if Ervin overruled a precedent because it was incorrect, then why couldn't the justices whom the senator repeatedly condemned do the same? Able to see that Ervin was flustered, Fortas eschewed any overt charges of hypocrisy. Instead, he delivered his zingers in a backhanded way.

Fortas: I am not criticizing your opinion, sir.

The rejoinder instigated a longer defense by Ervin.

Fortas: I am not quarrelling with you, Senator.

After a lengthy back and forth about stare decisis, Ervin—clearly still upset about the North Carolina decision—returned to it.

Ervin: I never voted to overrule but one case.

Fortas: Is that right? Well, forgive me for personalizing this. I guess I got a little carried away.

Savoring the victory, Fortas sat quietly, sometimes "doodling parallelograms" as Ervin spent the last two hours of the session reading from the Court's opinions. If Eastland had one of his baseball scorecards handy, he would have recorded a blowout for Fortas after the first day.

With their hopes of a dismantling Fortas's defenses dashed, the opposition was desperate to pin something on the justice. When Griffin's aides reviewed Fortas's testimony that night, they found an inconsistency. In an article in *The New York Times* a year earlier, Fred Graham mentioned a phone call Fortas had made to Lazarus, the department store chain CEO, to rebut the executive's criticism of the administration. Sensing Ervin's wounds from his give-and-take with the justice, Griffin's assistant made the senator an offer the next day: "We thought you might like to have a little fun with the Justice," he said, "since he had a little fun with you—and your . . . decision yesterday."

After another dull review of the Court's opinions by Ervin on the second day of Fortas's testimony, spectators began to shuffle in and out of the room. The senator was losing the once-captive audience until he brought the room to a standstill when reading an excerpt from the Graham article. Convinced that Fortas was trapped, "I would be glad," Ervin asked the justice, "to have any comments you make on that."

To inoculate Fortas from this kind of charge, Christopher had sent his assistants within the Justice Department to search far and wide to develop a list of justices conducting extra-judicial work. They discovered a practice dating back to the early days of the Republic. George Washington had chosen Chief Justice John Jay to lead the negotiations on a treaty with Britain. Justices in the 1800s were appointed to arbitral panels charged with resolving disputes between countries. William Howard Taft asked Hughes to determine second class postal rates. FDR tapped Owen Roberts to lead the study of the Pearl Harbor attack and sent Robert Jackson to Nuremberg to serve as America's chief prosecutor. And, of course, Johnson had picked Warren to lead the investigation of Kennedy's assassination. In all of these instances, however, the extra-judicial assignments were known to the public. To further shield Fortas, the agency dug out instances when justices had advised presidents outside of the public's eye. It found that a range of presidents, including Washington, Jackson, Lincoln, Andrew Johnson, Theodore Roosevelt, Wilson, Warren Harding, Hoover, FDR, and Truman received advice—legal and otherwise—from sitting justices. None of these relationships had breached the capital's customs.

Chief Justice John Marshall, the most revered justice in American history, also fulfilled multiple functions for President John Adams. After being sworn in as chief justice, he stayed on as Secretary of State for a month. Though it was Marshall's oversight in submitting a judicial commission that put in motion the dispute that would culminate in *Marbury v. Madison*, Marshall didn't recuse himself from arguably the most important case in the Court's history, the very case which ingrained the Court's powers of judicial review into the Constitution.

Fortas's dalliances were not so different in comparison, and to some of his supporters the issue was pointless. In fact, everyone had known of Fortas's close professional relationship with Johnson back in 1965, and few seemed to mind at the time. "It's like having Einstein as a crony," Harry Kalven, a professor at the University of Chicago said in defending the justice's relationship with Johnson. "There's nothing wrong with a crony if he's as good as this one." But now, as his detractors charged Fortas with an impropriety under a set of rapidly shifting mores (similar to how "nannygate" derailed Zoe Baird's chance to become the attorney general some two decades later) the White House cried foul. "Who better" Christopher asked defensively, "for a nominee to have as his friend than the President? Would Senator Griffin prefer that the nominee be a friend of a friend of the President? Or perhaps a friend of a tycoon? Or of a big contributor? Or of a shady lobbyist?"

Maintaining his composure, Fortas regurgitated this information, and to punctuate how prepared he was to rebuff anything the committee could throw at him, provided the authors, titles, and page numbers of his sources as if he was reading his answers from a law review article. In the face of Ervin's persistent harangue, Fortas allowed for one of his few minor concessions. "I called a friend," he acknowledged. "I told him at that time, as a citizen, that I was very distressed about a statement attributed to him that I considered to be wrong."

Ervin couldn't otherwise dent Fortas's defenses. "[T]wo things have been vastly exaggerated," Fortas said when Ervin brought up a *Newsweek* article describing the justice's critical role in the White House. "One is the intimacy of my relationship with the President, and the other is my proficiency as a violinist. They are still exaggerated."

"Well do you put yourself in a class with Jack Benny as a violinist," Ervin quipped, referring to the comedian who played the instrument in many of his acts. "No, sir, I am not as good as he is. He is really quite good," Fortas responded. He could have said the same of his own performance.

"Mr. Chairman, that completes my interrogation of the nominee," Ervin said, announcing his capitulation. After Ervin finished, the remaining senators—friendly liberal Democrats—either praised the nominee or lobbed him easy questions he could crush out of the park. Day two ended with another Fortas rout.

To accommodate the overflow of spectators, the Committee moved the session from its cramped chamber to the Caucus Room for the third day of Fortas's testimony. Originally intended as a meeting room for party caucuses, the space hosted some of the most important hearings in the Senate's history, from the sinking of the *Titanic,* to the attack on Pearl Harbor, to McCarthy-era blood-baths. One of those bloodbaths involved Owen Lattimore, who, in fending off accusations from McCarthy of being a Soviet agent, endured the longest congressional interrogation in U.S. history—with Fortas at his side.

Designed in the Beaux-Arts style by a pair of French-trained New York architects, the rectangular room provided a grand setting with marble walls, a dozen Corinthian columns, and crystal chandeliers suspended from an orn-ate ceiling. Three French windows flooded the 4,000 square-foot space with natural light. Big enough to seat more than 300 people, it was the perfect site for the gladiatorial battle that the eager spectators were about to witness. If Ervin was the challenger in the "undercard," then Thurmond—the second half of the duo Fortas felt were the "principal mouthpieces of evil"—was the "marquee" in the highly-anticipated main event.

Brown was the key to understanding Thurmond's rage. "The most devas-tating and relentless assault on the Constitution is coming from the Supreme Court itself," he wrote in *The Faith We Have Not Kept.* "The date when that blow was struck was 1954." While *Brown* may have topped Thurmond's list, it was simply the gravest of the Warren Court's many transgressions. Of the more than 170 state and federal laws that the Court invalidated, the cases that most troubled Thurmond—civil rights, Red Monday, school prayer, reappor-tionment, criminal procedure, and censorship—also offended large segments of the public. The cultural manifestations of these rulings were equally abhor-rent to him. He blamed the justices for encouraging moral depravity, coddling criminals, and giving comfort to flag-burning hippies. Though it seemed like a stretch, Thurmond also placed the blame for the riots erupting in America's cities squarely on the justices' shoulders: "the court," he wrote to constituents during the hearings, "is a significant factor in the ever-increasing chaos which confronts our Nation."

The justices weren't alone in propelling the social and cultural transfor-mations Thurmond found so distasteful. But for him, the Court bore more responsibility for the country's pitiful condition than any other institution. "Why such indignation?" he asked in *The Faith We Have Not Kept*, published months before the hearings:

> Because proven criminals are freed.
> Because subversives are given unlimited access to our society.
> Because our children are being deprived of the moral foundation they need to become good citizens.
> Because the very foundations of law have been eroded.
> No nation can long survive if such conditions are not checked....
> The Supreme Court has changed law from something absolute to something relative. It has made law whimsical. It has denied the very essence of law.

It's not as if Thurmond hadn't tried to check the Court over the years, but in each instance the justices had managed to dodge his best shots. Finding himself on the losing end of the Warren Wars, Thurmond—much like Ervin—became convinced that the best way to influence the Court was through its membership. What is surprising is that it took Thurmond and his confederates so long to implement this idea. With few exceptions, little of the antagonism directed at the Court had seeped into the confirmation process until 1968. And when Warren's adversaries did put up roadblocks in the nominations of Potter Stewart and Thurgood Marshall, they failed to do much more than splash mud on these inevitable confirmations. But now, in what turned into a "eureka moment," the Court's detractors looked at the addition of a new justice as the key front in their struggle over the judicial body. "Under our constitutional form of government," Thurmond wrote in a newsletter sent to South Carolina residents, "the American people have no opportunity to repudiate individual justices at the ballot box." The only solution in his eyes was to replace the Court's liberals with conservatives. When looked at from this perspective, his willingness to trample on just about every custom governing the confirmation process didn't look so unhinged after all. Over time, Thurmond's outlook became commonplace. But in 1968, it was revolutionary.

After years of riding solo, Thurmond now saw the chance to do more than bellow spiteful diatribes. "Oftentimes my opposition vote stood alone," he told his colleagues in early July. "Those who have wailed about the damage the Supreme Court has done the country now have a chance to let the people speak through their new president regarding the court leadership." Thurmond also recognized the long-term impact of what was at stake just when such considerations were becoming the norm. A letter to his constituents during the hearings encapsulated his thought process:

> This is a matter which will affect the lives of all Americans in a most fundamental way. If this body confirms the nomination of Fortas to be Chief Justice, it will insure the continuation of the Supreme Court as a radical influence on the American political scene for the next 20 to 30 years.

The fusion of these viewpoints transformed the confirmation process from a predictable, almost mundane ritual—that, with few exceptions, nominees had in previous instances comfortably navigated—into an all-out war. This unprecedented attempt—not to mention the unorthodox tactics used in the process—to sabotage a nomination politicized the confirmation process and established the framework for the acrimonious confirmation battles undertaken by future generations.

Here, finally, was Thurmond's last and best chance to win a battle against his archenemy. The senator did not squander the opportunity. "First, it is my contention that the Supreme Court has assumed such a powerful role as a policymaker in the Government," Thurmond opened, "that the Senate must necessarily be concerned with the views of the prospective Justices." The passage summarized the Court's politicization since Warren had taken office. The rest of Thurmond's opening elaborated on this historic shift:

> Ideally, the Supreme Court is thought to be removed and insulated from politics. . . . However, in the last decade and a half, the Court has made so many decisions affecting the lives of the American people in very fundamental ways that it would

seem to me that the Senate . . . is entitled to consider these views, much as the voters do with regard to candidates for the Presidency.

After this philosophical preamble, Thurmond returned to form, berating Fortas for four hours through a review of the rulings he abhorred. His pugilistic style made Ervin's punches from a day earlier seem like a sparring session. When Fortas declined to answer yet another question on constitutional grounds, a practice Frankfurter first began in 1939, the senator cut him off.

Thurmond: You have expressed your views to the President when he has called you down there (the White House), and over the telephone; haven't you?

Fortas: No, sir; never.

Thurmond: And he got the benefit of your views on matters; did he not?

Fortas: Never.

Thurmond: Why shouldn't a Senator have the benefit of your views?

Fortas: Senator, all I can say is that I hope and trust that the American people will realize that I am acting out of a sense of constitutional duty and responsibility.

Thurmond: Well, I am disappointed, even more so, in you, Mr. Justice Fortas.

Fortas's curt responses to Thurmond's longwinded diatribes made the hearing progress more like an arraignment than a question-and-answer session. More than fifty times—up until then a new record—Fortas refrained from responding to Thurmond's questions in various forms: "With all respect, Senator, the same answer," the justice said. "I am afraid I have to make the same answer. . . . For the same reason—because of constitutional limitations upon me—I must decline to address myself to that. . . . Senator, with the greatest respect, my response must be the same. . . . I must respond the same way, I regret to say." Fortas's refusals eerily reminded some in attendance of the witnesses who, badgered by McCarthy, resorted to "taking the Fifth" in the same room more than a decade earlier.

Imitating McCarthy, Thurmond—whom *Time* named "the gentleman Torquemada" after the Spanish Inquisition's infamous interrogator—fired back with caustic retorts. "You refuse to answer the question," he uttered, or some variation of it. On and on he went like a boxer swinging wildly but unable to land any punches.

Thurmond's angular nose and chin, high cheekbones, and thick eyebrows endowed him with a hawk-like mien. And those narrow, piercing eyes zeroed in on Fortas as the senator began his final assault against the beleaguered justice. With so many notorious rulings at his disposal, Thurmond settled for *Mallory v. United States*, a 1957 case in which the Court had freed a confessed rapist because police had held him too long prior to his arraignment, to pounce on Fortas. Eclipsed by Red Monday and predating *Miranda*, it was one of the Court's earliest criminal procedure holdings to instigate widespread recriminations. In July, 1958, amid the Red Monday legislation cooking in Congress, a House bill overturning the ruling passed 294-79. The following month, the Senate passed a modified version of this bill by a 65-12 count. The overwhelming support for the measure should have saved it from the machinations Johnson employed to torpedo HR 3 and the Jenner-Butler bill. But a parliamentary maneuver disposed of it, leaving the Court's enemies empty-handed. It was just one of the many setbacks Thurmond had endured in his endless effort to neuter the Warren Court. Now, fourteen years of pent-up fury boiled to the surface like a volcano on the verge of erupting.

"Why did he go free," Thurmond screamed, deviating from the script prepared by his staff. "A criminal, a convict, a guilty man, who committed a serious rape on a lady in this city. . . . Do you believe in that kind of justice?"

Through years of experience testifying before Congress, Fortas had relied upon his extemporaneous wit and sharp argumentative skills to take on some big foes. "Never embarrassed," a *New York Times* reporter wrote of the poker-faced justice, "never taken by surprise—or if so, never showing it—he is the ultimate unflappable man." And so far, he had remained unruffled by Thurmond's inquest with the only sign of nervousness his occasional tendency to fiddle with a pitcher of water on his desk. But, nothing in Fortas's background had prepared him for Thurmond's latest outburst. Just as Fortas again brought up the "constitutional limitation" inhibiting him from responding, the senator interjected with a crescendo. "Mallory—I want that word to ring in your ears. Mallory. . . . ," Thurmond bellowed, getting louder and angrier with every utterance of the assailant's name. "Mallory, a man who raped a woman, admitted his guilt, and the Supreme Court turned him loose on a technicality." Wasn't the decision, Thurmond shouted, "calculated to encourage people to commit rapes and serious crimes? Can you as a Justice of the Supreme Court condone such a decision . . . ?"

Flushed and visibly shaken for the first time, Fortas rested his head in his hands before glancing over to Eastland for a lifeline. Three years earlier, Fortas had thanked Eastland for his "courtesy and understanding" in overseeing his confirmation. "I shall never forget your kindness," Fortas had written to the chairman at the time. In fact, Fortas had been so grateful as to have invited the chairman to a ceremony celebrating his ascension to the Court. But now looking over a document, Eastland made no effort to rein in Thurmond, let alone make eye contact with Fortas. Isolated and helpless, and with a look of stunned disbelief on his face, the justice sat in "angered and outraged silence" for a few moments. Leaning towards the microphone, he appeared to be preparing to burst out with a snappy retort. None ever came.

No other confirmation hearing would contain such a remarkable exchange until Brett Kavanaugh, in a fiery defense against accusations of sexual assault, was to duel with the Judiciary Committee a half century later in 2018. Unlike Fortas, who would have to suffer through another ten weeks of humiliation before learning of his fate, Kavanaugh was appointed to the Court within days after his outburst.

CHAPTER 11

"MR. OBSCENITY"

The smut industry takes its direction from the High Court's decisions.
— JAMES CLANCY, TESTIFYING BEFORE THE
SENATE JUDICIARY COMMITTEE, JULY 22, 1968

JULY-AUGUST, 1968

Adult entertainment. Pornography. Smut. Filth. Whatever one called it, obscenity gave the Warren Court fits. For no lack of trying, the justices never managed to establish a workable legal standard balancing free speech rights against censorship boards resolved to uphold Victorian-era values. In *Roth v. United States*, a 1957 case involving state and federal obscenity statutes, the Court declined to grant First Amendment protections to obscene materials. Establishing this principle was the easy part. The tough part was figuring out just what constituted obscenity. One person's art, after all, was another's perversion. The justices settled on a test applying various value judgments to define obscenity: "whether, to the average person, applying contemporary community standards, the dominant theme of the material, taken as a whole, appeals to prurient interest." The formula was riddled with ambiguity. Just who was "an average person?" What were "contemporary community standards?" What factors would this hypothetical "average person" consider in determining whether the "dominant theme of the material . . . appeals to prurient interest?" It was easy to see why these vague criteria left the justices twisted like pretzels. "I have reached the conclusion," Justice Potter Stewart wrote in a state of exasperation in 1964, that censorship is "constitutionally limited to hard-core pornography. I shall not today attempt further to define the kinds of material I understand to be embraced within that short-hand description, and perhaps I could never succeed in intelligibly doing so. But I know it when I see it." The difficulty confronting the Court was the fact that Stewart's entirely subjective definition was as valid as any other formulation the justices had conceived.

Their inability to establish workable guidelines turned the Court into a makeshift censorship tribunal, often requiring the justices to view films brought to them on appeal to determine, on a case-by-case basis, whether the cinematic creations fell under the First Amendment's aegis. Justice John Marshall Harlan, who was going blind, endured the indignity of having a clerk summarize each movie's content to him. Over time, the process used by what commentators satirically named the "High Court of Obscenity" evolved into a farce, making the justices easy targets for caricature.

The burgeoning demand for sexually explicit materials during the 1960s exacerbated the Court's headaches. *Playboy* magazine, the standard-bearer of the industry, saw its circulation climb to four million by the decade's end, second only to *Reader's Digest*. The era's sexual awakening brought the magazine's founder, Hugh Hefner, into mainstream life where previous generations of pornographers had never reached. He appeared on Johnny Carson's *Tonight Show* and attracted leading writers and public intellectuals—including Justice William Douglas—to publish their work in his magazine alongside photographs of naked models.

While many Americans welcomed this sexual revolution, social conservatives cringed at the nation's slide into libertinism. The number of "obscenity complaints" received by the Post Office tripled from 1957 to 1965 and 73% of the public found "nudes in magazines objectionable." The standard set out in *Roth* would have been difficult to apply during any era. Doing so under these circumstances placed the Court squarely in the middle of the nation's culture wars.

Now largely remembered for his role in the 1980s Lincoln Savings and Loan scandal, Charles Keating was a corporate lawyer living in Cincinnati when in 1958 he dedicated his life to fighting pornography. A charismatic leader educated in the Jesuit tradition, Keating founded the Citizens for Decent Literature (CDL) in 1958 to replace the outdated Catholic organizations that had served as quasi-official decency commissions in the past.

To avoid being labelled an antiquated prude and an enemy of free speech, CDL relied on pseudo-science and the Court's convoluted legal standards to redirect the conversation away from traditional religious mores towards pornography's purported hazards. CDL's 1963 film, *Perversion for Profit*, narrated by George Putnam, the handsome Los Angeles-based television news anchor, epitomized this strategy. "I'd like to begin with a fact," Putnam stated in the film's opening. "A simple yet shocking fact. It is this. A floodtide of filth is engulfing our country in the form of newsstand obscenity and is threatening to pervert an entire generation of our American children." Once the viewer of porn has been defiled, Putnam exclaimed in his stentorian voice, "it is practically impossible to adjust to normal attitudes." Melodramatic, packed with sensationalistic imagery, and designed to petrify viewers like an old-fashioned sex-ed movie, *Perversion for Profit* aired at the local chapters of the American Legion, Elks lodges, and Catholic organizations. "They constantly portray abnormal sexual behavior as being normal," Putnam explained minutes into his presentation, holding a poster board of a giant black octopus with twelve tentacles stretched across a map of the United States. "They glorify unnatural sex acts. They tell youngsters that it's smart," he said, placing a verbal emphasis at the end of each clause of his statement to elevate its dramatic value, "it's thrilling, it provides kicks to be a homosexual, a sadist, and every other kind of deviancy." Besides rising crime rates, venereal disease, homosexuality, and juvenile delinquency, the film blamed pornography for the "moral decay. . . . [that] weakens our resistance to the onslaught of the communist masters of deceit."

As the preeminent anti-obscenity group of the era with 300 chapters and more than 100,000 members, CDL led the growing charge against pornography. By 1967, a bevy of congressmen and leading clerics filled up its governing committee. Besides reaching out to the public through its films and magazines, CDL drafted model legislation for state legislatures, filed amicus briefs with the Court, and hosted workshops for law enforcement. The latter made for a natural partner. Law enforcement agencies from the FBI to local police precincts demonized pornography. "There has not been a sex murder in the history of our department in which the killer was not an avid reader of lewd magazines," a Detroit police inspector told *Reader's Digest* in 1965. To many in the law enforcement community, pornography's dangers went far beyond sex crimes. Chicago's Police Superintendent blamed "obscene literature . . . for criminal behavior from vicious assaults to homicide."

Americans disgusted by this upsurge of sexual content cared little for the free speech rights of members of the adult industry. They were viewed not as artists but as carriers of a disease that society needed to be inoculated against. That inoculation came in various forms. California Governor Ronald Reagan supported an anti-porn referendum in California, and New York City, no hotbed of puritanism, created an anti-pornography commission chaired by the mayor. The federal government followed suit in 1967, forming a commission to find ways to curb obscenity. Riding this backlash against the era's rapidly changing sexual mores, Keating graduated from speaking before parochial schools and local civic groups to national acclaim and paved the way for a new wave of politically engaged organizations preaching family values. Along with James Clancy, a CDL lawyer, he testified before the House in 1965, affirming his position as the nation's foremost expert on the issue. (Nixon later appointed Keating to the presidential commission on obscenity.)

Invited by Thurmond, Clancy and Keating returned to a far bigger stage on July 22, 1968. Speaking sporadically during their appearance, Keating allowed Clancy to take the lead before the Judiciary Committee.

Unlike the far right witnesses who spun tales of communist conspiracies with little to back up their assertions, Clancy, a former sex crimes prosecutor in Los Angeles, came to the hearings well-versed. His clinical takedown of the Court offered a case-by-case rundown of 26 obscenity rulings during the 1966-67 term covering the entire gamut of the adult industry: twenty paperbacks (with titles such as *Lust School* and *Sin Servant*), a dozen bondage guides (*English Spanking School* and *Traveling Saleslady Gets Spanked*), ten "girlie" magazines (*High Heels*), and eight films (*June Tracy*).

Clancy's analysis revealed that by reversing twenty-three of the lower court rulings that censored these materials, the justices set aside the "community standards of thirteen States."

His well-crafted indictment began to go off-course when Clancy tried to pin the blame for these rulings on Fortas. Though the justice had sided with the majority in all of these instances, the Court processed twenty of them without providing an opinion explaining its reasoning. Of the three remaining cases which included opinions, none were authored by Fortas. This made it difficult to discern much about Fortas's views on the topic or differentiate him from the other justices. "A more precise understanding of his philosophy in the obscenity area," Clancy testified, "can be gained from a consideration" of *Schackman v. California*, a case involving three striptease films—*0-7*, *0-12*, and *D-15*. Applying the standard set out in *Roth*, a federal judge found the movies were "unequivocally and incontrovertibly obscene and pornographic in the hard-core sense."

The justices didn't think so, overturning the lower court with no explanation. "Because of this decision," Clancy told the committee, "such films . . . are now appearing in neighborhood movies, and . . . in open-air theaters." Offering no proof, he then launched the most extreme accusation made during the hearings. "The smut industry takes its direction from the High Court's decisions, advancing a giant step forward each time that the U.S. Supreme Court hands down a decision adverse to the people's interest. . . . I have been following the developments in this area for ten years," Clancy insisted, "and can say, without exaggeration," that the Court's rulings "were the causative factor which brought about . . . a release of the great deluge of hard-core pornography ever witnessed by any nation." Just in case the senators failed to appreciate the link between the Court and the smut trade, Clancy returned to the topic a few minutes later in his testimony:

> we have a set of decisions . . . which . . . is an open invitation
> to every pornographer to come into the area and distribute
> millions of copies—and I am not exaggerating—millions and
> millions of copies of what historically had been regarded even
> in France as hard-core pornography.

The irony of Clancy's assertions was that Warren despised pornography. He told his clerks that if he caught someone trying to sell obscene materials to his daughters, he would "go out and find the guy and tear him apart." Anything but a cultural warrior, "Warren's great strength was his simple belief in the things which we now laugh at," Justice Stewart noted years later, "motherhood, marriage, family, flag, and the like." Deemed a puritan by his clerks, who were typically fresh out of law school, Warren had to set aside his personal distaste for pornography to tackle these cases. Obscenity is "the most difficult area" of the law, the chief justice told a reporter after his retirement, because it required the Court to "balance two constitutional rights with each other." The government had a "right to have a decent society" but the Constitution shielded a person's free speech rights against government overreach. How far could people "go under the First Amendment," Warren asked, still searching for an answer that had eluded him, "without offending the right of the government to maintain a decent society?"

Encouraged by Eastland and Thurmond throughout his testimony, Clancy's assertions went unchallenged by the committee, which didn't bother to call any artists or law professors or free speech advocates to counter Clancy's conclusions or elaborate upon the challenging balancing act the justices faced. This should have come as no surprise; injecting subtlety and nuance into a multilayered debate was not Thurmond's style. One person in particular may have appreciated an invitation, however. Brennan received a greeting card adorned with a rabbit and blue and yellow colored eggs decorating its border. Its message read: "This is a season of the year filled with many unusual delights." The cover was clearly aimed at misdirection: pictures of two nude models were on the other side of the card. It was signed "Love & Kisses" by Hugh Hefner. Then again, under the circumstances, Fortas was probably better off without Hefner's public endorsement.

While obscenity drew new members to the Warren Court's growing list of detractors, the Court's prohibition of prayer in public schools in 1962 (*Engel v. Vitale*) secured its standing as the leading enemy of social and religious conservatives years before anti-war protestors, black militants, flower children, and other bedrocks of the counter-culture threatened everything traditionalists held dear.

Typically vigilant about couching its arguments in secular terms, CDL nevertheless took the opportunity to couple school prayer with obscenity even as the underlying constitutional issues involved had little in common. The opening *Engel* provided to smear the justices as agents of depravity was simply too expedient to forego. Divorced three times, married to a woman forty-two years his junior, and having contributed to *Playboy* made Douglas, in particular, the poster child within the Court for the cultural transformations social conservatives found so repugnant. "William O. Douglas scandalizes America with his third divorce in the offing," Keating wrote to CDL's members. "This man is instrumental in uprooting religion from our schools and in flooding our land with obscenity." George Wallace, the Alabama governor who earned acclaim during his nationally televised gamesmanship to block the integration of the University of Alabama, also equated the two disparate issues. "The Supreme Court . . . has ruled that you cannot even say a simple prayer in a public school, but you can send obscene literature through the mail," he bellowed at a campaign stop during his 1968 presidential run.

Engel prompted many prominent voices that had remained on the sidelines of the Warren Wars to speak out against the justices for the first time. Billy Graham, the most influential evangelist of the era, denounced the "dangerous trend" of barreling "toward secularism." While other leading Protestants as well as many Jewish groups supported the ruling, top officials within the Catholic Church led the charge against *Engel*. New York's Cardinal Francis Spellman, the nation's preeminent Catholic cleric, complained the ruling struck "at the very heart of the Godly tradition in which America's children have for so long been raised." Cardinal James McIntyre in Los Angeles, who had endorsed Warren's nomination during the crucial hours after Chief Justice Fred Vinson's passing, must have felt betrayed by the chief justice. "The decision is positively shocking and scandalizing to one of American blood and principles," he said. "It is not a decision according to law, but a decision of license." As with other controversial rulings of the era, the Cold War infiltrated any discussion of the decision's merits. "You can imagine to what extent the Communists will use that decision as propaganda," lamented Boston's Cardinal Richard Cushing. Encouraged by Catholic leaders, parochial school attendance peaked in the mid-1960s. In the Midwest and the South, many children had no need to enroll in private institutions: up to two-thirds of the public schools continued to sponsor prayers.

Religious figures were not alone in their contempt. Herbert Hoover and Eisenhower assailed *Engel* as did a majority of the nation's 42 largest newspapers. The *Wall Street Journal* called the prohibition a "violent wrecking of the Constitution's language." The editors of the *Los Angeles Times* were equally "outraged by this perverse decision." The Hearst newspaper chain considered the decision "a misrepresentation of the Constitution." The *National Review* had a field day in what turned into an "I told you so" moment for the publication. "We have moved a long way . . . toward despotism if we and our children may not express our faith . . . where and when we choose," the magazine protested in a lengthy editorial published in July, 1962:

> *The justices . . . are caught so tightly in the coils of their ideological obsessions that they no longer see the Republic's foundations. . . . [T] he First Amendment, as redefined by the Court, becomes a despotic weapon to prevent the American people from the natural and normal expression of their religious faith.*

A fortnight later, Buckley continued to pound away at the justices: "ours has become the only nation outside the Iron Curtain where it is unlawful to pray in public schools."

Just when it seemed that the American public couldn't get more outraged by the Court's rulings, the justices trampled upon a widespread practice dating back to the colonial era. Half of the nation's 35,000 school districts allowed school prayer in the 1950s. Indeed, for many in the country, *Engel* represented something far worse than misguided legal thinking, it was profoundly un-American: a Methodist bishop compared *Engel* to "taking a star or stripe off the flag." Whatever barometer one deployed, it was clear the negative reaction to *Engel* far surpassed the Court's other unpopular opinions. A Gallup Poll revealed that 79% of Americans approved of Bible-reading and prayer in public schools. Letters to newspapers came in at a three-to-one ratio against the ruling and nearly all the mail received by Congress on the topic stood in opposition to *Engel*. The justices also found themselves inundated with hate mail, some 5,000 letters and telegrams alone in the first month after issuing *Engel*—a new record.

Engel gave southern politicians something new to grouse about. "They put the Negroes in the schools," complained an Alabama congressman, "and now they've driven God out." Southern politicians may have taken the lead but the Court's critics among the political literati came from all corners of the country. A Long Island politician condemned *Engel* as "the most tragic in the history of the United States." Connecticut Senator Prescott Bush, the forefather of two future presidents and a moderate on social issues—he served as Planned Parenthood's first treasurer in 1947—found the decision "unfortunate" and "divisive." No matter the region, the response was nearly universal: every governor other than New York's Nelson Rockefeller denounced the justices.

Congressmen submitted more than 150 bills seeking to overturn *Engel*. Among these proposals, some of the zingers from Red Monday returned only to fade away like the nighttime streaks of a meteor shower. One proposal, a constitutional amendment with a legitimate shot of succeeding, emerged from this stockpile of dread and resentment. It wasn't sponsored by Thurmond, Eastland or any of the other southerners whose legislative counterattacks flopped. Nor did it originate from someone with stout conservative credentials or religious affiliations. The surprising father of this constitutional amendment was none other Dirksen. "How strange that we spend hundreds of millions of public funds every year to . . . harden the muscles of American youth," he complained to the press, "but when it comes to hardening the spiritual muscles through . . . prayer, it becomes enshrouded in quaint legalism and the jargon of church and state. Give Caesar what he requires but give God a little also." The Minority Leader spent a great amount of political capital in the four years after *Engel* pursuing the awesome task of amending the Constitution with a proposal that would have amounted to the first modification of the Bill of Rights in the nation's history. Following lengthy hearings and floor debates, his crusade to reverse *Engel* came to an end on September 21, 1966. The 49-37 Senate tally in favor of the Amendment reflected the significant popularity of his measure but fell nine votes shy of the two-thirds needed to get the proposal to the next stage of the amendment process. It was by no means an embarrassing outcome but it revealed once again how difficult it was to undo the Court's rulings through the legislative process—a lesson Fortas's attackers remembered all too well.

JULY–AUGUST, 1968

Thurmond had always been an unabashed showman. His calisthenics before the press and long-winded filibusters attested to this trait. In one of the more bizarre moments, in 1964 he wrestled Texas Senator Ralph Yarborough to the ground over the selection of an administrator he disliked. Flipping through pornographic magazines (*Nudie-Fax* seemed to be his favorite that day) during Deputy Attorney General Warren Christopher's testimony on July 23, he had reached a new low. In a phone call with the president, Smathers called Thurmond a "real nut" for this latest mischief. But for Thurmond, it was far easier to cast the justices as extremists for shielding adult content than to attack them over *Brown*, which was widely accepted outside of the South. What public figure, after all, would openly defend pornography? Certainly Hugh Hefner (and later Larry Flynt) volunteered but not many others outside the adult industry were eager to risk their reputations over the issue. Even if an elected official found adult materials socially tolerable during an age of sexual awakening or appreciated the constitutional tradeoffs involved, openly backing the purveyors of the smut trade would destroy his electoral prospects. For these very reasons, mainstream free-speech advocates also largely remained on the sidelines of the obscenity debate throughout the 1960s, leaving it up to the Court to uphold the Constitution's edicts and bear the brunt of the criticism for taking a principled stand on the subject.

If Thurmond's open perusal of nude magazines during the hearing weren't enough to embarrass the Judiciary Committee, his exchange with Christopher could have won the award for the most awkward moment of the hearings. After handing Christopher three pornographic magazines, Thurmond began his inquisition.

Thurmond: If you were a judge on the Supreme Court, would you hold such material as this obscene?

Christopher: Senator, I am not able to answer that question. . . .

Thurmond: Does it shock you that this material is so readily available . . . ?

Christopher: No, I am not surprised by it, Senator.

Thurmond: You are not surprised by it—in view of the decisions by the Supreme Court permitting it to be sold?

Christopher: Were you asking a question, Senator?

Thurmond: . . . I ask you why—upon what your answer is based . . .

Christopher: Because it has become commonplace in our society . . .

Thurmond: And why is it commonplace? Because the Supreme Court has made it commonplace, hasn't it?

In the nineteenth century, Henry Clay, Daniel Webster, and the upper chamber's other illustrious statesmen helped establish the Senate's self-congratulatory attitude, its sense of superiority and gravitas over the House. It says something about the Senate and its disdain for the Warren Court that Thurmond's colleagues allowed him to disgrace the world's greatest deliberative body without a single reprimand.

With all of this pornography swirling around the Capitol, it was inevitable the senators would get their hands on it. Eastland assigned three members of the Judiciary Committee—Arkansas's John McClellan, Hawaii's Hiram Fong, and Michigan's Philip Hart—to watch *0-7*, one of the films Clancy had detailed in his testimony, and report back to the committee. Disgusted by what they saw, Fong and McClellan couldn't bring themselves to back Fortas under any circumstance. "If the issue was whether this film was hardcore pornography," McClellan exclaimed at a closed door session of the Judiciary Committee on July 24, "and if the Court decision held it was not, I could not vote for my brother who made such a ruling on a film like that." He insisted that everyone on the committee watch the film to get a better understanding of the Court's lax attitude. "It is hardcore pornography, there is no question about it," Fong concurred. "And in my judgement," Thurmond added, "there could be no more hardcore pornography than there is—I cannot imagine what it would be." Later in the meeting, Thurmond described his mission to the capital's downtown where he found magazines depicting naked "men or women... in all kinds of positions." Was there nothing the 65-year-old senator wouldn't do for the sake of the Republic?

To circumvent the committee's refusal to publicly air *0-7* at the hearings, Thurmond invited members of the press and his fellow senators to watch the film in the Judiciary Committee's regular hearing room. Tame by present-day standards, *0-7* depicted a woman—wearing a garter belt and transparent panties—exposing her breasts, bottom, and pubic region. Twisting and turning her body throughout the silent film, the dramatic moment of the movie took place when she lowered her panties to expose her genitalia for a fleeting second. About fourteen minutes long, *0-7* was a popular peep-show in the penny arcades in Los Angeles.

The audience at Thurmond's peep-show wasn't as impressed. After all of his colleagues turned down his invitation, the senator managed to lure twenty members of the press to the first viewing. A female reporter from *The New York Times* told those in attendance not to think of the event as a "witch hunt but as a bitch hunt." Forced to make do without a screen, Thurmond used a coin-operated projector to show the film against a wood-paneled wall, making the woman's body appear as if it was shedding skin. Instead of responding with indignation, the journalists giggled and cracked jokes throughout the episode. It wasn't the loftiest moment for the Senate or the Washington press corps.

Realizing *0-7* was too tame to induce the desired outrage, Eastland sent an aide to Michigan to find a copy of *Flaming Creatures*, another one of the pornographic films on Clancy's list. While it was defended by Susan Sontag as an experimental, avant-garde art film intended for private audiences, when Eastland and a handful of senators and reporters watched the 40-minute film in the Capitol, they identified every form of deviancy the chairman needed to hang Fortas: gang rape, homosexuality, and graphic sexual acts. One senator complained the movie explored "transvestitism." Another told a reporter it "was so sick, I couldn't even get aroused." One viewer lashed out at Fortas on the Senate floor. "I am not going back," he swore, as if he had returned from the Underworld. "I have seen one Fortas film—I have seen enough." For those senators unwilling to watch *Flaming Creatures*, the ever-officious Thurmond ordered his staff to distribute black-and-white stills from the film.

As Thurmond added new entries to what came to be dubbed the "Fortas Film Festival," airing the movies in the Senate's recording studio and in various offices, senators trickled in to watch the reruns. The episode sparked off "a sudden seizure of the jollies." Members of the House complained their Senate colleagues had all the fun and Senate aides chuckled when they saw their bosses recruit other senators to the viewing sessions. Rumors spread of Thurmond's goal of airing the films in the holiest spot in the Capitol—the Senate floor. Washington's finest wondered whether "ole Strom had gone bananas at last."

Over the course of several weeks, many of the thirty senators who watched the films were left stunned. "Even those Senators, such as myself, who started the offensive against Justice Fortas on more lofty grounds," Griffin confessed, "attended the screenings and were shocked by what we saw." Near universally, they could not comprehend why the justices would unleash these monstrosities upon the public. "If you want to find a socially redeeming feature in the films," Griffin's aide told the senator, "you can say they provided work for the models." The president thought Griffin was just putting on an act. "He wasn't worried about pornography," he told Clark. "Anybody'd look at his face and tell he's not—that doesn't bother him!"

Whether or not these senators were genuinely appalled or just playing the part, the repercussions for Fortas were devastating. "[T]he movies were what the opposition needed to make their positions jell," Dirksen told the White House staff. One southerner began calling Fortas "Mr. Obscenity". The moniker was as crass and artless as it was effective. Senators looking for a reason to vote against Fortas now found one. Fortas's remaining backers lost heart when the opposition managed to equate a vote for Fortas into an endorsement for degeneracy. "[W]hen the debate gets underway it won't do Abe Fortas any good," a liberal senator told *Newsweek*, "it won't do the Supreme Court any good and it won't do the country any good." "You know this obscenity thing will be the issue that gets Fortas," Eastland boasted to a member of Griffin's staff. "Once the public is aroused, it'll be all over." It was aroused all right:

mail coming into the Senate—a barometer of constituent views—was pouring in 25 to 1 against Fortas.

Ideal fodder for late-night talk shows, the Fortas Film Festival practically invited parodies from the press corps. Avoiding this satirical tone, Kilpatrick approached the issue with the outmost sincerity. The film he watched during one of the Senate's screenings, he wrote, "is utterly without redeeming social importance. It goes far beyond community standards of decency. This was the verdict not only of the trial jury, but of every judge . . . until the conviction was overturned by" Fortas and four other justices. Seeing how outraged the public had become, Kilpatrick pressed to have the nomination rest on this one issue above all of Fortas's reputed sins. "Boil the issue down to this lip-licking slut," his column urged, "writhing carnally on a sofa, while a closeup camera dwells lasciviously on her genitals. . . . Is this what the Constitutions means?"

Considering how difficult it was to discern Fortas's specific role in the obscenity cases, the incident—like no other episode in the drawn-out confirmation—exemplified how Fortas's nomination had turned into a trial of the Warren Court. "Perhaps Justice Fortas was not the cause," Griffin acknowledged, "but after these hearings he was regarded as a symbol of the liberal philosophy . . . exhibited by the highest court in the land."

As the leading liberal on the Judiciary Committee, Michigan Senator Philip Hart had the unpleasant task of being the point man for the administration. Revered for standing up for the weak and vulnerable, "Hart proved that a saint could actually get elected to the Senate," Senator Douglas once said. Soft-spoken, reserved, and incapable of feigning the histrionics mastered by some of his peers, Hart's graying beard and quiet delivery gave him the appearance of a deliberative professor. He was the only living senator to have a Senate building named after him even though he never chaired a major committee or sponsored a historic bill. His colleagues honored him because he personified the ideals they strived for. He wasn't the most powerful senator. He wasn't the most accomplished senator. He was simply known as the "The Conscience of the Senate."

A veteran legislator who had steered some of the era's iconic legislation

MICHAEL BOBELIAN

through the Senate, Hart became the "nerve center" of the chamber's liberal bloc when Hubert Humphrey departed to become vice president. Working closely with Christopher, Hart tried to counter every one of the opposition's moves. He lobbed softballs at Fortas during the justice's testimony and vouched for Fortas to the press. While conceding that *0-7* was a "dirty movie," he unsuccessfully tried to turn the conversation to the First Amendment rather than the film's merits.

Urging his colleagues at the Judiciary Committee's executive session on July 24 to vote on the nomination so that it could be sent to the full Senate for a final vote, he tried to shoot down McClellan's request for another week. Concerned by the continuous delays the nomination endured, Hart knew that with the political conventions slated for August, Congress would not reconvene until September, putting the nomination at further risk. None of his entreaties worked. Eager to dig deeper into obscenity, the one issue that had really caught on with the public, Fortas's enemies within the committee managed to postpone a vote.

By the end of July, the opposition to the nomination had become formidable, coalescing around what Griffin characterized as a "grab bag of anti-Fortas issues." Fueled and amplified by their resentment of the Warren Court, Fortas's detractors had their pick of weapons to bludgeon the nomination: Johnson's "lame duck" status, charges of cronyism, and now, obscenity. Their target agreed with the assessment. "It's been pretty bloody," Fortas wrote to Douglas, his former mentor and closest friend on the Court, days after his testimony. "All the accumulated venom about practically everything seems to have come to a focus."

Meanwhile, when members of Johnson's team—Clark and Christopher from the Justice Department, Fortas's former law firm partner Porter, and Manatos, Temple, Califano and others from the White House staff—met on July 24, they still counted 57 to 65 senators in opposition to a filibuster. Fortas's camp was still capable of winning but the dwindling headcount reflected the growing anxiety in the White House. Less than a week later, Barefoot Sanders urged the president to rally Fortas's "discouraged" backers, reach out to undecided senators, and commandeer the cabinet to orchestrate a media blitz.

For those "absolutely opposed" to the nomination, Sanders suggested doing "anything we can . . . to make life miserable" for them. Despite his pessimism, Sanders ended the four-page memo on an optimistic note. "So it is possible," he concluded, "the Republicans might fold in September after a token fight."

He must not have been paying attention to Nixon's campaign.

CHAPTER 12

"REPUBLICANS SHOULD ADHERE TO THE PRINCIPLES OF THE PARTY OF LINCOLN"

AUGUST, 1968

Narrowly defeated by Kennedy in 1960 and left for dead after his humiliating loss in the 1962 California governor's race—the defeat Warren and Kennedy gleefully celebrated on Air Force One— Nixon made one of the most improbable comebacks in political history. Soaring through the 1968 primaries, he emerged as the odds-on favorite to capture the Republican nomination heading into the summer. To hold on to his lead though, Nixon had to fend off two rivals from the opposite ends of the GOP's ideological spectrum: New York Governor Nelson Rockefeller, the leader of its liberal wing, as well as the conservative favorite, California Governor Ronald Reagan. In an era when delegates at the party's convention rather than primaries determined the ultimate victor, Nixon eyed the South to clinch the nomination. It was a simple matter of arithmetic. The 356 southern delegates at the convention constituted nearly half the number needed to win. If Nixon could capture the vast majority of these delegates, as Barry Goldwater had done four years earlier, he could secure victory in the first round and avoid the type of open contest that had doomed frontrunners in the past.

It didn't take a political genius to ascertain the South's wish list. Upholding "law and order," protecting the textile industry, and maintaining a strong military in the face of anti-war protesters and draft-dodgers were of paramount importance to the region. But nothing eclipsed the South's obsession with civil rights. Petrified that their boundless efforts to stall *Brown*'s implementation had finally run their course, southern politicians wanted the Justice Department to back away from its strident push to desegregate the region's schools and craved the addition of new justices amenable to perpetuating the cat-and-mouse games local governments employed to postpone integration indefinitely. The sense of urgency was palpable, all the more so because the Court on May 27, 1968 rejected a southern school district's "freedom of choice" plan, the last and best hope in a long line of schemes devised to evade *Brown*.

Since 1964, Nixon had been traversing the nation campaigning for Republicans, and like an anthropologist doing field-work, was on the prowl for information to gauge the electorate's mood. The feedback he gleaned from southern audiences helped him craft his message in 1968. Nixon never publicly uttered a racial epithet. Nor did he issue harangues against civil rights advocates. He didn't deliver hate-filled speeches about integration either. In fact, Nixon publicly endorsed, albeit halfheartedly, the twin pillars of integration, *Brown* and the 1964 Civil Rights Act, and presented himself as the wise, respectable alternative to Wallace. But Nixon had mastered the ways—discreet, subtle, yet unambiguous ways, to let southerners know he would fulfill their wishes.

This turnabout on civil rights was among the most cynical moves of his career. In an effort to grab credit for *Brown*, Nixon had praised the GOP in 1956 for securing "the greatest advance for the rights of racial minorities since the Emancipation Proclamation." As Eisenhower stumbled his way through the issue, African-American leaders considered Nixon their principal ally in the White House. Jackie Robinson went as far as thanking Nixon for his valiant stance. Calling for a "strong civil rights platform" at the 1960 convention, Nixon unequivocally maintained this posture well into the decade: in an op-ed celebrating the GOP's gains in the South in 1966, he warned Republicans "not to go prospecting for the fool's gold of racist votes. . . . Any Republican victory that would come of courting racists," he cautioned, "would be a defeat for our future in the South, and our party in the Nation. . . . Republicans should adhere to the principles of the party of Lincoln." As the most recognized Republican of the era to complete this about-face, Nixon's opportunistic reversal on civil rights blazed a path for the party's eventual takeover of the region.

To implement his "Southern Strategy," Nixon turned to the region's king-maker Strom Thurmond. Serving as Goldwater's point-man in the South in the 1964 presidential election had established Thurmond as the GOP's leading figure in the region. The senator's patronage, Nixon acknowledged, "was essential to me." Heading into the 1968 Republican convention, Nixon had to woo Thurmond away from Reagan. "I love the man," Thurmond said of the former actor. "He's the best hope we've got." Unable to match Johnson's powers of persuasion, Kennedy's aura, and Reagan's John Wayne-like muscularity, charming an audience was not Nixon's forte. What he lacked in charisma he made up for in concocting one of the most calculated political campaigns the nation had seen. "I was doing serious courting and hard counting," Nixon admitted in regard to his meetings with southern Republicans on May 31 and June 1, 1968 in Atlanta. Encouraged by Harry Dent, Thurmond's chief advisor and the progenitor of the Southern Strategy, Nixon turned to the Court to demonstrate his bona fides to southern leaders. In a far-reaching presentation, Nixon emphasized that the "most important" thing he could accomplish in office would be to "appoint sound people to the . . . Court." Conceding that no one could undo *Brown*, Nixon vowed to undercut it by appointing justices who would tolerate the South's desire to integrate at a snail's pace. "That grabbed Strom Thurmond like nothing else," Dent remembered. Salivating at the prospect of a sympathetic judiciary, Thurmond pledged to deliver the South in return. The alliance paid immediate dividends for Nixon. In Thurmond's public endorsement three weeks later, he professed that Nixon "offers America the best hope of recovering from . . . a power-grasping Supreme Court."

To ward off the "stop Nixon" drive forged by Reagan and Rockefeller at the Republican convention in Miami Beach, Nixon needed to hold on to the 298 southern delegates informally committed to him. Since their pledge to Nixon resembled an arranged marriage more than a sincere commitment, the region's delegates preferred their "first love," the tall and handsome California governor brandishing unimpeachable conservative credentials. Though he had remained coy about his interest in the job, when Reagan finally revealed his desire to head the party's ticket, the southern delegates flocked to his side like paparazzi at a celebrity sighting.

Reagan may have been the more appealing candidate but Nixon had locked in the kingmaker as his patron. Acting as Nixon's "fire brigade," Thurmond came to the rescue each time Nixon's hold over a southern delegation waned. Shuffling from meeting to meeting, it sometimes meant reassuring them about Nixon's dedication to their principles. Other times, it meant refuting rumors of Nixon eyeing a liberal running mate. More often than not, it required him to pull back the southern delegates from Reagan's magnetic grasp. "We must quit using our hearts and start using our heads," he pleaded. "I love Reagan, but Nixon's the one."

To firm up his flagging support, Nixon also met with delegates from seven southern states at the Hilton Plaza two days before the balloting on August 6. It was one of the bigger contingents of delegates he would have to appeal to during the four-day convention. Nixon was a professional pettifogger. Whether the slight came from his distracted mother, arrogant classmates, biased reporters, elitist Ivy Leaguers, the righteous Warren or the fickle Eisenhower, Nixon collected these snubs to motivate himself. And like a bloodhound on a hunt, he identified these grievances within the electorate better than any politician of his era. He built his 1968 presidential run on the resentments of the so-called "silent majority"—blue-collar workers, suburbanites, social conservatives, and white southerners. Tired of serving as a punching bag for the nation's liberals, no group was more resentful than the South's white population of its pariah status. Nixon exploited this inferiority complex during his meeting with the southern delegates. "I don't believe you should use the South as a whipping boy," he exclaimed while working his way through a list of issues like bullet points in a PowerPoint presentation. When asked about the Fortas nomination, he explained in private what he had said only once in public: "I think that [the] chief justice should represent the mandate of the future and not Johnson's mandate of the past." The crowd applauded the declaration and the question offered him the opportunity to transition to one of his favorite talking points: "If I have the chance to appoint justices to the Supreme Court," he added, "they will be the kind of men I want—and I want men who are strict constructionists; men that interpret the law and don't try to make the law."

Combined with Thurmond's backing, Nixon's superior organizational reach and last-minute reassurances clinched the victory. Earning three-fourths of the southern delegates, he inched past the finish line with only 25 votes to spare.

For the vice-presidential pick, Nixon promised he "wasn't going to stuff a ... running mate down the throat of the South." Having given Thurmond veto power over the selection, Nixon sidestepped the six untouchables Thurmond blacklisted—including the party's leading liberal, Rockefeller, New York's Mayor John Lindsay, and Senator Charles Percy of Illinois—but also skipped over the kingmaker's two favorites for the job—Griffin and Reagan. Maryland Governor Spiro Agnew was a dull yet satisfactory choice, a running mate the historian Dan Carter called "a rather dignified clone of George Wallace" who Nixon felt could help him "win the entire rimland of the South."

Coming off his victory at the convention, Nixon carried the Southern Strategy over to the general election. In doing so, he ratcheted up what his immediate predecessors had set in motion. After Reconstruction, the South had operated as a one-party region dominated by Democrats. The "solid South" rarely strayed from its devotion to the Democratic Party regardless of the appeal—or lack thereof—of its presidential candidates. 1904 marked a perfect example of this phenomenon. Theodore Roosevelt, the Republican candidate that year, won the popular vote by nearly twenty points yet couldn't capture a single southern state. His Democratic counterpart, an obscure judge from upstate New York, was neither a southern stalwart nor a magnetic figure. The results were so lopsided at times, it was if the Democratic candidates were running unopposed: for eleven consecutive presidential contests starting in 1900, Democrats received more than 90% of South Carolina's votes. The exceptions to this dominance were few and far between. Between 1880, the first election after Reconstruction, to 1948, every Democratic presidential candidate won Arkansas. Alabama, South Carolina, and Mississippi broke with the party only in 1948 to support Thurmond's Dixiecrats. Virginia, Texas, Florida, and North Carolina also strayed only once, and that came in 1928 when their voters recoiled at the prospect of supporting a Catholic candidate, Al Smith. Georgia deserved the award for loyalty. To find a non-Democratic winner in the Peach

State, one had to travel back to Zachary Taylor in 1848.

The GOP's futility in the region had amounted to a concession of more than one hundred electoral votes before the first ballots were cast. Unable to break the Democratic stranglehold, Republicans finally found an opening in the late 1940s when a fissure between northern liberals and southern conservatives loosened the Democrats' monopoly, allowing Eisenhower to capture nearly half the South's electoral votes in 1952. Eager to build on this fragile beachhead, Eisenhower sought to increase the party's appeal to southern voters. In an era when the issue of civil rights exploded onto the national scene, that meant accommodating the South's desire to maintain the racial status quo. South Carolina's Governor James Byrnes made this clear to Eisenhower at a meeting in the White House early in his presidency, telling him that presidential support for integration "would forever defeat any possibility of developing a real Republican... party in the South." Eisenhower took this message to heart, but try as he might to placate the South, his unwillingness to back the region's defiance of *Brown* limited the GOP's gains.

Republicans found new opportunities to make headway in the South when Kennedy and Johnson sponsored civil rights legislation and ramped up the government's enforcement of *Brown*. In a pair of prescient articles published in 1963, James Kilpatrick openly asked white southerners: "Why stay a Democrat? ... I used to believe that, on balance, the South has benefited from ... one-party government; today I am not so sure of this." Pointing to Goldwater's popularity in the region, his headline in the *National Review* weeks later declared: "The South Goes Back Up for Grabs." Overcoming a century of Democratic dominance did not occur overnight. Liberal Republicans like Rockefeller remained staunchly committed to Lincoln's ideals and more than 80% of congressional Republicans voted for the 1964 Civil Rights Act. Unable to change their spots instantaneously, the GOP's takeover of the South was gradual and sporadic.

Barry Goldwater was the trailblazer in this change of course. Well before the conservative bellwether headed the Republican ticket in 1964, Goldwater had already established himself as one of the Court's most outspoken critics outside the South. "I have great respect for the Supreme Court . . . but I cannot believe that I display that respect by submitting abjectly to abuses of power by the Court," he wrote in *The Conscience of a Conservative*, his 1960 book that came to serve as a bible for conservatives. Condemning the Court for its "unconstitutional trespass into the legislative sphere, . . ." he criticized the justices in a manner that sounded as though it could have come right out of the Southern Manifesto. "In effect," Goldwater wrote of *Brown*, "the Court said that what matters is not the ideas of the men who wrote the Constitution, but the *Court's* ideas. . . . I am therefore not impressed," he declared, "by the claim that the Supreme Court's decision on school integration is the law of the land."

With a handful of exceptions, the Court had played an inconsequential role in presidential politics even when its unpopularity could have been exploited for electoral gain. In 1935, FDR blasted the Court during his "horse and buggy" speech for its continued demolition of his New Deal initiatives. Congress also introduced dozens of anti-Court measures at the start of 1936. Yet, despite persistent pleas from fellow Democrats during the presidential election that year, Roosevelt refused to turn the Court into a campaign issue, going as far as scrubbing out any mention of the institution from the party's platform.

By 1964, Republicans had found electoral opportunities in the Warren Court's controversial rulings: "Attacking the Supreme Court, on apportionment, for shielding Communists and for ruling out school prayer could become a potent vote-getter," a Michigan congressman observed months before the election. Goldwater harnessed this rage for his presidential run. "I weigh my words carefully when I say that of all three branches of Government," he announced in a major policy speech delivered to the American Political Science Association in September, 1964, "today's Supreme Court is the least faithful . . . to the principle of legitimacy in the exercise of power." Irate at the Court's takeover of "legislative power," Goldwater contended that the job of "keeping the law up to date should be in the hands of the legislatures . . . not just in the hands of the nine appointed Justices." The Court's many offenses—what he dubbed as "jackassian" rulings—allowed Goldwater to customize his remarks for the diverse set of audiences he encountered on the campaign trail. In Florida, he blamed the Court for the collapse of "law and order." The justices, he explained, "say that a criminal defendant must be given a sporting chance to go free even though nobody doubts in the slightest that he is guilty." "I am firmly convinced," he told southerners, "that the Constitution does not require the States to maintain racially mixed schools." And to a Mormon crowd, he asked: "is this the time in our nation's history . . . to ban Almighty God from our school rooms?"

The level of Court-bashing made it seem, as Anthony Lewis of *The New York Times* observed, that Goldwater was "running against the nine justices instead of Lyndon B. Johnson." This was no exaggeration. Throughout the campaign, Goldwater repeatedly linked the Warren Court to his opponent: "the trend of constitutional interpretation under the influence of the prevailing Democratic Party doctrine has been such that the Constitution is now widely held to mean only what those who hold power for the moment choose to say that it means," he declared in a speech typifying this strategy. Though Johnson deflected Goldwater's attempts to wed his candidacy to the judicial body, he had, like Kennedy, publicly embraced the Court's agenda. To Warren's delight, this support ended the isolation endured under Eisenhower but allowed Goldwater to successfully paint the Court as Johnson's ally. Aligning the Warren Court with the Democrat Party had far bigger repercussions beyond the 1964 election. The public's view of the Court began to take on a partisan and ideological quality not seen in previous generations. Polling data bore this out: 90% of Goldwater's supporters were critical of the Court while 80% of voters with favorable views of the Court backed Johnson.

Goldwater further hitched his candidacy to the Court by promising to appoint like-minded justices that would "redress constitutional interpretations in favor of the public." "When vacancies occur," Goldwater swore, "we want men appointed to the Court who will support the Constitution, not scoff at it." In another speech, he asked: "Do you want Lyndon Johnson's cronies or men who will respect the Constitution . . . ?" On the campaign trail, Thurmond reaffirmed Goldwater's message:

...a vote for Barry Goldwater is a vote to end judicial tyranny. Barry Goldwater as President will appoint real constitutional lawyers to the U.S. Supreme Court.

The overt association of Goldwater's candidacy with future nominations
broke new ground in presidential politics. While Court observers watched in
horror at his politicization of the judicial body, Goldwater's audiences roared
in approval. He hadn't forged these diatribes from scratch after all. Court antagonists had already built the bonfire. All he did was throw in a match, and
there was no organization more eager to add fuel to that fire than the John
Birch Society.

Founded in 1958 by Robert Welch, Jr.—a former Boston confectioner who
sat on the board of the National Association of Manufacturers—the Birchers
were on a mission to stamp out communists and their sympathizers—whom
they referred to as "comsymps." Preying on the same fears exploited by Mc
Carthy, Welch subscribed to conspiracy theories that would have made the
late Wisconsin senator seem mild-mannered by comparison. Having already
smeared Eisenhower as a "card-carrying Communist," the Birchers considered Warren their arch enemy. In its recruitment pamphlet, the Society
blamed Warren for his "long...powerful, and open pro-Communist support"
and alleged that Eisenhower picked the chief justice to perpetuate a communist conspiracy. The Red Monday decisions provided obvious targets for the
Society, but *Brown*, which Welch considered a communist plot, also raised the
group's suspicion. "It is obvious that the Warren-led Court intends," the Society exclaimed without an iota of irony, "to declare the whole Constitution ...
unconstitutional." Welch offered a cure to rid the nation of this cancer: "the
way to make the Justices ... behave is to impeach the ringleader."

Preposterous and radical in equal portions, Welch's "Impeach Earl Warren" campaign nevertheless helped position the Society as the pinnacle right-
wing group of the era. Armed with hundreds of billboards calling for Warren's removal—including one greeting spectators at the Indianapolis 500
Raceway—the Society's campaign raised its profile, doubling its income by

1963. The team of 35 people Welch assigned to lead the impeachment efforts generated pamphlets, buttons, and even matchbooks putting out various versions of the same slogan: "CURB THE SUPREME COURT: Help Impeach EARL WARREN." Or the more diabolical: "SAVE OUR REPUBLIC! IMPEACH EARL WARREN." A "Warren Impeachment Packet" sold for $1; billboard posters cost $20. Nothing was too outlandish for the Birchers. In 1962, the Society rewarded a $1,000 prize (worth about $8,000 in 2019) to a UCLA student for submitting the best essay on the topic. A year later, 75 protestors chanted "Impeach Earl Warren" for two hours in the middle of a ceremony at the New York City Bar Association honoring the chief justice. The picketers tossed their placards at Warren and his wife as they were on their way out of the venue. Unfazed by the assault, Warren greeted them with a smile and hung a *New Yorker* cartoon on his office wall depicting a parody of the iconic painting *Whistler's Mother*, in which she is embroidering an "IMPEACH EARL WARREN" pillow.

That was Warren's usual disposition—to brush off these invectives with humor no matter how alarming they seemed. One letter from Aptos, California, typified the degree of hatred directed at the chief justice: "Greetings on your 75th anniversary!" it began. "We hope to read your obituary . . . before you reach your 76th birthday." Of all the hate bombs hurled at Warren, the Birch campaign made the most headway, revealing the depth and breadth of the animosity directed at the Court. That hostility even penetrated what should have been the heart of Warren country. Officials found 2,000 impeachment pamphlets in Los Angeles's Earl Warren High School.

AUGUST, 1968

Goldwater's ability to capture five southern states in the 1964 presidential election despite getting trounced in one of the nation's most lopsided elections set the stage for Nixon four years later. Nixon's primary obstacle to duplicating Goldwater's success was Wallace, whose third-party run bedeviled Nixon's Southern Strategy. If Wallace takes "most of the South," Nixon confessed to Harry Dent, his leading strategist in the South, he wouldn't win enough electoral votes elsewhere to clinch the election.

Ironically, Wallace's start as racial moderate earned him the NAACP's endorsement in the 1958 governor's primary race. After losing that primary, however, he promised, "I will never be out-niggered again," and just like Arkansas' Faubus, he reinvented himself as an ardent segregationist. Rooted in racial animus, Wallace's 1968 campaign resembled Thurmond's Dixiecrat rebellion. But it had far broader sectional appeal than Thurmond's experiment twenty years earlier. Wallace's American Independent campaign assembled a series of populist economic policies and blended them with a raging ferocity against civil rights and the counter-culture. It was tailor-made for the South, where Wallace polled strongly, but also tapped into disenchanted voters elsewhere: Wallace captured more than 10% of the vote in Alaska, Delaware, Idaho, Indiana, Kansas, Maryland, Michigan, Missouri, Nevada, Ohio, and Oklahoma in the general election.

Nixon's sectional appeal, which had worked so effectively at the GOP convention, continued into the general election. Since only 30% of Americans favored liberal justices, Nixon was able to turn to the same grievances Goldwater had relied upon four years earlier. With law and order emerging as the nation's largest domestic concern in 1968, Nixon seized on what had already become a pastime for the American right: blaming the Court for rising crime rates.

A series of rulings starting with *Mallory* in 1957 came to a highpoint with *Miranda v. Arizona*, the 1966 case questioning whether the Fifth Amendment's right against self-incrimination applied to police interrogations. Warren could have limited the ruling to providing an answer. Instead, he used the case as an opportunity to practically create a field manual for every police district in the country, giving birth to the "*Miranda* rights" familiar to anyone who has watched a police procedural on television. Was it a sign of wisdom or hypocrisy that several of his precepts overturned the heavy-handed practices Warren employed as a district attorney? Either way, it opened Warren up for additional criticism.

The usual critics were on the frontlines of these attacks: "Enough has been done for those who murder and rape and rob," Ervin exclaimed. "It is time to do something for those who do not wish to be murdered or raped or robbed."

But what severely damaged the Warren Court's reputation were the biting dissents from Tom Clark, John Marshall Harlan, and Byron White, who labelled Warren's majority opinion a "constitutional straitjacket." Adding to the animus directed at Warren, White's dissenting opinion legitimized those detractors who linked these criminal procedure rulings to rising crime rates: "the Court's rule will return a killer, a rapist or other criminal to the streets . . . to repeat his crime whenever it pleases him."

Less than a quarter of Americans supported *Miranda,* and law enforcement was equally outraged. Boston's police commissioner dreaded that "criminal trials no longer will be a search for truth, but a search for technical error." Reno's police chief summed up the sentiment of police departments from across the country, characterizing *Miranda* as "another shackle. . . . Some day they may give us an equal chance with the criminals." State and federal judges, including Warren Burger, criticized the ruling. The best-selling author Truman Capote even chimed in, telling a Senate subcommittee that in "wailing about the rights of the criminal suspect," the Court ignored "the rights of the victims." Under the Court's limitations, he added, the killers profiled in *In Cold Blood* "would not even have been brought to trial, much less convicted."

It's difficult to appreciate the degree of contempt directed at the Court's criminal procedure rulings at the time. Criminals going free on "technicalities" became a common refrain as did recriminations against "soft on crime" judges. On top of the volumes of criticism and the hand-wringing over Warren's latest atrocity, the government established various commissions, held countless hearings, and hosted numerous law enforcement conventions decrying the Court's role in rising crime rates. Dozens of legislative proposals bounced around Congress. Weeks before Warren announced his retirement, Ervin tried to sneak a particularly harsh anti-Court rider into the Omnibus Crime Control and Safe Streets Act of 1968. The "real 'enemy' of the . . . bill," *The New York Times* explained in an editorial, "is not the criminal but the United States Supreme Court. It is the 'Warren Court' that is really under attack."

The public's attitude made it easy to draw such a conclusion. Seventy-eight percent of the respondents in a poll taken in 1968 felt the judiciary unfairly impeded law enforcement and Gallup listed "law and order" as the nation's most important domestic issue for the first time. These concerns didn't simply originate from fear-mongering politicians eager to exploit the issue. Crime was up, staggeringly so: the murder rate rose more than 50% during the 1960s, rapes and assaults more than doubled, and robberies nearly tripled.

AUGUST, 1968

Many Americans blamed the Court for rising crime rates and the proliferation of riots. Nixon exploited this connection on the campaign trail, practically attacking the Court as often as he railed against the Johnson administration. With Thurmond looking on from a few steps away, "our courts... have gone too far," Nixon declared during his acceptance speech at the GOP convention, swinging his right hand as if smashing a gavel, "in weakening the peace forces as against the criminal forces in this country." The convention's roar obliged him to pause for a moment. "[T]he first civil right of every American," he continued, "is to be free from domestic violence." In his campaign publication, *Toward Freedom From Fear*, he blamed *Miranda* and other cases for emboldening criminals. Referring to a "barbed wire of legalisms," he put the onus on the Court for allowing seven of eight criminals to go free—a statistic that was markedly wrong. Just as Clancy had claimed that pornographers were inspired by the Court's obscenity rulings at Fortas's hearings, Nixon argued that the "tragic lesson of guilty men walking free from hundreds of courtrooms across this country has not been lost on the criminal community."

On the campaign trail, Nixon merged these accusations with his critique of Hubert Humphrey. At one stop in Ohio, Nixon described how three confessed murderers went free because of the Court. "That's happening in thousands of cases all over America," he explained. Why wasn't his opponent equally outraged? Nixon supplied the answer: "Perhaps Mr. Humphrey's respectful silence on these far-reaching matters may stem from the fact that he has spent four years in obedience school."

Mimicking Goldwater's strategy, Nixon tweaked his message for each audience, emphasizing law and order in the Midwest while largely sticking to civil rights in the South. He dredged up fears of a communist takeover to a group of veterans and unearthed the dangers of pornography to a women's association. "It doesn't make me happy to say this," one of Nixon's advisors conceded, "but I think he's attacking the Supreme Court because he's convinced that's what the voters want." Nixon was right. A July, 1968 Gallup Poll revealed that only 36% of Americans held a favorable view of the Court, down nine points from a year earlier.

The Court-bashing portion of Nixon's typical stump speech ended with a pledge to appoint "strict constructionists" who would practice self-restraint and were "thoroughly experienced and versed in the criminal laws of the land." Listing Frankfurter and Harlan as his archetypes, "I'll never make a liberal appointment to the Supreme Court," he vowed. It was a bold move. No presidential candidate other than Goldwater had so closely tied his candidacy to the selection of justices. Yet, because of Nixon's success, this link became the norm: from the oft-cited "tough on crime" judges the GOP continually praised through the 1980s to Donald Trump's release of a list of potential nominees vetted by the Federalist Society in 2016.

Nixon's over-the-top pronouncements could not match Wallace, the linguistic maestro who attributed many of the nation's problems to the justices:

> In the period of the past three decades, we have seen the . . . Supreme Court transgress repeatedly upon the prerogatives of the Congress and exceed its authority by enacting judicial legislation. . . . We have seen them, in their solicitude for the criminal and lawless element of our society, shackle the police and other law enforcement agencies. . . . This is one of the principal reasons for the turmoil and the near revolutionary conditions which prevail in our country today. . . .

On top of *Brown*, Wallace railed against the usual laundry list of the Court's controversial rulings and promised to enact legislation returning prayer to schools and undoing the Court's restrictions on law enforcement. Nixon's campaign adviser Patrick Buchanan aptly described Wallace's ability to serve as a beacon for the hostility directed at the judicial body:

There was a tremendous counter revolution to what the Supreme Court was doing in the 50s and early 60s with its decisions on school prayer, and its decisions on integration, and its decisions later on, on abortion and things like that. . . . Governor Wallace was the first to hit these directly head-on to pick up on these issues and address these concerns of middle America. And he became really the tribune of middle America, the tribune of the people.

Wearing a smirk as he delivered his words with undiminished fury, Wallace never bothered to soften his approach the way Nixon had with his nuanced code-words. Implicit claims were of no use to him; his accusations were unequivocally explicit. In an interview with Kilpatrick published in the *National Review*, Wallace called the Court "a sorry, lousy, no-account outfit. . . . You can see what's happened: murder, rape, assault; and the criminals just laughin' while the police are crying for help." He exclaimed at one rally: "The Supreme Court is fixing it so you can't do anything about people who set cities on fire." In a typical campaign speech, he accused the Court of patronizing "convicted criminals, Communists, atheists, and clients of vociferous left-wing minority groups" in its quest to "destroy constitutional government in our country." Who else could the Court possibly encourage in its quest to destroy America? No matter how outlandish these statements sounded—such as the time he claimed Warren lacked "enough legal brains . . . to try a chicken thief"—these rants garnered the loudest applause at Wallace's rallies.

The reaction from Wallace's northern sympathizers was no different. His arrival on October 24 in Madison Square Garden set off a firestorm, attracting the KKK, the American Nazi Party—whose members donned "I like Eich" buttons in honor of the Holocaust's mastermind, Adolf Eichmann—and other right wing groups alongside 2,000 left-wing protestors. With 3,000 policemen playing referee, the two sides mocked, teased, and ranted at each other: Wallace's critics screamed "2-4-6-8 we don't want a fascist state" as his supporters hollered "Commie faggots!" in response. The performance inside the Garden was equally noxious. "The Supreme Court . . . has hand-cuffed the police," Wallace roared to the 16,000 in attendance while standing behind bullet-proof glass, "and tonight if you walk out of this building and are knocked in the head, the person who knocks you in the head is out of jail before you get in the hospital, and on Monday morning, they'll try a policeman about it." Whatever else one might think of Wallace, he had a knack for encapsulating the over-simplified view of the Court's criminal justice opinions in just a few words, and inducing outrage in the process. And just in case anyone wondered what ailed the nation, Wallace made sure to turn the mirror away from his audience towards the nine men in the Marble Palace. "Well, . . . you aren't to blame," he assured them. "[W]e don't have any sick society. We have a sick Supreme Court."

The impact of Nixon's campaign on Fortas's nomination, although indirect, was still substantial. When Johnson named Fortas to replace Warren on June 26, Nixon told the press that he should have allowed the incoming president to select the chief justice. After that initial outburst, he said little more. It wasn't for lack of desire. "Privately," Buchanan confessed, "Nixon wanted the Fortas nomination killed, but he did not want our fingerprints on the murder weapon." Having branded himself as the rational, sane moderate in contrast to Wallace, Nixon was afraid of being criticized for politicizing the confirmation. He remained noncommittal in public while privately encouraging Republicans to torpedo the nomination. Despite his public silence, his frequent criticism of the Court throughout his campaign boosted the anti-Fortas forces in the Senate. And his repeated vows to appoint justices to undo Warren's accomplishments made it clear to Fortas's opponents that if they successfully blocked his ascension, Nixon would reward them with a far more desirable alternative.

CHAPTER 13

"I RUINED HIS LIFE"

AUGUST–OCTOBER, 1968

With the Fortas Film Festival progressing fitfully, like a pebble intermittently digging into the sole of one's foot, the opposition prepared for its final push. A strategy session among thirteen congressional staffers on August 23 made it clear that not one of the senators represented at the meeting was wavering from his commitment to defeating Fortas. The aides agreed to divide up the work by subject matter. One person signed up for the lame duck issue. Another agreed to harp on cronyism. Thurmond's representative seized the "pornography issue" for his boss.

After Congress reconvened on September 4, Thurmond invited a police officer from Los Angeles to testify about *0-7*. The appearance of the vice agent was overkill; had it been up to Thurmond, that obscure art film would have received more attention than that year's Oscar winner—*Oliver!*.

When Griffin had started his lonesome crusade back in June, everyone from the press to Dirksen had dismissed him as an overmatched rookie out to slay a dragon with a pogo stick. His surprising performance earned him respect and contempt in equal doses. "Does he think he's still in the House?" a veteran senator grumbled of Griffin's behavior. "This is the Senate; this is the club. We don't do it that way." Griffin's boldness made it clear that he was not afraid of flouting the Senate's norms or defying his party's leadership. Now, with an assist from Thurmond, he prepared to deliver a knockout blow to Fortas's candidacy.

On July 19, a "man named O'Neil" from the American University Law School contacted Griffin's office to reveal that Fortas was teaching a seminar on social justice. The payment structure for the course, the source emphasized, appeared "very questionable." As far as the university employee knew, Fortas's former law partner, Paul Porter, raised the funds for the class from Fortas's friends and former clients. That fact alone made the arrangement dubious. The $15,000 in compensation, about seven times the typical remuneration for similar work and more than a third of Fortas's annual salary as a justice, turned this teaching gig into an ethical time-bomb. "If this is true," Griffin's aide told the senator immediately after finishing the conversation, "it'll break the case against Fortas."

On July 30, Griffin hinted at the possibility of unleashing new, damning details about Fortas's candidacy to a group of journalists at the National Press Club. After the talk, Fred Graham of *The New York Times* asked a senate staffer: the "Senator is just puffing—right?" Having enticed the reporter, the senator's assistant told Graham of the $15,000 payment. When the reporter failed to expose the payment arrangement, Griffin tried to coax the law school's dean, B.J. Tennery, to divulge its secrets. That also failed. With nowhere else to turn, Griffin passed the information on to the Judiciary Committee where Thurmond—a former collegiate track star—snatched it as if he was running the anchor leg of a relay race at the Olympics. In a phone call with Thurmond, Tennery at first refused to disclose the course's funding information. But when threatened with a subpoena, the dean succumbed to the senator's demands.

Testifying before the Judiciary Committee on September 13, Tennery disclosed the donors' names, including Gustave Levy (chairman of the New York Stock Exchange and an investment banker at Goldman Sachs), Troy Post (director of various companies), Maurice Lazarus (vice-chairman of Federated Department Stores), John Loeb (director of various companies), and Paul Smith (general counsel at Philip Morris). Solicited by Porter, they contributed $30,000 to pay the justice and cover the cost of tuition for the seventeen students enrolled in the class. "I do not believe that there is any law school dean in this country who would not have been overjoyed at the opportunity to have Mr. Justice Fortas as a teaching colleague," Tennery explained. "And I suggested to him . . . that he should be paid," the dean testified to the committee. "He left the amount entirely to my discretion." While no one had qualms about his motivation for bringing in a sitting justice to teach a course, the last portion of the dean's confession was patently suspicious.

In a rapid succession of questions, Thurmond was unable to get Tennery to admit that Fortas was the mastermind behind the payment arrangement. Thwarted on his first try, Thurmond then tried to loosen some other nugget of inculpatory information.

Thurmond: Could you tell us the highest salary paid to anyone any previous year for any seminar?

Tennery: . . . I can't recall that specifically, but I can tell you, I think what you would like to know. It certainly was considerably less than the Justice got.

Thurmond: . . . Would you mind telling us the largest salary paid any one individual... in any seminar prior to this one?

Tennery: I would say . . . it would be somewhere in the neighborhood of maybe $2,000.

That's all Thurmond needed.

No one could prove that Fortas was behind the ploy or whether he knew the donors' identities—which he did. It didn't matter. His critics had enough salacious material to tarnish him for his involvement in a scheme funneling an extraordinary sum of money from friends and former clients whose firms might come before the Court.

Already on the defensive, Fortas's supporters lost hope. "We were still counting" votes an advisor explained, until the seminar fee "destroyed us." Blindsided by yet another embarrassing revelation, some of Fortas's backers wondered why he didn't simply turn down the job once he was nominated. "I can't understand it. I just can't," William Proxmire, the Wisconsin senator, exclaimed in the Senate dining room, throwing his arms up in the air in frustration. "He's a wealthy man. His wife has a lucrative law practice. They have no children . . . to send through college. Why did he do it?"

Porter wept when discussing the fiasco with Califano. Having worked so hard to get his closest friend confirmed—turning his law firm into a "command post" for the undertaking—he unwittingly played a key role in Fortas's unmaking. Unfortunately for Porter, there was little time left for Fortas's supporters to stage a rally after suffering another lethal blow. Johnson pestered Senate liberals to continue to fight on. His staff diligently pounded out strategy memos and lobbied senators. The ABA and ad hoc legal groups organized by Porter and Christopher also entered the scene with last-ditch efforts, and the AFL-CIO made a final push. After the seminar disclosure, their support proved futile.

Watching his dear friend's prospects sink in slow motion, Porter lashed out at his allies. "Where in the hell are you and the rest of my liberal friends," he challenged John Kenneth Galbraith. "Whether we win this battle or not, I would not be pleased to reflect upon the studied indifference of my liberal friends on this issue." Johnson was equally disappointed with the Senate's liberals: "I just wish we had some talkers and hell-raisers on our side," he told the attorney general. They weren't the only senators to disappoint him. The president's floor leaders all but capitulated. "My own impression," Barefoot Sanders wrote to the president in mid-September, "is that Mansfield and Dirksen are going to do whatever they have promised . . . but that neither is approaching this fight with any enthusiasm, confidence, or sense of outrage."

Besides Dirksen and Hart, Johnson relied on Majority Leader Mike Mansfield to lead the nomination fight. After a stint as Johnson's Whip—or "errand boy"—in the late 1950s, Mansfield took over as Majority Leader in 1961 when Johnson moved on to the vice presidency. The two were a contrast in styles. Whereas Johnson was ambitious, manipulative, and domineering, Mansfield was self-effacing, transparent, and keen on transforming the Senate into a deliberative body of equals. "Mansfield was a consensus man" who tried to get his colleagues to agree on a position, observed Smathers, who served with both men. "Johnson himself was the consensus on all . . . legislation. . . . Johnson would decide what he wanted to do, then he would get those senators to go with him. Mansfield was exactly the opposite."

When told by *Time* magazine that he would appear on the cover, "That is bad news," Mansfield answered back, as if diagnosed with a fatal disease. "Publicity is something I don't need." Mansfield was humble to the point of shunning the title of "leader." "In the Senate," he told a reporter, "the word 'leader' is a misnomer. You don't lead. You try to see what the Senators want and then you follow. I am a follower."

Six feet tall and thin, with big ears jutting out from a narrow angular face, Mansfield was soft spoken, mild-mannered, and slow to anger. "There's not a nicer guy alive than Mansfield," explained Smathers. He was "the most saintly guy that I know." Maintaining a small staff and modest office, Mansfield shunned both Johnson's ostentatious displays of power and the dark arts he used to wield it. "I am neither a circus ringmaster, the master of ceremonies of a Senate nightclub, a tamer of Senate lions, or a wheeler and dealer," Mansfield declared on the Senate floor in response to criticism of his leadership. Mansfield restored the authority that Johnson had usurped back to committee chairmen and empowered the junior senators to break up the cabal his predecessor had relied upon to control the institution. Mansfield may have been naïve in the president's eyes but was beloved by his colleagues for freeing them of Johnson's despotic rule.

These attributes didn't make him a pushover, however. Born in Manhattan, Mansfield was shipped to Montana at the age of seven to live with his aunt when his mother died. He then dropped out of school at fourteen to sneak into the Navy. By the age of nineteen, he was the youngest person in the state to have seen combat in WWI. That wartime experience in his youth may not have hardened his empathic worldview but it certainly toughened him enough for the political arena. Although he would never reach Johnson's lofty heights, Mansfield was nevertheless at the helm when the Senate enacted the laundry list of Great Society legislation. As the decade progressed, however, Mansfield, an expert on the Far East who had taught Asian history at the University of Montana, drifted apart from Johnson over Vietnam.

Mansfield said and did all the right things in the early stages of the confirmation fight. He vowed to block any "talkathon" and undercut Griffin's charges: "If President Johnson is a lame duck," Mansfield told reporters in June, "anyone who even ran for a second term as president would have to be considered a lame duck." But the White House felt he practically invited a filibuster and failed to pressure the opposition by declining to schedule the Senate around the clock—a tactic Johnson had deployed to break the South's will during past filibusters.

At last, the Judiciary Committee voted 11-6 in favor of the nomination on September 17. On the eve of the debate scheduled to commence on September 25, the final vote predictions pouring into the White House were pessimistic. The damage done by the American University disclosure was now fully apparent. The Justice Department anticipated a 44-36 head count to end the filibuster, about fifteen fewer supporters than early September and well short of the margin needed for victory.

For the first time anyone could remember, Republicans led a filibuster with southern Democrats playing a supporting role. Directed by Griffin, Tower, and Tennessee's Howard Baker, it was a desultory affair lacking the dramatic showdowns of the past. With everyone expecting the opposition to prevail, no more than a half dozen senators were present at any given time. Johnson's primary floor leader, Hart, largely remained slumped in his chair. In all, nine senators spoke on Fortas's behalf while 22 of them delivered speeches opposing his confirmation. "The victory was ours," a senate aide explained, "it was just a matter [of] when they wanted to surrender." Johnson pondered giving up but decided to proceed after Fortas asked for an official vote.

As the three-month saga inched towards its inevitable conclusion, Johnson endured one more humiliation. Midway through the filibuster, Minority Leader Dirksen made an announcement that came as a surprise to all but those watching him closely enough to recognize the warning signs. Although a key element of the president's strategy, Johnson repeatedly worried about Dirksen's commitment. "We've got to get this thing through . . . early because if it drags out. . . . Dirksen will leave us," the president warned White House Special Counsel Larry Temple. Skeptical of the president's concerns, Temple pointed to all of Dirksen's boastful statements in favor of the nomination. "Just take my word for it. I know him. I know the Senate," Johnson answered back. "Dirksen will leave us if we get this thing strung out very long." While still pledging himself to Fortas, Dirksen's confident declarations grew dimmer over the summer. Unable to mask his pessimism from the press—Fortas's chances "are not roseate" he announced when Congress reconvened—Dirksen's tone shifted to one of acquiescence in September. "What worries me is Dirksen's quit us," Johnson told Clark on September 12. "He's just not giving us the support he ought to."

Citing the American University lecture and an obscure ruling (*Witherspoon v. Illinois*) involving jury selection in a death penalty case, Dirksen, as the president had predicted, officially rescinded his support on September 27. "If, as a result of the Court's decision," Dirksen announced, "twenty-four convicted murderers are to have their sentences . . . set aside, what do I say to the people of Illinois . . . ? What do I say when they allege that I had this one chance to protest and failed to do so?" It was all a ruse. The fact was that Dirksen's office received few complaints about *Witherspoon*. And hours before making the announcement, he had tried to cajole Griffin to support a resolution declaring there was no vacancy after all—a theory bandied about in the early days of the nomination by Fortas's opponents—a transparent face-saving measure Griffin turned down.

Contemporary media outlets as well as historians pointed to Dirksen's yearning to join the winning side of the contest along with his desire to maintain control over his caucus in the face of Griffin's rebellion as the primary motivations behind his sudden about-face. Those factors certainly mattered, but Warren had a revelation about the Minority Leader that has gone largely ignored. "Dirksen has already tried to ruin the Court," the chief justice said in a phone call months earlier when explaining his decision to resign. He was right. Dirksen may have backed Fortas's elevation out of his allegiance to Johnson, but he despised the Warren Court for the reapportionment and school prayer rulings.

Since both Russell and Dirksen were Johnson's personal friends and political allies, and were best situated to quell the factions within the Senate opposed to Fortas, the president had no choice but to ask them for help. This was by no means a tactical error on the president's part—that came through the selection of Fortas and Thornberry over more confirmable nominees. Perhaps the president should have listened to his advisors or, as he had sarcastically put in a phone call with Dirksen on the eve of announcing the nominations—the *St. Louis Post-Dispatch*. Forced to rely on Russell and Dirksen under the circumstances, it hurt Johnson's cause that both men loathed the Warren Court.

After twenty-five hours of floor debate spread over five days, the chief justice's enemies finally had Warren's heir-apparent in their cross-hairs. With Griffin's and Fortas's wives looking on from the gallery, the senators bellowed out their votes, "aye" or "nay," on October 1, 1968. Exhausted by months of fourteen-hour days, Griffin recorded each vote on his tally sheet. After fifteen minutes, the 45-43 count was fourteen votes shy of the two-thirds necessary to quash the filibuster. On the bottom of his tally sheet, Griffin wrote in an oversized font: "We Win!"

What accounted for the defeat? 45% of the American public favored Fortas's ascension (compared with 25% in opposition) as did 45% of newspapers (compared to 24% in opposition). Newspaper editors were not impressed with the cronyism and lame duck charges. Neither was Eastland. No one had bothered to note that even if the counsel Fortas provided to Johnson was unbecoming a justice, it was going to end in three months when the president's term came to an end. These critiques as well as the questionable circumstances surrounding Warren's retirement were effective in preventing a quick confirmation, allowing the opposition to rally and find more damning evidence with which to sink Fortas—namely claims of Fortas's endorsement of pornography and the scandal surrounding the American University seminar payment. Johnson's weakened hold over the Senate, particularly its liberals who lacked much energy throughout the confirmation, along with the emergence of a partisan attack led by Griffin also contributed to Fortas's defeat. But what really doomed Fortas was his association with the Warren Court.

Even as he publicly announced that he would not send another name to the Senate, Johnson pondered nominating Tom Clark, Hart, Goldberg or Thomas Kuchel, a Republican moderate from California. The president also considered making a recess appointment and leaving it up to the Senate to determine the nominee's fate after the New Year. The backlash against Eisenhower, who had made three recess appointments to the Court, doomed this option as well. In 1960, Hart oversaw the passage of a resolution urging an end to the practice. It would have been unimaginable for the conscientious senator to support Johnson's nominee under these circumstances. The fact that Johnson blocked Eisenhower's recess appointments near the end of his second term also made it that much more difficult for the president to take this route.

Nixon's next move made it all but impossible. Warren's son-in-law, John Daly, contacted the Nixon camp to let them know that the chief justice wanted to stay until the end of the term in June 1969 to ensure the smooth operation of the Court. On December 4, 1968, Nixon called Warren to agree to the chief's proposal, and well aware of Warren's enmity towards him, asked whether the chief justice would administer the oath at Nixon's inauguration. That this would even have been an open question reflected the level of disdain that the two men held for one another. When Nixon publicized his understanding with Warren to the public, Johnson immediately recognized Nixon's shrewdness. Making a last-minute recess appointment after Warren publicly agreed to stay on until the end of the Court's term would only confirm suspicions that Warren and Johnson had conspired to block Nixon from naming Warren's successor. "That's about the effect of it," Johnson told Warren in a phone call on December 5. To him, the matter was done. Yet that didn't stop Warren from making one final plea to the president to make a recess appointment despite the potential uproar it would cause. "There is no such legal effect or moral effect so far as I'm concerned," Warren said in response. "You are the president until the twentieth of January," the chief justice continued, "and if you chose to make an interim appointment tomorrow, I just assure you it would be a happy situation for me." Remarkably audacious, that conversation truly exposed the depth of Warren's hatred for Nixon.

Ultimately, Johnson turned down Warren's last-minute pitch.

While these machinations played out in the White House, Fortas received condolence letters from friends and colleagues as if he was mourning the death of a family member. "It is just about the darkest day I have spent at the

White House," Califano wrote in a hand-written message on October 3. Fortas remained an associate justice, but that too felt like a consolation prize after his public humiliation. In what turned out to be the last major domestic contest of his presidency, Johnson was also overcome with remorse. "Abe Fortas is a good, fine patriotic and courageous a human as I have ever known. He's been victimized in a terrible way," Johnson confessed after he left the White House. "I made him take the Justiceship. In that way I ruined his life."

Outgoing President Lyndon Johnson
and Incoming President Richard Nixon
share thoughts in the Oval Office at
the White House, January 20, 1969.

PART IV

Chapter 14

"Screaming for his Scalp"

OCTOBER, 1968–MAY, 1969

While making his rounds of various federal agencies on October 28, 1968, William Lambert of *Life* magazine received a tip from a low-level bureaucrat. "Why don't you look into the relationship between Fortas and Wolfson," his unnamed source suggested. The reference was to the justice's potential link to Louis Wolfson, a Wall Street financier and the architect of the hostile takeover that would become the staple of corporate raiders in the 1980s. Coming off a Pulitzer Prize for exposing corruption in the Teamsters, Lambert signed up with the magazine's group of investigative journalists known internally as "the spooks" in 1963. Perhaps, had the timing been different, the fastidiously dressed journalist would have pursued a different, more promising lead. But Fortas's unlikely loss had electrified Washington and—combined with the American University disclosures still fresh on everyone's minds—the potential for a scandal involving the justice and a financier convicted of federal securities violations captivated Lambert.

Lambert and Fortas had butted heads before. In a face-to-face meeting in 1964 when the justice served as Johnson's fixer, Fortas "tried like hell" to kill the reporter's probe into Johnson's finances. The justice was just as unforthcoming this time around as were others the reporter contacted. Lambert had never come across such tight-lipped sources before. One of his contacts told him: "Don't ask me any questions; don't even tell me anything. I don't want to know." Already intrigued by the prospect that Fortas was hiding something, the stonewalling piqued Lambert's curiosity.

The reporter wasn't the only person in Washington interested in Fortas's ties to Wolfson. Attorney General Clark grew concerned when Robert Morgenthau, the U.S. Attorney in New York who had overseen Wolfson's prosecution, informed him of Lambert's inquiries on November 8. Having been blindsided by the American University debacle, Clark visited Fortas in the justice's home to fend off a similar fiasco. "I paid that money back," Fortas told Clark, referring to a payment made to the justice for serving on the board of the Wolfson Foundation, a philanthropic organization Fortas took an interest in to promote racial and religious cooperation. "I decided that I couldn't do it." Satisfied with Fortas's response, Clark recommended that the justice reach out to Lambert to put the issue to rest. Comforted by the fact that no article appeared in *Life* over the next fortnight, Clark dropped the matter.

Lambert never did. In the coming weeks, he learned that Fortas's former law firm had represented several companies affiliated with Wolfson. On its own, that connection didn't set off any alarms. Arnold, Fortas & Porter had many well-heeled corporate clients. What Lambert discovered next was far more disquieting. After making a handful of calls, he unearthed a $20,000 payment from the Wolfson Foundation to the justice. It was the proverbial tip of the iceberg but with Fortas and Wolfson refusing to meet with him, Lambert's investigation gained little traction. Unaware of the dead ends hobbling Lambert and heeding Clark's advice, Fortas asked Porter to meet with Lambert to put an end to the reporter's meddling. Was his approach understandable? Certainly. Was it a sound move? One would think so. But no matter how rational or strategic or cunning Fortas may have been, his decision to send Porter as his emissary nevertheless backfired. During his meeting with the journalist, Porter divulged that Fortas had returned the money to Wolfson's philanthropic organization. From Porter's perspective, that fact should have cleared up any questions of impropriety. For Lambert, this new morsel of information was the point at which he knew he "had a story." The questions unleashed by Porter's disclosure were indeed enthralling. Why would the justice affiliate himself with a white-collar criminal? Why was Fortas paid so handsomely by a nonprofit organization? And, most of all, if the payment was above-board, then why did the justice return the money? By giving new life to Lambert, Porter again became an unwitting source of trouble for his closest friend. As he kept digging for more clues in the ensuing months, Lambert uncovered additional details of Wolfson's legal problems as well as a record of a meeting between the justice and the financier at Wolfson's Florida ranch. There was a hint of smoke but certainly no fire. Lambert's discoveries, as titillating as they were, didn't meet the threshold the star reporter needed to go to print.

Lambert's investigation had again stalled—until serendipity struck. It was as if the gods were lighting the way for the stymied reporter—or from Fortas's standpoint, punishing him for some gross failure to appease them. On April 1, 1969, Lambert noticed that Fortas had recused himself from Wolfson's appeal of his conviction to the Court. Unlike other members of the judiciary, the justices functioned without a set of ethical guidelines, allowing them to make their own determinations about conflicts of interest or other ethical quandaries. Careful to avoid the appearance of impropriety, the justice's past affiliation with Wolfson's legal team, who were members of Fortas's old law firm, constituted a sound justification for the recusal. Fortas made the right choice but in doing so, inadvertently rekindled Lambert's interest just when it may have fizzled away for good.

Determined to substantiate his findings, Lambert visited Will Wilson, the head of the Criminal Division at the Justice Department. Their meeting on April 10, 1969 turned out to be far more instructive to Wilson than to Lambert, who did most of the talking during their 40-minute conversation. Wilson was so transfixed by what he heard, it was as if Lambert had brought food to a starving person. The federal prosecutor immediately began an avid search for ties between the justice and Wolfson. His eagerness to get to the bottom of any wrongdoing was not simply driven by his responsibilities as head of the Criminal Division. Something else, something far more personal motivated Wilson. He loathed Johnson. The two had crossed paths in 1960 when Johnson, desperate for help in a state dominated by conservative Democrats, recruited Wilson to help him deliver Texas to Kennedy's ticket. In the ensuing years, Johnson declined his requests each time Wilson asked for help to advance his career. Feeling betrayed, Wilson switched parties to campaign for Nixon in 1968. He disliked Fortas just as much. Convinced that the justice didn't belong on the Court and had only reached his exalted position because of his friendship with Johnson, Wilson finally had a chance to exact his long-awaited revenge. "I knew what kind of a potential coup we had," he confessed years later to Fortas's biographer Bruce Allen Murphy. "In all candor, we wanted Fortas off the Court." For the second time in many months, Fortas became a target of those holding a grudge against Johnson. What made these developments all the more excruciating was that his foes exploited the justice's own foibles in furtherance of their vendetta against his former patron. If Fortas had been Shakespeare's contemporary, the playwright could have placed him near the top of his list of tragic figures.

When Nixon's Attorney General John Mitchell took control of the case from Wilson, the agency's investigation intensified as if it was trying to locate Lee Harvey Oswald's accomplice. Mitchell's lack of previous government experience made him an unusual choice to serve as the nation's chief law enforcement officer. A veteran of WWII who worked nights to get through Fordham Law School, he became one of the leading municipal bond lawyers in the country. "He was so good, he had it made," a young lawyer at his firm remembered. "He could pick his clients and . . . go home to Rye to play golf at four in the afternoon." Nixon so came to trust Mitchell after working together in the New York City law firm that Nixon joined in 1963, he made Mitchell his campaign manager over more established politicos. The feeling was mutual. Mitchell's blind allegiance to the president eventually led to his downfall, but in this instance, his unwavering willingness to do Nixon's bidding paid dividends for a president eager to reshape the Court. Already guaranteed the opportunity to replace Warren, who remained on track to retire that coming June, the surprising developments opened the door for Nixon to replace another of the Court's liberals. The addition of two justices so early in his presidency offered him the opportunity to recast the Court from a liberal stronghold into a conservative bastion and cultivate voters clamoring for this transformation.

The lead characters in this developing melodrama converged at the East Room of the White House on April 23 to honor the departing chief justice.

Hosted by Nixon, 110 guests donning black ties and long dresses—including Warren's family, Fortas, and Mitchell, as well as current and former justices and cabinet officials—were in attendance. Outfitted with three crystal chandeliers and parquet floors, the biggest room in the White House was regularly used to host dances and banquets. No luxury was spared for this occasion. The tables were decorated with organdy tablecloths and floral arrangements of orange lilies, daisies, carnations, and snapdragons while the guests ate with vermeil flatware and flower-decorated china. The sumptuous menu included crabmeat, filet mignon, and Caesar salad followed by mousse Nesselrode for dessert. A half-hour performance of opera and folk music by Mildred Miller, a leading soprano affiliated with New York's Metropolitan Opera, punctuated the event as did the endearing toasts to Warren, which brought Fortas to tears. It was indeed a celebratory evening. Despite their mutual animosity, the president warm-heartedly honored Warren's half-century of public service, as focused on "humanity and fair-play" and the chief justice told the audience that he was leaving "without malice in my heart." There may not have been any in his heart on the festive occasion but there was plenty of malice lurking elsewhere in the room. While Nixon and Mitchell performed their roles according to protocol and put on happy faces for those in attendance, they were plotting Fortas's demise in a two-faced performance that could have come right out of *The Godfather*.

In fact, five hours before hosting Warren's farewell party, Nixon had made his intentions clear during a meeting with FBI Director J. Edgar Hoover. After a brief review of the details unearthed by Mitchell's investigators, Nixon declared that Fortas "ought to be off" the Court. There was a constitutional process for removing a justice from office. If the House impeached Fortas, the Senate would have to convict the justice by a two-thirds majority to dismiss him from the Court. It would inevitably be a drawn-out process requiring a lengthy investigation and, considering that both the House and Senate were controlled by Democrats, it might not even end with Fortas's removal. Seeking to avoid this tedious path and potentially risky outcome, Nixon realized that he didn't need to actually get Fortas impeached. The mere threat of it might be enough to dispose of the embattled justice.

Other than Justice Samuel Chase's impeachment in 1804, there was no precedent for investigating a sitting justice and even less precedent for removing one from office. To guide the Justice Department through these murky waters, Mitchell called upon William Rehnquist (the future chief justice) from the Office of Legal Counsel, a department within the agency charged with providing legal advice to the president. Rehnquist concluded that if the agency found evidence of wrongdoing, then the justice would have no immunity from a criminal prosecution.

The potential threat of an indictment gave Nixon and Mitchell the leverage they needed to intimidate the justice. The Justice Department called a grand jury to examine Fortas's former firm, asked the FBI to investigate whether Fortas tried to use his office to hinder an SEC probe targeting Wolfson, and made multiple attempts to have its agents meet with Wolfson to get him to flip against the justice.

Unaware of these developments, Lambert visited the Justice Department a second time to verify his findings. "I will not run the story unless I have confirmation of it," Lambert told his contact in the department. At this point the agency's investigation had uncovered no evidence that Fortas had intervened on Wolfson's behalf or received the $20,000 payment as compensation for doing so. That didn't stop a senior official at the agency from giving Lambert the assurances he needed to go ahead and publish his findings. Perhaps there was no fire after all but if the president and the attorney general could blow out enough smoke, they might fool everyone into thinking there was one.

From an historic perspective, Nixon's actions were unthinkable. No justice had ever resigned under a cloud of scandal and Justice Chase's impeachment ended in his acquittal. Taken within the context of the previous four years, however, Nixon's attempt to expunge Fortas marked a natural progression in the battle for the Marble Palace. Johnson had pushed out two justices to make room to install his favorites. Warren timed his retirement to deny Nixon the opportunity to select his successor. The Senate shattered nearly every precedent during Fortas's nomination to put its imprint on the future direction of the judicial body. After this succession of events, Nixon's eagerness to exploit the "unexpected gift" handed to him by Lambert didn't seem so radical after all.

Released on May 4, 1969, Lambert's article failed to reveal that Fortas had intervened with prosecutors on Wolfson's behalf. Lambert had only found smoke—not fire—but his article drew negative inferences from the incomplete set of facts at his disposal. "Ostensibly, Justice Fortas was being paid to advise the foundation," the reporter wrote. "Whatever services he may or may not have rendered, . . . Fortas' name was being dropped . . . by Wolfson . . . in [an] effort to stay out of prison." Despite the gaps in the story, the implication was clear: Fortas may have used his esteemed position to aid Wolfson.

The reaction to Lambert's exposé was swift and one-sided. It was not a surprise that they would be the first in line to call for Fortas's removal from the Court: Thurmond demanded Fortas resign and Griffin, who had recently introduced a bill requiring federal judges to disclose their finances, expressed his disgust to the press. What was far more troubling for the justice was that his former allies kept their distance like he was a leper. "Thank God that he didn't get to be Chief Justice," Fortas's former law partner, Thurman Arnold uttered. Embarrassed by the revelation, Senator Hart declined to speak out on the justice's behalf. He had good reason to remain hushed. Some of his constituents mocked him for having served as Fortas's advocate months earlier. "How do you now feel about Honest Abe—Fortas, not Lincoln" one of them asked in a letter. That was at least a clever pun compared to a handwritten note Hart received: "Last year's invective that you spewed at those who opposed Fortas' nomination . . . is not egg on your face but excrement." Fortas's former champions in the legal community were also dismayed by the latest disclosures. The ABA accused Fortas of conduct "clearly contrary" to judicial ethics and Alexander Bickel, a leading constitutional law professor at Yale Law School, urged the justice to clear his name or quit. Several federal judges pleaded to Fortas to fulfill his "duty to the Court and to the country" and resign.

Clifford, the former defense secretary, was one of the few exceptions to this chorus of outrage. He offered to help Fortas defeat the "wolves howling out in the forest" but of those Democrats who were still in office, few came to Fortas's defense when lawmakers from both parties called for a congressional investigation. Bloodthirsty Republicans began to openly discuss ways to pressure Fortas to resign and Gerald Ford, the House Minority Leader, publicly contemplated commencing impeachment proceedings. Opinion-makers within the press were equally revolted. Justice Black's wife fittingly recorded their sentiments in her diary: "Editorials screaming for his scalp." The visceral reaction proceeded exactly as Nixon had hoped. "The cloud gathering over Justice Fortas makes it a good probability that he will be forced to resign," Buchanan reported to the president days after the *Life* article appeared on news-stands.

Fortas was resolute at first. "I'm going to ride this thing out," he insisted to a friend. His reputation as a Washington operator rested on his strategic thinking, calculated words, and extensive connections. Paradoxically, all of those strengths failed him during the biggest crisis of his life. Months earlier, Fortas had advisors within the Justice Department and the White House guiding him through the confirmation process. With Douglas in Brazil and the White House staffed with adversaries, Fortas entered this new battlefield alone. Instead of making a full disclosure or issuing a mea culpa like Nixon in his famous 1952 "Checkers speech", Fortas's lawyerly retort to the article issued in the form of a pithy press release, read as if he were responding to a cross-examination. What made the response seem especially implausible was the obvious inconsistency of his denial. Just two paragraphs after claiming that he had "not accepted any fee . . . from . . . the Wolfson Family Foundation," he acknowledged returning "the fee." Among the poisonous clouds swirling over the Court in 1969, his narrowly tailored denials backfired. Instead of snuffing out the fire encircling him, his response poured gasoline over it.

On May 6, Mitchell's team uncovered the key detail in the contract between the justice and the foundation. Wolfson had arranged for Fortas to receive annual payments of $20,000 for his entire life that would revert to his wife upon the justice's death. Mitchell didn't need the agency's best investigators to realize the discovery's repercussions. The remuneration surpassed half of Fortas's annual salary and consumed a large portion of the foundation's budget, which doled out only $77,680 in grants in 1966. The questions were obvious and foreboding. Why would the foundation agree to pay the justice so lavishly?

And why would it set up what amounted to a lifetime pension for a person (and his spouse) who had no previous affiliation with it? There seemed to be no innocent explanations.

Fortas's lapse in judgment cost him yet again. Why did he risk so much to enter into a dubious arrangement? According to his biographer, Fortas's "obsession for having enough money" was a likely contributor. Similar monetary considerations explained his reluctance to join the Court in the first place, an honor that nearly any lawyer would have otherwise jumped at. It's not as if Fortas had not been warned about entering into a financial relationship with Wolfson. Recognizing the potential for trouble, Fortas's clerk had cautioned the justice about the arrangement with the foundation in January, 1966. At the time, the justice dismissed his assistant, telling him: "mind your own business." Perhaps it wasn't about the money. Perhaps he stayed with the foundation out of sympathy for Wolfson, whose wife was dying of cancer just as his legal troubles with federal prosecutors were underway. "I can't kick this guy in the teeth under these circumstances," Fortas told Porter at the time. If so, then why did Fortas resign from the foundation a few days after the conversation with his clerk but waited until after Wolfson was indicted by federal prosecutors eleven months later to return the $20,000? Wolfson certainly asked for Fortas's help and the justice came close to providing it. Fortas had even offered to "give anything to protect" Wolfson at one point but ultimately never intervened with government investigators. "It would have been like lighting a fuse on our own dynamite," he told Wolfson. Fortas was indeed innocent of any wrongdoing but this sequence of events—amplified by the White House's gradual release of damning details and rumors that Fortas had asked Johnson to pardon Wolfson in the last days of his presidency—was easily construed as the actions of a guilty man.

Throughout the brewing crisis, Nixon remained aloof when asked about the scandal, almost as if he were a disinterested observer. (He maintained the same posture in his memoirs published in 1978 in which he expressed his "sympathy" for the embattled justice.) Serving as Eisenhower's hatchet-man in the 1950s, he appreciated the need to let others bloody their hands to allow a president to remain above the fray. As part of Nixon's game of misdirection, a senator told the press that Nixon had appealed to Republican congressmen not to exploit Fortas's mishap for partisan gain. The reality was that Nixon encouraged the very same group to remain on the offensive during a private meeting he hosted. In another instance, the White House tried to mislead the press by leaking Nixon's alleged reluctance to plunge ahead with impeachment proceedings. And when Douglas Kiker of NBC described the White House's "intense private pressures" on the justice as an "ominous . . . partisan" move, the president ordered his communications office to rebut the charge. Just as he had sought to keep his "fingerprints" off Fortas's confirmation fight months earlier, Nixon aimed to keep his role in this saga a secret.

There was no playbook for what Nixon was orchestrating. Much like Griffin nine months earlier, he was winging it. And just like the Michigan senator's, the president's strategy had worked to perfection. Badgered from all quarters and bereft of allies, Fortas appeared ready for a knockout blow. Vice President Agnew was typically the attack dog in the administration, but in this case, Nixon drafted his attorney general to serve as Fortas's executioner. Despite lacking much political experience, Mitchell managed to play the role immaculately. He didn't disclose the incriminatory facts all at once to the public. He let innuendo do the work. When asked by congressional Republicans on May 6 whether there are "more developments" that have not yet "come to light," the attorney general simply answered "Yes." The brevity of details had the effect of magnifying what little information was made available, allowing the public to convict Fortas through sheer conjecture.

Hoping Warren would pressure Fortas to quit, Nixon dispatched Mitchell to meet secretly with the chief justice on May 7. Inside Warren's office, the attorney general showed the chief justice documents exposing all the gory details of Fortas's relationship with Wolfson and the financier's expectation that he would receive help from the justice with federal prosecutors. Before he left, Mitchell made it clear that yet more damaging material would come to light unless Fortas resigned. Though Warren managed to maintain a poker face throughout the meeting, he was appalled by what he considered a "matter of intense controversy and emotion." For the chief justice, the mere appearance of an impropriety was enough to besmirch the Court. It didn't take long for

Warren, a stickler for ethics, to make up his mind. "He can't stay," Warren told his assistant after Mitchell's departure. Soon afterwards, Warren visited all the justices in order of seniority. Typically, the sociable chief justice would have paused to converse with their secretaries and clerks. Visibly shaken by Mitchell's disclosures, he cast aside his usual conviviality on this occasion, abruptly entered his brethren's offices, and shut the door behind him to deliver the news.

When *Newsweek* disclosed the details of Mitchell's visit to the Marble Palace, the dominoes fell quickly. Senator Walter Mondale became the first Democrat to call for Fortas's resignation on May 10. "[T]he cloud over the Court has been darkened," Maryland's Joseph Tydings—another Democrat—announced on the Senate floor. "Mr. Justice Fortas must resign," he declared. "He must resign immediately."

While Thurmond and Griffin piloted the public case against Fortas, Mitchell kept hinting of the pending release of new, more damaging information and the existence of a "criminal investigation." The FBI amped up the administration's full-court press. Hoover leaked Fortas's legal but unseemly tax shelters to the press and the character assassination turned vulgar when rumors materialized of an FBI investigation into Fortas's alleged homosexual relationship with a teenager. The media set up camp in front of Fortas's home and followed him everywhere he went. Hounded by the press and disparaged within the halls of Congress, Fortas also faced the compilation of revelations and gossip circulated by the White House that raised the brewing tempest to a Level Five hurricane. Yes, there was no playbook for Nixon to follow. But he could have written one on how to convert an ethical blunder into a red-hot scandal.

Despite the embarrassing disclosures and endless pressure, Fortas still refused to yield.

Just as the president had hoped, the chief justice landed the final blow. Disappointed and disillusioned, Warren recruited Black to advise Fortas to resign. Ironically, the moderate temperament that once prevailed over the Court had allowed Black to maintain his seat after his membership in the KKK had been exposed. Little of that moderation remained when it came to the Court thirty years later. In a two-hour meeting on May 10, Black told Fortas to resign "for the good of the Court." Much of Congress, including the justice's erstwhile supporters, were hoping for the same outcome in order to avoid a long, drawn-out impeachment process that would further sully the Court and weigh heavily on the legislators. On May 13, Fortas met with Douglas and Porter at his Georgetown mansion to review his options.

It was a heartbreaking moment for the two justices. Their relationship dated back to the New Deal when Fortas emerged as Douglas's protégé. Douglas had recommended Fortas for teaching positions at choice law schools, including Yale, Columbia, and the University of Chicago in the early 1940s. "He is an outstanding person," he wrote to Northwestern University's dean in one these reference letters. Fortas managed Douglas's legal affairs upon entering the private sector and over time they developed a close friendship. "I have read many times your letter upon the occasion of my mother's death," Fortas wrote to Douglas in 1946. "I cannot tell you how much it means to me." They threw each other parties and exchanged gifts over the years. On top of the sherry, wine, and other traditional gifts that Fortas had bestowed upon Douglas, he even bought his mentor a horse. To mark Douglas's twenty-fifth anniversary on the Court, Fortas wrote an encomium honoring him for the *Yale Law Journal* in 1964. Douglas returned the favor a year later, helping Johnson recruit Fortas to the Court, allaying the concerns of Fortas's wife over his nomination, and hosting a reception to celebrate Fortas's appointment. Now, as the two men met upon Douglas's return from Brazil, their jubilation had turned to grief. Their misery was all the more agonizing due to the twist of fate that had taken Fortas from the pinnacle of his career just a few months earlier to his current situation on the brink of infamy.

Douglas encouraged the beleaguered justice to stay on. But it was too late. Desperate to stop the increasingly tawdry accusations, and convinced that his critics would not stop short of an impeachment, Fortas submitted his resignation the next day at a meeting with his brethren. "There has been no wrongdoing on my part," he assured his colleagues, before explaining his reasons for resigning:

It is my opinion, however, that the public controversy relating to my association with the Foundation is likely to . . . adversely

affect the work and position of the Court. . . . In these circumstances . . . it is not my duty to remain on the Court, but rather to
resign in the hope that this will enable the Court to proceed . . .
free from extraneous stress.

An unspoken fear also motivated him. Fortas hoped that by falling on his
sword, he would satiate the Court's foes, and in doing so, spare Douglas from
facing the same fate.

CHAPTER 15

"The Least Considered Aspect of Presidential Power"

JUNE, 1969–APRIL, 1970

Early in his presidency, Nixon received a memo contending that the Court was "the least considered aspect of Presidential power." Obvious to a modern-day observer, it was a point few would have made at the time. Reaffirming Nixon's evolving views, the memo underscored the president's "opportunity to influence the course of national affairs for a quarter of a century. . . . " Nixon echoed this sentiment in announcing his nomination of Warren Burger to take over as chief justice: "I think it could fairly be said that our history tells us that our Chief Justices have probably had more profound and lasting influence on their times and on the direction of the Nation than most Presidents have had."

The fact that Burger and Nixon had separately converged upon Warren on Eisenhower's behalf at the 1952 convention happened to be an odd coincidence. Burger's first name was also coincidentally Warren and his middle name was Earl. Burger's bona fides were what mattered to Nixon. The judge had established himself as a reliable conservative since his appointment to the D.C. Circuit Court of Appeals in 1956. It was unusual for a federal judge to publicly criticize a higher court but it paid dividends for Burger. He had spoken out against the Warren Court during Red Monday, but it was his 1967 speech frowning upon the Court's criminal justice cases that captured Nixon's attention. To further his standing with the president, Burger continued to pound away at Warren in the months leading up to his nomination. Ostensibly focused on mundane bureaucratic matters, his seven-page memorandum sent to the White House in March, 1969, did just that by fixating on the Warren Court's criminal jurisprudence. These cases were "the most glaring example of the Justices bungling into an area where they are totally lacking in experience," Burger complained. "Yet they rashly plunged in." His observations grew more damning as the memo progressed. Burger concluded, "The hard fact is that Chief Justice Warren did not have the support of Congress, the legal profession or the public" and that the "new Chief Justice will come to office at a time when the Court's prestige is perhaps at its lowest ebb in history." Clearly auditioning for the job by the end of the memo, Burger recommended that "the Supreme Court must be 'rehabilitated' in the public confidence." Nixon had mastered the art of drawing upon a person's resentments to get his way. It seemed that Burger could brandish these skills as well. Proceeding with minimal input from the Justice Department, the president became convinced that Burger was committed to undoing Warren's legacy.

Burger checked off all the other boxes for Nixon. At sixty-one, he was young enough to serve a significant number of years. He also espoused Frankfurter's philosophy of judicial self-restraint, and openly embraced Nixon's position on the raging issue of the day—criminal justice. More importantly, he had no close ties to the president. In the lead-up to Burger's nomination Nixon's speechwriter Patrick Buchanan warned: "Because of the suspicion and skepticism about the Court's integrity in the wake of the Fortas thing, it seems… important that the President's first choice not in any way be construed as 'Nixon's Fortas.'" Nixon highlighted this point to the press during his announcement: "Now, because of the Fortas matter, I determined that the appointee should not be a personal friend." This declaration marked a turning point in the criteria used for the selection of justices. Anyone with a hint of cronyism was now off limits, wiping out the many senators, cabinet officials, and governors who used to constitute the pool of candidates for the Court. Burger's thirteen years on an appellate court also gave him the kind of judicial experience Warren's critics had long coveted in a chief justice. He had one final distinction in his favor. Burger's flowing white hair, baritone voice, and a statesmanlike mien fit the archetype of the position better than anyone since Charles Evans Hughes, whom a colleague once claimed resembled the Almighty. Burger may not have matched Hughes's godlike persona, but "he looks, acts and talks like a Chief Justice," Dirksen observed.

The selection brought Nixon widespread praise. Along with the press and the law enforcement community, all the principle figures who had opposed Fortas—Thurmond, Eastland, Dirksen, Russell, and Griffin—lauded this new choice. With little to object to in Burger's record, his nomination flew through the Senate. The confirmation hearings lasted less than two hours and on June 9, seventeen days after Nixon had announced the pick, the Senate confirmed Burger 74-3. For a moment, at least, the confirmation process looked much like it had in the pre-Fortas era.

It's hazardous to dabble in counter-factual histories; "What if" scenarios are best left to novelists and screenwriters. In this instance, however, it's worth speculating a bit. What if, for his second pick, Nixon had settled on another conventional center-right jurist out of the ranks of the judiciary? Would that have relegated the Fortas debacle to a one-time blip in an otherwise tranquil series of confirmations dating back to the 1890s? Neither of the two most contentious nominations of the twentieth century prior to Fortas—Louis Brandeis's drawn-out confirmation in 1916 and John Parker's rejection in 1930—had left a lasting imprint. In both instances, all the key players in the confirmation process reverted back to their traditional roles, restoring the appointment of justices to a predictable and unexciting routine. It's worth asking: if Nixon had acted differently, would Fortas's nomination have been another short-lived exception? We will never know. What we do know is that the Fortas episode represented a fundamental break with the past. It was the moment when, like an inter-species pathogen, the politicization of the Court fomented during Warren's tenure had now crossed over to infect the confirmation process. Though he stumbled his way through a makeshift, error-prone strategy, Nixon cemented and built upon this metamorphosis, forging a template for modern judicial politics to be fine-tuned by future generations.

Eager to tap a southerner for Fortas's empty seat, Nixon nominated Clement Haynsworth on August 18. A native of South Carolina, Haynsworth was by all accounts an affable and capable judge from the U.S. Court of Appeals for the Fourth Circuit. A "product of Greenville aristocracy," Haynsworth was a graduate from Furman University, named after his great-grandfather, and Harvard Law School, making him the latest in a long line of respected lawyers in his family. Haynsworth was vetted by the attorney general from a list of 150 candidates, backed by Harry Dent, the mastermind behind the southern strategy, and approved by "Uncle Strom." His age, judicial philosophy, and previous judicial experience met all of Nixon's criteria.

The strategy behind the nomination emulated Johnson's thinking and also marked an evolutionary leap in political opportunism. Like his immediate predecessor, Nixon saw the Court as another means to propel his vision and looked to avoid the mistakes made by Truman, Eisenhower, and Kennedy in selecting ideologically unreliable jurists. But there were some important distinctions. The Court had never stood at the top of Johnson's agenda. Nixon, on the other hand, considered refashioning the Court his primary domestic goal. Unlike Johnson, Nixon also tried to put his stamp on the Court in a far more public way. Johnson dodged Goldwater's attempts to link the Democratic Party to the Warren Court in the 1964 election. Nor did Johnson overtly cater to his political base in nominating Marshall, Fortas, and Thornberry. Nixon, on the other hand, actively campaigned against the Court and was far more calculating about how voters would perceive his nominees.

Nixon's primary electoral concern remained Wallace. In May, Dent, now a member of the White House staff, reported that Wallace was still the "big factor in the South" who could "have a profound effect" on the next presidential race. To strengthen his presence in the region, Nixon assigned southerners to government posts, coddled its textile industry, and fired Leon Panetta (the future Defense Secretary under Barack Obama), who had been vigorously pushing for integration as a high-ranking official at the Department of Health, Education, and Welfare. No tactic seemed out of bounds. So eager to placate the region, the president issued a directive forbidding any White House official from making a statement that might offend the South. The coup de grace of this strategy was to appoint favorable justices. "No section of the Nation better reflects the forces that resulted in your election than the South," Thurmond explained to Nixon in May, 1969, "and I hasten to add no section can contribute more effectively to your re-election in 1972. Perhaps the greatest concern in the South centers on the Supreme Court," he added, as if the president needed reminding. "No act of your administration would be regarded with more favor, or more deeply appreciated, in the South than an appointment of an outstanding Southerner to one of the present vacancies on the Court." Thurmond's words reinforced what Nixon and Dent were already plotting. What Nixon didn't account for was the potential backlash to his blatantly politicized selection.

While Haynsworth's name was still swirling in Washington's leak-infested rumor-mill, AFL-CIO president George Meany pressed Nixon to reconsider the nomination. One of the last titans of the labor movement's glory years, Meany had no qualms about challenging the president. Originally from the Bronx, he worked his way up the AFL's ranks to oversee its merger with the CIO in 1955, turning the combined entity into a fifteen-million-strong force. Meany exuded an uncommon combination of refinement and brawn. With closely cropped white hair, that had receded up his scalp, and wearing custom tailored suits, the only visible vestiges of his blue-collar past were his hands, callused from his work as a plumber in Manhattan in earlier days. As a rabid anti-communist, he had no dreamy visions of establishing a global labor utopia. While he focused on wages, working conditions, and other economic issues relevant to his members, he was willing to use the union's political capital to achieve other goals. Administering the labor union not as a special interest group but what he considered the "people's lobby," Meany positioned the AFL-CIO to play a vital role in many of the legislative achievements of the era.

Rebuffed by the president, Meany launched his first volley two days after Nixon's announcement. Calling Haynsworth "hostile to workers and Negroes," the union chief urged the Senate to reject the nomination. Days later, the AFL-CIO launched a national campaign by mobilizing local chapters to lobby the Senate. With Meany taking charge, he appeared on national television to denounce the nominee.

What accounted for this full-court press from an institution that had taken little interest in the Court's membership for nearly four decades? Meany made no secret that Haynsworth's labor and civil rights rulings terrified him. But his strongest justification rested on a familiar theme—dubious ethics. Ironically, it was the union's interest in one of Haynsworth's cases in 1963 that opened the door to the charge. The case arose when Deering Milliken, a South Carolina textile mill, closed down its plant after an affiliate of the AFL-CIO won an election establishing the union as the mill workers' representative. As part of a 3-2 majority, Haynsworth overturned a holding by the National Labor Relations Board, which had found that Deering's closure violated federal law. It wouldn't go down as an historic case, but at the time, represented a major blow to the labor movement. The file the union had put together on Haynsworth at the time uncovered that, on top of owning one-seventh of Vend-A-Matic, a food vending supplier operating in three of Deering's mills, the judge had also served as the supplier's vice president and director. Citing a conflict of interest, Meany argued that Haynsworth should have recused himself from presiding over the case.

Operating in the wake of Fortas's resignation, the union followed a simple strategy of repeating the accusations made against the fallen justice. "We had a Supreme Court judge who resigned just a few months ago because his conduct was considered unethical," Meany reminded viewers during his interview with ABC News, "and there was nothing in that case that even approaches the conflict of interest that I feel is proven on the record . . . by Judge Haynsworth." The argument was as specious as it was effective. Yes, a year after ruling on the Deering case, a buyout of Vend-A-Matic earned Haynsworth $455,307 on an original investment of $2,300. But there were plenty of points in the judge's favor. Haynsworth was unaware of the relationship between Deering and Vend-A-Matic during the case, Deering comprised just 3% of Vend-A-Matic's sales, and both a judicial review and Robert Kennedy—the attorney general in 1964—had cleared Haynsworth of any wrongdoing.

Soon after Labor Day, Meany asked Andrew Biemiller, the AFL-CIO's legislative director, "How many votes have you got in the Senate against this guy?"

"We start with eight," Biemiller responded.

"Can we triple it?," his boss asked.

"We can double it certainly, triple it maybe," Biemiller said.

"All right," Meany said. "We're in it all the way."

Even if the number were quadrupled, the union faced a daunting task. Fortas may have been rejected less than a year earlier but from whatever angle one viewed the situation, the idea of the Senate turning down another nomination seemed a longshot. The American public preferred conservative justices over liberal ones by a nearly two-to-one margin, and Nixon's approval rating hovered around 60% and only months into his term, he was no lame duck. Within the Senate, the same coalition of southern Democrats and conservative Republicans who had teamed up against Fortas still carried the numbers to prevail.

To overcome the long odds, Biemiller recruited Indiana Senator Birch Bayh. In some ways, he was a natural pick. Union officials had developed a close relationship with Bayh through generous campaign donations and a large contingency of UAW workers in his state. Yet, he was not the AFL-CIO's first choice. Just months into his second term, Bayh stood outside of the chamber's inner circle. Nor was he particularly liberal. In a state Nixon had carried by 250,000 votes, Bayh was reelected by a 71,000 vote margin. To thrive under these circumstances, Bayh navigated a centrist path, forming alliances with groups who were historic rivals. "Birch is pretty smooth," said a Washington insider who had seen Bayh in action. He had to be. How else could he have corralled the AFL-CIO and the U.S. Chamber of Commerce to join forces behind his push to abolish the Electoral College?

Despite some of Bayh's shortcomings, the AFL-CIO had no one else to turn to. None of the Republicans on the Judiciary Committee would dare to betray the president, and its southern members rejoiced over Haynsworth. Afraid of being charged with hypocrisy for opposing Haynsworth on ethical grounds after championing Fortas, Hart bowed out of any leadership role. Just weeks after the scandal of Chappaquiddick, Edward Kennedy also declined to serve as the public face of the resistance. That left Bayh as the opposition's default leader.

For those who knew Bayh well enough to call him "B^2," they never doubted his ability to meet this challenge. Born in 1928 in Terre Haute, Indiana, Bayh spent his summers on his grandparents' farm and became president of the 4H club in high school, the first of many leadership posts. At Purdue University, he won a light-heavyweight championship in boxing and was crowned the student body president. In 1959, he became the youngest Speaker of the Indiana House of Representatives. Only thirty-four when he entered the Senate in 1963, Bayh landed the chairmanship of the Subcommittee on Constitutional Amendments. It was a curious destination for someone who had failed the bar exam on his first attempt. Yet, he parlayed the obscure posting into a consequential platform. Bayh grabbed national headlines by commandeering the Twenty-Fifth Amendment that modified presidential succession into the Constitution. He was also responsible for the Twenty-Sixth Amendment to reduce the voting age to eighteen, making him the only person other than the Founding Fathers to author two constitutional amendments. Though Bayh had remained on the sidelines during the Fortas-Thornberry debacle to focus on a tight reelection, his oversight of Dirksen's reapportionment and school prayer amendments throughout the 1960s made him a veteran of the Warren Wars.

Bayh brought one more attribute to the equation—a hefty dose of courage. This was on full display when he and Ted Kennedy were both in a plane crash in Massachusetts in 1964. Knocked unconscious when the plane came down during a storm in an apple orchard, Bayh awakened to find the pilot dead and Kennedy out cold. Though he suffered a hip injury, Bayh managed to drag himself and Kennedy out of the wreckage.

Thin, of medium build, with thick, closely cropped hair, Bayh rarely deviated from a monotone delivery and spoke at a steady pace with few breaks to punctuate his message. He may not have been a stellar orator but the AFL-CIO didn't need a Dirksen-like performer to contest Haynsworth. It needed a steady and bold voice like the one Griffin had provided a year earlier.

The AFL-CIO didn't go after Haynsworth alone. It reunited with the NAACP to resurrect one of the most potent political alliances of the era. The Court had always remained of paramount importance to this coalition. The two organizations had come to the Warren Court's defense during Red Monday and had been on the frontlines of the battle against Dirksen's reapportionment amendment. Despite their participation in the legislative battles surrounding the Warren Court, they had not set foot into the confirmation arena since 1930. Thirty-nine years later, they broke that streak stretching across twenty-seven nominations.

Haynsworth's hearings that September lacked the drama of Fortas's exchanges with Ervin and Thurmond. The main theme to emerge was the participation of twelve special interest groups—a record at the time—testifying against the nominee. The AFL-CIO alone had three witnesses—Meany, Biemiller, and an in-house lawyer, Thomas Harris. The UAW and nearly half a dozen other affiliates of the AFL-CIO also sent representatives to testify. Clarence Mitchell, the NAACP's legislative director, led a bevy of civil rights leaders opposing the nomination. Together, these groups put on a media blitz, sent out more than a quarter million pamphlets as part of a national grass roots campaign, and urged their local chapters to lobby the Senate. The AFL-CIO called it "one of our biggest fights on the Hill."

The impact on Haynsworth was devastating. What seemed like a clear path to victory in mid-August had then turned sour a month later. The long-term impact on the Court was equally significant. Despite Johnson's attempts to wield them on his behalf, outside groups, lobbyists, and campaign donors ended up playing a modest and largely behind-the-scenes role in the Fortas nomination. That dynamic changed dramatically this time around. Advocacy organizations, special interest groups, and major voting blocs had, since the 1880s, intermittently gotten themselves involved in confirmations. But in none of these instances did they come close to matching the exploits of Haynsworth's adversaries. As the momentum increased, their presence became even more pervasive. In the coming decades, ideologically driven organizations and groups closely tied to social issues would play an ever-increasing role in the nomination of justices, culminating in the Federalist Society's outsized influence in curating potential nominees for Donald Trump.

Bayh and his allies conducted the most comprehensive financial review of any judicial nominee in history, scrutinizing hundreds of documents related to Haynsworth's assets. For a man with more than $730,000 in investments, it was a laborious task. The quest for any scintilla of wrongdoing repeatedly forced Haynsworth to rummage through old files. The enormity of the task was equally burdensome on his inquisitors. It would have taken a team of forensic accountants to dissect all of the information made available to the Judiciary Committee. Stretched thin by the magnitude of the task, Bayh spent countless hours reviewing the financial records on his own. All of this sleuthing was rewarded when the UAW uncovered a genuine conflict of interest that proved to be far more damning than Vend-A-Matic.

Releasing information in small doses over a period of weeks, it was as if the opposition were out to slowly poison Haynsworth through its disclosures. The primary charges lodged at the nominee were: the financial imbroglio with Vend-A-Matic; Haynsworth's participation in cases involving companies in which he had some financial interest (usually through the ownership of a parent company); and his refusal to recuse himself from cases involving clients of his former law firm. No one accused Haynsworth of violating the law but there was no doubt of his skirting ethical standards that, in the wake of Fortas's entanglements with American University and the Wolfson Foundation, had become far more exacting. Summing up every iota of damning information he and his allies had dug up, Bayh's fourteen-page account of Haynsworth's wrongdoing in the Judiciary Committee's official report read like he was indicting a criminal mastermind rather than a judge who should have acted with greater care.

Assuming the Senate would rubber-stamp the nomination, the attorney general and Nixon were caught off-guard. They weren't the only ones to make that assumption. "How's this for confidence," a senior vice president of the public relations giant Hill & Knowlton asked the president in October when referring to the firm's listing of Haynsworth as a justice in the latest printing of its government directory. They should not have been so presumptuous. Days after Fortas resigned, a staff member warned John Ehrlichman, one of Nixon's primary domestic advisors, to conduct vigorous background checks "on our candidates . . . to spot any trouble ahead of time." He was right. Embittered by Fortas's demise, Senate liberals were intent upon putting any objectionable nominees through the same scrutiny. "Haynsworth would have been confirmed in a minute ten years ago," a White House aide noted. "But his appointment came at a time when Christ himself would have drawn at least one 'no' vote on principle alone."

Belatedly but vigorously, the White House fought back. "We can stimulate mail too," Nixon ordered. "There should be letters and wires from the Farm Bureaus, Southern bar associations, the National Rifle Association and our other friends; they have got to be energized." Under Nixon's direction, his staff recruited these conservative groups to shill for the nominee and called in favors from local politicians, those who benefited from the president's patronage, business executives, and campaign donors. Buchanan launched a media campaign, ghostwriting editorials and calling upon conservatives with a large following—including Kilpatrick, Buckley and Phyllis Schlafly—for help. While Buchanan focused on swaying public opinion, Roman Hruska, one of the point-men for the White House in the Senate, and Rehnquist at the Justice Department, generated point-by-point rebuttals to every charge made against Haynsworth.

No matter how comprehensive, no matter how on-point, and convincing the arguments to nominate him, Haynsworth's opponents were left unsatisfied at every turn. The problem for the nomination's defenders was that the details of the charges didn't matter as much as the perception that Haynsworth had breached ethical norms. "In a room full of lawyers I could explain what the differences are between Haynsworth and Fortas," a senator told Nixon at a meeting in the White House. "But what comes through to a lot of guys on our side is that the man on the street is not going to understand."

By the end of the hearings on September 26, many Republicans counseled the president to withdraw the nomination. Goldwater complained to Nixon that even constituents who were so far to the right that they considered the icon of conservatism a "Socialist," urged a withdrawal. "Look, I'm glad to have a strict constructionist on the Court," the Arizona senator explained to the president, "but why must we be embarrassed?" Griffin, who had been promoted to Senate Minority Whip after Dirksen died on September 7, was the most prominent voice preaching a strategic retreat. "I disagree with Presidents who have said the Senate must confirm any nominee for the Supreme Court who is not 'unfit,'" Griffin said in justification of his position. "That may be an appropriate test for Executive branch appointments," he continued, reiterating a point he had made a year earlier, "but the Senate has a higher, co-equal responsibility in determining who shall sit on the Supreme Court." When the Michigan senator publicly announced his opposition on October 8, he struck a major blow to the nomination.

Nixon cared little for Griffin's principled stance. Rather than withdrawing the nomination, the president vowed to "destroy Griffin," and ordered his underlings to cut off all Republican traitors. Angered by the unexpected resistance, the president came to see the nomination as a barometer of his leadership. "All the liberals . . . the *Washington Post* and *The New York Times* would praise me highly if we withdraw him, but I don't intend to do that. . . . If we cave on this one," he told his staff in mid-October, "they will think that if you kick Nixon you can get somewhere."

Just as Griffin had endured countless entreaties a year earlier, some Republican senators suffered through the same experience, much of it during face-to-face meetings in the Oval Office. Often heavy-handed, the tactics backfired. Johnson may have twisted arms, observed one senator, but Nixon "twists throats." Lobbied by local bar associations, corporate executives, and major campaign donors, Ohio Senator William Saxbe warned that the pressure was "as strong as anything we've seen." To lure Saxbe to the other side, a mortgage broker offered the senator a chance to get in on an investment promising a million dollars in profits. If that was the carrot dangled to entice Saxbe, the White House brandished the stick to try to frighten him into submission by probing his finances for damaging information. Hugh Scott, the new Minority Leader, warned the White House to back off, or he would "announce publicly . . . against Haynsworth." The extensive lobbying also grated on Delaware Republican John Williams: "nothing in Haynsworth's record troubled [me] as much as the tactic . . . used by the White House," he said. Renowned for his integrity, when the senior statesman turned against the nominee, a half dozen of his colleagues followed suit.

At the end, the administration's campaign could not surmount the sense of hypocrisy felt by some Republicans. "I do not believe that I can adopt a double standard," the chair of the Republican Conference, Margaret Chase Smith, wrote to Nixon, echoing the mood of several of her colleagues. On November 21, the Senate rejected Haynsworth 45-55 with 17 of 43 Republicans voting against the nomination. Nixon blamed the debacle on the antipathy towards the South and the attorney general's fumbling of the nomination. But the explanation, as one senator put it, was more straightforward: "Had there been no Fortas affair. . . . , Haynsworth . . . undoubtedly would have been confirmed."

Feeling betrayed by his own party and furious at labor and civil rights groups as well as his favorite villain—the liberal press—Nixon was infuriated. Yet, Haynsworth's defeat did serve his political purpose. The nominee's demise boosted Nixon's standing in the South, helping him become "a thumpingly popular President in Dixie." Griffin and other Republicans who had urged a withdrawal were unable to grasp the fact that a hard-fought defeat would boost Nixon's profile in the South just as much as a victory by exhibiting his loyalty to the region. Nixon's staff made sure to hit home this point, milking the president's refusal to withdraw the nomination as often as possible in their appeals to southern audiences. Reflecting the region's sentiments, Thurmond expressed his "deep personal appreciation" for the president's "firm commitment" to the nomination. In that sense, the nomination worked exactly as planned. "You know," a White House staffer observed, "the President really believes in that Southern strategy—more than he believes in anything else."

Nixon's next pick doubled down on that belief. He ordered Dent "to go out and this time find a. . . judge farther down South and further to the right." George Carswell emerged from this search. A graduate of Duke University and Mercer University's law school, Carswell served in the Navy during WWII and moved to Tallahassee, where he practiced law before becoming a U.S. Attorney. Eisenhower appointed him to the federal bench in 1958 and in June, 1969, Nixon elevated him to the Fifth Circuit Court of Appeals. Since his recent escalation to the appellate body had gone so smoothly and Haynsworth's downfall should have quenched a desire for revenge by Senate liberals, no one inside the White House expected a rough confirmation.

Yet, the trouble began immediately. On January 20, 1970, the day after the formal announcement, the NAACP's Mitchell set off the alarm, warning Bayh and his other allies that Nixon was trying to "change the direction of the court." Tall, thin, with a widow's peak and wispy mustache, Mitchell was among the most influential African-Americans in the nation at that time. As the NAACP's chief lobbyist and the founder of the Leadership Conference on Civil Rights—an umbrella organization of religious, civil rights, and labor groups—he played an integral role in passing the civil rights laws of the 1960s. Popularly known as the "101st Senator" due to his immense, overarching influence within the Senate, Mitchell employed a low-key yet forceful style, preferring to listen to those he sought to sway, instead of dictating terms while standing by to stir public opinion among their constituents when necessary.

Civil rights groups had been the junior partners in the opposition to Haynsworth. But, far more alarmed by Carswell—whom it considered to be an existential threat to the gains it had made up to that point—the NAACP took the lead this time around. Mitchell had good reason to be concerned.

In the popular telling of the civil rights movement, the Court's role in the drama begins and ends with *Brown*. The reality was that the Warren Court shielded and sided with civil rights advocates at nearly every stage of their crusade. It validated the sit-ins, marches, and other forms of protest employed throughout the South, shielded the NAACP from intimidation, and safeguarded the civil rights legislation of the 1960s from constitutional scrutiny. It was the potential threat to this wide-ranging support that made Carswell's nomination so frightening to Mitchell.

The challenge for Mitchell was that no senator was eager to jump into another drawn-out battle just weeks after the Haynsworth affair had left them exhausted. An aide predicted that the Senate would have confirmed anyone "unless he has committed murder"—and, what's more—only if he had done so "recently."

Once again, the White House underestimated the intensity of the opposition, going so far as to ruminate over the details of Carswell's swearing-in ceremony. The microscope that now was focused on nominees were now under reflected that intensity. In order "to show how far the digging has gone," a senate aide wrote, an investigator "in Florida reports that he has made contact with a women [sic] who works in the local Federal prison and has volunteered to ask prisoners if they have any gripes against the judge."

What the NAACP and members of the press unearthed made Haynsworth's civil rights record look rosy by comparison with Carswell's. While running for a state senate seat in 1948, Carswell extolled the virtues of "white supremacy" and declared segregation as the "only practical and correct way of life." In 1953, he drafted a white-only charter for boosters of the Florida State University football team. Three years later, he helped establish a segregated golf course on public property to circumvent a judicial decree directing municipal golf courses to desegregate. Carswell's claim that he was unaware of the purpose of transferring the golf course from the municipality to private hands defied credulity. He must have been "the only one in Northern Florida" to be ignorant of the scheme, Kilpatrick wrote. In 1966, the judge sold a piece of property with a restrictive covenant limiting its occupancy to white people in violation of the law. A Princeton professor summed up the criticism, arguing that Carswell's "chief qualification appears to be an abiding unwillingness to protect the constitutional rights of black Americans." Blindsided by revelations the Justice Department had failed to uncover, when Nixon read about them for the first time, he simply wrote on the margin of the memo—"My God!"

As appalling as it was, Carswell's civil rights record wasn't by itself going to sink his nomination. Bayh had based his opposition of Haynsworth on ethical grounds. With Carswell, he found an easier, less ambiguous vulnerability to expose—his incompetence.

Here, Bayh and his allies found help from an unlikely ally—the legal community. With the ABA taking the lead on confirmations for decades, other legal groups had stayed on the sidelines. Lawyers, bar associations, professors, and law school deans jumped into the fray this time around. Derek Bok, the dean of Harvard Law School (and later to become the president of the university) warned of Carswell's low "level of competence." "I am impelled to conclude," Yale Law School Dean Louis Pollak testified before the Judiciary Committee, "that the nominee presents more slender credentials than any nominee for the Supreme Court put forth in this century." That put Carswell on the bottom of a list of forty-eight nominees. Other scholars were equally critical. Nine professors from Florida State University Law School called on the president to nominate a "truly distinguished Southern jurist" instead of Carswell. Twenty-five professors from U.C. Berkeley's Boalt Law School advised the Senate not to lower its standards by accepting Carswell. Twenty-three professors from Harvard Law School jointly lamented Carswell's lack "of commitment to those moral and legal principles which can now serve to bind our nation together."

The NAACP and AFL-CIO were experienced hands in Washington. Bok and Pollak were renowned legal minds. It was the emergence of these ad-hoc groups that personified the willingness of new interest groups to enter the confirmation battlefield. Based out of Columbia Law School, the Law Students Concerned for the Court put out a study in March assessing Carswell's reversal rate as a district court judge. What the organization lacked in name recognition it made up for in analytical rigor. Its research exposed Carswell's shoddy record as a jurist: the nominee was reversed 58.8% of the time, almost three times the national average of federal judges. To make matters worse, Carswell seemed to show no improvement over time. The report also pointed out that Carswell's opinions were cited by other courts at about half the rate of other judges—a clear indication that they carried far less weight as precedents. "Every index applied by the study to the judicial performances of Judge Carswell and of other judges during the same time period," the group concluded, "found Carswell's rating far below the average of his peers."

An assembly of lawyers with far greater standing provided an equally devastating assessment of Carswell's credentials. More than two hundred former Court clerks, the most prestigious job available to a young lawyer, declared their "united . . . opposition to the confirmation of Judge Carswell. . . . The record shows him to be of mediocre ability," they pronounced. Dean Acheson, the former secretary of state, was the most prominent member on the list, that also included future justice Stephen Breyer as well Richard Posner, Guido Calabresi, John Ely, and Lawrence Tribe, all of whom would go on to become renowned jurists and legal thinkers.

No amount of spin-control could repair Carswell's reputation after these condemnations. Nixon's congressional liaison put it best to the president: "They think Carswell's a boob, a dummy. And what counter is there to that? He is." The White House team echoed this sentiment. Its meetings "were increasingly punctuated by groans of frustration and hoots of disbelief as our nominee's ineptitude became more and more apparent. . . ." one member recalled. "Few if any of us thought he was well qualified for the Supreme Court, but the issue was that we could not endure a second straight defeat on a Supreme Court nomination."

Just when it couldn't get worse for Carswell, Hruska capped off the bungled nomination with a gaffe for the ages. In an attempt to downplay Carswell's flimsy credentials, the Nebraska senator said, "Even if he were mediocre, there are a lot of mediocre judges and people and lawyers, and they are entitled to a little representation, aren't they?" A source of laughter and bemusement, the blunder provided the opposition with one of its catchiest talking points.

On March 30, 1970, Saxbe passed along the Senate's reservations to the president. Though acknowledging Carswell was a "bad egg," the combative Nixon still refused to back down. Instead, the president sent a biting letter back to Saxbe on April 1 reflecting his anger at the changing dynamics of judicial politics:

> What is centrally at issue in this nomination is the constitutional responsibility of the President to appoint members of the Court—and whether this responsibility can be frustrated by those who wish to substitute their own philosophy or their own subjective judgment for that of the one person entrusted by the Constitution with the power of appointment. The question arises whether I, as President of the United States, shall be accorded the same right of choice in naming Supreme Court Justices which has been freely accorded to my predecessors of both parties. . . . [I]f the Senate attempts to substitute its judgment as to who should be appointed, the traditional constitutional balance is in jeopardy and the duty of the President under the Constitution impaired.

What Nixon had not yet realized was that, after Fortas, the Senate would never return to its accommodating ways when confronted with an unappealing nominee. Zealously safeguarding its new, muscular role in the confirmation process, the world's most deliberative legislative body scolded the president for his attempted power-grab. "The interpretation" promoted by Nixon, Bayh said in a four-hour speech on the Senate floor the next day, "is wrong as a matter of constitutional law, wrong as a matter of history, and wrong as a matter of public policy." Griffin reaffirmed the sentiment, one which he had loudly espoused a year earlier. "Unfortunately, for too many years," he said a few minutes after Bayh, "the Senate did not assert itself . . . and in too many instances the Senate was a rubberstamp. No one could be more pleased than I am that now the Senate is truly exercising its . . . power." Misreading the situation, Nixon's aggressive posture cost him a handful of wavering senators. Scott warned the White House: "one more stunt like that and Carswell will get two votes."

One by one, liberals and moderates in both parties gravitated towards the opposition. Nearly every vote-count put together in February and March of 1970 showed declining support for Carswell even as the confirmation's backers held on to a majority. The vote was expected to be so close that Bayh concocted a strategy to prevent Agnew from breaking a potential tie in the Senate with a final vote, which as vice president, he was empowered to do. It turned out to be an unneeded contingency plan. On April 8, 1970, the Senate rejected Carswell 45-51 with thirteen Republicans voting with the opposition. No president other than Johnson had suffered consecutive confirmation losses since Grover Cleveland. Humiliated by the historic setback, Nixon managed to exploit the failure. Speeches from the Oval Office were primarily reserved for major policy announcements. A day later, however, Nixon used the dramatic backdrop to pander to the South's sense of victimization: "With yesterday's action, the Senate has said that no Southern . . . judge . . . can be elevated to the Supreme Court. . . . I understand the bitter feeling of millions of Americans who live in the South about the act of regional discrimination that took place."

"Richard Nixon was a hero in the South," Dent observed when he traveled to the region after the defeat. "No action by the president," he said, referring to the two nominations, "did more to cement the sinews of the southern strategy."

He was right: the region handed Nixon his largest margin of victory in 1972.

It seemed like Fortas's seat on the Court was snake-bitten. Weeks after *Baker*, the 1962 reapportionment case, an embittered Frankfurter suffered a massive stroke and was forced to retire from the Court. Bound to a wheelchair and barely able to speak, he blamed *Baker* for his condition. Living out his remaining four years in a debilitated state, he generated enough verve to vilify the Court's "reprehensible decisions" every chance he could. Too ill to remain on the frontlines of the struggle against Warren and his allies, and frustrated with the praise heaped upon them by "liberal approvers," he recruited others to his cause, urging legal scholars to "sharpen your pens" and strike at his former colleagues, if for nothing else but to "get under their skins." Hoodwinked by Johnson, Goldberg, the next holder of this seat, regretfully resigned after three years. Then came the final act of Fortas's Shakespearean tragedy. The seat had been empty for nearly a year when Carswell was rejected, making it the first time the judicial body had operated with eight justices for that long. The time had come for Nixon to find a suitable nominee.

"If they vote him down," Nixon had dared a group of Republican senators when Carswell's candidacy began to falter, "we'll send them somebody from Mississippi." The *National Review* had the same notion, satirizing a nomination of "Cletus Gaptooth of Shotgun, Miss." The president decided against going through with his threat. Skipping over another southerner, Nixon instead picked Harry Blackmun, an appellate judge from Minnesota whom he tried to portray as a carbon copy of Haynsworth and Carswell. The selection was nothing of the sort and the Senate knew it, confirming Blackmun 94-0 on May 12, 1970.

The two failed nominations represented the biggest setbacks of Nixon's presidency until Watergate. The implications were far more historic for the Court. The transformation that had taken place during Fortas's nomination was now entrenched, and Nixon's next move was about to raise the stakes for the institution one notch higher.

CHAPTER 16

"DOUGLAS IS THE NEXT ONE . . ."

APRIL–DECEMBER, 1970

O f all the speeches that Gerald Ford made in his twenty-eight years in public office, the one he delivered to the House of Representatives on April 15, 1970 was the most peculiar. Before 325 of his peers in a setting that a reporter described as a "Roman circus," he railed against William Douglas for two hours. Occurring less than a week after Carswell's defeat, another harangue against one of the Court's liberals seemed par for the course. What made this speech different, and far more sinister than the hundreds of others that Thurmond, Eastland, and company had been spewing for years was Ford's attempt to turn the long-held resentments of the Court into action.

A fiscal conservative and social moderate with bipartisan appeal, Ford espoused a middle-of-the-road brand of Republicanism. Affable and unpretentious, with an even-keeled personality, his demeanor seemed to match his political philosophy. "Everybody liked Jerry Ford," Griffin remembered. Still athletic at fifty-six—in college at the University of Michigan he had steered the offensive line for a pair of national championship teams—Ford exuded an earnest, no-nonsense Midwestern ethos, all of which made him an unlikely political assassin.

Since Warren's fateful meeting with Johnson nearly two years earlier, the tug-of-war over the Court's membership and the zeal to determine its direction for a coming generation had shattered traditions once thought to be inviolable. But, just when it seemed that no one could disrupt the status quo any further, Ford managed to do just that. This time the target was Douglas. "I believe . . . that he is unfit and should be removed," Ford said of the justice at the end of his speech. "I would vote to impeach him."

Forced to contend with Griffin's filibuster, Thurmond's adult film spectacle, Fortas's scandalous resignation, the longest vacancy on the Court since Reconstruction, and a record number of rejections not seen since the mid-nineteenth century, the nation was hard-pressed to find examples from the past to illuminate this turn of events. The constitutional mechanism for removing members of the judiciary had rarely been invoked: of the thousands of judges to serve in the federal courts over nearly two centuries, only nine had been impeached by the House and only four of them were found guilty by the Senate. Justice Samuel Chase, the only member of the Supreme Court to be targeted with impeachment, survived his trial back in 1805. Within this historical context, the notion of impeaching a justice seemed farfetched. Ford's attempt to expel Douglas made it clear that the norms governing the Court, no matter how well-established, no longer carried the day. Ford's speech did not emerge as an isolated incident, but was the culmination of the political warfare that had been surrounding the Court ever since the justices had issued *Brown* nearly sixteen years earlier. And though Warren was no longer chief justice, it was the opening salvo in one of the final clashes of the Warren Wars.

The idea to impeach Douglas germinated soon after Fortas's ouster and quickly spread through the capital. "The word here went out from the High Command," Douglas wrote to his sister just days after Fortas's resignation, "that the first to go would be Abe, the second myself, and the third one Brennan." Dismayed that his attempt to inoculate his friend may have been futile, Fortas wrote to Douglas on May 28, 1969: "I should be in anguish if I thought that my own decision aggravated your problem—because I hoped that it would . . . relieve the pressure on you. . . . I hope to God it will." In hindsight, Fortas's willingness to sacrifice himself, rather than appeasing those determined to get rid of the Court's liberals, encouraged the conservative opposition to put on a repeat performance. Elated by Fortas's downfall, Thurmond made this clear to his constituents a fortnight after Fortas resigned: "Douglas is the next one who must go."

Only one man had the wherewithal to turn these words into action. Like a puppeteer working the strings behind the scenes, Nixon sought to oust another one of the Court's liberals. Early in his presidency, Nixon ordered the IRS to audit Douglas, and the FBI had long been tapping Douglas's phones. When Nixon grew frustrated by the unexpected opposition to Haynsworth during the fall of 1969, the idea of impeaching Douglas advanced from an abstract concept to become an active campaign. To move things along, the president asked Mitchell to investigate the stock ownership of all the justices to expose the types of conflicts of interest that had doomed Haynsworth. Although typically willing to do Nixon's bidding, the attorney general resisted this time around, however. If the president's meddling into the justices' confidential tax records "was ever discovered," Mitchell warned, and "that this matter was being looked into through what one could call a rather devious means, it would present real trouble for the President." Reprising his role as chief executioner, the attorney general turned to Will Wilson, the same Justice Department official who had been in charge of the Fortas probe, to build a case against Douglas.

Over time, this nascent idea, whispered and bandied about at first and mentioned by the press through occasional leaks, turned into a bare-faced threat. "If the Senate does not confirm Carswell," Ford said during the ill-fated nomination, "we'll impeach Douglas." Ford's blunt statement was the clearest signal yet that the highly politicized battle over the Court's membership that first erupted with Fortas's nomination in June 1968 had now spread to the sitting justices.

Using the successful removal of Fortas as its prototype, the White House sought to mask its role from the public. Donald Rumsfeld, the future Secretary of Defense under George W. Bush who was at the time the director of the Office of Economic Opportunity, suggested a pithy statement pointing out that the "Douglas matter" fell "solely within the jurisdiction of the Congress." Another aide insisted that the White House "disassociate [itself] even more clearly." To do so, the administration needed a congressman to be the frontman for Douglas's removal. Ford, a straight-shooter who had never mastered the dark arts of politics, went to the head of the line based on his relationship with the president. Nixon and Ford had established an enduring bond when both men were reaching the crossroads of their careers in 1965. Ford had just risen to House Minority Leader while Nixon was in the early stages of resurrecting his own career. Ford became "a Nixon man" from the start, and remained deeply loyal to the president throughout Nixon's 1968 campaign and presidency. That loyalty, combined with his leadership position within Congress, made him the ideal vessel for Nixon's latest move on the Court. Despite Ford's denials of Nixon's meddling, even some inside the White House doubted his veracity. "I only hope, against hope" wrote Patrick Moynihan— the future New York senator, then serving as one of Nixon's domestic advisors—"that it does not soon appear in the press that we were involved."

Both professionally and personally, Douglas personified all that conservatives loathed like no other member of the Court. His career as a liberal stalwart was unassailable. It's true that Warren had been the Court's indisputable leader and Brennan, a masterful tactician and vote-counter, served as his right-hand man. Douglas's stubborn adherence to his principles kept him from reaching their degree of influence, but neither Warren nor Brennan—nor Black, Fortas, or Goldberg, for that matter—could match Douglas's uncompromising liberalism. Douglas's categorical fealty to these principles made him a star among liberals and a villain among conservatives. His private life was similarly infuriating to his detractors. In contrast to his brethren, who led upstanding lives, Douglas lived far more like a strapping playboy than the staid jurists the American public was used to seeing on the Court. In 1970, he was on his fourth marriage—to a law student forty-four years his junior whom Joan Crawford once called a "child" at a White House dinner—at a time when not a single justice had ever been divorced. "In all candor," Mississippi Congressman Thomas Abernathy complained, Douglas "would do himself and his country a favor if he would quietly resign from the High Court and devote full time to that in which he appears to be most learned and proficient—linking the highways of matrimony." Rumors of extramarital affairs and the justice's pursuit of younger women caromed throughout Washington. "We all had the feeling that nobody's wife was safe around Bill," said one of his closest friends.

Douglas's lofty standing in the counter-culture added to his dreadful reputation within conservative circles. A star on college campuses—in his book, *Points of Rebellion*, the justice practically encouraged the nation's youth to openly revolt at a time when conservative Americans cringed at the increasing demonstrations staged by students, civil rights advocates, and anti-war protestors. The book's most provocative passage called "today's Establishment ... the new George III," in reference to the king of England during the American Revolution. "Whether it will continue to adhere to his tactics, we do not know. If it does," Douglas concluded near the end of the book, "the redress, honored in tradition, is also revolution." "The kindest thing I can say about this ninety-seven-page tome is that it is quick reading," Ford continued in his speech before the House. "It is a fuzzy harangue evidently intended to give historic legitimacy to the militant hippie-yippie movement."

Points of Rebellion could not match the outrage induced by Douglas's other works. The justice authored four pieces for Hefner's publication. While *Playboy* at least showcased several prominent and respected writers of the time, *Evergreen*, an erotic magazine that published an excerpt of *Points of Rebellion* just days before Ford's speech, catered less to the mainstream. The issue in which Douglas's piece appeared included an article espousing "Sexual Adventure in Marriage," a nude pictorial, and a cartoon titled "George III" of Nixon bedecked with a crown. "I am simply unable to describe the prurient advertisements, the perverted suggestions, the downright filthy illustrations," Ford said in disgust, "and the shocking ... four letter language it employs. ... There are nude models of both sexes in poses that are perhaps more shocking than the postcards that used to be sold only in the back alleys of Paris and Panama City."

Ford's sentiments were widely shared. Douglas's usual litany of hate-mail mushroomed as news of his personal shortcomings spilled into the public over the years. Called a "silly old fool," a "dirty old man," and "senile," critics repeatedly demanded his resignation. Others weren't so kind as to wish for his retirement. A handwritten note on floral-decorated stationery asked him to have "the common decency to retire or drop dead." "BY GOD," another irate critic wrote: "I HOPE SOME DAY WE GET TO HANG YOU ALONG WITH DEAN ACHESON, . . . HENRY KISSINGER, DANIEL (FAT-

FACE) P. MOYNIHAN and some others . . . who would look good with a rope around their necks."

Despite his disavowals to the contrary, Ford's encapsulation of these sentiments near the end of his speech revealed the true reasons behind his call for impeachment:

> Douglas appears to represent . . . the pornographic publishing trade . . . and [the] intellectual incubators for the New Left. . . . Douglas does not find himself in this company suddenly or accidentally or unknowingly, he has been working at it for years, profiting from it for years, and flaunting it in the faces of decent Americans for years.

Of all Douglas's alleged iniquities, his affront to these "decent Americans" more than anything else put a bulls-eye on his back, so much so that Keating—the anti-porn crusader—offered to help Ford convict Douglas.

As appalling as they were to many Americans, Ford strained to link these tawdry episodes to impeachable transgressions. "Writing . . . articles for notorious publications of a convicted pornographer is bad enough," the House Minority Leader told his colleagues during his speech. "Taking money for them is worse. Declining to disqualify one's self," he continued, "is inexcusable." Ford claimed Douglas had failed to recuse himself from an obscenity case involving Ralph Ginzburg, owner of a publication for which Douglas had written an article. But the bulk of the charges—the ones that were the most threatening to Douglas—focused on the justice's relationship with the Parvin Foundation, an association Ford claimed closely tied Douglas "to the international gambling fraternity." For a decade, Douglas had served as president of the foundation that annually funded dozens of students from developing nations to fellowships at Princeton University and hosted a series of conferences to foster international cooperation. On the surface, the foundation's goals were benevolent. It was the fortune made by its backer Albert Parvin from Las Vegas casinos, and the existence of SEC and IRS investigations into his business practices that cast a long shadow over Douglas's involvement. Ford alleged that Douglas had been engaging in the practice of law while serving on the foundation in clear breach of federal law. Ford's most salacious accusations, though, were less concerned with such technical violations. They linked Parvin to the underworld figures Bugsy Siegel and Meyer Lansky, as well as Wolfson, of all people, in an attempt to associate Douglas with unsavory characters.

While Ford kept adding logs to the bonfire during his long-winded speech, Andrew Jacobs Jr., an Indiana Democrat, filed an impeachment resolution to ensure that the House Judiciary Committee—and not a special investigating committee preferred by Ford—would oversee the process. By getting his resolution filed before Ford's, Jacobs's wily parliamentary maneuver left the investigation in the hands of Emmanuel Celler, the House Judiciary Committee chairman. A pro-labor New Dealer who had overseen the passage of several civil rights measures, Celler had long used his post on the committee to defend the Court from its naysayers. While the most consequential moments of the Warren Wars took place in the Senate, Celler fought on the frontlines of these struggles in the House. A veteran of Red Monday and the Dirksen amendments, the 82-year old congressman from Brooklyn returned to the battlefield to protect one of the two remaining members of the original Warren Court. Taking advantage of the opening provided by Jacobs's ploy, Celler established a five-member subcommittee to investigate the impeachment charges made by Ford and installed himself as its chairman.

Ironically, for the third time in many months, Nixon's hardball tactics backfired. Douglas had planned on retiring in the summer of 1970. But now, determined to clear his name, he resolved to stay on the Court. "I do not propose to bend to any such pressure," the justice assured Parvin. Conscious of the severity of the charges made against him and pressed by his friends to acquire top-notch legal representation, the justice avoided repeating Fortas's mistake of defending himself on his own. He hired Simon Rifkind, a former federal judge who was a named partner in an elite New York law firm, to lead a team of superstars including Ramsey Clark and Warren Christopher.

Dubbed "a real pack rat" by Rifkind for his meticulous record-keeping—the justice preserved what most people would have discarded, including envelopes on which he doodled random thoughts—Douglas transferred all the files of his finances, speeches, and travels to Rifkind's team in order to counter every allegation lodged against him no matter how inconsequential. When Parvin resisted handing over his personal correspondence with Douglas that related to his divorce and other matters, Douglas insisted that they be turned over to Rifkind's team as well. When the subcommittee inquired about gifts from Parvin, Douglas's secretary reached out to his ex-wives in order to be as thorough as possible in their responses. Retracting into his shell like a turtle under siege, the justice muzzled his usual self-assuredness and deferred all important decisions to Rifkind, asking for the counselor's authorization on his travel plans, speeches, and publications to avoid supplying new ammunition to his detractors.

With so few precedents to rely upon, it was unclear what standards the House should apply to assess the merits of Ford's charges. Ford had called for a broad and flexible approach to judging Douglas's behavior: "an impeachable offense," he argued in his April speech, "is whatever a majority of the House of Representatives considers to be at a given moment in history." In a formal memorandum submitted to Celler, Ford expanded on this idea, proposing a standard granting Congress wide latitude in removing a justice "whose proven conduct, either in the administration of justice or in his personal behavior, casts doubt on his personal integrity and thereby on the integrity of the entire judiciary." Rifkind argued for a narrower definition requiring impeachment only in instances of "criminal conduct." Celler's subcommittee incorporated concepts from both sides. "For a judge to be impeached," the subcommittee concluded, "it must be shown that he has committed treason, accepted a bribe, or has committed a high crime or misdemeanor." It conceded that behavior amounting to "serious derelictions of duty owed to society" could be grounds for impeachment, as Ford had argued, but concluded that any such indiscretion must involve Douglas's actions "in his judicial capacity" and not his "non-judicial misconduct which occurs off the bench and does not constitute a crime." Simply put, Ford's accusations against Douglas's personal indiscretions may have sullied the justice's personal reputation, but as long as they didn't involve or interfere with Douglas's duties as a judge or were illegal, Celler's subcommittee determined that they weren't grounds for impeachment.

This position infuriated Ford's team. "[I]t is wholly a whitewash, almost a commendation, of Justice Douglas' every act over the past decade," Ford's aide wrote of Celler's take on Douglas's behavior. "Not one word of criticism, censure or concern for propriety." As the subcommittee's views became apparent through the spring and summer of 1970, it became clear that Rifkind's team only had to contend with refuting Ford's substantive charges and not defending Douglas's lifestyle.

Celler's subcommittee spent months meticulously reviewing the materials submitted by Ford and Rifkind. After more than 30,000 man-hours of work summarized in a 924-page report, the subcommittee on December 3, 1970 officially exonerated Douglas of all Ford's charges on a 3-1 party-line vote (one of the Republican members abstained). One by one, members of the subcommittee acquitted Douglas of any wrongdoing. It turned out that Douglas's publisher had placed the excerpt of his book in *Evergreen* without the justice's knowledge. Douglas had published his article in Ginzburg's magazine prior to the publisher's appeal to the Court, clearing him of any conflicts of interest charges. Douglas and Parvin were indeed close friends, but unlike Fortas, who was promised $20,000 a year in lifetime payments for no clear tasks other than to provide guidance, Douglas earned his remuneration for actively running a foundation. When lawyers combed through the time and expenses Douglas had incurred in fulfilling these duties, they concluded that the justice had worked for the equivalent of 25¢ an hour. The subcommittee also found that the speaking fees and reimbursements the justice had received for delivering speeches across the world were not back-handed payoffs to compensate Douglas for special favors. Moreover, the justice's work for the foundation did not involve legal matters, but purely administrative ones. That cleared Douglas of the more technical charges. Douglas may have flirted with danger by spending so much of his time moonlighting outside of the Court (earning $377,260 from these activities during the 1960s, nearly as much as his judicial salary over that span of time) and certainly lived an unorthodox lifestyle by the age's standards, but he had not broken the law. In regard to the most incendiary charge, accusing Douglas, of fraternizing with criminals, Celler's report found no evidence that "Douglas ever associated with or even met" with "underworld characters or members of some organized gambling fraternity."

What had commenced with great momentum—kick-started by Ford's combative speech in April—ended with a thud seven months later. "Ford blew it," Wilson grumbled. All that Ford did with the materials the Justice Department handed over to him, Wilson complained, was waste it on that "dang fool speech." Douglas's victory put an end to Nixon's attempts to target the Court's other liberals. Going forward, the president would have to reshape the judicial body the old-fashioned way—by waiting for a vacancy. He didn't have to wait very long.

Chapter 17

"I'm Not from the South, I'm Not a Woman, and I'm Not Mediocre"

SEPTEMBER–DECEMBER, 1971

When back-to-back retirements by Justices Black and Harlan in September of 1971 opened the door for Nixon to leave a bigger mark on the Court than all but a handful of his predecessors, a chorus of presidential aides insisted on a fresh approach. Buchanan urged swift action to prevent labor and civil rights groups from building "public support" as they had done with Haynsworth and Carswell and lobbied for an "impeccable" southerner to divide the Democratic frontrunners in the coming election: "either they kick their black friends in the teeth, or they kick the South in the teeth." Bud Krogh, the "plumber" who ordered the break-in of the office used by the *Pentagon Papers* author Daniel Ellsberg's psychiatrist just weeks earlier, focused on the "unwavering objective" of selecting an ideologically sound candidate with "a powerful, proven intellect." Krogh formulated an instruction manual to take advantage of the "unique opportunity for the President to secure control of the Court. . . . Only if . . . young men are selected," he insisted, "can we hope to maintain ideological control of the Court for a full generation." "We simply can't afford to play catch up ball with a nomination again," Krogh argued. He was, in essence, calling for the type of professionalized and systematic approach presidents would eventually develop over the coming decades. The president followed Krogh's advice in piecemeal fashion, embracing some suggestions yet unable to resist toying with controversial picks who could potentially scuttle his long-term vision for the Court.

Nixon's worst characteristics—the paranoia, cynicism, and excessive combativeness that led to his downfall—were on full display during his quest for another southerner. This time around, he fixated on Virginia Congressman Richard Poff. Despite his good-standing among his peers across the political spectrum, Poff had to contend with the fallout from Carswell. He would have to pass the same litmus test on civil rights and demonstrate his credentials were worthy of a seat on the high court. In a heartfelt mea culpa, Poff admitted to succumbing to the wave of pressure sweeping the region to sign the Southern Manifesto. "He did what any damn southerner should do," Nixon told Mitchell in Poff's defense. The very stance on civil rights that advanced Poff's political fortunes now haunted him on the national stage. Poff's legal qualifications were also thin. Other than his tenure on the House Judiciary Committee, Poff's graduation from the highly-ranked University of Virginia Law School constituted the peak of his legal career. He had little experience practicing law and never served as a judge. The fact that he had sponsored legislation requiring justices to have five years of judicial experience further highlighted this blemish. With all of these potential liabilities marring Poff's candidacy, Nixon's aides warned that selecting the congressman risked another embarrassing defeat.

Nixon resented their concerns over Poff's spotty credentials. "Warren is a dumb Swede," he growled, referring to the former chief justice at a meeting with his aides on September 28. "All this bullshit about distinguished judges just makes me sick to my stomach. . . . Shit," he insisted, Poff is "brighter than those other people. And hell, who knows how distinguished he'll become."

Poff was more concerned with the impact his nomination would have on his family than with any of these other shortcomings. He understood that the new scrutiny nominees faced would put his life under a magnifying glass. To Nixon's screening team, he confessed to having an affair in the 1950s, but it was the disclosure of an innocuous revelation that led him to remove himself from contention. Poff had not told his twelve-year-old son of his adoption. "He is a very sensitive child," the congressman explained to the

White House aide, John Dean. "We consulted a psychologist, and we were told to wait." So nervous of the impact this revelation might have on his son, Poff would stay awake in the middle of the night agonizing over it. "I can't risk going forward with this thing. . . . I love him, and would feel terrible if my ambitions hurt him," Poff told Dean. On October 2, just days after he had climbed to the top of Nixon's list, Poff formally withdrew his nomination for what he claimed was to avoid "a long and divisive confirmation battle." Ironically, weeks later, Poff was compelled to reveal the very secret for which he had given up a potential Court seat when a reporter exposed the true reason behind his withdrawal.

After Poff bowed out, Nixon flirted with the idea of selecting Senate Majority Whip Robert Byrd, a Democrat from West Virginia whose accomplishments as a lawyer made Carswell look like Oliver Wendell Holmes. The senator had graduated from American University Law School in 1963 but never practiced law. If that wasn't enough to strike him from consideration, the fact that Byrd once belonged to the KKK and staged a fourteen-hour filibuster opposing the 1964 Civil Rights Act should have grounded his candidacy. Though counseled by his advisors to dump Byrd, Nixon's resentment at missing out on Poff made these negative attributes all the more appealing. Byrd's "more reactionary than Wallace," the president boasted. After Haynsworth and Carswell, his relationship with the Senate had reached a low not seen since Woodrow Wilson's feud with the chamber over the League of Nations. Even as his congressional liaisons reported near unanimous opposition to Byrd's candidacy, even from a senator who had vowed to "never cross the President," Nixon relished the fact that Byrd's nomination would tie the legislative body up in knots. "In Byrd," wrote William Shannon, a frequent contributor to *The New York Times* editorial page, "the President has found a candidate whose record appalls and flabbergasts his adversaries, but one whom the Senate in its craven clubbiness could hardly fail to confirm." On every level, his consideration of Byrd for the job encapsulated Nixon's calculating and cynical mindset, what Dean called the "equivalent of throwing a stink bomb into the Senate."

None of this was uncommon for Nixon. Speculating over how his enemies might react to his moves was a favorite pastime of his. Two openings on the Court gave him ample opportunity to play out this game. "I just want to beat the bastards on this," he told Mitchell, his primary interlocutor on the nominations. The president took great pleasure in misdirecting the press with "red herrings," and if his antics were incendiary, then all the better. "As far as Byrd's thing, let it ramble around a bit up there," he told Mitchell on October 11. "I'll bet you they're regurgitating all over the place . . . because Poff . . . , compared to Byrd, is a flaming liberal. . . . It teaches them a lesson."

Nixon also mulled over an equally divisive pick: Herschel Friday, an Arkansas lawyer who once represented southern school districts resisting integration. Dismissed as an "avid redneck segregationist" by Nelson Rockefeller, he too would certainly face strong opposition from civil rights leaders and Republican liberals essential to a successful confirmation.

While contemplating which southerner to pick, Nixon sought to break new ground by selecting a woman for the second opening, a move that reflected the flourishing identity politics of the era. Forging a strategy mimicked by future Republican presidents, i.e. Reagan and George H. W. Bush—with respectively Sandra Day O'Connor and Clarence Thomas—Nixon planned to cast himself as a champion of equality and diversity. "It isn't a man's world anymore," he conceded to Mitchell. Nixon's motives were hardly egalitarian or sincere, however. Sexist comments made throughout his deliberations exposed his true sentiments. "I don't think a woman should be in any government job... because they are erratic and emotional," he told Mitchell in late September. Yet no other under-represented group would boost his reelection chances more. "In a political sense, it comes right down to cold turkey," Nixon explained to the attorney general. "I lean to a woman only because . . . we got to pick up every half a percentage point we can."

The president's interest in a female nominee signified the growing impetus for the idea. A bevy of women's groups, the president's wife, and mail pouring into the White House pressed Nixon to select a woman, and Griffin, Bayh, Hart, and other senators also chimed in with their preference for a female justice. With so few seasoned Republican judges within the ranks of the federal judiciary and even fewer conservative women judges to pick from, however, the White House struggled to find a viable candidate. In a meeting with Republican senators, Nixon called the pool of female candidates "a bag of bags." After an extensive search, he finally settled on California appellate judge Mildred Lillie. After finishing her studies at Boalt Law School (Warren's alma mater), Lillie worked in the public and private sectors. Starting in 1947, she served on California's Municipal Court, later jumped to the Superior Court, and in 1958, began to serve in the California Court of Appeal. She may have lacked Burger's judicial pedigree but, unlike Poff and Byrd, had no disqualifying marks on her record.

Pressured by John Volpe, the Secretary of Transportation, Nixon also explored the possibility of picking an Italian-American judge for one of the two vacancies. Ever mindful of the political ramifications involved, Buchanan had articulated the benefits of selecting a justice of Italian descent a year earlier. "Politically, the elevation of a Catholic Italian-American to . . . the Court would mean ten million Italians would light candles in their homes for the President." "My view is that," Buchanan reiterated at the end of September, 1971, "we get the most brilliant and qualified Italian-American . . . in the nation—and then . . . play up his Italian background." Others in the White House also identified these benefits. Seeing "enormous symbolic value to . . . Italians," Chuck Colson—another one of the "plumbers" who was later sent to prison for his role in the Watergate scandal—felt that the increasingly conservative constituency "strategically located in . . . key states" could be "cultivated." "Every play we make to those Catholics is good," Nixon explained to the attorney general. Refusing to resurrect the "Jewish seat" that once belonged to Brandeis, Frankfurter, Goldberg, and Fortas, and that dated back to 1916, Nixon displayed no appetite to appeal to Jewish voters. Asked by Mitchell when he would appoint a Jew to the Court, Nixon bluntly replied: "after I die."

Taking all of these factors into consideration, Lillie came the closest to being Nixon's ideal candidate. She was a woman, a Catholic, and, through her marriage to an Italian-American, might be able to placate Volpe. Unable to resist the positive coverage he expected to receive in the press, Nixon made Lillie the presumptive favorite among the various women vetted by his aides. "This woman story is going to be big," Nixon assured the attorney general. "I can't wait."

The American Bar Association began to grade the professional qualifications of potential appointments to the federal judiciary after WWII and formally reviewed Court nominees starting with Harlan in 1954. And though no one was bound to its conclusions—the ABA's committee on the federal judiciary recommended Carswell, after all—its endorsements added extra heft to a president's choices. The six potential candidates Mitchell sent to the ABA included Byrd, Lillie, and Friday. When the press published the leaked list on October 13, the reaction was uniformly negative: "there was considerable dismay," *The New York Times* reported, "because the list did not include any of the leading judicial figures who had been mentioned in earlier speculation." Rowland Evans and Robert Novak echoed the widespread belief that the selections amounted to a collection of mediocrities largely meant to appeal to southern segregationists.

Embarrassed by the proposed names, Burger threatened to resign. "Fuck him," Nixon bellowed, when he heard about the chief justice's ultimatum. "Let him resign." The president wasn't finished. "Fuck the ABA" he also declared. "They're such a bunch of sanctimonious assholes." The episode turned comical when John Ehrlichman denied ever hearing the "quoted obscenity . . . attributed" to the president. It was among the most benign lies of a presidency rampant with deceit and vulgarity.

The leaked list of potential candidates exposed Nixon's basest political instincts. Selecting Byrd would pit northern and southern Democrats against one another while a conservative woman would be untouchable by the Left. "You know John, it must really make you feel happy that you would be the attorney general to have made the first recommendation of a woman on the Court," Nixon said in a cynical tone, as Mitchell began to chuckle. "When I get with that new Women's lib, why I'll be their hero," Mitchell joked in return, inducing H.R. Haldeman, who was listening in on the conversation, to burst out in laughter. The interaction typified Nixon's conversations with Mitchell, who was often his partner in these sessions. In another discussion about Lillie, the attorney general assured the president that the judge possessed "a good personality. . . . I think we'll see that she's not one of these frigid bitches."

The ABA's leak so embarrassed Nixon, it finally put an end to his gamesmanship. Other than his nomination of Warren Burger, he had misfired with each vacancy on the Court. Pressured to move swiftly to contain the fallout of the ABA's disclosure, Nixon set a deadline for October 21, giving him a week to zero in on two confirmable nominees.

For a southerner, the White House settled on 64-year-old Lewis Powell, the former president of the ABA out of Virginia, who was widely renowned as one of America's finest lawyers. Besides his stellar credentials, Powell carried an inoffensive civil rights record. Powell had declined similar overtures a year earlier due to his poor eyesight. This time around, he couldn't resist the president's personal appeal, which came via a combination of flattery and a call to duty. "We think that nominating you would be very, very important," Nixon told Powell in a phone call on October 19. When Powell expressed his concern that he might not be able to serve very long, Nixon dismissed his worries, and turned the conversation back to Powell's sense of duty. "If I determine that your appointment at this time is what the Court needs," Nixon continued, "would you undertake it?" Powell conceded to Nixon's direct appeal, and with that, Nixon finally had a southerner widely respected across the nation. In hindsight, had the president wooed Powell earlier, he could have saved himself and the nation a good deal of agony.

Powell's age and infirmity persuaded Nixon to search for a younger nominee for the second vacancy. With Millie still in the running despite the fallout from the ABA leak, Nixon eyed Dirksen's son-in-law, 45-year-old Tennessee Senator Howard Baker. Baker was caught off-guard by the unexpected offer: "We sort of knocked Howard off his feet" Mitchell reported back to the president. When the senator hesitated—"I guess he's searching his soul," Mitchell told Nixon— he forced Nixon to search for a backup should he falter.

This odd sequence of events is what opened the door for William Rehnquist. Dean had proposed Rehnquist for one of the two vacancies weeks earlier (a move Dean would later regret). After the idea bounced around the administration, it began to mature into a real possibility by mid-October. Mitchell laid out the case for Rehnquist to Nixon on October 19—just two days before the president's self-imposed deadline. With Carswell's thin credentials still a blot on the president, it helped Rehnquist's cause that no one could accuse him of mediocrity. After graduating as valedictorian of Stanford Law School, he clerked for Justice Jackson, an honor bestowed upon only the best law graduates, and as the head of Office of Legal Counsel at the Justice Department, he was a lawyer's lawyer much like Fortas. These gold-plated credentials made up for his lack of judicial experience and the absence of any noteworthy accomplishments as a public official. Rehnquist had a couple of other things in his favor. At 47, he could serve on the Court well into the next century and as a Goldwater acolyte, he was a hard-nosed ideologue, a distinction that differentiated him from anyone else under consideration. Mitchell described him as an "arch-conservative," an ideologically driven lawyer the likes of which had rarely been seen on the Court. The *National Review* went further in calling him a "Counterrevolutionary" (emphasis in original) who would not just impede but reverse the Warren Court's achievements.

Nixon resisted the idea at first. The first time he met Rehnquist, the president thought he was a "clown" for wearing a pink shirt and psychedelic tie. Nixon's impression didn't change after listening to Mitchell's initial pitch. Rehnquist's conservatism was appealing and his brilliance would rebut any claims of mediocrity that had dogged Carswell and the list handed over to the ABA. But in Nixon's eyes, Rehnquist wasn't distinguished enough to impress the public. He wasn't a judge. He wasn't a congressman. He wasn't a governor. To the outside world, Rehnquist was an obscure bureaucrat. Besides, he was the wrong gender, nationality, and religion. "I suppose he's a damn Protestant," Nixon barked to Mitchell. Conscious of the president's criteria as the point-man vetting candidates in the Justice Department, Rehnquist joked that he had no chance to gain the nomination: "I'm not from the South, I'm not a woman, and I'm not mediocre."

Convinced that selecting Rehnquist earned "zero political benefit for the president," Ehrlichman agreed with Nixon's assessment. At the time, Nixon's search for an ideologue was difficult to align with his aim to enhance his electoral prospects. The challenge of balancing these conflicting goals threw the White House into a maelstrom, leading Nixon to mull over a host of candidates as he settled on a pair of finalists. Fordham's former Dean William Mulligan, William French Smith—who later became Reagan's attorney general—and several others were briefly under consideration even as the president neared the finish line. Nixon also considered nominating Powell and Baker. Despite these considerations, the idea of selecting Rehnquist snowballed when Nixon began to appreciate the long-term benefit of selecting an ideologically driven justice.

It was Rehnquist's good fortune that the ABA's next move furthered his candidacy. By an 11-1 vote, it deemed Lillie "unqualified" for the Court on October 20. The low grade gave the president cover, allowing him to position himself as a champion of women while skipping over Lillie for a male candidate. Even before the official word came from the ABA, Nixon looked for ways to exploit Lillie's negative rating. "We're going to have to put it on them," he told Mitchell, and referring to the ABA, he added, "Let them take the rap." The fact that the White House's top female candidate was disqualified by a panel composed entirely of men thrilled him. "I think the eleven to one is brilliant," Nixon boasted to Mitchell when the ABA's vote became public, "because it's a . . . stacked jury. All men. . . . Jesus, that's great," he continued. "That's great." Striking Lillie off the list for good left Baker and Rehnquist as the two contenders heading into the final moments of the selection process.

Baker remained noncommittal leading up to Nixon's scheduled announcement date. "I can't find him," Mitchell told the president. "You know he promised to call me back . . . and I can't even find him." Baker's continued indecision combined with the ABA's categorical rejections of the other potential picks made Nixon more receptive to the idea of picking Rehnquist. On October 21, the morning of the president's announcement, Baker said he was willing to serve but wouldn't be upset if Nixon chose someone else. By the time he called to deliver his tepid acceptance, Nixon had changed his mind. "Baker," Dean recalled, "dithered himself right out of the job."

Ultimately, Rehnquist's reputation as a top-notch legal mind compared with Byrd, Lillie, and Friday combined with his steadfast ideology made him attractive enough for the president to overcome the nominee's lack of appeal to potential voters. But in selecting Rehnquist, Nixon had unknowingly picked a justice who was ahead of his time. Decades later, Republican voters would become far more preoccupied with a nominee's ideology than his religion, ethnic heritage, gender, or geographic origin.

The purity of Rehnquist's ideology also frightened Democrats. Though the Senate handily confirmed Powell 89-1, it put Rehnquist through a long inquisition. Once again led by Bayh, the opposition uncovered damaging materials from Rehnquist's past. "I realize that it is an unpopular and unhumanitarian position, for which I have been excoriated by 'liberal' colleagues," Rehnquist had written in a two-page memo as Justice Jackson's clerk, "but I think *Plessy* . . . was right and should be re-affirmed." If the memo reflected Rehnquist's views, it was automatic grounds for disqualification in the eyes of Senate liberals who relied on *Brown* as a litmus test before *Roe v. Wade* took over that role. Rehnquist explained that the memo reflected Justice Jackson's—not his— views and was put together at the justice's behest in preparation for a Court conference. For anyone who knew Jackson well, the explanation strained credulity. Another clerk vouched for Rehnquist while Jackson's former secretary disavowed Rehnquist's portrayal. The dueling stories couldn't break the tie and, nearing the end of the session, the Senate was in no mood for a fight. "You have fully discharged your responsibilities on this issue," Bayh's assistant wrote to him on December 8, "and have made as complete a fight as you could have, given the disinterest of your colleagues and the media." He was right. One of the senators leading the opposition complained that it "was time to vote and get out of town." On December 10, 1971, the Senate did just that, confirming Rehnquist 68-26, and with it, put an end to the most tumultuous era in the Court's history.

Epilogue: 1987 and Beyond

Nearly nineteen years to the day after Fortas's bruising loss, his ghost would resurface to haunt Robert Bork. Other than the absence of a filibuster, the parallels between the two aborted nominations were clear to anyone who was witness to both historic battles. It was fitting then that Joseph Califano—who had a front-row seat to Fortas's tragedy as Johnson's domestic advisor—reminded Bork's supporters of the consequences of what they had wrought: "Conservative Republicans and Democrats who seek to declare Judge Bork's views off-limits and decry the tactics of his opponents had better bone up on recent history," Califano wrote in "The '68 Version of the Bork Debate," an op-ed printed in *The New York Times*. "The similarities" between Fortas and Bork, "are striking: a lame-duck President nominating a brilliant lawyer . . . who shared his political philosophy, a time of transition for the Court and a desire to reverse a host of split decisions." The resemblances between the two events did not end there, however. Thurmond's "searing criticism of Justice Fortas as soft on criminals, obscenity and subversives," Califano pointed out, "makes . . . [Edward] Kennedy's comments about Judge Bork seem as dreary as a Harvard Law Review treatise." Califano recounted some of the groundbreaking moves made by Senators Robert Griffin and Howard Baker, the duo administering the filibuster, as well as the outburst of Thurmond screaming "Mallory" at the top of his lungs as Fortas sat helplessly a few feet away. "Opponents of the nominations made no apologies for using every procedural device at their disposal," Califano reiterated, and then pressed Bork's foes to resort to the same tactics if necessary:

> The history lesson is important. . . . Senators who conclude
> that [Bork's] views are incompatible with their vision of the

Court have the same obligation in 1987 as Senators Thurmond, Baker and others had in 1968: to oppose the nomination, by filibuster if necessary.

The greatest irony of the Bork affair was in the role reversal between liberals and conservatives. This time around, Thurmond took charge of defending a beleaguered and widely-reviled nominee from attacks that he condemned as unfair and unprecedented. Careful to avoid uttering Fortas's name during the extensive hearings and debates, Thurmond railed against Bork's opponents for deviating from the practices and traditions that had long governed the confirmation process. He conveniently skipped over the adult film festival, his tirade during the hearings, the filibuster, and the other ways he had mercilessly violated long-held norms and customs back in 1968. Throughout the summer and fall of 1987, Thurmond insisted that Bork's stellar credentials as a scholar and jurist along with his upstanding character—and not his conservative ideology—were the only legitimate factors the Senate should take into consideration.

Repeatedly, Thurmond's rivals relied on his statements from 1968 to make their case against Bork. The most frequently cited passage that they quoted to validate their actions encompassed Thurmond's views on how the Senate should evaluate a nominee:

> To contend that we must merely satisfy ourselves that Justice Fortas is a good lawyer and a man of good character is to hold a very narrow view of the role of the Senate, a view which neither the Constitution itself nor history and precedent have prescribed.

"Senator Thurmond was correct when he said that then," Ohio's Howard Metzenbaum argued in a typical display of the manner in which Thurmond's adversaries redirected his words against Bork. "[T]hose views are equally correct today."

Metzenbaum's declaration was a stark reminder of how the Fortas affair had put an end to the Senate's deferential attitude. Thurmond, Griffin, and others had made this abundantly clear throughout 1968. There was not going to be a return to those halcyon days when the Senate quickly and routinely confirmed justices when faced with an undesirable nominee. Maine's George Mitchell, the future Majority Leader, fittingly summed up the feelings of those accused of bending the rules to thwart Bork. "It is ironic to hear some of those who opposed Justice Fortas because of his legal philosophy," Mitchell proclaimed in a speech on the Senate floor, "now argue that it is wrong for the Senate to consider Judge Bork's philosophy." On October 23, 1987, the Senate rejected Bork 42-58.

For better and worse, the politicization of the Court, and the revolution it sparked in the confirmation process instigated by Fortas, Warren, Johnson, and Nixon, resonates to this day. The changes these individuals set in motion opened up the judicial body to women and underrepresented minorities, ushering in a welcome metamorphosis for an institution previously bereft of these voices. Both by design and happenstance, they also marshaled in an era of brilliant jurists—something that was not always the case for most of the nation's history.

But they also left behind a perilous legacy.

It wasn't that presidents of previous epochs had ignored the ideological viewpoints of their nominees. Since the birth of the Constitution in the 1780s, the Court had been a political body. But it was designed by the Founding Fathers—and operated as such for most of its history—to be the least politicized of the three branches. With that in mind, the Constitution's authors decided to appoint rather than elect the justices and grant them lifetime tenure. Johnson's emphasis on his appointments' judicial philosophy, when harnessed by later generations more inclined towards partisanship and ideological extremism, turned the Court into a den of dogmatic justices. As both parties purged themselves of moderates over the past half century, they also began to drive the centrists on the Court towards extinction. The numbers bear this out: Nixon, Reagan, and the two Bushes selected nine of the ten most conservative justices out of the last forty-five, while Clinton's and Obama's picks ranked among the most liberal.

While Johnson inspired the nation's current obsession with ideological purity, Nixon's politically calculated selections became the norm for future presidents. Here again, context matters. Presidents were always mindful of the political repercussions in their judicial appointments. But few if any could match the ferocity with which Nixon pounced on the Court during his 1968 presidential run, and the deliberate efforts he made to woo southerners through his nominations. Nixon's success in using the Court to lure voters encouraged his successors to mimic his strategy. Taken to new heights over the next fifty years, a pledge to appoint ideologically sound justices became a mainstay of presidential campaigns and a key way to gratify constituents.

It's also not the case that the justices prior to Warren's arrival were Solomon-like sages who administered their duties free of ideological or partisan bias. The Warren Court's revolution in so many areas of American life combined with the backlash it engendered led to a clear and noticeable shift, however. What had been a random, accidental, and ad hoc process of developing liberal and conservative coalitions within the Court up to the 1960s had practically turned into an exact science by the century's end. As the justices became more closely aligned with their respective political parties, they stripped the Court of its last vestiges as a neutral arbiter. No ruling exemplified this transformation more than *Bush v. Gore*.

The Warren Court's sweeping changes, and its willingness to assist those unable to make inroads through the political branches—a case in point being the NAACP's decades-long failure to get an anti-lynching bill through Congress—also showcased the Court's potential to circumvent lawmakers and enact policies that might otherwise be unpopular with large segments of the public. By the twenty-first century, the NAACP's legal strategy—born out of frustration and necessity rather than from a desire to subvert the political process—became the norm for both liberals and conservatives. The extension of the NAACP's approach in recent years has led to the expansion of gun rights, unlimited corporate participation in elections, and the legalization of gay marriage through judicial decree. Operating under this precept, many advocates have become convinced that it is far easier to influence five justices to push forth their political agenda rather than attempt to appeal to thousands of state and federal legislators and the broader public. The confluence of all of these forces hyper-politicized the Court, and magnified the electorate's view of the justices in purely ideological and partisan terms.

Beside the quest for ideological purity and the increased partisanship of the confirmation process, the emphasis that Johnson and Nixon placed on a nominee's race, gender, religion, or ethnicity became commonplace even as the significance placed on each of these characteristics has shifted over time. It was therefore no coincidence that the two groups who had their hopes dashed by Nixon in 1971—women and Italian-Americans—were both rewarded through Reagan's picks of Sandra Day O'Connor and Antonin Scalia. While a justice's religion is now considered largely an afterthought, the race and gender of a potential nominee remain of paramount importance, particularly among Democrats.

A would-be justice also now requires stellar credentials to make a president's short list of preferred candidates. In response to Carswell's embarrassing qualifications and the persistent criticism of Warren's lack of judicial experience, modern presidents have sought to address both concerns: since Rehnquist's appointment, only Elena Kagan, who was nominated but not confirmed to serve as an appellate judge in 1999, arrived on the Court without having served on the judiciary. While stocking the judicial body with brilliant legal minds has raised the Court's profile, the exclusion of governors, senators, and cabinet officials has been a detriment to the judicial body. Their absence has deprived the institution of the skills and background that elected officials can bring to the job—namely the experience of reaching compromises among feuding factions and a keen, real-world understanding of the legislative and regulatory processes the Court is regularly asked to rule upon. The last historic shift to emerge from the Johnson-Nixon era was the end to the selection of presidential confidants and the emergence of the outsized role that special interest groups have come to play as gatekeepers for judicial appointments.

Several recent nominations exemplify the lasting influence of this transformation.

As the replacement for the retiring O'Connor, Harriet Miers would have been the Court's second female justice. Although her gender worked in Miers's favor, her nomination in 2005 violated four of the precepts noted above. She was criticized as George Bush's crony for serving in the White House and—whether true or not—was depicted as a legal lightweight, which after Carswell constituted automatic grounds for disqualification. Finally, lacking judicial experience and portrayed as ideologically wishy-washy by the very conservatives to whom the president was trying to placate, Miers's nomination was withdrawn. When applying the post-Fortas paradigm to her candidacy, it's easy to diagnose why her nomination sputtered.

Justice Antonin Scalia's unexpected death in 2016 also showcased the aggressive posture first adopted by the Senate in 1968. Republican senators based their refusal to consider Merrick Garland on the same specious argument Griffin had made about Johnson's lame-duck status. Senate Democrats tried to avenge Garland by filibustering Neil Gorsuch. That too borrowed from Griffin's playbook and their effort was just as politically motivated. Finally, the process used to select Brett Kavanaugh—a favorite of evangelicals and the Federalist Society—as well as his astonishingly partisan testimony in which he attacked Senate Democrats, all point back to Fortas's failed nomination as the historic crucible for this rancor.

Other than Thurmond and Griffin, none of the major participants involved in the Fortas affair lived long enough to witness the long-term impact of their actions. Thurmond eventually denounced Jim Crow on his way to earning the respect of his peers. His devotion to healthy living paid dividends: he served in the Senate past his hundredth birthday. After leaving the Senate in 1979, Griffin served eight years on the Michigan Supreme Court. He was elected—not appointed—to the judicial position.

Everett Dirksen never stopped his crusade to stave off the Court's reapportionment orders. When he died on September 7, 1969, one of the items in his briefcase included a letter concerning the constitutional convention he had long sought to launch.

Richard Russell and Johnson—the teacher and student, the father-figure and the son whom he longed to make president—remained close for two decades despite their differences over civil rights. But, after the misunderstanding over Russell's desire to get Alexander Lawrence a seat on the federal bench, Johnson and Russell never met again as friends. When Russell died in 1971, Johnson did not attend his funeral.

Philip Hart remained widely respected among his colleagues. Days before his death in 1976, the Senate unanimously voted to have a federal building named after him, the first time they had done so for a living member of the chamber.

After thirty-six years and five months on the job, William Douglas finally retired in 1975 as the longest serving justice in U.S. history, a record that stands to this day. Ironically, Gerald Ford appointed his successor. Considering the enmity between the two, Douglas would have been pleasantly surprised in Ford's selection of John Paul Stevens.

Despite all the criticism he faced over the years, Warren remained among the most vaunted justices in the Court's history. Even in retirement, he did not stop defending the Court from its naysayers. In his last public speech, delivered at Morehouse College on May 21, 1974, he condemned a plan under consideration to create a new appellate body that would weaken the Court's standing. "The proposal," he told the graduates, "should challenge the interest of every person who believes that the Supreme Court was intended to be… the last forum to which all Americans have free access for the adjudication of their constitutional rights."

Nixon's role in Watergate was Warren's other primary obsession during his final days. Referring to Nixon derisively, Warren told a reporter months before his death: "Tricky is perhaps the most despicable President this nation has ever had." The sight of his closest associates, Justices William Brennan and William Douglas, at his bedside on July 9, 1974 stirred the ailing Warren into an energetic conversation about Nixon's showdown over the Watergate tapes. To assuage his fears that Chief Justice Warren Burger might support Nixon's request to block access to the tapes, they informed Warren of the Court's unanimous ruling against the president. Two hours later, Warren died, content in the knowledge of his rival's defeat and comforted by the fact that the Court he helped fashion—more than anyone other than John Marshall—stood on the right side of history. He became the first justice to receive the honor of having his body lie in state in the Court building. Exactly one month after Warren's death, Nixon resigned.

Warren's allies from 1968 fared far worse. No politician after WWII rivalled Johnson's command over the government. It was as if the accumulation and deployment of power represented more than a fulfillment of his Texas-sized ambitions; it bestowed him with some kind of life-sustaining force. Deprived of that vitality once he was out of the White House, Johnson abandoned the healthy habits that had kept him alive since his heart attack in 1955. His relapse, characterized by rapid weight gain and a return to chain-smoking, presaged a quick decline. He died in 1973 of a heart attack at the age of 64. For the legislative grandmaster, the circumstances surrounding the last congressional battle of his presidency made the loss all the more heartbreaking. "The irony of that episode . . . that made the circumstance all the more agonizing for me personally," Johnson reflected in his memoir, "was that Abe Fortas had never wanted to sit on the Supreme Court in the first place."

Neither Johnson's ailing health nor the reverberating sting of Fortas's demise weakened the relationship between the two men, however. "You've been there when I needed you through a lot of years," Johnson wrote to Fortas in 1971, "and I'll never forget that." Days before his death, Johnson wrote another heartfelt message to the justice: "There is no other friendship like Abe Fortas' [sic], and no one's is more appreciated." The feeling was mutual. To mark the president's passing, Fortas honored Johnson with a stirring encomium in *The New York Times* titled "He Was America." Despite the good will between the two men, there was no denying that Johnson's actions put into motion his friend's demise. The magnitude of Fortas's defeat made it a quintessentially Shakespearean story. In June, 1968, he was a near-certainty to replace Warren as chief justice. Less than a year later, he resigned in disgrace. Fortas may have been careless in serving as Johnson's confidant while sitting on the bench, and he should have steered clear of the dubious financial arrangements that tarnished his reputation. But at the end, he was the collateral damage of the fallout over Warren's legacy more than a man in charge of his own destiny.

Fortas was not a superstitious man. So instead of looking for some mysterious curse to make sense of his misfortune, the fallen justice wondered whether *Life* ran William Lambert's story exposing the Fortas-Wolfson relationship to retaliate against him for his dissenting opinion in a previous case involving a sister publication. It's more likely that nothing more than journalistic curiosity had inspired Lambert, who earned a George Polk award for his investigative piece. In yet another irony, Wolfson offered Fortas the same position on his foundation in 1973 and proposed to pay $20,000 a year for his services. "The only difference," the financier explained, "is that this would be on a year-to-year basis and not a lifetime arrangement." So tarnished by the Wolfson scandal, Fortas was unable to return to his old firm, which expunged him from its name. Never able to restore his reputation, Fortas died in 1982 as the only justice to resign under a cloud of scandal.

Fortas was the last man standing among the close-knit group of friends and associates who stood by his side during his painful saga. His devotion to Warren never wavered: he served as an honorary pallbearer for Warren and in an essay honoring the chief justice, Fortas declared that Warren "deserved the title of Super-Chief." Fortas saved his warmest words for Douglas. In the eulogy he delivered at the justice's funeral, Fortas said: "Bill Douglas was my beloved teacher, friend, and colleague for fifty years. We shared joys and sorrows, triumph and disaster, achievement and defeat, acclaim and calumny." That Warren and Douglas still carry this acclaim while Fortas is stranded in infamy reaffirms the fact that Fortas was—and still remains—the greatest casualty in the battle for the Marble Palace.

Acknowledgments

O f the many people who helped me during this long journey, some deserve special recognition. *Battle for the Marble Palace* would not have been possible without my editor, Tim Schaffner. I will forever appreciate his passion for this project, his belief in me, and the many improvements he made to the book in every stage of the process. I also want to thank Jeffery Kurz for his shrewd editorial suggestions which improved this story in myriad ways. Writing a book is a collaborative effort and though we were spread across three states, I could not have found better partners. Sean Murphy at Schaffner Press also deserves credit for shepherding the project through its final stages and David Ter-Avanesyan for conjuring up a dazzling design for the book. I am also indebted to Scott Manning and Abigail Welhouse for their enthusiastic backing and sage advice. They too were wonderful collaborators. My agent, Jennifer Carlson, was with me every step of the way. She has guided and buttressed me through more than a dozen years together.

In researching *Battle for the Marble Palace*, I examined more than twenty archives and collected nearly 10,000 documents, photos, and audio-visual files. I had plenty of help along the way. Both the Association of Centers for the Study of Congress and the Dirksen Congressional Center provided generous grants to fund my research. Melanie Locay, Carolyn Broomhead, and Jay Barksdale at the New York Public Library helped arrange access to the library's research rooms. The time I spent as a Wertheim and Allen scholar and a Shoichi Noma Researcher at the institution proved to be invaluable. The assistance provided to scholars are some of the hidden gems among the many treasures offered by the library. The librarians at Columbia University always offered helpful answers to my queries and those at Baruch College processed dozens of inter-library loans. Sarah Waitz and William Davis assisted me at the National Archives, Jonathan Eaker tracked down photos at the Library of Congress, and Betty Koed, Katherine Scott, Heather Moore, and Daniel Holt at the Senate Historical Office directed me to vital sources. The oral histories conducted by Senate historians were pivotal to my understanding of the institution's power dynamics in the 1950s and '60s. The extensive oral histories conducted by the Bancroft Library at UC Berkeley contained a mountain of information about Earl Warren during his years in California and his time as chief justice. They too were crucial to my research. Frank Mackaman at the Dirksen Congressional Center was indispensable both in guiding me through the Center's archival holdings and helping me obtain research grants. Allen Fisher at the Lyndon Johnson Presidential Library answered a barrage of questions and tracked down every one of my challenging requests for information. He and the entire staff at the library helped make my stay in Austin a pleasure. The same could be said for the archivists—including Meghan Lee-Parker, Pamela Eisenberg, Ryan Pettigrew, and Keri Matthews—at the Richard Nixon Presidential Library. With their help, I was able to blaze through thousands of documents in days instead of weeks and steer through the massive collection of audio recordings of Nixon's presidency. The librarians at the Library of Congress's manuscript division, including Jeffrey Flannery and Ryan Reft, were always willing to assist me no matter how many questions I asked of them during my multiple trips there. Robert Ellis at the National Archives helped me track down transcripts of oral arguments while Geir Gundersen, Stacy Davis and John O'Connell at the Gerald Ford Presidential Library guided me through the voluminous records I reviewed. Evelina Stulgaityte at the University of Texas School of Law, Kristen Nyitray at Stony Brook University, Emily Swenson at the Bentley Historical Library, and John Fierst at the Clarke Historical Library were thoughtful enough to make arrangements to make my visits more productive. Leah Richier, Ginger Frere, and Jennifer Duplaga expertly gathered documents from the archives I couldn't visit in person. Kimberly Springer at Columbia University and Michael Maire Lange at UC Berkeley assisted me with questions regarding their respective oral history collections. Michael Frost and the archivists at

Yale's Sterling Library provided critical assistance in helping me research Abe Fortas's papers. Chuck Papirmeister, the law librarian at the Senate Judiciary Committee, Jan Hebbard at the Richard Russell collection, Patricia Evans at the Supreme Court library, and Lesley Martin at the Chicago History Museum Research Center directed me to key collections. I am especially appreciative of Kate Cruikshank for navigating me through the Birch Bayh papers. During my stay in Bloomington, she also recommended some of the best restaurants I had a chance to dine in during my many travels for this book. If you've ever wondered how writers recreate the past, look no further than these archivists and librarians who largely go unrecognized for the admirable work they do to preserve, catalog, and share the rich history of our nation.

I primarily relied on these archival and oral history collections, periodicals from the era (accessed largely through electronic databases), and congressional documents to compose this book. *Battle for the Marble Palace* also builds upon the research and findings of others. The bibliography provides a complete list of the works I relied upon but the ones I found most compelling are worth highlighting here. Bernard Schwartz's *Super Chief* provided an insider's account of the Warren Court while Lucas Powe Jr.'s *The Warren Court and American Politics* was critical to my understanding of the political controversies surrounding the judicial body. Richard Kluger's *Simple Justice* remains the preeminent work on *Brown v. Board*. Together with Mark Tushnet's scholarship, one gets a profound—and often overlooked—appreciation of the Court's role in the civil rights movement. Though there are no all-inclusive guides to the legislative struggles surrounding the Warren Court, there are some excellent works on individual battles. Walter Murphy wrote a blow-by-blow account of Red Monday while J. Douglas Smith explored Everett Dirksen's attempts to undo the Court's reapportionment rulings. The scholarship on the nomination process put forth by Henry Abraham, David Yalof, and John Maltese was highly informative while the titles by John Dean, Wil Haygood, Kevin McMahon, Stephen Carter, John Frank, and John Massaro offered valuable insights into individual confirmations. Since the 1960s have been the topic of countless books and documentaries, I'm going to limit this list to the two books that sparked my interest in the era: Theodore White's *The*

Making of the President 1968 and Allen Matusow's *The Unraveling of America*, which captivated me as an undergraduate nearly thirty years ago. The three presidents at the heart of this book have been the subjects of wonderful studies. Stephen Ambrose along with Chester Pach Jr. and Elmo Richardson gave me a deep understanding of Dwight Eisenhower's views on civil rights. The most informative accounts, from my perspective, of Lyndon Johnson's political career were written by Joseph Califano Jr., Robert Dallek, and Robert Caro, whose work is second to none. Ambrose and Richard Reeves produced stellar biographies of Richard Nixon. Of the various books to tackle Earl Warren's life, the ones authored by John Weaver, G. Edward White, and Jim Newton, most of all, were my favorites. Stephen Wermiel and Seth Stern as well as Juan Williams penned other superb judicial biographies. Robert Shogan produced an incisive account of Abe Fortas's travails despite not having access to the treasure-trove of archives available to later generations. I found the books authored by Bruce Allen Murphy and Laura Kalman to be especially comprehensive and perceptive. Their first-rate accounts guided me throughout my research. Liva Baker, Dan Carter, Nadine Cohodas, Joseph Crespino, John Kyle Day, Harry Dent, Eric Foner, William Hustwit, Harry McPherson, Rick Perlstein, Samuel Shaffer, and William White authored other instructive titles touching upon different elements of this story. My hope is that *Battle for the Marble Palace* will add to this bountiful of scholarship.

Several renowned scholars advised me along the way. Jesse Choper, Walter Dellinger III, and Terrance Sandalow provided keen insights on the Court and dug deep into their memory banks of the time they spent with the justices. Richard Friedman, my constitutional law professor, was kind enough to meet with me in Ann Arbor to guide me in the early stages of my research. I am thankful to Lucas Powe Jr. for sharing his ideas over lunch in Austin and to Jim Newton for the hospitality he showed me at his home where we entered into a rich discussion about Earl Warren. All of them offered me wise counsel for which I am grateful.

Battle for the Marble Palace gives me the opportunity to honor the two teachers who had the biggest impact on my life. The late Sidney Fine, with whom I had the good fortune of taking four courses with at the University of Michigan decades ago, has long been an inspiration for me. I repeatedly called upon the lessons he taught me during the preparation of this book. Samuel Freedman, my professor at the Columbia University Graduate School of Journalism, deserves the most credit for helping me to become an author. To this day, I review my notes from his class before starting any major project and his words of wisdom still echo in my ears. I cherish his continued mentorship and friendship.

For a project years in the making, a few individuals who provided encouragement along the way deserve special mention, including Alice Sparberg Alexiou, Cerisse Anderson, Levon Avdoyan, Jeremy Bogaisky, Kevin Coyne, Fred Ebrahemi, Benjamin Hudson, Allan and Mary Jalon, Joshua Kors, Marc Mamigonian, Bedross Der Matossian, Josh Mills, Andrea Murad, Dave and Claudine Rodriguez, Matt and Priyanka Schneider, James and Elina Thatcher, and Dan Wise. The numerous conversations with James Humphrey during my visits to the nation's capital helped me sharpen my ideas. Patrick Landers was kind enough to house me in Washington D.C. and always championed my work, even during its nascent stages. Dennis and Mary Papazian treated me like a member of their family when I stayed in their home during my research of the Fortas archives. They have been great friends and mentors for many years. Vikram Reddy was always there to brainstorm ideas, inject moments of levity through the toughest of moments, and provide endless encouragement over a span of many years. I couldn't have asked for more from a friend.

Last of all, I want to thank my family. One part researcher, one part editor, and one part fact-checker, my wife Edina helped me at every stage of the book's production. She has been my tireless supporter. And finally, I want to recognize my children, Zabelle and Andrew, for their enduring patience and understanding when I spent months away from home digging through archives and missed our family vacations to finish this manuscript. One of my greatest joys as a writer and father will be the day they read these pages.

Notes

Abbreviations Used in Notes

Abbreviations for Consulted Archives

—Bayh-IU: Birch E. Bayh Senatorial Papers, Modern Political Papers Collection, Indiana University

—Brennan-LOC: William J. Brennan Papers, Manuscript Division, Library of Congress

—Burton-LOC: Harold H. Burton Papers, Manuscript Division, Library of Congress

—Clark-TLL: Tom C. Clark Papers, Tarlton Law Library, University of Texas Law School

—Dirksen-DCC: Everett M. Dirksen Papers, The Dirksen Congressional Center

—Douglas-CHM: Paul H. Douglas Papers, Chicago History Museum

—Douglas-LOC: William O. Douglas Papers, Manuscript Division, Library of Congress

—Fortas-SML: Abe Fortas Papers, Manuscripts and Archives, Sterling Memorial Library, Yale University

—Frankfurter-LOC: Felix Frankfurter Papers, Manuscript Division, Library of Congress

—Griffin-CHL: Robert P. Griffin Papers, Clarke Historical Library, Central Michigan University

—Hart-BHL: Philip A. Hart Papers, Bentley Historical Library, University of Michigan

—Javits-SBU: Jacob K. Javits Collection, Stony Brook University

—Jenner-ISL: William E. Jenner Papers, Indiana State Library

—Russell-RBRL: Richard B. Russell Jr. Collection, Richard B. Russell Library for Political Research and Studies, University of Georgia

—Talmadge-RBRL: Herman E. Talmadge Collection, Richard B. Russell Library for Political Research and Studies, University of Georgia

—Warren-LOC: Earl Warren Papers, Manuscript Division, Library of Congress

—SJC-NA: Records of the Committee on the Senate Judiciary and Related Committees, 1816-1968, National Archives

Abbreviations for Materials at Presidential Libraries

—Dwight D. Eisenhower Presidential Library, Abiline, Kansas (DDEL)

—Gerald R. Ford Presidential Library, Ann Arbor, Michigan (GRFL)

GFCP – Gerald Ford Congressional Papers
GFCP:PSS – Gerald Ford Congressional Papers: Press Secretary and Speech File
VP – Gerald Ford Vice Presidential Papers
—Lyndon B. Johnson Presidential Library, Austin, Texas (LBJL)
OFWHA – Office Files of the White House Aides
OPF – Office of the President File
PP – Personal Papers
SF-CBS – Special Files, CBS Interviews
WHCF – White House Central Files
WHCF-SF-AFHT – White House Central Files, Special File Pertaining to Abe Fortas and Homer Thornberry
—Richard M. Nixon Presidential Library, Yorba Linda, California (RMNL)
NARA – National Archives & Records Administration (Telephone Transcripts)
POF:ANSS – President's Office Files: Annotated News Summaries Series
POF:PMS – President's Office Files: President's Meeting Series
PPF – President's Personal Files
WHCF:ANF – White House Central Files: Alphabetical Name Files
WHCF:SF – White House Central Files: Subject Files
WHSF:SMOF – White House Special Files: Staff Member and Office Files
WHSF:SF – White House Special Files: Subject Files
WHSF:SF-CF – White House Special Files: Subject Files-Confidential Files

Abbreviations for Oral Histories

CSAOHP	California State Archives State Government Oral History Program, Center for California Studies, California State University, Sacramento
CUOH	Columbia University Center for Oral History
EWOHP	Earl Warren Oral History Project at the Bancroft Library, University of California, Berkeley
GRFOH	Gerald R. Ford Oral History Collection – Gerald R. Ford Presidential Library
LCEW	Law Clerks of Chief Justice Earl Warren, Bancroft Library, University of California, Berkeley
LBJOH	Lyndon B. Johnson Oral History Collection – Lyndon B. Johnson Presidential Library
RMNOH	Richard M. Nixon Oral History Collection – Richard M. Nixon Presidential Library
RROHC	Richard B. Russell Library Oral History Documentary Collection, University of Georgia
SOHP	Southern Oral History Program – Center for the Study of the American South, University of North Carolina, Chapel Hill
USSHO	United States Senate Historical Office

Abbreviations for Hearings

—Nomination of Abe Fortas (AFCH)

Hearing Before the Committee on the Judiciary, U.S. Senate, Eighty-Ninth Congress, First Session, on Nomination of Abe Fortas, of Tennessee, to be an Associate Justice of the Supreme Court of the United States, August 5, 1965, Volume 7.

—Nominations of Abe Fortas and Homer Thornberry, Part 1 (AFHTCH1)

Hearings Before the Committee on the Judiciary, U.S. Senate, Ninetieth Congress, Second Session, on Nomination of Abe Fortas, of Tennessee, to be Chief Justice of the United States and Nomination of Homer Thornberry, of Texas, to be Associate Justice of the Supreme Court of the United States, July 11, 12, 16, 17, 18, 19, 20, 22, and 23, 1968, Volume 9A.

—Nominations of Abe Fortas and Homer Thornberry, Part 2 (AFHTCH2)

Hearings Before the Committee on the Judiciary, U.S. Senate, Ninetieth Congress, Second Session, on Nomination of Abe Fortas, of Tennessee, to be Chief Justice of the United States and Nomination of Homer Thornberry, of Texas, to be Associate Justice of the Supreme Court of the United States, Part 2, September 13 and 16, 1968, Volume 9A.

—Nomination of George Harrold Carswell (GHCCH)

Hearings Before the Committee on the Judiciary, U.S. Senate, Ninety-First Congress, Second Session, on Nomination of George Harrold Carswell, of Florida, to be Associate Justice of the Supreme Court of the United States, January 27, 28, and 29 and February 2 and 3, 1970, Volume 11.

—Nomination of Robert Bork (RBCH)

Hearings Before the Committee on the Judiciary, U.S. Senate, One Hundredth Congress, First Session, on the Nomination of Robert H. Bork to be Associate Justice of the Supreme Court of the United States, September 15, 16, 17, 18, 19, 21, 22, 23, 25, 28, 29, and 30, 1987 (Parts 1-5).

Abbreviations for Commonly Cited Periodicals & Government Journals

CR	Congressional Record
CT	Chicago Tribune
CSM	Christian Science Monitor
LAT	Los Angeles Times
NR	National Review
NW	Newsweek
NYT	New York Times
USNWR	US News & World Report
WSJ	Wall Street Journal
WP	Washington Post
WS	Washington Star

Abbreviations for Commonly Cited Names

JC	Joseph Califano
WC	Warren Christopher
ED	Everett Dirksen

WD William Douglas
GRF Gerald R. Ford
AF Abe Fortas
FF Felix Frankfurter
RG Robert Griffin
JJ Jacob Javits
LBJ Lyndon B. Johnson
MM Mike Manatos
RN Richard Nixon
RR Richard Russell
LT Larry Temple
EW Earl Warren

PROLOGUE

15 *brain surgeon*: Schwartz & Lesher, *Inside*, 236; Murphy, *Fortas*, 10, 13.

16 *He's the wisest*: Murphy, *Fortas*, 115.

17 *stage center*: Interview with Walter E. Dellinger III; "Fortas for Warren," *NYT*, June 27, 1968.

17-18 *since Brown*: Day, *Southern Manifesto*, 74; "Thurmond Urges Johnson Not to Fill Court Vacancy," *Charleston News & Courier*, June 22, 1968.

18 *The trouble began*: Thurmond, *Faith*, 13.

18-19 *The chief fountain*: Thurmond, *Faith*, 25.

19 *As pornography*: Gallup, *The Gallup Poll, Vol. 3*, 2201; *CQ Almanac 1964*, "Congress Fails to Act on School Prayer Amendments;" Dierenfield, "Public Response."

20 *great confidence*: Frum, *How We Got Here*, 18.

20 *In its contest*: Thurmond, *Faith*, 158-59. Griffin made a similar statement a fortnight earlier. See, July 2, 1968 *Capitol Cloakroom*, Griffin-CHL B227.

20 *If the Senate*: July 22, 1968 Strom Thurmond newsletter, Fortas-SML B97.

20-21 *to commit rapes*: Fred Graham, "Fortas Testifies he Rebuked Critic of War Spending," *NYT*, July 18, 1968; AFHTCH1, 191; John Mackenzie, "Thurmond Badgers Fortas But Gets Few Replies," *Boston Globe*, July 19, 1968; Crespino, *Strom Thurmond's America*, 216; Shogan, *A Question of Judgment*, 170.

22 *Bork's nomination*: Despite the widely-held belief of the prominence of the Bork nomination, Bruce Allen Murphy, Laura Kalman, and a few other scholars have also pointed to Fortas's nomination in 1968 as the turning point in the confirmation process. My research builds on their work by focusing on the changes in the Senate's attitude towards the

selection of justices, the ideological and electoral calculations Johnson and Nixon took into account in appointing justices in comparison to their predecessors, and the increasingly politicized role of the judicial body in electoral politics. This book also explores the critical—yet in many cases, obscure—episodes in which the Warren Court's critics tried but failed to curb, resist, and undermine the judicial body. Ultimately, it was this futility that led these detractors to set out to control the Court's membership. In doing so, they upended years of customs and traditions to thwart Fortas's ascension. When these tactics became entrenched during Nixon's nominations of Clement Haynsworth and G. Harrold Carswell, they established the template for the modern-day selection of justices. These series of combative nominations, when explained through the context of what I call the "Warren Wars," made this epoch—and not the Bork nomination in 1987—the turning point in the confirmation process.

CHAPTER 1

27 *Between eight*: President's Daily Diary, June 26, 1968, LBJL; Lawrence Altman, "Navy confirms Johnson had surgery for skin cancer," *NYT*, June 29, 1977.

27 *With time*: June 26, 1968 Albert Jenner letter to Ramsey Clark, LBJL WHCF-SF-AFHT B1; December 20, 1968 WC memo to LT, LBJL WHCF-SF-AFHT B3. The ABA began reviewing judicial nominees in 1945.

27-28 *Johnson provided*: President's Daily Diary, June 26, 1968, LBJL; December 20, 1968 WC memo to LT, LBJL WHCF-SF-AFHT B3; June 26, 1968 telephone conversation No. 13144, LBJL.

28 *Unable to meet*: June 26, 1968 telephone conversation No. 13145, LBJL; LBJOH – Eastland (Interview I), 13.

28 *never whips*: "The Authentic Voice," *Time*, March 26, 1956; Robert Sherrill, "James Eastland: Child of Scorn," *Nation*, October 4, 1965.

28 *His maternal*: "The Authentic Voice," *Time*, March 26, 1956; Haygood, *Showdown*, 133-36.

29 *Born months*: Robert Sherrill, "James Eastland: Child of Scorn," *Nation*, October 4, 1965; "The Authentic Voice," *Time*, March 26, 1956; Douth, *Leaders in Profile*, 216; White, *Citadel*, 192-93.

29 *Eastland believed*: "The Authentic Voice," *Time*, March 26, 1956; Day, *Southern Manifesto*, 28.

29 *The difference between*: Driver, "Supremacies," 1092.

29 *Eastland gobbled*: "Died," *Newsweek*, March 3, 1986; Cohodas, *Strom Thurmond*, 372.

30 *1965 profile*: Robert Sherrill, "James Eastland: Child of Scorn," *Nation*, October 4, 1965.

30 *Branding the justices*: Day, *Southern Manifesto*, 27, 30; "The Authentic Voice," *Time*, March 26, 1956.

30 *As chairman*: LBJOH – Jacobsen (Interview III), 3-4; LBJOH – Eastland (Interview I), 10.

30-31 *committee's southerners*: "Thurmond Urges Johnson Not to Fill Court Vacancy," *Charleston News & Courier*, June 22, 1968; Lyle Denniston, "Senate battle expected on Warren successor," *WS*, June 22, 1968; Marjorie Hunter, "Senate coalition may block action on Warren's post," *NYT*, June 23, 1968.

31 *one of the best*: Johnson, *Vantage Point*, 547.

31 *The findings Eastland*: December 20, 1968 WC memo to LT, LBJL WHCF-SF-AFHT B3.

32 *Having surveyed*: December 20, 1968 WC memo to LT, LBJL WHCF-SF-AFHT B3.

32 *The president's congressional*: June 25, 1968 MM memo to LBJ, LBJL WHCF-SF-AFHT B1.

32 *At 10:37*: President's Daily Diary, June 26, 1968, LBJL.

34 *The law on the side*: http://www.frederick-douglass-heritage.org/quotes/.

34 *Forced to occupy*: http://history.house.gov/Exhibitions-and-Publications/BAIC/Historical-Essays/Fifteenth-Amendment/Legislative-Interests/.

34 *The whites esteem*: Kluger, *Simple Justice*, 44.

34 *They are to be returned*: EJI, *Lynching in America*, 8.

34 *The dismantling*: Foner, *Reconstruction*, 587, 590.

35 *A southern newspaper*: Foner, *Reconstruction*, 590, 595.

35 *employed to reenslave*: Foner, *Reconstruction*, 594; Woodward, *Origins*, 213.

35 *until 1973*: http://history.house.gov/Exhibitions-and-Publications/BAIC/Historical-Data/Black-American-Representatives-and-Senators-by-Congress/. On the local level, more than 2,000 African-Americans were elected to office during Reconstruction. See, http://history.house.gov/Exhibitions-and-Publications/BAIC/Historical-Essays/Fifteenth-Amendment/Reconstruction/.

35-36 *The most piteous*: Kluger, *Simple Justice*, 50.

36 *Popular games*: http://www.ferris.edu/jimcrow/what.htm; http://www.ferris.edu/HTMLS/news/jimcrow/violence.htm.

36 *From 1877*: EJI, *Lynching in America*, 5; Haygood, *Showdown*, 172; Ayers, *Vengeance & Justice*, 246.

37 *The federal response*: http://www.foxnews.com/story/2005/06/13/senate-apologiz-es-for-not-passing-anti-lynching-laws.html; https://www.naacp.org/nations-premier-civ-il-rights-organization/; http://history.house.gov/Exhibitions-and-Publications/BAIC/Historical-Essays/Temporary-Farewell/Anti-Lynching-Legislation/.

37 *In need of southern*: Kluger, *Simple Justice*, 166-67.

38 *not confer the*: United States v. *Reese*, 92 U.S. 214, 217 (1875).

38 *On top of*: Kluger, *Simple Justice*, 61.

38 *Court's dimmer lights*: Kluger, *Simple Justice*, 72.

38 *Gauged by this*: Plessy v. *Ferguson*, 163 U.S. 537, 550-51 (1896).

39 *The present decision*: Plessy v. *Ferguson*, 163 U.S. 537, 560 (1896).

39 *Why it is*: EJI, *Lynching in America*, 9; Kluger, *Simple Justice*, 67, 86; Friedman, *History of American Law*, 506-07; Woodward, *Origins*, 212, 355.

39 *violent recriminations*: EJI, *Lynching in America*, 10-14.

40 *We couldn't get*: Williams, *Thurgood Marshall*, 82, 95-96.

40 *During the 1940s*: https://www.naacp.org/naacp-legal-team/naacp-legal-history/.

40 *underlying logic*: Sweatt v. *Painter*, 339 U.S. 629 (1950).

41 *unprepared to overrule*: Tushnet, *Making*, 191; Schwartz, *A History*, 287; Kluger, *Simple Justice*, 592-93.

41 *Clark also equivocated*: Kluger, *Simple Justice*, 614-15; Tushnet, *Making*, 193-94; CUOH – Marshall, 28, 84.

41 *purely a private*: Frankfurter, *From the Diaries*, 335-36.

41 *Mayflower Hotel*: Kluger, *Simple Justice*, 598-99.

41-42 *Hugo Black . . . believed*: Tushnet, *Making*, 189, 192-93; Kluger, *Simple Justice*, 596, 601, 605-06, 612-13, 617; Schwartz, *Super Chief*, 76-77.

42 *Though the fractured*: Douglas, *Autobiography*, 114; Tushnet, *Making*, 187; Schwartz, *Super Chief*, 72; Newton, *Justice for All*, 307; Kluger, *Simple Justice*, 618.

42-43 *a similar impression*: http://www.aoc.gov/capitol-buildings/supreme-court-building; Toobin, *The Nine*, 1.

43 *Court's legacy*: https://www.supremecourt.gov/about/buildinghistory.aspx; https://www.supremecourt.gov/about/courtbuilding.aspx; Schwartz, *Super Chief*, 27.

43 *Upon taking his oath*: Weaver, *Warren*, 198; Kluger, *Simple Justice*, 668.

43 *nine separate law firms*: Schwartz, *Super Chief*, 31.

45 *His resilience*: CUOH – Schmidt, 77, 201; Schwartz, *Super Chief*, 32-33.

45 *Jackson coveted*: Schwartz, *Super Chief*, 35; "Jackson Attacks Black for judging ex-part-ner's case," *NYT*, June 11, 1946.

45 *Jackson should be*: Newton, *Justice for All*, 267; Schwartz, *Super Chief*, 35.

45 *Albany Law School*: Schwartz, *Super Chief*, 37.

46 *At the risk of*: January 11, 1955 FF memo the Court, Warren-LOC B353.

46 *more umbrage*: Powe, *Warren Court*, 6; Feldman, *Scorpions*, 61-64.

46 *Compared with his*: Feldman, *Scorpions*, 321; Kluger, *Simple Justice*, 605.

46-47 *Beyond their philosophical*: Schwartz, *Super Chief*, 35; Feldman, *Scorpions*, 306; May 29, 1954 WD memo to FF, Warren-LOC B353.

47 *After the second*: Schwartz, *Super Chief*, 83-84; Warren, *Memoirs*, 4, 296; Weaver, *Warren*, 150

47 *case's outset*: Schwartz, *Super Chief*, 84-85; Warren, *Memoirs*, 285.

47-48 *His next words*: December 11, 1972 EW speech at Civil Rights Symposium, LBJL SF-CBS, B3; Schwartz, *Super Chief*, 86.

48 *I don't see how*: Schwartz, *Super Chief*, 86.

48 *This opening volley*: Schwartz, *Super Chief*, 85.

48 *To keep anyone*: Schwartz, *Super Chief*, 86-88; Kluger, *Simple Justice*, 681-83; Tushnet, *Making*, 210.

48-49 *One by one*: Schwartz, *Super Chief*, 87-89; Tushnet, *Making*, 210-11; Kluger, *Simple Justice*, 684-86; Newton, *Justice for All*, 311-12.

49 *Warren was aware*: Schwartz, *Super Chief*, 31-32.

49 *By some process*: Fortas, "Chief Justice Warren," 406; Kluger, *Simple Justice*, 669; Schwartz, *Super Chief*, 31.

49-50 *with one voice*: "Ends a Busy Term, Draws a Heavy Fire," *Time*, June 25, 1956; Schwartz, *Super Chief*, 89-90; Newton, *Justice for All*, 313; Kluger, *Simple Justice*, 697.

50 *When the justices*: Kluger, *Simple Justice*, 698; Newton, *Justice for All*, 316-17, 321; Schwartz, *Super Chief*, 96-98.

50 *Jackson dropped*: Feldman, *Scorpions*, 400-02; Tushnet, *Making*, 212-13; Kluger, *Simple Justice*, 691-95, 701; Warren, *Memoirs*, 286; Newton, *Justice for All*, 321.

50-51 *By the spring*: Feldman, *Scorpions*, 400, 402; Kluger, *Simple Justice*, 695-96; Schwartz, *Super Chief*, 94, 96; Newton, *Justice for All*, 322.

51 *This would have been impossible*: Schwartz, *Super Chief*, 82.

51 *As we Justices marched*: Luther A. Huston, "1896 ruling upset," *NYT*, May 18, 1954; Warren, *Memoirs*, 3, 286; Williams, *Thurgood Marshall*, 225; Newton, *Justice for All*, 324; Kluger, *Simple Justice*, 704; Schwartz, *Super Chief*, 102.

52 *We come then*: *Brown v. Board of Education*, 347 U.S. 483, 493 (1954).

52 *We conclude unanimously*: Kluger, *Simple Justice*, 710. According to Kluger, Warren spoke the word "unanimously" in the courtroom: it wasn't part of the official ruling later published by the Court.

52 *No one screamed*: CUOH – Marshall, 99; Warren, *Memoirs*, 3; Williams, *Thurgood Marshall*, 226; Newton, *Justice for All*, 325; Kluger, *Simple Justice*, 711.

53 *politicians all stepped*: LBJOH – Warren (Interview I), 6.

53-54 *For a man convinced*: "The Authentic Voice," *Time*, March 26, 1956; Robert Sherrill, "James Eastland: Child of Scorn," *Nation*, October 4, 1965.

55 *The chairman dismissed*: June 26, 1968 MM memo to LBJ, LBJL WHCF-SF-AFHT B1; Johnson, *Vantage Point*, 547.

55 *When Johnson had named*: June 23, 1968 telephone conversation No. 13135, LBJL; Johnson, *Vantage Point*, 547; LBJOH – Eastland (Interview I), 13.

55-56 *The president already suspected*: Johnson, *Vantage Point*, 547; LBJOH – Eastland (Interview I), 13.

CHAPTER 2

57 *Beginning in 1925*: CUOH – Schmidt, 111, 115.

58 *considered him the favorite*: W.H. Lawrence, "Eisenhower nominated on the First Ballot," *NYT*, July 12, 1952.

58 *Steering clear*: Frank, *Ike and Dick*, 22, 29; McCullough, *Truman*, 887.

58 *Capturing more*: Deadlocked conventions had unraveled favorites before. In 1912, House Speaker James Clark began with the early lead over Woodrow Wilson, capturing 440½ delegates to Wilson's 324. Clark's support peaked on the tenth ballot before beginning a painstakingly incremental decline. Wilson took his first lead on the 30th ballot and even-

tually prevailed sixteen roll calls later. Twelve years later, in 1924, the Democrats plunged into another marathon. With 60 different candidates receiving votes, the convention remained deadlocked for sixteen days until the exhausted favorites—New York governor Al Smith and William McAdoo—released their delegates, allowing the dark horse John Davis to win by default on the 103rd ballot. See, Link, *Wilson*, 448-49, 458; Peter Carlson, "The Ballot Brawl of 1924," *WP*, March 4, 2008; Jack Shafer, "1924: The Wildest Convention in U.S. History," *Politico Magazine*, March 7, 2016.

59 *Most Admired Man*: Gallup, *The Gallup Poll, Vol. 2*, 1038; EWOHP – Wollenberg, 153.

59 *Balloting began*: W.H. Lawrence, "Eisenhower nominated on the First Ballot," *NYT*, July 12, 1952; LeAnn Spencer and Andy Davis, "South Side Landmark Heads for Extinction," *CT*, May 28, 1999; Anthony Boylan, "Amphitheatre Gets Its Final Curtain Call," *CT*, May 30, 1999.

59 *Alabama began the process*: W.H. Lawrence, "Eisenhower nominated on the First Ballot," *NYT*, July 12, 1952.

59-60 *Warren's gubernatorial victories*: White, *Warren*, 137.

60 *Warren's popularity*: Warren, *Memoirs*, 155, 171-72, 200, 234; EWOHP – Dinkelspiel, 36; EWOHP – Faries, 37; EWOHP – Warren Jr., 24-25; EWOHP – Brown, 29; White, *Warren*, 131.

60-61 *Warren was horrified*: CUOH – Schmidt, 72; EWOHP – Mailliard, 32; EWOHP – Hansen, 64, 66; EWOHP – Warren Jr., 59-60; Colleen O'Connor, "'Pink Right Down to her Underwear,'" *LAT*, April 9, 1990; Weaver, *Warren*, 176; Baker, *Miranda*, 123.

61 *Earl of Warren*: EWOHP – Adams, 31; EWOHP – Jorgensen, 69; "Ends a Busy Term, Draws a Heavy Fire," *Time*, June 25, 1956.

61 *Earl Warren Special*: EWOHP – Dinkelspiel, 2; Weaver, *Warren*, 181; Perlstein, *Nixonland*, 36.

61 *chair the delegation*: Warren, *Memoirs*, 251; EWOHP – Jorgensen, 68; EWOHP – Dinkelspiel, 1-2, 6; Weaver, *Warren*, 181-82.

61 *Eisenhower over Warren*: EWOHP – Jorgensen, 68-69, 91; EWOHP – Dinkelspiel, 1-6; EWOHP – McCormac, 8; EWOHP – Lynn, 15a-16a; EWOHP – Brown, 28; EWOHP – Mellon, 7; Newton, *Justice for All*, 244, 246; Weaver, *Warren*, 182; Warren, *Memoirs*, 251; Frank, *Ike and Dick*, 31; Perlstein, *Nixonland*, 36; Pach & Richardson, *Eisenhower*, 22; Ambrose, *Eisenhower* (Vol. I), 538.

62 *end of the train*: EWOHP – Jorgensen, 69; EWOHP – Hansen, 89; Lawrence E. Davies, "Bar disputed men, Warren proposes," *NYT*, July 5, 1952; Newton, *Justice for All*, 248.

62 *Once at the convention*: EWOHP – Dinkelspiel, 2, 5-6, 11; EWOHP – Jorgensen, 69; EWOHP – Crocker, 19; EWOHP – Wollenberg, 151; "Road Signs in California," *Time*,

June 16, 1952; Seymour Korman, "Warren Here," *CT*, July 6, 1952.

62 *Illinois gave*: Felix Belair Jr., "Minnesota starts a July snowball," *NYT*, July 12, 1952; W.H. Lawrence, "Eisenhower nominated on the First Ballot," *NYT*, July 12, 1952.

62 *The general tallied*: W.H. Lawrence, "Eisenhower nominated on the First Ballot," *NYT*, July 12, 1952.

63 *Minnesota went ahead*: EWOHP – Stassen, 4; W.H. Lawrence, "Eisenhower nominated on the First Ballot," *NYT*, July 12, 1952.

63 *Just to rub it*: EWOHP – Warren Jr., 20-22, 26-27; LCEW – Kranwinkle, 13-14; Drew Pearson, "Earl Warren Jr. Says Nixon Double-Crossed His Father," *Free Lance-Star*, May 17, 1962; Newton, *Justice for All*, 378, 382, 396; White, *Warren*, 142.

63 *Nixon's humiliation*: Newton, *Justice for All*, 397.

63 *To his final days*: LCEW – Rosett, 16; LCEW – Schmidt, 18; Schwartz, *Super Chief*, 21, 680-82; CUOH – Schmidt, 71; Schwartz & Lesher, *Inside*, 17.

64 *truly great men*: CUOH – Schmidt, 325; Richard Amper, "The Trumans Join Judaic Law Class," *NYT*, September 15, 1957.

64 *For more than seven years*: Ambrose, *Eisenhower* (Vol. II), 191.

64-65 *With his popularity*: Warren, *Memoirs*, 291.

65 *more to make civil rights*: December 11, 1972 EW speech at Civil Rights Symposium, LBJL SF-CBS B3; Warren, *Memoirs*, 289, 292.

65 *continue Warren's legacy*: CUOH – Schmidt, 61-63, 73.

65-66 *congruent political views*: LCEW – Kranwinkle, 23; LBJOH – LBJ (Reminiscences), 16; February 20, 1965 Juanita Roberts letter to EW, LBJL WHCF FG431/J B346; March 1, 1966 EW letter to LBJ, LBJL WHCF FG431/J B346; May 11, 1967 dinner invitation, LBJL WHCF FG431/J B346; November 22, 1967 LBJ letter to EW, LBJL WHCF FG431/J B346; January 16, 1968 EW letter to LBJ, LBJL WHCF FG431/J B346; March 19, 1966 LBJ letter to EW, LBJL WHCF FG431/J B346; Califano, *Triumph*, 41; CUOH – Schmidt, 63.

66 *The two most powerful*: March 13, 1967 Drew Pearson notes, LBJL PP Drew Pearson G246; April 30, 1968 LBJ letter to EW, LBJL WHCF FG431/J B346; May 13, 1968 Jim Gaither memo to LBJ, LBJL WHCF FG431/J B346; May 14, 1968 LT memo to LBJ, LBJL WHCF FG431/J B346; May 27, 1968 Nina Warren letter to LBJ, LBJL WHCF FG431/J B346.

66 *On June 13, 1968*: June 11, 1968 Jim Jones memo to LBJ, LBJL WHCF FG431/J B346; President's Daily Diary, June 13, 1968, LBJL.

CHAPTER 3

67 *When rumors of Warren's departure*: June 21, 1968 Billy Graham letter to LBJ, LBJL WHCF FG535/A B360; June 22, 1968 Mike Mansfield memo to LBJ, LBJL WHCF FG431/J B346; June 24, 1968 Harry McPherson memo to LBJ, LBJL WHCF FG431/J B346.

67 *Near the end*: Newton, *Justice for All*, 492; Murphy, *Fortas*, 270.

68 *For his first pick*: Yalof, *Pursuit of Justices*, 20-21; Schwartz, *Super Chief*, 57.

68 *Truman cherry-picked*: Yalof, *Pursuit of Justices*, 30-33; Yalof, *Pursuit of Justices*, 30; Kluger, *Simple Justice*, 242; Schwartz, *Super Chief*, 73; Kluger, *Simple Justice*, 587.

69 *Tom Clark was my biggest*: Schwartz, *Super Chief*, 57-58.

69 *worst of the Truman appointees*: Schwartz, *Super Chief*, 58; McCullough, *Truman*, 216; Yalof, *Pursuit of Justices*, 37.

70 *I am back here*: Warren, *Memoirs*, 260; EWOHP – Brownell, 1-3; Clayton Knowles, "Court Job Open to Warren," *NYT*, September 4, 1953; Lawrence E. Davies, "Warren Bars 4th Term Bid," *NYT*, September 4, 1953; Ambrose, *Eisenhower* (Vol. II), 23. Another version of the story claims Nixon urged Eisenhower to select Warren to get the governor out of California. See, Schwartz & Lesher, *Inside*, 17.

70 *To beef up*: EWOHP – Brownell, 4, 56; "Gov. Warren Takes Himself Out," *LAT*, September 4, 1953; Lawrence E. Davies, "Warren Bars 4th Term Bid," *NYT*, September 4, 1953; "Message to the Governor," *Time*, August 10, 1953; "Chief Justice Vinson Dies of Heart Attack in Capital," *NYT*, September 8, 1953; "Chief Justice Vinson Dead," *LAT*, September 8, 1953.

70-71 *His infectious bonhomie*: Newton, *Justice for All*, 1-2, 205; Weaver, *Warren*, 162, 196; EWOHP – Cavanaugh, Introduction, 2-6; EWOHP – Brien, 30-31; EWOHP – Henderson, 18, 21.

71 *Cavanaugh was reluctant*: EWOHP – Cavanaugh, 33-34; John Dart, "Biographer Details a Cardinal's 'Regime,'" *LAT*, June 7, 1997.

71 *Warren vacillated*: EWOHP – Cavanaugh, 34.

72 *As news of Vinson's death*: Richard Strout, "Republican Likely to Fill Vinson Post," *CSM*, September 8, 1953; "Chief Justice Vinson Dead," *LAT*, September 8, 1953; Dewey L. Fleming, "Mourning Set for Vinson," *Baltimore Sun*, September 9, 1953; Lawrence E. Davies, "Warren Advanced for Chief Justice," *NYT*, September 9, 1953; James Reston, "U.S. Mourns Vinson," *NYT*, September 9, 1953.

72 *Reluctant to name Warren*: EWOHP – Brownell, 6; Eisenhower, *Mandate for Change*, 228;

Pach & Richardson, *Eisenhower*, 141.

72 *Black ended his decade*: Powe, *Warren Court*, 13; Clifford, *Counsel*, 216; McCullough, *Truman*, 888.

73 *Because Bill is over in Chungking*: EWOHP – Faries, 26; Newton, *Justice for All*, 8. Knowland sent a letter to Eisenhower recommending Warren for the job on September 25, 1953. See, Branyan & Larsen, *Documentary History*, 1075.

73 *Brownell's search*: "Chief Justice Rumor Shifts to Jackson," *Austin American Statesman*, September 11, 1953; "Jackson for Chief Justice, Warren as Associate Urged," *Boston Globe*, September 12, 1953.

73 *Jackson carried a black mark*: EWOHP – Brownell, 7-8, 59-60; William H. Stringer, "Warren Unofficially 'In,'" *CSM*, September 29, 1953; "One Law for All," *Time*, October 12, 1953; Yalof, *Pursuit of Justices*, 48; Eisenhower, *Mandate for Change*, 227.

73 *John Foster Dulles*: Warren, *Memoirs*, 261; Pach & Richardson, *Eisenhower*, 141; October 23, 1954 Ike letter to E.E. Hazlett Jr., DDEL; James Reston, "U.S. Mourns Vinson," *NYT*, September 9, 1953; Albert Clark, "Supreme Court Selections," *WSJ*, September 9, 1953; Warren B. Francis, "Warren and Dewey Top Vinson Successor List," *LAT*, September 9, 1953; Joseph Paull, "Govs. Dewey, Warren Lead for Court Job," *WP*, September 9, 1953; Eisenhower, *Mandate for Change*, 227; Weaver, *Warren*, 192; Yalof, *Pursuit of Justices*, 48.

73-74 *No one better fulfilled*: EWOHP – Brownell, 9-10.

74 *Do you think…associate justice*: EWOHP – Mailliard, 43.

74 *On September 27, 1953*: EWOHP – Brownell, 25-26, 65-66; "Secret Warren Talk Reported With Brownell," *LAT*, September 28, 1953; "One Law for All," *Time*, October 12, 1953; Weaver, *Warren*, 192; Schwartz, *Super Chief*, 5-6.

75 *same degree of consideration*: EWOHP – Brownell, 28, 68, 60; Warren, *Memoirs*, 261; EWOHP – Hagerty, 6; Ambrose, *Eisenhower* (Vol. I), 538; October 23, 1954 Ike letter to E.E. Hazlett Jr., DDEL; "One Law for All," *Time*, October 12, 1953; EWOHP – Olney, 386; EWOHP – Barnes, 79-80.

75 *I could start off*: James Reston, "Eisenhower names Warren to be chief justice of U.S.," *NYT*, October 1, 1953; "Eisenhower Backs Leak of News Tips," *NYT*, October 1, 1953; "The Calculated Leak," *Time*, October 12, 1953.

75-76 *showed any concern*: EWOHP – Brownell, 11, 67; Warren, *Memoirs*, 270. See also, "Chief Justice Warren," *WP*, October 1, 1953.

76 *They weren't alone*: William H. Stringer, "Warren Unofficially 'In,'" *CSM*, September 29, 1953. See also, "Hear Warren is Choice for Chief Justice," *CT*, September 29, 1953; W. H. Lawrence, "Warren is Slated for Appointment as Chief Justice," *NYT*, September 29, 1953.

76 *A survey of legal experts*: Weaver, *Warren*, 178.

76 *There wasn't really*: EWOHP – R. Warren, 36.

76-77 *Just how did this play out*: "Governor Earl Warren Interview," *Longines Chronoscope*, April 11, 1952; EWOHP – Sweigert, 43, 94; William H. Stringer, "Warren Unofficially 'In,'" *CSM*, September 29, 1953; White, *Warren*, 132; "Who's Who in the GOP: Warren," *Time*, April 12, 1948.

77 *very tough prosecutor*: EWOHP – Brownell, 70; EWOHP – Brown, 58; EWOHP – Warren Jr., 33.

77 *A key proponent*: EWOHP – Sweigert, 150; EWOHP – Feigenbaum, 51; EWOHP – J. Warren, 51.

77 *His liberal views*: EWOHP – Brownell, 70.

78 *My boy*: Warren, *Memoirs*, 14-16.

78 *Like many residents*: Warren, *Memoirs*, 17, 26; Newton, *Justice for All*, 22.

78 *Deprived of an education*: Warren, *Memoirs*, 16-17, 19-23; Newton, *Justice for All*, 21-22.

78 *I saw every man*: Warren, *Memoirs*, 30.

78-79 *In 1908*: Warren, *Memoirs*, 36, 39, 42-43; Newton, *Justice for All*, 26, 36, 40-41.

79 *I remember how shocked*: Warren, *Memoirs*, 47-50.

79 *I believe the preservation*: Newton, *Justice for All*, 89-95; Warren, *Memoirs*, 124-26.

79 *championing of rights of the little*: EWOHP – Faries, 32.

79-80 *there was little in*: Harold Lord Varney, "Earl Warren," *American Mercury*, August, 1958.

80 *Examination of Earl Warren's*: "Man of the West," *Time*, January 31, 1944.

80 *biggest damn fool*: Eisenhower, *Mandate for Change*, 230; Yalof, *Pursuit of Justices*, 67.

80 *conferences in tears*: LCEW – Reitz, 17; LCEW – Rosett, 20; Schwartz, *Super Chief*, 216-17.

80-81 *Catering to Catholic voters*: Yalof, *Pursuit of Justices*, 55, 57, 59.

81 *Those two are very important*: Stern & Wermiel, *Justice Brennan*, 139.

81 *The Court's lurch to the right*: Devins & Baum, "Split Definitive," 19; Landes & Posner, "Rational," 46; Epstein et al, "Ideological Drift," 1492; Yalof, *Pursuit of Justices*, 79.

82 *high regard for*: LBJOH – Jacobsen (Interview III), 13-15.

82 *The best way to describe*: LBJOH – O'Brien (Interview XIII), 24.

82 *c/o White House*: Fred Rodell, "The Complexities of Mr. Justice Fortas," *NYT*, July 28, 1968; "Chief Confidant to Chief Justice," *Time*, July 5, 1968; Murphy, *Fortas*, 115, 119; Shogan, *A Question of Judgment*, 97.

82-83 *Born in 1910*: Richard Harwood, "'A Legal Machine'… 'A Gentle Man,'" *WP*, May 16, 1969; Murphy, *Fortas*, 3-5.

83 *Southwestern college*: Murphy, *Fortas*, 7.

83 *lawyer's lawyer's lawyer*: "LBJ Picks a New Chief Justice," *Newsweek*, July 8, 1968; Murphy, *Fortas*, 10, 13.

83 *poet in South America*: LBJOH – O'Brien (Interview XIII), 22; AFCH, 2; AF biographical materials, Fortas-SML B199; Fred Rodell, "The Complexities of Mr. Justice Fortas," *NYT*, July 28, 1968; Shogan, *A Question of Judgment*, 70; "Chief Confidant to Chief Justice," *Time*, July 5, 1968.

83-84 *best single argument*: Fred Rodell, "The Complexities of Mr. Justice Fortas," *NYT*, July 28, 1968; Murphy, *Fortas*, 85, 87. Harlan told his clerks Fortas was "the most brilliant advocate to appear in my time." See, Schwartz & Lesher, *Inside*, 236.

84 *indoor plumbing*: Caro, *Path to Power*, 58.

84 *been born today*: "The General Manager," *Time*, June 22, 1953.

84 *got no sense*: USSHO – Smathers, 56-57; Caro, *Path to Power*, 46, 95-97.

85 *You never forget what poverty*: USSHO – Smathers, 71; http://www.lbjlibrary.org/lyndon-baines-johnson/timeline; https://www.npr.org/templates/transcript/transcript.?storyId=180880018; https://www.senate.gov/artandhistory/history/common/generic/VP_Lyndon_Johnson.htm.

85 *firmly in their camp*: http://www.lbjlibrary.org/lyndon-baines-johnson/timeline; Evans & Novak, *Johnson*, 8; Caro, *Master of the Senate*, 112-13; Evans & Novak, *Johnson*, 7.

86 *what the hell's*: Califano, *Triumph*, xxv.

86 *Court's inner workings*: July 21, 1965 telephone conversation No. 8370, LBJL; Dallek, *Flawed Giant*, 233.

86 *To Abe Fortas*: Murphy, *Fortas*, 127.

87 *no desire to leave*: Galbraith, *A Life*, 456; July 13, 1968 memo to LBJ, LBJL OPF Arthur Goldberg B5; LBJOH – Goldberg (Interview I), 1-2.

88 *tough to say no*: Warren, *Memoirs*, 358; LBJOH – Warren (Interview I), 20.

88 *hypnotic experience*: Califano, *Triumph*, 43.

88 *agreed to switch jobs*: LBJOH – Califano (Interview XVIII), 3; Murphy, *Fortas*, 170-71; Kalman, *Long Reach*, 62; June 24, 1968 LBJ memo, LBJL OPF Arthur Goldberg B5.

88 *surprising rabbit*: Rowland Evans & Robert Novak, "Inside Report: LBJ's Bold Surprise," *New York Herald Tribune*, July 22, 1965. "Nobody was able to fathom what prompted Arthur to agree," Larry O'Brien explained. LBJOH – O'Brien (Interview XIII), 21.

88-89 *at the U.N.*: LBJOH – Goldberg (Interview I), 1-2, 18; July 26, 1965 Arthur Goldberg letter to LBJ, LBJL WHCF FG535/A B360; July 26, 1965 Arthur Goldberg letter to the "Brethren," Warren-LOC B355; February 17, 1967 W.W. Rostow memo to LBJ, LBJL OPF Arthur Goldberg B5.

89 *earned only $39,500*: AFCH, 5; Dallek, *Flawed Giant*, 233; "Justice Abe Fortas on the Spot," *Newsweek*, May 19, 1969. In 2018, an associate justice earned $255,300.

89 *government-by-crony*: LBJOH – Porter (Interview I), 29; Murphy, *Fortas*, 168; AFCH, 6.

89 *painful searching*: July 19, 1965 AF letter to LBJ, LBJL WHCF FG535 B34.

89 *On July 21, he again rebuffed*: Beschloss, *Reaching for Glory*, 401; Murphy, *Fortas*, 175-77; Califano, *Triumph*, 27.

89 *until the end of time*: Shogan, *A Question of Judgment*, 111.

89 *don't be surprised*: July 28, 1965 telephone conversation No. 8406, LBJL.

90 *off the hook*: LBJOH – Porter (Interview I), 30.

90 *Take this job*: Murphy, *Fortas*, 180.

90 *alongside the press corps*: LBJOH – Fortas, 19; Califano, *Triumph*, 35.

90 *soaked with sweat*: LBJOH – Porter (Interview I), 30.

90 *As if partaking*: https://millercenter.org/the-presidency/presidential-speeches/july-28-1965-press-conference.

90-91 *sad for you personally*: August 11, 1965 AF letter to WD, Douglas-LOC B1782; July 29, 1965 Orrin Evans letter to AF, Fortas-SML B89; July 28, 1965 Arthur Goldberg telegram to AF, Fortas-SML B92; July 30, 1965 Robert Baker letter to AF, Fortas-SML B89.

91 *nonetheless coveted*: Emma Brown, "Nicholas Katzenbach dies: Lawyer, who served as attorney general, shaped civil rights policy in 1960s," *WP*, May 9, 2012; Kalman, *Long Reach*, 86.

91 *son to become attorney general*: September 22, 1966 Robert Kintner memo to LBJ, LBJL WHCF FG431/J B346; LBJOH – T. Clark (Interview I), 18; October 3, 1966 Tom Clark

letter to EW, Fortas-SML B152; Haygood, *Showdown*, 15; Califano, *Triumph*, 205-06; Kalman, *Long Reach*, 87-90.

92 *My judgment is that*: January 25, 1967 telephone conversation No. 11408, LBJL.

92 *keep Clark*: Califano, *Triumph*, 206; March 1, 1967 Liz memo to LBJ, LBJL WHCF FG431/J B346.

92 *shield his legacy than Fortas*: CUOH – Schmidt, 216; Califano, *Triumph*, 308; Johnson, *Vantage Point*, 545, 547. Fortas voted with Warren at a higher percentage than any other justice other than Brennan. See, "Chief Confidant to Chief Justice," *Time*, July 5, 1968.

CHAPTER 4

93-94 *one of his plays*: William Barry Furlong, "The Senate's Wizard of Ooze," *Harper's*, December, 1959; "Washington Conversation," CBS, March 5, 1961; "The Leader," *Time*, September 14, 1962; Ben Bagdikian, "'The Oil Can is Mightier Than the Sword,'" *NYT*, March 14, 1965.

94 *Senate in 1951*: http://bioguide.congress.gov/scripts/biodisplay.pl?index=d000360.

94 *loveable ham*: USSHO – Valeo, 775.

94 *earnestly earnest*: "Washington Conversation," CBS, March 5, 1961; William Barry Furlong, "The Senate's Wizard of Ooze," *Harper's*, December, 1959.

94 *blatant reaction*: Ben Bagdikian, "'The Oil Can is Mightier Than the Sword': Senator Dirksen," *NYT*, March 14, 1965.

94 *Oleaginous Ev*: "The Leader," *Time*, September 14, 1962.

94 *but lived*: Shapiro, *Last Great Senate*, 22.

94 *Shakespearean actor*: USSHO – Ferris, 47.

95 *cloak of the poet*: USSHO – Tames, 12.

95 *hoarse baritone*: USSHO – Valeo, 776.

95 *snake-oil salesman*: William Barry Furlong, "The Senate's Wizard of Ooze," *Harper's*, December, 1959.

95 *I never know where*: William Barry Furlong, "The Senate's Wizard of Ooze," *Harper's*, December, 1959; McPherson, *A Political Education*, 73.

95 *new circumstances*: "Close-Up," ABC, February 7, 1965.

96 *my tenure*: Warren, *Memoirs*, 306.

96 *great issue*: August 23, 1964 JJ New Conference, Javits-SBU Series, Subseries 1, Press Releases B32.

96 *two-thirds of its seats*: Emerson, "Malapportionment," 125-26; Smith, *On Democracy's Doorstep*, 16-21; *CQ Almanac 1964*, "Court Reapportionment Decree Challenged."

96 *Un-Representatives*: Smith, *On Democracy's Doorstep*, 17-19; Emerson, "Malapportionment," 126.

97 *Maryland in 1867*: Untitled charts, Hart-BHL B156.

97 *25 to 30 seats*: October 8, 1961 University of Virginia release, Brennan-LOC I-63; Emerson, "Malapportionment," 127; *CQ Almanac 1962*, "Supreme Court Opens Door to Districting Litigation."

97 *allowing 37 percent*: *Baker v. Carr*, 369 U.S. 186, 188, 191, 253 (1962).

97 *600%*: October 8, 1961 University of Virginia release, Brennan-LOC I-63.

97 *pigs and chickens*: Holman Harvey & Kenneth O. Gilmore, "Reapportionment: Shall the Court or the People Decide?," *Reader's Digest*, March, 1965.

97 *where the money is*: Smith, *On Democracy's Doorstep*, 54.

97-98 *through this process*: Schwartz, *Super Chief*, 67; CUOH – Schmidt, 137.

98 *reach of the judiciary*: Warren, *Memoirs*, 307-08; CUOH – Schmidt, 65, 82, 84, 131, 179-80, 349; LCEW – Bice, 32; Schwartz, *Super Chief*, 267. That very limitation convinced Tom Clark, who had steadfastly supported Felix Frankfurter's insistence on keeping the Court out of the political minefield of reapportionment during deliberations, to eventually view the case through Warren's eyes. "I am sorry to say that I cannot find any practical course that the people could take," Clark wrote apologetically to Frankfurter explaining his reversal, "except through the Federal Courts." March 7, 1962 Tom Clark letter to FF, Clark-TLL BA119.

98 *historic significance*: In *Baker*, the Court held that the question of reapportionment, which had remained outside the bounds of judicial review, was now ripe for judicial oversight. The mandate to institute one-person, one-vote legislative districts came through a series of rulings in 1963 and 1964. Without knowing the exact parameters the justices would lay down, many states nevertheless began to reapportion their legislative districts soon after *Baker*.

99 *resentment into action*: Fred J. Cook, "The Federal Union Under Fire," *Progressive*, September, 1963; *CQ Almanac 1965*, "State Apportionment Plan Loses in Senate."

99 *and wrong right*: "Toward the Total State," *NR*, April 10, 1962.

99 *subvert Baker*: *CQ Almanac 1965*, "State Apportionment Plan Loses in Senate."

99 *curtail Warren's powers*: Council of State Governments, "Amending the Constitution to Strengthen the States in the Federal System," *State Government*, Winter 1963; Alexander C. Vassar, ed., *The Legislators of California*, March 2011; CSAOHP – Lowrey, iii, 71, 73, 77.

99-100 *21-20*: Council of State Governments, "Amending the Constitution to Strengthen the States in the Federal System," *State Government*, Winter 1963; Anthony Lewis, "10 States Ask Amendment to Gain Districting Rights," *NYT*, April 14, 1963.

100 *dismaying dimensions*: "Upsetting the Constitution," *NYT*, April 15, 1963.

100 *considered the proposals*: Arthur J. Freund, 1963 Roll of the States, Warren-LOC B659; Swindler, "Current Challenge," 11; June 10, 1963 EW letter to Arthur Freund, Warren-LOC B660.

100 *speak out*: June 28, 1963 EW letter to Frank Burleson, Warren-LOC B659; October 14, 1963 EW letter to Jacob D. Fuchsberg, Warren-LOC B659.

100 *proposals might go*: June 10, 1963 EW letter to Arthur Freund, Warren-LOC B660. Freund as well as and a law review article by Charles Black, a Yale law professor, began to galvanize some opposition to the amendments.

100-01 *watchmen for the Constitution*: Warren, "Dedication," 386-94. Warren repeated these sentiments at a law conference weeks later. See "Warren Cautions on Amendments," *NYT*, May 23, 1963; Kenneth Crawford, "Reaction's Refuge," *Newsweek*, June 3, 1963.

101 *nationwide campaign*: June 14, 1963 Arthur J. Freund letter to Richard Bentley, Warren-LOC B659; June 17, 1963 Henry Loble letter to EW, Warren-LOC B659; June 25, 1963 Frances T. Freeman Jalet letter to EW, Warren-LOC B659; July 6, 1963 Walter F. Mondale letter to EW, Warren-LOC B659; Memorandum: The First Seventeen Months of the States' Rights Amendments: December 6, 1962 – May 6, 1964, Warren-LOC B659.

101 *jump into the fray*: Anthony Lewis, "Opposition Slows Amendment Push," *NYT*, May 19, 1963.

101 *sinister and radical*: Walter Lippmann, "The Assault on the Union," *Newsweek*, June 10, 1963.

101 *danger of burning down*: "Tampering With the Form of Government," *WSJ*, June 25, 1963; "Who's for the Constitution?" *NYT*, May 10, 1963; May 31, 1963 Thomas Madden letter to EW, Warren-LOC B659; June 24, 1963 David Berger letter to EW, Warren-LOC B659; July 3, 1963 David Berger letter to EW, Warren-LOC B659; Memorandum: The First Seventeen Months of the States' Rights Amendments: December 6, 1962 – May 6, 1964, EW LOC B659; "3 Amendments Fail in North Carolina," *NYT*, June 21, 1963; "Stalled at Sixteen," *New Republic*, August 31, 1963; "The States' Rights Amendments," *Time*, June 7, 1963.

101 *one-vote principle*: *CQ Almanac 1964*, "Court Reapportionment Decree Challenged." The *Wall Street Journal* predicted that the number of state legislatures controlled by

metropolitan areas would jump from 10 to 30. See, Joseph Sullivan, "Redistricting Upset?," *WSJ*, July 9, 1964.

101-02 *cities or economic interests*: Reynolds v. Sims, 377 U.S. 533, 562 (1964).

102 *sagacious conclusion*: Warren, *Memoirs*, 309-10; "After Redistricting Decision," *USNWR*, July 6, 1964.

102 *of his generation*: "WE MUST ACT NOW!... To Preserve Freedom," *Nation's Agriculture*, January, 1966; "A Look Ahead by the Republicans," *USNWR*, January 17, 1966.

102 *seemed assured*: Richard Lyons, "Senate in Upheaval Over Dirksen Rider," *WP*, August 12, 1964; Richard Lyons, "Redistricting Faces New Threat," *WP*, August 14, 1964; E.W. Kenworthy, "Districting Fight Threatens Drive For Adjournment," *NYT*, August 15, 1964; E.W. Kenworthy, "Mansfield Drops Plan to Adjourn," *NYT*, August 16, 1964; E.W. Kenworthy, "Liberals Keep Up Districting Fight," *NYT*, August 18, 1964.

102 *fight in decades*: August 2, 1965 UAW Washington Report, Bayh Subcommittee on Constitutional Amendments & Subcommittee on the Constitution, 1963-1980 B20.

103 *over six weeks*: Robert Albright, "Cloture Move Fails in Senate," *WP*, September 11, 1964; *CQ Almanac 1964*, "Court Reapportionment Decree Challenged."

103 *formidable lead*: E.W. Kenworthy, "G.O.P. Will Unite on Redistricting," *NYT*, January 6, 1965; Smith, *On Democracy's Doorstep*, 254.

103 *power of majorities*: Hearings before the Subcommittee on Constitutional Amendments of the Committee of the Judiciary, 1965, 149, 278.

104 *walls by barbarians*: "How Reapportionment Threatens Business," *Nation's Business*, December, 1964; "What happened in Delaware redistricting could occur in your own state legislature," *Nation's Business*, June, 1965.

104 *promotes mob rule*: "Robert Moses Warns Against 'Mob Rule,'" *Nation's Business*, December, 1964. Moses issued similar warnings to Javits. See January 15, 1965 Robert Moses letter to JJ, Javits-SBU Series 2 B124.

104 *objectives at the state level*: November 30, 1965 Joseph Tydings letter to George Meany, Douglas-CHM Part 1 Series 2 Subseries 6 B561; August 2, 1965 UAW Washington Report, Bayh-IU Bayh Subcommittee on Constitutional Amendments & Subcommittee on the Constitution, 1963-1980 B20; Hearings before the Subcommittee on Constitutional Amendments of the Committee of the Judiciary, 1965, 722; *CQ Almanac 1965*, "State Apportionment Plan Loses in Senate."

105 *siding with Dirksen*: July 26, 1965 vote tally, Dirksen-DCC 2377; July 26, 1965 Paul Douglas letter to Sol Rabkin, Douglas-CHM Part 1, Series 2, Subseries 6 B562; *CQ Almanac 1965*, "State Apportionment Plan Loses in Senate."

105 *I do*: December 14, 1965 ED speech, Dirksen-DCC 2318; July 26, 1965 tv debate, Javits-

SBU Series 2 B119.

105 *local ordinances*: CSAOHP – Whitaker, 5-6; Jill Lepore, "The Lie Factory," *New Yorker*, September 24, 2012.

105 *apportion the California legislature*: CSAOHP – Whitaker, 5-6, 102; Jill Lepore, "The Lie Factory," *New Yorker*, September 24, 2012; Smith, *On Democracy's Doorstep*, 33.

105-06 *firm of that kind*: 111 *CR* 19349.

106 *Government of the People*: "The Plan of Campaign for the Committee for Government of the People," Dirksen-DCC 2265; September 20, 1965 Clem Whitaker letter to Clyde Flynn, Dirksen-DCC 2265.

106 *Texas Instruments*: September 17, 1965 dinner materials, Dirksen-DCC 2265.

106 *the oil industry*: October 16, 1965 Clem Whitaker letter to Gabriel Hauge, Dirksen-DCC 2267; October 16, 1965 Clem Whitaker letter to J. Ed Warren, Dirksen-DCC 2267; October 25, 1965 Clem Whitaker letter to Gordon Reed, Dirksen-DCC 2273; December 13, 1965 Clem Whitaker letter to Gordon Reed, Dirksen-DCC 2273.

106-07 *recruiting materials*: "Reapportionment of State Legislatures and its Relationship to Business," Dirksen-DCC 2273; Reapportionment Fact Sheet, Dirksen-DCC 2274.

107 *top end*: October 16, 1965 Clem Whitaker letter to J. Ed Warren, Dirksen-DCC 2267; October 16, 1965 Clem Whitaker letter to Lamont du Pont Copeland, Dirksen-DCC 2267; Misc. lists, Dirksen-DCC 2267; November 15, 1965 Kenneth McGuiness letter to Committee for Government of the People, Dirksen-DCC 2281.

107 *wife's name*: October 1, 1965 ED letter to Ralph Cordiner, Dirksen-DCC 2266; October 18, 1965 list, Dirksen-DCC 2268; October 25, 1965 J. Ed Warren speech, Dirksen-DCC 2273; November 16, 1965 Karl Bendetsen letter to Gabriel Hauge, Dirksen-DCC 2271; November 30, 1965 "Report No 1," Dirksen-DCC 2271; "List One," Dirksen-DCC 2267; "List Two," Dirksen-DCC 2267; "Oil Industry," Dirksen-DCC 2267.

107 *notable participants*: October 1, 1965 ED letter to Ralph Cordiner, Dirksen-DCC 2266; October 25, 1965 J. Ed Warren speech, Dirksen-DCC 2273; October 1, 1965 ED letter to Roger Blough, Dirksen-DCC 2266; October 1, 1965 ED letter to Lamont du Pont Copeland, Dirksen-DCC 2266; October 1, 1965 ED letter to Rodney Markley, Dirksen-DCC 2266; October 1, 1965 ED letter to Lloyd Miller, Dirksen-DCC 2266; December 15, 1965 ED letter to William Young, Dirksen-DCC 2273; Draft of invitation letter, Dirksen-DCC 2273; February 16, 1966 Clyde Flynn memo to ED, Dirksen-DCC 2278; January 19, 1966 Press Release, Dirksen-DCC 2275.

108 *justice of our cause*: January 19, 1966 Press Release, Dirksen-DCC 2275; February 21, 1966 Progress Report, Dirksen-DCC 2278.

108 *New York Daily News*: March 15, 1966 Press Release, Dirksen-DCC 2287; March 17, 1966

Press Release, Dirksen-DCC 2287; May 6, 1966 Summary of Report, Dirksen-DCC 2284; "Distribution of Materials," Dirksen-DCC 2286; Untitled report, Dirksen-DCC 2288.

108 *two-thirds threshold*: March 20, 1966 "One Man – One Vote" broadcast, Dirksen-DCC 2282; April 18, 1966 Andrew J. Biemiller letter to Paul Douglas, Douglas-CHM Part 1, Series 2, Subseries 6 B563; February 14, 1966 ED letter to Gabriel Hauge, Dirksen-DCC 2278; *CQ Almanac 1966*, "Senate Lets Reapportionment Ruling Stand."

108 *dead issue*: September 15, 1966 Clyde Flynn memo to ED, Dirksen-DCC 2332.

108-09 *direct election of senators*: "Districting Foes Press New Drive," *NYT*, December 13, 1964; American Enterprise Institute, *A Convention*.

109 *34-state threshold*: Fred Graham, "Efforts to Amend the Constitution on Districts Gain," *NYT*, March 18, 1967; June 21, 1967 Clyde Flynn memo to ED, Dirksen-DCC 2332; 1967 memo listing state-by-state actions, Dirksen-DCC 2297; February 28, 1967 ED letter to Margaret Chase Smith, Dirksen-DCC 2302; March 28, 1967 Clyde Flynn memo to Frank Meyer, Dirksen-DCC 2304; *CQ Almanac 1967*, "Hearings Held on Constitutional Conventions."

109 *Fred Graham wrote*: Fred Graham, "Efforts to Amend the Constitution on Districts Gain," *NYT*, March 18, 1967.

109 *broad-scale attack*: 113 *CR* 9342-43.

109 *constitutional nightmare*: Theodore Sorensen, "The Quiet Campaign to Rewrite the Constitution," *Saturday Review*, July 15, 1967.

109 *profound constitutional crisis*: "On to Philadelphia!," *NR*, April 4, 1967.

109-10 *limit the scope*: August 9, 1967 Philip Hart letter to Robert Dye, Hart-BHL B58; American Enterprise Institute, *A Convention*; "The Mysterious Convention," *NYT*, March 23, 1967;

110 *hot topic*: To avoid any chaos, Ervin invited the nation's leading constitutional scholars to help draft a bill resolving these ambiguities. See, *CQ Almanac 1967*, "Hearings Held on Constitutional Conventions."

110 *testified before legislative*: April, 1967 Clyde Flynn memo to ED, Dirksen-DCC 2305; May 16, 1967 memo to ED and Roman Hruska regarding Pennsylvania, Dirksen-DCC 2307; May 17, 1967 memo to ED and Roman Hruska regarding Iowa, Dirksen-DCC 2307; May 17, 1967 memo to ED and Roman Hruska regarding Ohio, Dirksen-DCC 2307; "A Constitutional Convention—The Facts," *USNWR*, June 5, 1967; June 15, 1967 Clyde Flynn memo to ED, Dirksen-DCC 2310.

110 *wisdom of our Founding Fathers*: May 8, 1967 ED letter to Ike, Dirksen-DCC 2292.

110 *short of his goal*: *CQ Almanac 1969*, "Constitutional Convention."

110-11 *called him every day*: LBJOH – Javits (Interview I), 3-4; USSHO – Scott, 151; USSHO – Smathers, 67; "Moment of Victory," *Time*, April 18, 1960; USSHO – Riddick, 259-60; USSHO – Valeo, 267, 304-05, 776; USSHO – Ferris, 22, 92; Ben Bagdikian, "'The Oil Can is Mightier than the Sword,'" *NYT*, March 14, 1965; Califano, *Triumph*, 42.

111 *Dirksen visited the White House*: President's Daily Diary, June 24, 1968, LBJL.

111 *Taj Mahal*: "Sense & Sensitivity," *Time*, March 17, 1958; "A Man Who Takes His Time," *Time*, April 25, 1960; Caro, *Master of the Senate*, 566, 569, 1018.

112 *five stars*: "Sense & Sensitivity," *Time*, March 17, 1958; "A Man Who Takes His Time," *Time*, April 25, 1960.

112 *Jewish supporters to contest*: Shaffer, *On and Off*, 83.

112-13 *departed satisfied*: Shaffer, *On and Off*, 83; President's Daily Diary, June 24, 1968, LBJL; Murphy, *Fortas*, 294, 296-97; Unpublished manuscript, 65, Griffin-CHL B284.

113 *little ruckus*: MacNeil, *Dirksen*, 333.

CHAPTER 5

114 *choicest American stock*: Caro, *Master of the Senate*, 164-65.

114 *antebellum glory*: Caro, *Master of the Senate*, 164-65.

114-15 *dig up on the subject*: Caro, *Master of the Senate*, 164, 167-68.

115 *leave your mind*: Caro, *Master of the Senate*, 165-66, 168.

115 *sitting senator*: Fite, "Richard B. Russell and Lyndon B. Johnson," 126; Caro, *Master of the Senate*, 169-70, 173-75.

115 *Roman presence*: Caro, *Master of the Senate*, 198.

115-16 *God Himself*: McPherson, *A Political Education*, 54.

116 *flat on the legislative*: USSHO – Valeo, 309.

116 *home life*: USSHO – Ferris, 26; USSHO – Smathers, 49; USSHO – Riddick, 275; Caro, *Master of the Senate*, 177, 207; Finley, *Delaying the Dream*, 156.

116 *man I Knew*: LBJOH – LBJ (Reminiscences), 25.

116 *rules as none other*: Caro, *Master of the Senate*, 179, 200; USSHO – Smathers, 48; McPherson, *A Political Education*, 54-55.

116 *budget after WWII*: Caro, *Master of the Senate*, 180.

117 *more coordinated army*: Finley, *Delaying the Dream*, 43, 85, 98, 121; White, *Citadel*, 87-88; "Dixiecrats go 'All Out' to Curb Supreme Court," *Philadelphia Tribune*, August 23, 1958.

117 *recruit allies*: Caro, *Master of the Senate*, 182, 185-86, 197.

117-18 *miscegenation is desirable*: Sam Jones, "Voice of the South," *NR*, July 27, 1957.

118 *permanent solution*: Caro, *Master of the Senate*, 191; Mann, *Walls of Jericho*, 230.

118-19 *do just that*: White, *Citadel*, 180, 190-91.

119 *revenge upon the North*: White, *Citadel*, 68.

119 *complete integration*: Finley, *Delaying the Dream*, 43, 123, 130; Gore, *Let the Glory*, 85.

120 *rule the country*: Sam Jones, "Voice of the South," *NR*, July 27, 1957; William White, "Ruling to figure in '54 campaign," *NYT*, May 18, 1954.

120 *ever assembled*: January 17, 1957 RR letter to John W. Turner, Russell-RBRL Subgroup C, Series I, B9; March 12, 1958 RR letter to C.R. Nichols, Russell-RBRL Subgroup C, Series I, B18; May 5, 1958 RR letter to James D. Maddox, Russell-RBRL Subgroup C, Series I, B18F20; September 11, 1958 RR letter to R.L. Carswell, Russell-RBRL Subgroup C, Series I, B18; September 16, 1958 RR letter to W.P. McFaden, Russell-RBRL Subgroup C, Series I, B18; November 6, 1958 RR letter to Tiffany Wilson, Russell-RBRL Subgroup C, Series I, B18; September 18, 1959 RR letter to Henry Long, Russell-RBRL Subgroup C, Series I, B18; Mann, *Walls of Jericho*, 229.

121 *Senate in 1949*: Russell and Johnson had occasionally worked together while Johnson was in the House. See, Fite, "Richard B. Russell and Lyndon B. Johnson," 127.

121 *figures on the stage*: Stern, "Lyndon Johnson and Richard Russell," 688-89; Fite, "Richard B. Russell and Lyndon B. Johnson," 128.

121 *There was no one that worked*: Murphy, *Fortas*, 97.

121 *office wall*: Fite, "Richard B. Russell and Lyndon B. Johnson," 132-33; Caro, *Master of the Senate*, 210-12, 382; USSHO – Scott, 238; McPherson, *A Political Education*, 54.

122 *shouter*: USSHO – Attig, 60.

122 *constant availability*: Califano, *Triumph*, 12.

122 *dictatorial fellow*: USSHO – Smathers, 55.

122 *side of his face*: Califano, *Triumph*, 14; USSHO – Tames, 100.

122 *along with everybody*: USSHO – Smathers, 48; USSHO – Riddick, 275.

122 *in-your-face style*: USSHO – Scott, 238; USSHO – Smathers, 47-48.

122-23 *very closely parallel*: Evans & Novak, *Johnson*, 33; Caro, *Master of the Senate*, 212, 221; Finley, *Delaying the Dream*, 111; "Sense & Sensitivity," *Time*, March 17, 1958.

123 *NAACP thought*: Stern, "Lyndon Johnson and Richard Russell," 689.

123 *for the reasoning*: May 18, 1954 LBJ speech, LBJL SF-CBS B1; May 28, 1954 LBJ letter to H.R. Wilson, LBJL SF-CBS B1.

123-24 *left him shattered*: Caro, *Master of the Senate*, 471; Finley, *Delaying the Dream*, 157; Stern, "Lyndon Johnson and Richard Russell," 690.

124 *victory would help*: Stern, "Lyndon Johnson and Richard Russell," 695.

124 *own expense*: USSHO – Riddick, 249; "The General Manager," *Time*, June 22, 1953; LBJOH – Eastland (Interview I), 2; Caro, *Master of the Senate*, 382, 472. Russell also felt that if selected as the party's leader, he would need to abandon his sectional interests as the representative of all of its members.

124 *never become president*: Mann, *Walls of Jericho*, 165.

124 *wanted him to sign*: Badger, *New Deal*, 73-74.

124-25 *I wasn't there when*: Caro, *Master of the Senate*, 599, 786-87; Day, *Southern Manifesto*, 118, 120.

125 *only guy*: President's Daily Diary, June 25, 1968, LBJL; USSHO – Smathers, 53; USSHO – Riddick, 250.

125-26 *ever get elected*: LBJOH – Temple (Interview I, Tape 6), 7.

126 *damned Republican*: Clifford, *Counsel*, 555-56; LBJOH – Clifford (Interview IV), 20.

126 *says is a great man*: June 25, 1968 telephone conversation No. 13140, LBJL.

126 *enthusiastically support*: LBJOH – Califano (Interview LXIII), 2; June 22, 1968 telephone conversation No. 13132, LBJL; June 25, 1968 telephone conversation No. 13138, LBJL; Johnson, *Vantage Point*, 545-46.

126 *I'm for you*: LBJOH – Thornberry (Interview I), 38-39; President's Daily Diary, June 25, 1968, LBJL.

126-27 *Russell acquiesced*: Fite, "Richard B. Russell and Lyndon B. Johnson," 133-34.

127 *patty-cake*: President's Daily Diary, June 25, 1968, LBJL.

CHAPTER 6

130 *Effective at your pleasure*: June 26, 1968 LBJ nomination announcement, RMNL

WHCF:SF FG51 B3.

130 *formally stepping down*: Murphy, *Fortas*, 272.

130 *candidacy falter*: June 25, 1968 Mary letter to LBJ, LBJL WHCF FG431/J B346; June 26, 1968 LBJ nomination announcement, RMNL WHCF:SF FG51 B3; President's Daily Diary, June 25, 1968, LBJL; December 20, 1968 WC memo to LT, LBJL WH-CF-SF-AFHT B3; LBJOH – Christopher (Interview I), 10-11; October 1, 1968 telephone conversation No. 13509, LBJL; Califano, *Triumph*, 308.

131 *Fortas's elevation*: June 26, 1968 LBJ nomination announcement, RMNL WHCF:SF FG51 B3.

131 *rosy assessment*: LBJOH – Temple (Interview I, Tape 5), 41.

131 *all but three*: AFCH, 1, 3-4; Murphy, *Fortas*, 184.

132 *Rabin*: June 27, 1968 Yitzhak Rabin letter to AF, Fortas-SML B94.

132 *A great day*: June 26, 1968 Marshall letter to AF, Fortas-SML B95.

133 *This is the business*: Unpublished manuscript, 15, Griffin-CHL B284; "WARREN RESIGNATION?," *WSJ*, June 14, 1968; September 25, 1968 RG chronology, Griffin-CHL B418.

133 *stand that day*: Unpublished manuscript, 16-19, Griffin-CHL B284; LBJOH – Griffin (Interview I), 7; September 25, 1968 RG chronology, Griffin-CHL B418.

133 *No other president*: LBJOH – Griffin (Interview I), 5-6.

133 *seen and not heard*: Unpublished manuscript, 19, Griffin-CHL B284.

134 *rank-and-file Democrats*: Aldo Beckman, "Sen. Griffin: Champion of Doing the Impossible," *CT*, July 14, 1968; Marjorie Hunter, "Leading Fortas Foe," *NYT*, September 28, 1968; Dennis Hevesi, "Robert P. Griffin Dies at 91," *NYT*, April 17, 2015.

134 *Soapy Williams*: E.W. Kenworthy, "Ford Will Oppose Halleck in House," *NYT*, December 19, 1964; John D. Morris, "G.O.P. Rivals Face Close House Test," *NYT*, January 2, 1965; Marjorie Hunter, "Leading Fortas Foe," *NYT*, September 28, 1968; Dennis Hevesi, "Robert P. Griffin Dies at 91," *NYT*, April 17, 2015.

134 *Super-Senator*: "The New Faces," *Newsweek*, October 28, 1968; George Clifford, "Sen. Robert Griffin A Power in Washington?," *Detroit Scope Magazine*, November 2, 1968.

134 *tongue-in-cheek*: June 21, 1968 RG Press Release, Griffin-CHL B292; September 25, 1968 RG chronology, Griffin-CHL B418; Unpublished manuscript, 21, Griffin-CHL B284.

134-35 *uncharted territory*: June 26, 1968 American Law Division memo to RG, Griffin-CHL B285; June 27, 1968 American Law Division memo to RG, Griffin-CHL B228.

135 *plot orchestrated*: June 24, 1968 RG Press Release, Griffin-CHL B418; Shogan, *A Question of Judgment*, 153.

135 *install a new administration*: Shogan, *A Question of Judgment*, 153; Unpublished manuscript, 22, Griffin-CHL B284; Shaffer, *On and Off*, 83-84.

135 *this young man*: Marjorie Hunter, "Leading Fortas Foe," *NYT*, September 28, 1968.

135 *waning control*: http://www.everettdirksen.name/dirksen_leadershipsenators.htm#null.

135 *was just awful*: Unpublished manuscript, 27-28, Griffin-CHL B284; September 25, 1968 RG chronology, Griffin-CHL B418; June 25, 1968 MM memo to LBJ, LBJL WHCF FG535/A B360.

135-36 *issue can be lost*: Unpublished manuscript, 29, Griffin-CHL B284.

136 *Reagan to power*: Jacques Steinberg, "George Murphy, Singer and Actor Who Became Senator, Dies at 89," *NYT*, May 5, 1992.

136 *colleagues to sign*: Shaffer, *On and Off*, 84.

136 *Griffin drafted*: Unpublished manuscript, 29, Griffin-CHL B284; September 25, 1968 RG chronology, Griffin-CHL B418.

136 *incumbent President*: June 26, 1968 RG letter, Griffin-CHL B418.

136 *inclusion of Hiram Fong*: June 26, 1968 RG letter, Griffin-CHL B418.

136 *restless the entire night*: Unpublished manuscript, 45, Griffin-CHL B284.

137 *source of his strength*: June 27, 1968 RG press conference, Griffin-CHL B292.

137 *report the news*: January 18, 1967 RG press release, Griffin-CHL B418; June 27, 1968 RG press conference, Griffin-CHL B292; Unpublished manuscript, 48, Griffin-CHL B284.

137 *have got . . . a vacancy*: June 27, 1968 Senate Judiciary Committee Executive Session, 117-20, 122.

138 *underestimated the opposition*: LBJOH – Nimetz (Interview I), 29.

138 *it doesn't work*: George Clifford, "Sen. Robert Griffin A Power in Washington?," *Detroit Scope Magazine*, November 2, 1968.

138 *downplaying the senator's*: Unpublished manuscript, 67, Griffin-CHL B284. See also, "Chief Confidant to Chief Justice," *Time*, July 5, 1968.

138 *But Pesky*: Unpublished manuscript, 42, 68, Griffin-CHL B284; "Fortas for Warren," *NYT*, June 27, 1968; "New Court Lineup," *WS*, June 27, 1968; June 26, 1968 Bob

Fleming memo to LBJ, LBJL WHCF-SF-AFHT B6; June 27, 1968 Bob Fleming memo LBJ, LBJL WHCF FG535/A B360.

138 *Just who do you*: Unpublished manuscript, 10, Griffin-CHL B284.

139 *same relationship now*: LBJOH – Moore (Interview I), 11.

139-40 *political marriages*: LBJOH – Temple (Interview I, Tape 5), 17-18; RROHC – Tom Johnson OHD-032.

140 *sent only Lawrence's name*: LBJOH – Temple (Interview I, Tape 5), 14.

140 *opposed Lawrence's candidacy*: LBJOH – Temple (Interview I, Tape 5), 14-15; LBJOH – Moore (Interview I), 17; Murphy, *Fortas*, 338-39.

140-41 *impediment to integration*: LBJOH – Temple (Interview I, Tape 5), 16-17; LBJOH – Moore (Interview I), 18.

141 *close to being one*: LBJOH – Jacobsen (Interview III), 4-5; LBJOH – Temple (Interview I, Tape 5), 19-20, 24-25.

141 *turned down before*: LBJOH – Moore (Interview I), 20; Fite, "Richard B. Russell and Lyndon B. Johnson," 136; RROHC – Tom Johnson OHD-032; Fite, *Russell*, 478.

141 *never support the appointment*: Murphy, *Fortas*, 341-43.

141-42 *I feel justified*: Murphy, *Fortas*, 344.

142 *asset to the President*: May 22, 1968 Tom Johnson memo to Jim, LBJL OFWHA LT B1.

142 *torpedo the appointment*: Murphy, *Fortas*, 346, 348-49; LBJOH – Califano (Interview LXIII), 9; LBJOH – Temple (Interview I, Tape 5), 25, 29; RROHC – Tom Johnson OHD-032.

142 *expressing his grievances*: Wayne Kelley, "A Conversation with Richard Russell," *Atlanta Magazine*, December, 1968; LBJOH – Moore (Interview I), 23.

142 *fond of Harry*: LBJOH – Temple (Interview I, Tape 5), 28.

142 *magnetic to me*: McPherson, *A Political Education*, 56.

142 *part-time schedule*: Murphy, *Fortas*, 335.

143 *Fortas-Thornberry ticket*: July 1, 1968 LT memo to LBJ, LBJL WHCF-SF-AFHT B2; LBJOH – Temple (Interview I, Tape 5), 28-29.

143 *nominate Mr. Lawrence*: July 1, 1968 RR letter to LBJ, LBJL OFWHA LT B1.

143 *support for Fortas*: LBJOH – Temple (Interview I, Tape 5), 31, 33.

144 *back to Georgia*: July 1, 1968 RR letter to LBJ, LBJL OFWHA LT B1.

144 *rupture over civil rights*: RROHC – Tom Johnson OHD-032.

144 *respect to your nominations*: July 1, 1968 RR letter to LBJ, LBJL OFWHA LT B1.

144 *to pay the price*: LBJOH – Califano (Interview LXIII), 5-6.

144 *great friendships*: LBJOH – Temple (Interview I, Tape 5), 33.

144 *president miscalculated*: LBJOH – Califano (Interview LXIII), 6-7.

144 *a little salute*: July 1, 1968 McPherson memo to LBJ, LBJL OFWHA LT B1.

145 *such an inference*: July 1, 1968 LBJ letter to RR, LBJL OFWHA LT B1.

145 *again as friends*: Fite, *Russell*, 479-80; LBJOH – Temple (Interview I, Tape 5), 36-37; July 9, 1968 MM memo to LBJ, LBJL WSCF FG535/A B360; Murphy, *Fortas*, 352, 357-58; "Alexander A. Lawrence, A U.S. Judge in Georgia," *NYT*, August 22, 1979; Stern, "Lyndon Johnson and Richard Russell," 699.

145 *have a prayer*: LBJOH – Califano (Interview LXIII), 8.

145 *called from Georgia*: Unpublished manuscript, 49-50, Griffin-CHL B284; LBJOH – Griffin (Interview I), 9. Based on an oral history given by Russell's assistant, Powell Moore, as well as office diaries, Bruce Allen Murphy argues that the initial exchange between Griffin and Russell took place in Russell's office and a phone call may have supplemented it. Griffin, on the other hand, claims the first contact took place while he was in Michigan. Considering the lack of accuracy when it comes to remembering exact chronologies, either version might be accurate. From a substantive standpoint, it's not very material. Regardless of whether they spoke in person or on the phone to initiate their alliance, there is no doubt that Russell and Griffin formed a coalition.

145-46 *legislative victories*: *CQ Almanac 1968*, "Conservative Coalition Shaped Major 1968 Bills."

146 *my efforts to return*: September 18, 1968 RR letter to W.A. Wilkes, Russell-RBRL Subgroup C Series I B17.

146 *I'll be with you*: LBJOH – Griffin (Interview I), 10; Shaffer, *On and Off*, 88.

CHAPTER 7

147 *your views*: AFHTCH1, 8.

147-48 *Warren and Johnson*: AFHTCH1, 9-11; July 2, 1968 WC memo to LT, LBJL WHCF-SF-AFHT B2; Murphy, *Fortas*, 323.

148 *will be destroyed*: Haygood, *Showdown*, 91-94.

148 *their joust*: AFHTCH1, 23.

148 *conflict with*: AFHTCH1, 25. Ervin made a similar argument to LT two weeks earlier. See, July 2, 1968 LT memo to LBJ, LBJL WHCF-SF-AFHT B2.

149 *on his throne*: AFHTCH1, 35.

149 *feet every time*: David Bruck, "Strom Thurmond's Roots," *New Republic*, March 3, 1982; "The Senator from South Carolina," *Time*, February 2, 1962; "How Strom Thurmond Does it," *Newsweek*, September 13, 1971.

149 *between meetings*: SOHP – Thurmond (A-0334); "The Senator from South Carolina," *Time*, February 2, 1962; Don Oberdorfer, "Ex-Democrat, Ex-Dixiecrat, Today's 'Nixiecrat,'" *NYT*, October 6, 1968; "How Strom Thurmond Does it," *Newsweek*, September 13, 1971.

149 *extravagant personalities*: McPherson, *A Political Education*, 82.

149 *not be believable*: Don Oberdorfer, "Ex-Democrat, Ex-Dixiecrat, Today's 'Nixiecrat,'" *NYT*, October 6, 1968.

149-50 *coffin lid*: William Chapman, "The Legend of Senator Strom Thurmond," *Progressive*, January, 1969; Don Oberdorfer, "Ex-Democrat, Ex-Dixiecrat, Today's 'Nixiecrat,'" *NYT*, October 6, 1968; Cohodas, *Strom Thurmond*, (pictorial insert) 15; "The Senator from South Carolina," *Time*, February 2, 1962; Bass & Thompson, *Strom*, 225.

150 *Ben Tillman*: SOHP – Thurmond (A-0334); David Bruck, "Strom Thurmond's Roots," *New Republic*, March 3, 1982; "The Senator from South Carolina," *Time*, February 2, 1962.

150 *not ashamed*: David Bruck, "Strom Thurmond's Roots," *New Republic*, March 3, 1982.

150 *advocate of white supremacy*: Westerhoff, *Politics of Protest*, 9; SOHP – Thurmond (A-0334); David Bruck, "Strom Thurmond's Roots," *New Republic*, March 3, 1982.

150 *that we reject*: Cohodas, *Strom Thurmond*, 303.

150 *Fort Sumter*: "How Strom Thurmond Does it," *Newsweek*, September 13, 1971.

150 *Centralized control*: Day, *Southern Manifesto*, 29.

151 *snarky comeback*: AFHTCH1, 39.

151 *take the lead*: LBJOH – Moore (Interview I), 21.

151 *60 Minutes*: Philip J. Hilts, "The Saga of James J. Kilpatrick," *WP*, September 16, 1973; Hustwit, "Caste to Color," 645, 663, 669.

152 *conservative perspective*: Hustwit, "Caste to Color," 639-40, 642, 657, 659-60, 663, 669; Adam Bernstein, "Columnist Explored Public-Policy Issues from Conservative Perspective," *WP*, August 17, 2010.

152 *fondness for Jim Crow*: Hustwit, *Kilpatrick*, 7-9.

152 *started a newspaper*: Hustwit, *Kilpatrick*, 9-11; Philip Hilts, "The Saga of James J. Kilpatrick," *WP*, September 16, 1973.

152-53 *social order*: Roberts & Klibanoff, *Race Beat*, 112.

153 *bankrupt family*: Philip Hilts, "The Saga of James J. Kilpatrick," *WP*, September 16, 1973; Hustwit, *Kilpatrick*, 17.

153 *fait accompli*: Hustwit, *Kilpatrick*, 10-11, 16, 23; Roberts & Klibanoff, *Race Beat*, 113; Adam Bernstein, "Columnist Explored Public-Policy Issues from Conservative Perspective," *WP*, August 17, 2010.

153 *white people*: Hustwit, *Kilpatrick*, 20-21; Finley, *Delaying the Dream*, 89; http://www.politico.com/magazine/story/2013/12/harry-f-byrd-jr-obituary-101429; "Giving Them Fits," *Time*, August 17, 1962; Gore, *Let the Glory*, 103.

153 *fabled jurists*: Philip Hilts, "The Saga of James J. Kilpatrick," *WP*, September 16, 1973; Hustwit, *Kilpatrick*, 25.

154 *3-4 inch book*: Hustwit, *Kilpatrick*, 29, 33-34.

154 *tyranny before*: Roberts & Klibanoff, *Race Beat*, 115; Hustwit, *Kilpatrick*, 44, 45, 54.

154 *defunct theory*: Hustwit, *Kilpatrick*, 49.

154 *stronghold in New England*: Banner, *Hartford Convention*, 118-19, 300.

155 *solemn mockery*: *U.S. v. Peters*, 9 U.S. 115, 136, (1809)

155 *it was formed*: Hyneman, *Trial*, 38.

155 *household word*: Hustwit, *Kilpatrick*, 49-52; Roberts & Klibanoff, *Race Beat*, 116.

156 *judicial junta*: Hustwit, "Caste to Color," 647.

156 *to amend it*: James Kilpatrick, "Right and Power in Arkansas," NR, September 28, 1957.

156 *taught us how*: Roberts & Klibanoff, *Race Beat*, 72.

156 *enforcing its orders*: Hustwit, *Kilpatrick*, 50, 60-61; Tushnet, *Making*, 240-41; Hustwit, "Caste to Color," 648.

156-57 *13,000 pamphlets*: Hustwit, "Caste to Color," 647; Hustwit, *Kilpatrick*, 57.

157 *make a stand*: Hustwit, *Kilpatrick*, 62.

157 *88 to 5*: Hyneman, *Trial*, 21; Gates, *Massive Resistance*, 105; Hustwit, *Kilpatrick*, 63.

157 *wrote to the editor*: Hustwit, *Kilpatrick*, 58, 64.

157 *illegal and unconstitutional*: Day, *Southern Manifesto*, 93.

157 *law review article*: James Byrnes, "The Supreme Court Must be Curbed," *USNWR*, May 18, 1956.

158 *tapped him to write*: Hustwit, "Caste to Color," 649.

158 *heavily mixed*: Hustwit, "Caste to Color," 650; Day, *Southern Manifesto*, 19.

158 *Hell He is Equal*: Hustwit, "Caste to Color," 655-56.

158 *two-to-one margin*: Gallup, *The Gallup Poll, Vol. 2*, 1249, 1333, 1420, 1502, 1507, 1518, 1527; Gallup, *The Gallup Poll, Vol. 3*, 1616, 1723, 2210; Day, *Southern Manifesto*, 65.

158 *going along*: CUOH – Marshall, 125.

158 *much as we got*: Warren, *Memoirs*, 290.

159 *believes that shit*: Bass & Thompson, *Strom*, 165.

159 *drafting process*: Day, *Southern Manifesto*, 90-91.

159 *price in the polls*: Day, *Southern Manifesto*, 4, 108-09; Aucoin, "Southern Manifesto," 188; *CQ Almanac* 1956, "Southern Congressmen Present Segregation Manifesto."

159-60 *in its implementation*: 102 *CR* 4459-60.

160 *political counterrevolution*: Aucoin, "Southern Manifesto," 178.

160 *plans to integrate*: Hustwit, "Caste to Color," 648.

160 *within the confines*: Hustwit, *Kilpatrick*, 63; Hyneman, *Trial*, 21.

160 *common foe*: Hustwit, *Kilpatrick*, 64; Hustwit, "Caste to Color," 648.

160-61 *local level*: Gore, *Let the Glory*, 100.

161 *end of the decade*: FBI, "Racial Tension and Civil Rights," March 1, 1956, DDEL; Day, *Southern Manifesto*, 9.

161 *business boycotts*: Day, *Southern Manifesto*, 10; "The Authentic Voice," *Time*, March 26, 1956; FBI, "Racial Tension and Civil Rights," March 1, 1956, DDEL.

161 *Senate floor*: Gore, *Let the Glory*, 101; Mann, *Walls of Jericho*, 162.

161 *never at all*: Roberts & Klibanoff, *Race Beat*, 72.

161 *rather than integrate*: Day, *Southern Manifesto*, 12-16.

162 *out of order*: Newton, *Justice for All*, 342.

162 *reaped the whirlwind*: James Kilpatrick, "Right and Power in Arkansas," NR, September 28, 1957.

162 *over the region*: Reed, *Faubus*, 165; Fadely, *Agitator Rhetorician*, 41-47, 55.

162 *way myself*: Peter Applebome, "Orval Faubus, Segregation's Champion, Dies at 84," *NYT*, December 15, 1994; Freyer, *Little Rock Crisis*, 23; Reed, *Faubus*, 166, 169, 188.

162-63 *referendum on interposition*: Reed, *Faubus*, 170, 173, 177-78, 180, 188-90; Freyer, *Little Rock Crisis*, 78, 80-81, 87-88.

163 *lower grades*: Cooper v. Aaron, 358 U.S. 1, 8 (1958).

163 *integration proceed*: Williams, *Thurgood Marshall*, 263.

164 *government domestically*: Diary entry, May 14, 1956, DDEL.

164 *disturbed the domestic scene*: July 22, 1957 Ike letter to E.E. Hazlett, DDEL.

164 *ossified racist*: Ambrose, *Eisenhower* (Vol. II), 125; Pach & Richardson, *Eisenhower*, 139; Luther A. Huston, "School bias arguments end; high court will rule later," *NYT*, December 10, 1953.

164 *own administration's policy*: Ambrose, *Eisenhower* (Vol. II), 142-43; Pach & Richardson, *Eisenhower*, 143.

164-65 *with past decisions*: Ambrose, *Eisenhower* (Vol. II), 190

165 *unequivocal enthusiasm*: Eisenhower, *Mandate for Change*, 230; Eisenhower, *Waging Peace*, 150.

165 *sit in school*: Warren, *Memoirs*, 291.

165 *deserved credit for Brown*: "Eisenhower asks south to be calm," *NYT*, May 20, 1954; July 22, 1957 Ike letter to E.E. Hazlett, DDEL; Eisenhower, *Waging Peace*, 150.

165 *improved racial relations*: Ambrose, *Eisenhower* (Vol. II), 327, 408; Young, *Documentary History*, 453.

165 *passionate and inbred*: Diary entry, May 14, 1956, DDEL.

165 *tacit approval*: July 22, 1957 Ike letter to E.E. Hazlett, DDEL; Ambrose, *Eisenhower* (Vol. II), 191, 409-10.

165 *it was rendered*: Garrow, *Bearing the Cross*, 119.

165-66 *opposed to it*: CUOH – Marshall, 126.

166 *ill-suited for*: Report by the Attorney General on the Administration's Efforts in the Field of Racial Segregation and Discrimination, January 26, 1955, DDEL; Ambrose, *Eisenhower* (Vol. II), 304, 306; Pach & Richardson, *Eisenhower*, 143.

166 *every legal means*: "The Transcript of Eisenhower News Conference on Foreign and Domestic Issues," *NYT*, March 15, 1956.

166 *progressively eliminated*: Young, *Documentary History*, 438; https://www.presidency.ucsb.edu/documents/republican-party-platform-1956.

166 *always act accordingly*: July 22, 1957 Ike letter to E.E. Hazlett, DDEL.

166-67 *enforce the court's directive*: September 24, 1957 Executive Order 10730, DDEL; September 24, 1957 Eisenhower Speech, DDEL.

167 *postpone integration*: Freyer, *Little Rock Crisis*, 145-46; August 28, 1958 Order by Supreme Court, *Aaron v. Cooper*, Clark-TLL BA73.

167 *faced by the school board*: *Cooper v. Aaron* transcript of oral arguments, August 28, 1958.

167 *circumvented entirely*: *Cooper v. Aaron* transcript of oral arguments, August 28, 1958.

167-68 *law of the land*: *Cooper v. Aaron* transcript of oral arguments, August 28, 1958.

168 *ruled by protocol*: https://www.supremecourt.gov/about/courtbuilding.aspx; Kluger, *Simple Justice*, 565-66.

168 *I never tried*: *Cooper v. Aaron* transcript of oral arguments, August 28, 1958.

168-69 *many a years*: *Cooper v. Aaron* transcript of oral arguments, August 28, 1958; Newton, *Justice for All*, 361.

169 *segregated institutions*: Claude Sitton, "Faubus Orders 4 Schools Shut," *NYT*, September 13, 1958.

169 *among the justices*: Freyer, *Little Rock Crisis*, 152; Stern & Wermiel, *Justice Brennan*, 143. A second round of oral arguments on September 11, 1958 was again filled with far more drama than substance.

169 *undertaken before*: Anthony Lewis, "Supreme Court Forbids Evasion or Force to Balk Integration," *NYT*, September 30, 1958; September 19, 1958 Harlan draft, Clark-TLL BA73; October 8, 1958 WD note, Douglas-LOC B199; Warren, *Memoirs*, 298; Schwartz, *Super Chief*, 299-300.

169-70 *reject these contentions*: *Cooper v. Aaron*, 358 U.S. 1, 4 (1958).

170 *ingeniously or ingenuously*: Cooper v. Aaron, 358 U.S. 1, 16-17 (1958).

170 *similarly restrained*: Cooper v. Aaron, 358 U.S. 1, 18-19 (1958).

170 *unanimously reaffirmed*: Cooper v. Aaron, 358 U.S. 1, 19 (1958). Few in the South were willing to make the same concession. After *Cooper*, much of the region continued to follow a path of defiance. Of the nearly three million African-American students living in the former Confederate states, only 2.14 percent attended schools with white children in 1964. In Alabama and Mississippi, that number was less than 0.1 percent. *CQ Almanac 1964*, "Only 2% of Southern Negroes in School with Whites." Those numbers improved in the mid-1960s. By 1968, 32 percent of black children attended integrated schools. See, Reichley, *Conservatives*, 177. The Court's reassertion of its authority didn't change much on the ground in Little Rock either. Faubus closed down the city's schools, earning him compliments from segregationists across the South who later plotted a presidential run on his behalf. See, Reed, *Faubus*, 246.

171 *racial separation*: Virginia Commission on Constitutional Government, "Did the Court Interpret or Amend," May 17, 1960.

171 *war is over*: Hustwit, "Caste to Color," 654.

171 *hundred newspapers*: Hustwit, "Caste to Color," 645, 663, 669; Adam Bernstein, "Columnist Explored Public-Policy Issues from Conservative Perspective," *WP*, August 17, 2010.

171 *huge district*: Philip J. Hilts, "The Saga of James J. Kilpatrick," *WP*, September 16, 1973.

171 *field of jurisprudence*: James J. Kilpatrick, "Taking a Look at Earl Warren's Court," *WS*, June 30, 1968.

172 *towards its function*: August 18, 1969 Sam Ervin letter to Jack Goldman, RMNL WHCF:SF FG51 B2.

172 *objection to Fortas*: The Senate confirmed eleven judicial nominations since Johnson announced his decision not to run for reelection on March 31. See, June 28, 1968 Robert Hardesty letter to Ralph Yarborough, LBJL OFWHA Robert Hardesty B9.

173 *a new President*: AFHTCH1, 46.

173 *same time*: AFHTCH1, 46.

174 *friend of Lyndon Johnson*: AFHTCH1, 56.

174 *power upon the Senate*: AFHTCH1, 41.

174-75 *prepared statement*: AFHTCH1, 44.

175 *such a time*: AFHTCH1, 51.

175 *polysyllabic scorn*: Philip Warden, "Winning Votes to Aid Fortas, Dirksen Says," *CT*, July

10, 1968; Oswald Johnston, "Dirksen Talk Backs Fortas," *Baltimore Sun*, July 13, 1968.

175 *offensive term*: AFHTCH1, 51.

175 *even in the room*: Lyle Denniston, "Dirksen, Griffin Feud Over Top Court Nominees," *WS*, July 13, 1968.

175 *shouted cronyism*: AFHTCH1, 52.

175 *guilty of cronyism*: AFHTCH1, 53-54.

175 *Newsweek reporter observed*: "A Day of the Latter Sort," *Newsweek*, July 22, 1968. A White House aide at the hearing had never seen Dirksen "more eloquent." See, July 12, 1968 LT memo to LBJ, LBJL WHCF-SF-AFHT B2. Christopher also thought Dirksen had won the exchange with Griffin. See, July 12, 1968 LT memo to LBJ, LBJL WH-CF-SF-AFHT B2.

175 *hold water*: AFHTCH1, 54; Philip Warden, "Dirksen Backs Court Choices by President," *CT*, July 13, 1968.

176 *assert ourselves*: AFHTCH1, 58; Fred Graham, "Dirksen Defends Johnson's Naming Friends to Court," *NYT*, July 13, 1968.

CHAPTER 8

178 *do with the nominee*: AFCH, 9, 11-13, 31. Another witness, Charles Callas, who appeared in both hearings received a far warmer reception in 1968. Fed up with one witness for rambling and another for labelling Fortas a communist simply for working in the same federal agency as one, McClellan also defended Fortas on multiple occasions.

178 *far more genuine*: In 1962, Eastland released a scorecard similar to the ones used in baseball games listing how each justice voted on communist-related cases. According to Eastland's count, Warren sided with the communists 62 out of 65 times. "This is the grim picture of . . . the Court," he declared on the Senate floor when showcasing his handiwork. "The Court must be restricted," he beseeched his colleagues. "Unless it is, it will not only snap and bite, but will tear to pieces and devour constitutional government."See, 108 *CR* 7601-04.

178 *America's sovereignty*: "Formal Call Made for Rightist Party," *NYT*, April 16, 1961; "The Ultras," *Time*, December 8, 1961; Courtney, *America's Unelected Rulers*, 51, 66, 110; Huntington, *Right-Wing*, 246-47.

178 *should be impeached*: AFHTCH1, 77.

179 *his valor*: Belknap, *American Political Trials*, 221; Elias, "Red Monday," 207.

179 *uphold the convictions*: Belknap, *American Political Trials*, 222.

179 *Hand's decision*: *Dennis v. United States*, 341 U.S. 494 (1951).

180 *HUAC blacklist*: http://www.writing.upenn.edu/~afilreis/50s/schrecker-blacklist.html.

180 *in the dam*: *Pennsylvania v. Nelson*, 350 U.S. 497 (1956).

180 *against self-incrimination*: *Slochower v. Board of Education*, 350 U.S. 551, 557 (1956).

180 *sensitive positions*: *Cole v. Young*, 351 U.S. 536, 547 (1956).

180 *witch-hunts*: Douglas, *Autobiography*, 92.

181 *Mississippi flood*: Schlesinger, *Robert Kennedy and His Times*, 234.

181 *Mississippi McCarthy*: Robert Sherrill, "James Eastland: Child of Scorn," *Nation*, October 4, 1965.

181 *Executive Branch*: Hearings before the Subcommittee to Investigate the Administration of the Internal Security Act and other Internal Security Laws of the Committee of the Judiciary, June 26, 1956, 3343-44.

181 *flat delivery*: McPherson, *A Political Education*, 77.

182 *pro-Communist influence*: Hearings before the Subcommittee to Investigate the Administration of the Internal Security Act and other Internal Security Laws of the Committee of the Judiciary, June 26, 1956, 3345.

182 *branches of our Government*: Hearings before the Subcommittee to Investigate the Administration of the Internal Security Act and other Internal Security Laws of the Committee of the Judiciary, June 26, 1956, 3345-47, 3355.

182 *70 Court-curbing*: *CQ Almanac 1956*, "Federal-State Powers."

182-83 *similar measures:* H.R. 11600, 84th Congress, June 5, 1956; H.R. 11795, 84th Congress, June 5, 1956; Pritchett, *Congress*, 27; S.J. Res. 45, 84th Congress, February 15, 1955; S.J. Res. 168, 84th Congress, May 9, 1956; S.J. Res. 3811, 84th Congress, May 9, 1956. Florida Senator George Smathers proposed five years of experience for incoming justices; Mississippi's John Stennis doubled that figure. S.J. Res. 3759, 84th Congress, April 30, 1956; S.J. Res. 264, 84th Congress, May 14, 1956.

183 *overturn Nelson*: Murphy, *Congress and the Court*, 73, 75; *CQ Almanac 1956*, "Federal-State Powers."

183 *floor of either chamber*: *CQ Almanac 1956*, "Federal-State Powers."

183 *taking notice*: Anthony Lewis, "Warren Assailed by Two Senators," *NYT*, June 27, 1956.

183 *their illegal conduct*: *Schware v. New Mexico Board of Bar Examiners*, 353 U.S. 232, 246 (1957).

184 *buried McCarthyism*: Sabin, *In Calmer Times*, 141.

184 *sanctions by previous judges*: Jencks v. U.S., 353 U.S. 657 (1957).

184 *it could cause*: Warren, *Memoirs*, 218, 312-13; CUOH – Schmidt, 331.

184 *of this nature*: Watkins v. U.S., 354 U.S. 178, 182 (1957).

184 *expression of it*: FF memo to EW, May 31, 1957, Warren-LOC B580.

184-85 *all but limitless*: "Inquiry reform seen inevitable," *NYT*, June 19, 1957; "The Court, Congress, Chaos," *Newsweek*, July 1, 1957.

185 *HUAC alone*: Horwitz, *The Warren Court*, 61.

185 *are indefensible*: Watkins v. U.S., 354 U.S. 178, 187 (1957).

185 *disloyal employees*: Service v. Dulles, 354 U.S. 363 (1957).

185-86 *for their impeachment*: "Impeach Justices, Thurmond Urges," *NYT*, July 8, 1957; 103 *CR* 10333. A group of southern Representatives also worked on impeachment plans. See, "Group in House Tries to Impeach Supreme Court," *Philadelphia Inquirer*, June 25, 1957.

186 *in its own hands*: "High Court Scored in Senate and House," *NYT*, June 25, 1957.

186 *must be curbed*: James Byrnes, "The Supreme Court Must be Curbed," *USNWR*, May 18, 1956.

186 *destroys this nation*: Sabin, *In Calmer Times*, 194.

186 *Lucius Rivers*: Murphy, *Congress and the Court*, 68.

186 *wholesale impeachment*: "A Resolution Requesting Impeachment of Six Member of the United States Supreme Court," GRFL CFCP BR13.

186 *law-abiding citizen*: Ross, "Attacks on the Warren Court," 25.

186-87 *historical proportion*: Lawrence Davies, "Law Group Head Hits High Court," *NYT*, June 25, 1957.

187 *America has ever received*: Newton, *Justice for All*, 354.

187 *a psychiatrist*: Murphy, *Congress and the Court*, 69, 92; Allen Drury, "Inquiry Curbs Decried," *NYT*, July 1, 1957; Sabin, *In Calmer Times*, 194; 103 *CR* A4941.

187 *constant attack*: Sam Jones, "Voice of the South," *NR*, July 27, 1957.

187 *Treason's Biggest Victory*: "U.S. Press Comment on Decisions in Watkins, Smith Cases," *NYT*, June 19, 1957; Elias, "Red Monday," 218; David Lawrence, "Treason's Biggest

Victory," *USNWR*, June 28, 1957.

188 *commonplace minds*: "Has Congress Abdicated," *NR*, June 29, 1957; Forrest Davis, "The Court Reaches for Total Power," *NR*, July 6, 1957.

188 *more fires*: Luther Huston, "Review of the Session," *NYT*, July 1, 1957.

188 *popular support*: Sabin, *In Calmer Times*, 188.

188 *been the instrument*: Schwartz, *Super Chief*, 200; August 31, 1957 letter from William Brennan to FF, Frankfurter-LOC R17.

188 *But how could you*: Stern & Wermiel, *Justice Brennan*, 130.

188-89 *distasteful justices*: Murphy, *Congress and the Court*, 12, 15-19.

189 *congressional inaction*: Murphy, *Congress and the Court*, 40.

189 *qualifications to future appointments*: *CQ Almanac 1958*, "Proposals to set aside Court decisions." Like the year before, most of these measures—such as capping judicial tenure or Eastland's proposal requiring federal judges to take an oath to refrain from issuing "any decision to alter the Constitution"—sank immediately. See, Elliott, "Court-Curbing Proposals in Congress," 604.

189 *time out*: *CQ Almanac 1957*, "Disclosure of FBI Files."

190 *man for traitors*: Ross, *Jenner*, 1, 8, 11, 17; Poder, *Jenner*, ii-iii.

190 *succession of blows*: Murphy, *Congress and the Court*, 123.

190 *gray area*: Undated memorandum regarding S. 2646, Jenner-ISL B15.

190-91 *review federal laws*: Hyneman, *Trial*, 48; *Congressional Digest*, Vol. 37 (May, 1958), 136; Elliott, "Court-Curbing Proposals in Congress," 606.

191 *dedicated apologia*: William White, "What the McCarthy Method Seeks to Establish," *NYT*, April 4, 1954.

191 *ghost-write*: S. 2646 Hearings (Part 2) (85th Congress), 638; https://spectator.org/59862_living-fire/.

191 *make it behave*: S. 2646 Hearings (Part 2) (85th Congress), 640, 642-43, 648-49.

191-92 *modicum of interest*: S. 2646 Hearings (Part 2) (85th Congress), 70, 113, 155; Ross, "Participation," 6. Most notably, an alliance between the NAACP and big labor shot down John Parker's nomination to the Court in 1930. Catholic organizations and business groups had also lobbied presidents in filling in openings. These instances proved to be exceptions to an otherwise hands-off policy.

192 *pigeonhole it for good*: CBS News Transcript, March, 10, 1958, Jenner-ISL B15.

192 *more palatable*: March 6, 1958 letter from John Butler to William Jenner, Jenner-ISL B15.

192 *apex of his influence*: McPherson, *A Political Education*, 78; https://www.senate.gov/artandhistory/history/common/contested_elections/130Tydings_Butler.htm; John Hess, "John M. Butler, 80; M'Carthy Supporter," *NYT*, March 17, 1978; Evans & Novak, *Johnson*, 45.

193 *grave concern*: August 7, 1958 NAACP Memo, Douglas-CHM B1338.

193 *come to fruition*: 104 *CR* 18734; *CQ Almanac 1958*, "Federal Preemption Doctrine."

193 *defense of it*: Warren, *Memoirs*, 321.

193 *address the conference*: "London Conference of Bar Opens Today," *NYT*, July 24, 1957.

193-94 *congressional Court bashers*: Luther Huston, "Churchill Calls U.N. Change Vital," *NYT*, August 1, 1957; John Nolan Jr., "Supreme Court v. A.B.A.," *Commonweal*, May 15, 1959; Luther Huston, "Bar Unit Assails High Court Trend," *NYT*, July 26, 1957; September 3, 1957 letter from EW to Charles Rhyne, Warren-LOC B754.

194 *report without objection*: Murphy, *Congress and the Court*, 93.

194 *a pariah*: Warren, *Memoirs*, 323.

194 *advancing the cause*: September 3, 1957 letter from EW to Charles Rhyne, Warren-LOC B754. Mortified, the ABA decided to sit on his resignation in the hopes that he would reconsider—which he firmly declined to do. News of his resignation would have thrown a match on to the simmering fire threatening the justices. But the denouement of the episode turned out to pour gasoline on that fire. After a long period of no communication between the two sides, an ABA spokesman broke the silence in January, 1959 by telling the press that Warren dropped his membership for failing to pay his dues. The false account further antagonized the chief justice. "I told you . . . that I at least wanted my children to have a record of the fact that their father had neither welched on his dues nor lied about his resignation," Warren wrote to the ABA president, demanding an "unequivocal letter" affirming his September, 1957 resignation. Unable to mend the relationship through Harlan, whom the ABA approached to serve as an intermediary, the ABA didn't send this letter certifying Warren's resignation until 1971. The long overdue communiqué included an apology. See, January 6, 1959 letter from Whitney North Seymour to John Marshall Harlan, Warren-LOC B355; June 23, 1959 letter from EW to Ross Malone, Warren-LOC B754; March 2, 1971 letter from Edward Wright to EW, Warren-LOC B754; Austin Wehrwein, "Bar Bids Congress Tighten Red Laws," *NYT*, February 25, 1959; Cohn & Bolan, "The Supreme Court and the A.B.A.," 233-35; McKay, "The Supreme Court," 618-22.

194 *printing the entire report*: John Nolan Jr., "Supreme Court v. A.B.A.," *Commonweal*, May 15, 1959.

194 *been more tolerant*: Warren, *Memoirs*, 331.

194 *hit was playing*: Gunther, *Learned Hand*, 652-53.

195 *Dumb Swede*: Newton, *Justice for All*, 347.

195 *enjoyed myself*: Schwartz, *Super Chief*, 276-77, 279.

195 *direction of public affairs*: David Lawrence, "Famous Judge Rebukes Supreme Court," *USNWR*, March 7, 1958.

195 *democratically elected branches*: Anthony Lewis, "Top Court Chided By Learned Hand," *NYT*, February 6, 1958; William Chamberlin, "Lawmakers in Black?," *WSJ*, March 28, 1958; Gunther, *Learned Hand*, 654-57.

195 *legislation to curb*: May 8, 1958 letter from JJ to Learned Hand, Javits-SBU S2B19.

195-96 *cannot be ignored*: 104 *CR* 3198.

196 *voices within*: Gunther, *Learned Hand*, 660; Dilliard "Senator Thomas C. Hennings," 436. The *National Review*, for one, mentioned Hand's critique at least twice on June 7 and June 21, 1958.

196 *Lawmakers in Black*: William Chamberlin, "Lawmakers in Black?," *WSJ*, March 28, 1958.

196 *legislative function*: David Lawrence, "Famous Judge Rebukes Supreme Court," *USNWR*, March 7, 1958.

196 *nose well tweaked*: S. 2646 Hearings (Part 2) (85th Congress), 164; Edwin Corwin, "Limiting the Judiciary," *NYT*, March 16, 1958. Eventually, the embarrassment of siding with the Court's enemies led Hand and the ABA not so much eat their words but, after some coaxing, grudgingly oppose the Jenner-Butler bill while maintaining their criticism.

196 *that boast*: Lawrence Davies, "High Court Urged to Limit Actions," *NYT*, August 21, 1958; "What 36 State Chief Justices Said About the Supreme Court—For the First Time, Here is the Full Text of Historic Report," *USNWR*, October 3, 1958.

196 *one-sided votes*: CQ *Almanac 1958*, "Federal Security Program;" CQ *Almanac 1958*, "Proposals to set aside Court decisions."

CHAPTER 9

198 *near miracle*: "The General Manager," *Time*, June 22, 1953.

198 *unusual power*: LBJOH – Thurmond (Interview I), 13.

198 *single most powerful*: USSHO – Smathers, 118. If Thurmond and Smathers were overstating Johnson's power, it was not by much: in the late 1950s, Johnson delivered his

own version of a State of the Union address rivaling that of the president. "Sense & Sensitivity," *Time*, March 17, 1958.

198 *party's leadership*: https://www.senate.gov/artandhistory/history/common/briefing/Majori-ty_Minority_Leaders.htm#4; Caro, *Master of the Senate*, 558; Evans & Novak, *Johnson*, 30.

199 *political arts*: USSHO – Smathers, 45, 112-13, 118; "Sense & Sensitivity," *Time*, March 17, 1958; USSHO – Paone, 92; USSHO – Scott, 40; "The General Manager," *Time*, June 22, 1953; Evans & Novak, *Johnson*, 103; http://niemanstoryboard.org/stories/robert-caro-part-1-on-finding-book-projects-reporting-sacrifice-and-sources/; McPherson, *A Political Education*, 52.

199-200 *particular fellow*: "The General Manager," *Time*, June 22, 1953; USSHO – Smathers, 53.

200 *as a sapling*: LBJOH – Javits (Interview I), 1.

200 *foreman of that job*: USSHO – Riddick, 258-59.

200 *vote in the evening*: USSHO – Smathers, 74; USSHO – Shuman, 213; USSHO – Scott, 304.

200 *into an ally*: After Richard Neuberger refused Johnson's overtures on an important vote, the Majority Leader still made sure to push Neuberger's pet project—the Hells Canyon Dam—through the Senate, converting Neuberger from a potential foe into a loyal ally. "Sense & Sensitivity," *Time*, March 17, 1958; "A Man Who Takes His Time," *Time*, April 25, 1960.

200 *man capitulated*: USSHO – Shuman, 124; Caro, *Master of the Senate*, 564.

200 *amazed yourself*: USSHO – Smathers, 75.

200 *come and ask*: USSHO – Ferris, 16, 68.

200-01 *balance in his favor*: USSHO – Smathers, 68.

201 *for an hour*: USSHO – Smathers, 119; Caro, *Master of the Senate*, 588; Murphy, *Fortas*, 100.

201 *elevated the majority*: USSHO – Smathers, 60; Caro, *Master of the Senate*, 560-62.

201 *Senate's consideration*: Murphy, *Congress and the Court*, 157; McPherson, *A Political Education*, 132.

201 *was among them*: "Democrats Clear Court Curb Bills," *NYT*, August 16, 1958; Allen Drury, "Johnson Seeks End of Session Saturday," *NYT*, August 20, 1958; Joseph L. Rauh Jr., "The Truth about Congress and the Court," *Progressive*, November, 1958; McPherson, *A Political Education*, 132; Pritchett, *Congress*, 36. The deal included a third House bill dealing with *Mallory v. U.S.*, a criminal procedure case.

201-02 *for three years*: Crespino, *Strom Thurmond's America*, 104.

202 *vote anyway*: Murphy, *Congress and the Court*, 166; Joseph L. Rauh Jr., "The Truth about Congress and the Court," *Progressive*, November, 1958; Bass & Thompson, *Strom*, 169-70. An alternative account of Thurmond's exploits during the filibuster claimed he wore a bag to collect his urine. See Crespino, *Strom Thurmond's America*, 117.

202 *result of this line*: 104 *CR* 18636.

202 *judgment of the Congress*: 104 *CR* 18646.

202 *class of litigants*: 104 *CR* 18647.

202-03 *heaven help*: 104 *CR* 18685-86.

203 *49-41 vote*: Murphy, *Congress and the Court*, 166.

203 *central dais*: Baker, "Traditions," 1, 14, 22.

203-04 *inside drawer*: Baker, "Traditions," 7, 19.

204 *officer's attention*: Baker, "Traditions," 19; USSHO – Shuman, 148.

204 *I offer an amendment*: 104 *CR* 18687-88; Murphy, *Congress and the Court*, 166.

204 *enter the Senate*: "The Making of a Maverick," *Time*, January 16, 1950; Smith, *On Democracy's Doorstep*, 230-31; https://www.bowdoin.edu/economics/curriculum-requirements/douglas-biography.shtml.

204 *outvoted 49-1*: "The Making of a Maverick," *Time*, January 16, 1950; "The Fin of the Shark," *Time*, January 22, 1951.

205 *win a convert*: "Sense & Sensitivity," *Time*, March 17, 1958. "Johnson made progress, not issues," McPherson observed, "Douglas the reverse." McPherson, *A Political Education*, 30.

205 *the ringmaster*: Mann, *Walls of Jericho*, 141.

205 *empty chamber*: USSHO – Valeo, 795; "A Man Who Takes His Time," *Time*, April 25, 1960; Caro, *Master of the Senate*, 566, 568; Evans & Novak, *Johnson*, 88.

205 *against the South*: 104 *CR* 18688.

205 *negotiated with Russell*: 104 *CR* 18690; Anthony Lewis, "Critics of Supreme Court Score a Victory in Senate," *NYT*, August 20, 1958; Rodney Crowther, "Senate Votes Down Bill to Curb Court," *Baltimore Sun*, August 21, 1958; Warren Unna, "Senate Shelves Curbs on Court," *WP*, August 22, 1958; Anthony Lewis, "Johnson Shows Mastery Again," *NYT*, August 25, 1958; Dallek, *Lone Star Rising*, 536. The Illinois Senator refused to relent: "if any Member thinks that by getting the bill… out of the way," he said, in response to Johnson's move, "he will . . . avoid facing the issue of whether the Senate approves or disapproves of the decisions of the Supreme Court in the desegregation cases, that Member is mistaken." He vowed to keep submitting his amendment to other pending

bills until the Senate came to consider it. "I am ready to stay here, not only all summer, but all fall—for . . . it happens that I am not running for office." Having induced a burst of laughter, Douglas added another wisecrack. "Furthermore," he said, "I keep in good physical condition, by exercising every morning. So I am willing to stay here until we face this issue." 104 *CR* 18691.

205-06 *HR 3 in its place*: 104 *CR* 18695-96, 18718; Willard Edwards, "Court Foes Keep Senate Battle Alive," *Chicago Tribune*, August 21, 1958.

206 *floor beforehand*: USSHO – Shuman, 126-27. Johnson explained his philosophy to Humphrey: "Now you don't just come right out on the floor and lay important bills right out in front of God and all those voters. That's not the way it's done. . . . You have to take it slow and easy, working your colleagues over like gentlemen—not on the floor but in the cloakrooms—explaining and trading, but always letting them see what's in it for them. Then when you're sure—Ivory soap sure, and you know you have the votes buttoned up in your back pocket—you come out statesmanlike on the Senate floor and, in the spirit of democracy, have a little debate for the people." USSHO – Zee, i.

206 *support HR 3*: LBJOH – Mitchell (Interview I), 3; Murphy, *Congress and the Court*, 162-64; "Antitrust Lawyers See Far-Reaching Effects in Court's DuPont Decision," *WSJ*, June 5, 1957.

206 *votes in mid-August*: Murphy, *Congress and the Court*, 162-63.

206 *romantic preconceptions*: Caro, *Master of the Senate*, 389.

207 *Thinking is never good*: Caro, *Master of the Senate*, 390, 393.

207 *learned a senator's vote*: "A Man Who Takes His Time," *Time*, April 25, 1960; USSHO – Valeo, 261; Caro, *Master of the Senate*, 392-93, 587-88; Evans & Novak, *Johnson*, 97, 113.

207-08 *with his butterfly*: USSHO – Valeo, 153.

208 *status at the committee level*: USSHO – Smathers, 54, 61-62; USSHO – Scott, 149; USSHO – Ferris, 21, 67-68.

208 *vote against you*: Caro, *Master of the Senate*, 390.

208 *prevailed 46-39*: Rowland Evans Jr., "Court, South and Lyndon," *Hartford Courant*, August 25, 1958; McPherson, *A Political Education*, 133; Murphy, *Congress and the Court*, 168; Caro, *Master of the Senate*, 1031; Warren Unna, "Senate Shelves Curbs on Court," *WP*, August 22, 1958; 104 *CR* 18748.

208 *Vote!*: 104 *CR* 18749; Murphy, *Congress and the Court*, 169.

208 *substantive vote*: LBJOH – Thurmond (Interview I), 12.

208 *sat paralyzed*: McPherson, *A Political Education*, 133.

208 *counsel at all times*: Evans & Novak, *Johnson*, 51.

209 *better adjourn*: LBJOH – McPherson (Interview I), 24-25; McPherson, *A Political Education*, 133.

209 *surprises of his tenure*: LBJOH – McPherson (Interview I), 25; Caro, *Master of the Senate*, 1031.

209 *mentor's advice*: Murphy, *Congress and the Court*, 169; Mann, *Walls of Jericho*, 233.

209 *move the Senate adjourn*: 104 *CR* 18750.

209 *motion is not debatable*: 104 *CR* 18750.

209 *prevailed 70-18*: 104 *CR* 18750; Anthony Lewis, "LBJ the Performer: Lyndon," *NYT*, August 10, 1980; Caro, *Master of the Senate*, 1031.

209 *there's still a way*: Caro, *Master of the Senate*, 1031; Evans & Novak, *Johnson*, 165-66.

209-10 *lambaste you*: Anthony Lewis, "LBJ the Performer: Lyndon," *NYT*, August 10, 1980; Caro, *Master of the Senate*, 1032.

210 *escape from quicksand*: Evans & Novak, *Johnson*, 166; Rodney Crowther, "Senate Rejects Curbs on Court," *Baltimore Sun*, August 22, 1958; Warren Unna, "Senate Shelves Curbs on Court," *WP*, August 22, 1958; "Triumph of Restraint," *WP*, August 23, 1958; Caro, *Master of the Senate*, 589-90; McPherson, *A Political Education*, 32; USSHO – Paone, 9, 14; USSHO – Zee, i, 123-24.

210 *Change your vote*: Caro, *Master of the Senate*, 595.

211 *on official business*: "How High Court Avoided Rebuke," *Chicago Tribune*, August 24, 1958; Drew Pearson, "Courage Shown in Vote on Court," *WP*, August 27, 1958; 104 *CR* 18928; Evans & Novak, *Johnson*, 166; McPherson, *A Political Education*, 134.

211 *to stay away*: Murphy, *Congress and the Court*, 171.

211 *Lausche to change*: Murphy, *Congress and the Court*, 171-72.

211 *anti-Court forces*: Caro, *Master of the Senate*, 396-97; Rowland Evans Jr., "Court, South and Lyndon," *Hartford Courant*, August 25, 1958; Drew Pearson, "Courage Shown in Vote on Court," *WP*, August 27, 1958.

211-12 *Johnson's overtures*: Murphy, *Congress and the Court*, 172; Bob Bernick Jr., "Wallace F. Bennett Dies in his Sleep," *Deseret News*, December 20, 1993; Brune, *Korean War*, 376.

212 *just hours earlier*: "How High Court Avoided Rebuke," *Chicago Tribune*, August 24, 1958; Rowland Evans Jr., "Court, South and Lyndon," *Hartford Courant*, August 25, 1958; Evans & Novak, *Johnson*, 166-67; Caro, *Master of the Senate*, 1033; Murphy, *Congress and the Court*, 172-73.

212 *seat in the gallery*: Murphy, *Congress and the Court*, 173; "How High Court Avoided Rebuke," *Chicago Tribune*, August 24, 1958.

212-13 *defeated 41-40*: Murphy, *Congress and the Court*, 170-71; Evans & Novak, *Johnson*, 166-67; Drew Pearson, "Courage Shown in Vote on Court," *WP*, August 27, 1958; Rowland Evans Jr., "Court, South and Lyndon," *Hartford Courant*, August 25, 1958.

213 *great triumphs*: Anthony Lewis, "41-40 Senate Vote Kills Bills Aimed at Supreme Court," *NYT*, August 21, 1958.

213 *switched it around*: LBJOH – Thurmond (Interview I), 12.

213-14 *batting average*: https://www.presidency.ucsb.edu/documents/remarks-the-accomplishments-the-89th-congress; Califano, *Triumph*, 145.

214 *willing to trade*: Califano, *Triumph*, 72-73.

214 *rest unknown*: June 27, 1968 MM & Barefoot Sanders memo LBJ, LBJL WHCF-SF-AFHT B1.

214 *someone begs him to*: June 26, 1968 MM memo to LBJ, LBJL WHCF-SF-AFHT B6; June 28, 1968 memo to LBJ, LBJL WHCF-SF-AFHT B1; June 29, 1968 Bill Heath report, LBJL WHCF-SF-AFHT B1.

214 *switch sides*: June 29, 1968 Bill Heath report, LBJL WHCF-SF-AFHT B1; June 29, 1968 LT letter to LBJ, LBJL WHCF-SF-AFHT B1; July 1, 1968 LT memo to LBJ, LBJL WHCF-SF-AFHT B2.

214 *with the White House*: June 25, 1968 MM memo to LBJ, LBJL WHCF-SF-AFHT B1; Murphy, *Fortas*, 365.

215 *end of June*: Califano, *Triumph*, 310.

215 *get beat*: LBJOH – Christopher (Interview I), 16; LBJOH – McPherson (Interview III), 29; Miller, *Lyndon*, 484.

215 *executives for help*: LBJOH – Califano (Interview LXIII), 3; Califano, *Triumph*, 128, 222-23; July 1, 1968 Jim Gaither memo to JC, LBJL WHCF-SF-AFHT B2; Unpublished manuscript, 62, Griffin-CHL B284.

215 *behest on July 8*: June 29, 1968 JC memo to LBJ, LBJL WHCF-SF-AFHT B1; July 10, 1968 Walter Reuther letter to JC, LBJL WHCF FG 535/A B360; July 8, 1968 Walker Cisler telegram to RG, LBJL WHCF FG 535/A B360.

215-16 *one way or another*: June 29, 1968 JC memo to LBJ, LBJL WHCF-SF-AFHT B1.

216 *Fortas to Eastland*: June 29, 1968 Jim Gaither memo to JC, LBJL WHCF-SF-AFHT B1; June 29, 1968 JC memo to LBJ, LBJL WHCF-SF-AFHT B1; July 1, 1968 LT memo to LBJ, LBJL WHCF-SF-AFHT B2; Murphy, *Fortas*, 317; July 10, 1968 Ross Malone

letter to James Eastland, Fortas-SML B94.

216 *great deal of pressure*: June 28, 1968 MM memo to LBJ, LBJL WHCF FG 535/A B360.

216 *doubtful Republicans*: June 27, 1968 Barefoot Sanders memo to LBJ, LBJL WH-CF-SF-AFHT B1; June 28, 1968 William Finley memo to WC, LBJL PP Ramsey Clark B128; June 29, 1968 memo, LBJL WHCF FG 535/A B360.

216 *rebutting Griffin*: June 27, 1968 MM & Barefoot Sanders to LBJ, LBJL WHCF-SF-AF-HT B1; June 28, 1968 AFL-CIO press release, LBJL WHCF-SF-AFHT B1; June 29, 1968 memo, LBJL WHCF FG 535/A B360; June 29, 1960 UAW telegram to JC, LBJL FG 535/A B360; June 29, 1968 JC memo to LBJ, LBJL WHCF-SF-AFHT B1; Califano, *Triumph*, 311; Dallek, *Flawed Giant*, 560; July 1, 1968 WC memo to LT, LBJL PP WC B13; July 10, 1968 WC letter to Wayne Morse, LBJL PP WC B13; Murphy, *Fortas*, 309.

216 *keep the heat*: July 11, 1968 Harry McPherson memo to LBJ, LBJL WHCF-SF-AFHT B5.

216 *editorial pages*: July 2, 1968 Irv Sprague memo to Barefoot Sanders, LBJL WH-CF-SF-AFHT B2.

216 *White House's solicitations*: July 17, 1968 Tom J. memo to Jim, LBJL WHCF-SF-AF-HT B5; Unpublished manuscript, 67, Griffin-CHL B284. See also, "Chief Confidant to Chief Justice," *Time*, July 5, 1968.

216-17 *statist liberals*: "The Political Court," *WSJ*, June 27, 1968; Louis M. Kohlmeier, "President Takes a Risk," *WSJ*, June 27, 1968; David Lawrence, "High Court Cynically Manipulated," *WS*, June 27, 1968; "Exit Warren," *NR*, July 16, 1968; "Enter Fortas," *NR*, July 16, 1968.

217 *lobbying campaign*: July 10, 1968 Larry Levinson memo to LT, LBJL WHCF-SF-AFHT B2; July 2, 1968 Jim Gaither memo to JC, LBJL WHCF-SF-AFHT B2; July 2, 1968 MM memo to LBJ, LBJL WHCF FG 535/A B360.

217 *they won't change*: July 2, 1968 Harry McPherson memo to MM, LBJL WHCF-SF-AF-HT B4.

217 *Grand Coulee Dam*: LBJOH – Califano (Interview LXIII), 15.

217 *aroused anti-Semitism*: LBJOH – McPherson (Interview III), 28; July 7, 1968 transcript of Lou Gordon Show, Griffin-CHL B418.

217-18 *ANTI-AMERICAN JEW*: July 18, 1968 "American Christian" letter to Eastland, SJC-NA; September 9, 1968 D.P. Glenn letter to Eastland, SJC-NA; September 22, 1968 James Fitzgerald letter to Eastland, SJC-NA.

218 *vote for that Jew*: Murphy, *Fortas*, 361. "After Marshall," Eastland apparently said at a cocktail party, "I could not go back to Mississippi if a Jewish chief justice swore in the next president." See, Murphy, *Fortas*, 299.

218 *bed with anti-Semites*: June 28, 1968 Irv Sprague memo to Barefoot Sanders, LBJL WHCF FG 535/A B360; July 2, 1968 Irv Sprague memo to Barefoot Sanders, LBJL WHCF-SF-AFHT B2; Murphy, *Fortas*, 320; Califano, *Triumph*, 310-11; July 11, 1968 Harry McPherson memo to LBJ, LBJL WHCF-SF-AFHT B5.

218 *anti-Semitic sentiments*: July 2, 1968 Harry McPherson memo to MM, LBJL WH-CF-SF-AFHT B4; July 2, 1968 George Reedy memo to LBJ, LBJL WHCF-SF-AFHT B4; July 10, 1968 Harry McPherson memo to LBJ, LBJL WHCF-SF-AFHT B5; July 8, 1968 Ernest Goldstein memo, LBJL WHCF-SF-AFHT B5; July 10, 1968 Ernest Goldstein memo, LBJL WHCF-SF-AFHT B5; June 29, 1968 Dr. William Wexler letter, LBJL WHCF-SF-AFHT B1; Murphy, *Fortas*, 320; September 18, 1968 American Jewish Committee Press Release, Fortas-SML B94.

218 *Wyman reported back*: June 28, 1968 Gene Wyman memo, LBJL WHCF-SF-AFHT B1.

219 *lowest dregs*: Shogan, *A Question of Judgment*, 156.

219 *agreed to contact Tower*: July 8, 1968 Ernest Goldstein memo, LBJL WHCF-SF-AFHT B5; July 10, 1968 Ernest Goldstein memo, LBJL WHCF-SF-AFHT B5.

219 *than Abe has*: LBJOH – McPherson (Interview VII), 3.

219 *grumbled to reporters*: Lyle Denniston, "Court-Issue Pressure Charged," *WS*, July 3, 1968.

219 *win this battle*: July 2, 1968 Capitol Cloakroom, Griffin-CHL B227.

219 *fancied than real*: Califano, *Triumph*, 312; July 2, 1968 Capitol Cloakroom, Griffin-CHL B227; Unpublished manuscript, 58, 80-82, Griffin-CHL B284.

219 *returning Arthur Goldberg*: June 28, 1968 RG Press conference, Griffin-CHL B292.

219 *lazy allegations*: July 8, 1968 Ernest Goldstein memo, LBJL WHCF-SF-AFHT B5; July 27, 1968 WABC-TV transcript, Javits-SBU Series 1 Subseries 1 Press Releases B41; Sidney Zion, "O'Dwyer Sees Bias in Senate Opposition to Fortas," *NYT*, July 24, 1968.

219-20 *solid evidence*: July 24, 1968 JJ press release, Javits-SBU Series 1 Subseries 1 Press Releases B41.

220 *tired of each other*: Califano, *Triumph*, 266.

220 *lowest point*: http://www.presidency.ucsb.edu/data/popularity.php?pres=36.

220-21 *public statement*: July 1, 1968 vote tally, LBJL WHCF FG 535/A B360; July 9, 1968 vote tally, LBJL WHCF-SF-AFHT B2; June 28, 1968 MM memo to LBJ, LBJL WHCF FG 535/A B360.

221 *vacation on Capri*: July 8, 1968 Barefoot Sanders memo to Postmaster General, LBJL WHCF-SF-AFHT B2; July 23, 1968 JC memo to LBJ, LBJL WHCF-SF-AFHT B7; Murphy, *Fortas*, 314.

CHAPTER 10

224 *Democrats to his right*: Fred Graham, "Fortas Testifies he Aided Johnson While a Justice," *NYT*, July 17, 1968; Ronald Ostrow, "Fortas Tells of Aid to LBJ," *LAT*, July 17, 1968; Nick Thimmesch, "Fortas Enters Round 2 Today, But OK is Already Seen Likely," *Newsday*, July 17, 1968; Unpublished manuscript, 103-04, Griffin-CHL B284; Shogan, *A Question of Judgment*, 164.

224 *unfortunate precedent*: Confirmation of Nomination of Earl Warren, Executive Session, Subcommittee of the Judiciary Committee, February 24, 1954, 134. While no justice confirmed by the Senate had ever testified, justices who were initially recess appointments had appeared before the Judiciary Committee.

225 *have any chance*: December 20, 1968 WC memo to LT, LBJL WHCF-SF-AFHT B3.

225 *counseled him to appear*: LBJOH – Christopher (Interview I), 12.

225 *not a novice*: LBJOH – Christopher (Interview I), 12. Fortas didn't seek input from Warren, who was hoping the justice wouldn't testify. See, Schwartz, *Super Chief*, 721; AFHTCH1, 103.

225 *winning a duel*: July 10, 1968 JC memo to LBJ, LBJL WHCF-SF-AFHT B5.

225 *remove all doubts*: July 11, 1968 Albert Gore letter to LBJ, LBJL WHCF-SF-AFHT B4.

225 *future cases*: AFHTCH1, 100-01.

226 *kissing babies*: Fred Rodell, "The Complexities of Mr. Justice Fortas," *NYT*, July 28, 1968.

226 *nothing more*: Robert Sherrill, "James Eastland: Child of Scorn," *Nation*, October 4, 1965; AFHTCH1, 104.

226 *close to lying*: LBJOH – Califano (Interview LXIII), 10. Califano mentioned several instances in his memoir of his discomfort with Fortas's role in the president's matters. Concerned of how their opponents might exploit any communications between Johnson and Fortas, the president's staff recommended that Fortas not attend "an off-the-record luncheon" to discuss Johnson's presidential library. See, July 23, 1968 JC memo to LBJ, LBJL WHCF-SF-AFHT B7.

226 *too close to a president*: Bass & Thompson, *Strom*, 199.

226 *Boss*: October 7, 1965 note to LBJ, LBJL WHCF-SF-AFHT B1; May 4, 1967 AF letter to LBJ, LBJL WHCF-SF-AFHT B1.

227 *occurs very seldom*: AFHTCH1, 104.

227 *eighty times*: LBJ-AF meetings chronology, LBJL WHCF-SF-AFHT B6.

227 *more cabinet meetings*: O'Brien, *Storm Center*, 89.

227 *copper markets*: November 25, 1966 LBJ letter to AF, LBJL WHCF FG431/J B346; Califano, *Triumph*, 110.

227 *enough for Abe*: February 12, 1967 JC memo to LBJ, LBJL WHCF-SF-AFHT B1.

227 *national broadcasters*: May 9, 1968 JC memo to AF, LBJL WHCF Confidential File, FG535 B34; June 6, 1968 AF memo to LBJ, LBJL WHCF FG431/J B346.

227 *managing the bill*: O'Brien, *Storm Center*, 91.

228 *absolutely clear*: AFHTCH1, 104.

228 *was a lie*: "The President has got too much respect for the independence of the Court for that and wouldn't want to embarrass Abe," McPherson explained. "But he has asked him an awful lot of things, which probably have gone on occasion too far." See, LBJOH – McPherson (Interview III), 30. Califano, on the other hand, provides several examples in his memoir of Johnson and Fortas discussing legal matters and issues that may come before the Court. While the president may not have asked about pending cases before the Court, Fortas did speculate on how the Court might rule on hypothetical matters.

228 *best lawyer*: Califano, *Triumph*, 157.

228 *numbers involved*: August 1, 1967 AF memo to Marvin Watson, Fortas-SML B156.

228 *election reform*: May 11, 1967 JC memo to AF, Fortas-SML B156.

228 *likely action*: Califano, *Triumph*, 86-87, 141, 148-49, 157-59.

228 *at these meetings*: Murphy, *Fortas*, 237.

228 *sought my help*: July 24, 1968 AF letter to John Marshall Harlan, Fortas-SML B95.

229 *before it was delivered*: AFHTCH1, 104-05.

229 *presidential counselor*: Murphy, *Fortas*, 392-403; Califano, *Triumph*, 216. An empirical analysis of confirmation testimony by Justin Wedeking and Dion Farganis concluded that Fortas "evidenced the lowest level of candor for any nominee" from 1955 to 2010. See, Wedeking & Farganis, "Supreme Court," 14.

229 *President's fixer*: "Fortas v. Fortas," *NR*, September 10, 1968.

229 *for a judgeship*: AFHTCH1, 103. Fortas reviewed Clark's judicial recommendations. See, Murphy, *Fortas*, 383-84.

229 *now for sure*: May 20, 1968 LT memo to LBJ, LBJL WHCF FG431/J B346; June 24, 1968 Jim J memo to LBJ, LBJL WHCF FG431/J B346.

229 *Fortas's fortress*: AFHTCH1, 106-07.

229 *biblical anecdotes*: Finley, *Delaying the Dream*, 140.

230 *true intent*: AFHTCH1, 108; Nick Thimmesch, "The Old Guard Questions Fortas," *Newsday*, July 17, 1968; James Kilpatrick, "Justice Abe Fortas Meets the Committee," *Hartford Courant*, July 20, 1968.

230 *heir apparent*: Fortas voted with Warren 86% of the time in their three terms together on the Court. See, Murphy, *Fortas*, 217.

230 *overruling prior decisions*: AFHTCH1, 110.

230 *I will always do*: AFHTCH1, 110-11.

230 *Fortas's retort*: Unpublished manuscript, 170, Griffin-CHL B284; James Kilpatrick, "Justice Abe Fortas Meets the Committee," *Hartford Courant*, July 20, 1968.

231 *little carried away*: AFHTCH1, 111-14.

231 *doodling parallelograms*: Fred Graham, "Fortas Testifies he Aided Johnson While a Justice," *NYT*, July 17, 1968; "162 Days Until Christmas," *Newsweek*, July 29, 1968.

231 *desperate to pin*: Fortas received rave reviews for his performance. See, July 16, 1968 MM memo to LBJ, LBJL WHCF-SF-AFHT B2.

231 *criticism of the administration*: Unpublished manuscript, 124-25, 171, Griffin-CHL B284.

231-32 *had a little fun*: Unpublished manuscript, 171, Griffin-CHL B284.

232 *comments you make*: AFHTCH1, 163-64; Fred Graham, "Fortas Testifies he Rebuked Critic of War Spending," *NYT*, July 18, 1968.

232 *extra-judicial work*: July 17, 1968 Paul Bower memo to WC, LBJL PP WC B13.

232 *Kennedy's assassination*: Additional Information with Respect to Extra Judicial Functions of Justices, Fortas-SML B96.

232 *from sitting justices*: July 12, 1968 WC memo, LBJL WHCF-SF-AFHT B2; July 17, 1968 memo to AF, LBJL WHCF-SF-AFHT B2.

232 *judicial review into the Constitution*: *CQ Editorial Research Reports 1968*, "Challenging of Supreme Court."

233 *good as this one*: July 12, 1968 WC memo, LBJL WHCF-SF-AFHT B2; "Chief Confidant to Chief Justice," *Time*, July 5, 1968.

233 *shady lobbyist*: July 12, 1968 WC memo, LBJL WHCF-SF-AFHT B2.

233 *I considered to be wrong*: AFHTCH1, 164-67; Fred Graham, "Fortas Testifies he Re-

buked Critic of War Spending," *NYT*, July 18, 1968.

233 *really quite good*: AFHTCH1, 168.

233 *completes my interrogation*: AFHTCH1, 168.

233-34 *for the third day*: Fred Graham, "Fortas Testifies he Rebuked Critic of War Spending," *NYT*, July 18, 1968.

234 *main event*: Fred Graham, "Delay on Fortas Likely in Senate as Hearing Ends," *NYT*, July 20, 1968; July 26, 1968 AF letter to WD, Douglas-LOC B1782.

234 *blow was struck*: Thurmond, *Faith*, 14.

234 *flag-burning hippies*: Thurmond, *Faith*, 5-11.

234 *confronts our Nation*: July 22, 1968 Strom Thurmond newsletter, Fortas-SML B97.

235 *essence of law*: Thurmond, *Faith*, 25.

235 *ballot box*: July 22, 1968 Strom Thurmond newsletter, Fortas-SML B97.

236 *regarding the court leadership*: Cohodas, *Strom Thurmond*, 393.

236 *20 to 30 years*: July 22, 1968 "Strom Thurmond Reports," Griffin-CHL B418.

236 *prospective Justices*: AFHTCH1, 180.

236-37 *candidates for the Presidency*: AFHTCH1, 180.

237 *I am disappointed*: AFHTCH1, 182-83; Powe, "The Senate and the Court," 893.

237 *I regret to say*: Fred Graham, "Thurmond Prods Fortas to Reply," *NYT*, July 19, 1968.

237 *decade earlier*: Richard Strout, "Fortas Grimly Silent Before Thurmond Barrage," *CSM*, July 20, 1968.

237-38 *gentleman Torquemada*: "The Fortas Film Festival," *Time*, September 20, 1968.

238 *65-12 count*: *CQ Almanac 1958*, "Mallory Rule."

238 *enemies empty-handed*: Allen Drury, "Aid Bill is Voted as 85th Congress Winds up Session," *NYT*, August 24, 1958; Anthony Lewis, "Johnson Shows Mastery Again," *NYT*, August 25, 1958.

238 *kind of justice*: AFHTCH1, 191; Crespino, *Strom Thurmond's America*, 216.

238 *unflappable man*: Fred Rodell, "The Complexities of Mr. Justice Fortas," *NYT*, July 28, 1968.

238-39 *such a decision*: AFHTCH1, 191; John Mackenzie, "Thurmond Badgers Fortas But Gets Few Replies," *Boston Globe*, July 19, 1968; Crespino, *Strom Thurmond's America*, 216; Shogan, *A Question of Judgment*, 170.

239 *ever came*: August 13, 1965 AF letter to James Eastland, Fortas-SML B92; September 17, 1965 James Eastland letter to AF, Fortas-SML B92; Fred Graham, "Thurmond Prods Fortas to Reply," *NYT*, July 19, 1968; Oswald Johnston, "Fortas Gives Defense of Court Record," *Baltimore Sun*, July 19, 1968; John Mackenzie, "Thurmond Badgers Fortas But Gets Few Replies," *Boston Globe*, July 19, 1968; Joseph Albright, "Thurmond Grills Fortas, DA-Style," *Newsday*, July 19, 1968; "162 Days Until Christmas," *Newsweek*, July 29, 1968; "As Controversy Mounts—Can Fortas Win Confirmation as Chief Justice?" *USNWR*, August 5, 1968.

CHAPTER 11

240 *appeals to a prurient interest*: Roth v. U.S., 354 U.S. 476, 481-85, 489 (1957).

240-41 *when I see it*: Jacobellis v. Ohio, 378 U.S. 184, 197 (1964). "In the decade following Roth…," Brennan's clerks observed years later, "it has been impossible to obtain any significant measure of consensus among the Justices on the problem of obscenity." Owen Fiss & Peter Strauss, Opinions of William J. Brennan Jr., October Term, 1965, Brennan-LOC II-6.

241 *targets for caricature*: Woodward & Armstrong, *The Brethren*, 239; Anthony Lewis, "Sex," *Esquire*, June, 1963.

241 *second only*: Powe, *Warren Court*, 355.

241 *magazines objectionable*: December 20, 1965 H.B. Montague letter to G. Robert Blakey, Brennan-LOC I-135; Gallup, *The Gallup Poll, Vol. 3*, 2201.

241-42 *commissions in the past*: Strub, *Perversion for Profit*, 87-88; Binstein & Bowden, *Trust Me*, 77-78, 88.

242 *purported hazards*: Strub, *Perversion for Profit*, 89; Whitney Strub, "Meet the spiritual forefather of conservatives' War on Women," Salon, April 13, 2014.

242 *kind of deviancy*: CDL, *Perversion for Profit*.

242 *masters of deceit*: CDL, *Perversion for Profit*; Strub, *Perversion for Profit*, 80.

242 *workshops for law*: Binstein & Bowden, *Trust Me*, 88; April 24, 1967 CDL letter to Brennan, Brennan-LOC II-3; Strub, *Perversion for Profit*, 103, 106; Binstein & Bowden, *Trust Me*, 88.

243 *assaults to homicide*: O.K. Armstrong, "The Damning Case Against Pornography," *Reader's Digest*, December, 1965.

243 *expert on the issue*: Charles Bennett, "New Smut Drive Planned by City," *NYT*, August 7, 1964; "Ronald for Real," *Time*, October 7, 1966; Binstein & Bowden, *Trust Me*, 95; Strub, *Perversion for Profit*, 84-85; Hearings before the Select Subcommittee on Education of the Committee of Education and Labor, (To Create a Commission on Noxious and Obscene Matters and Materials), September 1, 1965, 20, 22, 29.

243 *Nixon later appointed*: Strub, *Perversion for Profit*, 129.

243 *hearings well-versed*: AFHTCH1, 302. Though Clancy had lost ten of the twelve cases he brought as a prosecutor, he blamed the district attorney's office for lacking the zeal necessary to do the job correctly. See, Strub, *Perversion for Profit*, 106.

243 *June Tracy*: AFHTCH1, 292, 294, 1179-80.

243-44 *thirteen states*: AFHTCH1, 292. Clancy conveniently left out the controversial ruling, with Fortas and Warren joining the 5-4 majority, confirming the prosecution of Ralph Ginzburg for mailing circulars that provided instructions on how to obtain pornography but actually contained no obscene materials. See, *Ginzburg v. United States*, 383 U.S. 463 (1966).

244 *D-15*: AFHTCH1, 292, 294.

244 *hard-core sense*: *Schackman v. California*, 258 F. Supp. 983 (1966).

244 *witnessed by any nation*: AFHTCH1, 295-96.

244 *even in France*: AFHTCH1, 300.

245 *tear him apart*: CUOH – Schmidt, 69-70; "A Conversation with Chief Justice Earl Warren," McClatchy Broadcasting, June 25, 1969, Warren-LOC B846.

245 *motherhood*: Schwartz, *Super Chief*, 139.

245 *tackles these cases*: Schwartz, *Super Chief*, 221.

245 *maintain a decent society*: "A Conversation with Chief Justice Earl Warren," McClatchy Broadcasting, June 25, 1969, Warren-LOC B846.

245 *Love & Kisses*: Hugh Hefner letter to Brennan, Brennan-LOC II-3.

246 *flooding our land*: January 1, 1966 CDL form letter, Brennan-LOC II-3.

246 *through the mail*: Schlesinger, *History*, 3493-94.

246 *decision of license*: Alexander Burnham, "Edict is Called a Setback by Christian Clerics—Rabbis Praise it," *NYT*, June 26, 1962.

246-47 *Communists will use*: Anthony Lewis, "Both Houses Get Bills to Lift Ban on School Prayer," *NYT*, June 27, 1962.

247 *continued to sponsor*: Powe, *Warren Court*, 363; http://www.ncea.org/NCEA/Proclaim/
Catholic_School_Data/Catholic_School_Data.aspx; http://www.scholarsstrategynet-
work.org/brief/why-decline-catholic-schools-matters.

247 *42 largest newspapers*: Anthony Lewis, "Both Houses Get Bills to Lift Ban on School
Prayer," *NYT*, June 27, 1962; Dierenfield, "Public Response."

247 *violent wrecking*: Powe, *Warren Court*, 187.

247 *misrepresentation of the Constitution*: "Excerpts from Editorials on School Prayer
Decision," *NYT*, June 29, 1962.

247 *their religious faith*: "'God Save This Honorable Court," *NR*, July 17, 1962.

247 *pray in public schools*: "Thou Shalt Not Pray," *NR*, July 31, 1962.

247 *prayer in the 1950s*: *CQ Almanac 1962*, "Supreme Court Prayer Decision;" Dierenfield,
"Public Response."

247-48 *a new record*: Dierenfield, "Public Response." One congressman presented a petition
calling for the return of religion to schools signed by 170,000 people. See, O'Neill,
Coming Apart, 26.

248 *driven God out*: *CQ Almanac 1962*, "Supreme Court Prayer Decision."

248 *corners of the country*: *CQ Almanac 1964*, "Congress Fails to Act on School Prayer
Amendments."

248 *unfortunate and divisive*: Anthony Lewis, "Both Houses Get Bills to Lift Ban on School
Prayer," *NYT*, June 27, 1962.

248 *Rockefeller denounced*: *CQ Almanac 1962*, "Supreme Court Prayer Decision."

248 *counterattacks flopped*: "Constitutional Amendment to Permit Voluntary Prayer in Public Schools" undated ED press release, Dirksen-DCC 2072; *CQ Almanac 1962*, "Supreme
Court Prayer Decision."

248 *a little also*: "Constitutional Amendment to Permit Prayer in Public Schools" undated
ED press release, Dirksen-DCC 2072.

248-49 *amendment process*: *CQ Almanac 1966*, "Senate fails to Amend School Prayer Ruling."

249 *administrator he disliked*: https://www.senate.gov/artandhistory/history/minute/pinned.htm.

249 *latest mischief*: July 25, 1968 telephone conversation No. 13218, LBJL; John Corry,
"Strom's Dirty Movies," *Harper's Magazine*, December, 1968.

250 *has made it commonplace*: AFHTCH1, 360; "Senate Committee Asks Fortas to Testify
Again," *LAT*, July 24, 1968; John Corry, "Strom's Dirty Movies," *Harper's Magazine*,

December, 1968; December 20, 1968 lgm memo to Cecil, Griffin-CHL B418.

250 *report back to the committee*: Unpublished manuscript, 199, Griffin-CHL B284; "Fortas Feud Grows Louder," *WS*, July 28, 1968.

250-51 *kinds of positions*: July 24, 1968 Senate Judiciary Committee Executive Session, 19-21, 26.

251 *regular hearing room*: John Corry, "Strom's Dirty Movies," *Harper's Magazine*, December, 1968; Crespino, *Strom Thurmond's America*, 217; Frye, "Dialectic," 262.

251 *penny arcades*: *Target Smut* written script, Griffin-CHL B418; *Schackman v. California*, 258 F. Supp. 983 (1966); John Corry, "Strom's Dirty Movies," *Harper's Magazine*, December, 1968.

251 *witch hunt*: Fred Graham, "Senate Panel Bids Officials Explain Pro-Fortas Memo," *NYT*, July 23, 1968; John Corry, "Strom's Dirty Movies," *Harper's Magazine*, December, 1968.

251 *cracked jokes*: John Corry, "Strom's Dirty Movies," *Harper's Magazine*, December, 1968.

251 *Clancy's list*: Frye, "Dialectic," 264-65.

251 *graphic sexual acts*: AFHTCH1, 1172; Frye, "Dialectic," 247, 266.

251 *movie explored*: "Fleshing Out the Case," *Newsweek*, August 12, 1968.

251 *get aroused*: Shaffer, *On and Off*, 92.

251-52 *have seen enough*: Frye, "Dialectic," 266.

252 *from the film*: Murphy, *Fortas*, 448.

252 *bananas at last*: Saul Friedman, "4 Films: 'The End' For Fortas?" *St. Petersburg Times*, September 12, 1968; December 20, 1968 lgm memo to Cecil, Griffin-CHL B418; John Corry, "Strom's Dirty Movies," *Harper's Magazine*, December, 1968.

252 *for the models*: Unpublished manuscript, 201-02, Griffin-CHL B284.

252 *bother him*: September 12, 1968 telephone conversation No. 13413-4, LBJL.

252 *opposition needed*: September 16, 1968 MM memo to LBJ, LBJL WHCF FG431/J B342.

252 *Mr. Obscenity*: Marquis Childs, "Nixon Role Urged in the Fortas Case," *United Feature Syndicate*, September 13, 1968.

252 *country any good*: July 25, 1968 telephone conversation No. 13218, LBJL; "Fleshing Out the Case," *Newsweek*, August 12, 1968.

252 *public is aroused*: December 20, 1968 lgm memo to Cecil, Griffin-CHL B418.

253 *25 to 1*: July 30, 1968 George Reedy memo to LBJ, LBJL WHCF-SF-AFHT B7.

253 *Constitution means*: James Kilpatrick, "Suggestion: Let a Movie Decide Fortas' Fate," *WS*, August 13, 1968.

253 *court in the land*: Unpublished manuscript, 162, 204, Griffin-CHL B284.

253 *saint could*: USSHO – Shuman, 93; https://www.c-span.org/video/?73072-1/philip-hart-conscience-senate.

253 *they strived for*: https://www.senate.gov/artandhistory/history/common/generic/Featured_Bio_Hart.htm.

254 *film's merits*: Jones, *The Defeat*, 279; Califano, *Triumph*, 259; "Fortas Feud Grows Louder," *WS*, July 28, 1968.

254 *shoot down*: July 24, 1968 Senate Judiciary Committee Executive Session, 3, 19, 24.

254 *grab bag*: Unpublished manuscript, 206, Griffin-CHL B284.

254 *come to a focus*: July 26, 1968 AF letter to WD, Douglas-LOC B1782.

254 *57 to 65*: July 24, 1968 JC memo to LBJ, LBJL WHCF FG 535/A B360.

254-55 *token fight*: July 30, 1968 Barefoot Sanders memo to LBJ, LBJL WHCF-SF-AFHT B2.

CHAPTER 12

256 *frontrunners in the past*: Maxwell, *Indicted South*, 239.

257 *evade Brown*: *Green v. County Sch. Bd. of New Kent County*, 391 U.S. 430 (1968).

257 *Emancipation Proclamation*: Arthur Krock, "In The Nation," *NYT*, February 16, 1956.

257 *valiant stance*: Frank, *Ike and Dick*, 149, 153.

257 *party of Lincoln*: Richard Nixon, "GOP to be Reckoned With in South," *WP*, May 8, 1966; Westerhoff, *Politics of Protest*, 34; Perlstein, *Before the Storm*, 90.

258 *essential to me*: "Thurmond to Bolt Democrats Today," *NYT*, September 16, 1964; Charles Mohr, "Thurmond Joins Goldwater Drive," *NYT*, September 18, 1964; Nixon, *Memoirs*, 305. Nixon's courtship began years earlier. When asked by a reporter whether he was ashamed to welcome Thurmond into the party of Lincoln, Nixon fired back: "Strom is no racist. Strom is a man of courage and integrity." Perlstein, *Nixonland*, 89.

258 *hope we've got*: Cohodas, *Strom Thurmond*, 396.

258 *1968 in Atlanta*: Nixon, *Memoirs*, 304; Chester et al, *An American Melodrama*, 446.

258 *southern leaders*: Cohodas, *Strom Thurmond*, 396-97.

258 *like nothing else*: SOHP – Thurmond (A-0334); Don Oberdorfer, "Ex-Democrat, Ex-Dixiecrat, Today's 'Nixiecrat,'" *NYT*, October 6, 1968; Westerhoff, *Politics of Protest*, 43, 55; Dent, *Prodigal South*, 82.

258 *South in return*: "Thurmond Praises Nixon," *Times-Union & Journal*, June 2, 1968; Dent, *Prodigal South*, 207.

258 *power-grasping*: "Thurmond Throws Support To Nixon, Says He Offers America Best Hope," *Charlotte Observer*, June 23, 1968. Other southern Republicans also endorsed Nixon after the Atlanta meeting. See, Charles Pou & Hugh Nations, "Nixon Nearing Magic Number," *Atlanta Journal-Constitution*, June 2, 1968.

258-59 *celebrity sighting*: Carter, *Politics*, 329; Chester et al, *An American Melodrama*, 437-38. Seventy-five percent of the delegates identified themselves as conservatives. See, Perlstein, *Nixonland*, 131.

259 *Nixon's the one*: Dent, *Prodigal South*, 89-90; Carter, *Politics*, 330.

259 *professional pettifogger*: Perlstein, *Nixonland*, 21-43.

259 *make the law*: "What Dick Nixon Told Southern Delegates," *Miami Herald*, August 7, 1968.

260 *rimland of the South*: John Herbers, "Nixon Holds Most of Support in South by Promising Conservative Stand on Rights," *NYT*, August 8, 1968; Don Oberdorfer, "Ex-Democrat, Ex-Dixiecrat, Today's 'Nixiecrat,'" *NYT*, October 6, 1968; Nixon, *Memoirs*, 312; Dent, *Prodigal South*, 102; Carter, *Politics*, 332. Nixon also consulted with Buckley and Kilpatrick. See, Buchanan, *Greatest Comeback*, 304.

261 *defeat any possibility*: Eisenhower, *Diaries*, 246.

261 *not so sure*: James J. Kilpatrick, "Crossroads in Dixie," *NR*, November 19, 1963.

261 *Up for Grabs*: James J. Kilpatrick, "The South Goes Back Up for Grabs," *NR*, December 17, 1963.

262 *law of the land*: Goldwater, *Conscience of a Conservative*, 21-23. Goldwater also saw the potential for the GOP to lure away southern white voters by opposing civil rights. See, Carter, *Politics*, 218.

262 *scrubbing out*: Stephenson, *Campaigns and the Court*, 3, 149-50, 184; Leuchtenburg, *The Supreme Court Reborn*, 104-08; Simon, *FDR and Chief Justices Hughes*, 294, 296-98.

262 *potent vote-getter*: Joseph Sullivan, "Redistricting Upset?," *WSJ*, July 9, 1964.

262 *nine appointed Justices*: "Partial Text of Goldwater Speech: Raw and Naked Power," *WP*, September 12, 1964.

262 *set of audiences*: Perlstein, *Before the Storm*, 425.

262-63 *he is guilty*: Charles Mohr, "Goldwater Says He'd Curb Court," *NYT*, September 16, 1964.

263 *our school rooms*: Goldwater, *Conscience of a Conservative*, 20-21; Charles Mohr, "Goldwater Hits U.S. Moral 'Rot,'" *NYT*, October 11, 1964.

263 *running against*: Anthony Lewis, "Campaign: The Supreme Court Key Issue," *NYT*, October 11, 1964.

263 *typifying this strategy*: "Partial Text of Goldwater Speech: Raw and Naked Power," *WP*, September 12, 1964. Thurmond made the same connection that year, stating, "The Democratic Party has encouraged, supported, and protected the Supreme Court in a reign of judicial tyranny." See, Bass & Thompson, *Strom*, 192.

263 *publicly embraced*: September 13, 1964 Eric Goldman memo to LBJ, LBJL WHCF FG431/J B346; Fendall W. Yerxa, "Johnson Rejects High Court Issue," *NYT*, September 13, 1964.

263 *Polling data*: Murphy & Tanenhaus, "Public Opinion," 39-40.

263 *respect the Constitution*: Charles Mohr, "Goldwater Says He'd Curb Court," *NYT*, September 16, 1964; Anthony Lewis, "Campaign: The Supreme Court Key Issue," *NYT*, October 11, 1964; Charles Mohr, "Goldwater Hits U.S. Moral 'Rot,'" *NYT*, October 11, 1964.

264 *real constitutional lawyers*: Westerhoff, *Politics of Protest*, 37.

264 *comsymps*: John Wicklein, "Birch Society Will Offer $2,300 For Impeach Warren Essays," *NYT*, August 5, 1961; Mulloy, *The World*, 1, 9, 77; Schoenwald, *A Time*, 65.

264 *arch enemy*: Mulloy, *The World*, 12; John D. Morris, "Inquiry is Sought on Birch Society," *NYT*, March 31, 1961.

264 *communist conspiracy*: Paul Crowell, "Pickets Jeer Warren Here and Hurl Placards at Him," *NYT*, October 30, 1963; Huntington, *Right-Wing*, 60-61.

264 *declare the whole*: Robert Welch, "A Letter to the South on Segregation," *One Man's Opinion*, September, 1956; Schoenwald, *A Time*, 88.

264 *impeach the ringleader*: Epstein & Forster, *Report*, 41. The idea wasn't unique to the Society. Red Monday had instigated similar appeals and Dan Smoot, a former FBI agent who established a modest media empire through his anti-communist newsletters, called for Warren's removal in early 1961. "Warren is a socialist who thinks government has unlimited power. . . . He has the same attitude toward the Constitution that communists and all other socialists have," Smoot concluded. See, *The Dan Smoot Report*, January 30, 1961, Brennan-LOC II-115.

264-65 *cost $20*: Epstein & Forster, *Report*, 41-42.

265 *pillow*: John Wicklein, "Birch Society Will Offer $2,300 For Impeach Warren Essays,"

NYT, August 5, 1961; "Student at U.C.L.A. Wins Birch Contest," *NYT*, February 6, 1962; Paul Crowell, "Pickets Jeer Warren Here and Hurl Placards at Him," *NYT*, October 30, 1963; Schwartz, *Super Chief*, 281.

265 *alarming they seemed*: CUOH – Schmidt, 89; "A Conversation with Earl Warren," Brandeis Television Recollections, December 11, 1972; Warren-LOC B846.

265 *read your obituary*: March 19, 1966 J.B. Lewis Family letter to EW, Warren-LOC B667.

265 *Earl Warren High School*: "Anti-Warren Papers Found," *NYT*, May 1, 1963.

265-66 *clinch the election*: Carter, *Politics*, 328.

266 *ardent segregationist*: Fadely, *Agitator Rhetorician*, 49; "Wallace," *New Republic*, November 9, 1968.

266 *30% of Americans*: June 13, 1969 Harry Dent memo to RMN, RMNL WHSF:SMOF Dent B1; Safire, *Before the Fall*, 78; Murphy & Tanenhaus, "Public Opinion," 39.

266 *police procedural*: Miranda v. Arizona, 384 U.S. 436 (1966).

266 *opened Warren up*: For some of Warren's coercive tactics as a prosecutor, see, Newton, *Justice for All*, 59, 66 and White, *Warren*, 267.

266 *raped or robbed*: Nan Robertson, "Ervin Protests Curbs on Police," *NYT*, July 23, 1966.

267 *repeat his crime*: Miranda v. Arizona, 384 U.S. 436, 467, 542, 545 (1966). In the six months after *Miranda*, confessions by defendants charged with felonies (other than homicide) dropped from 49 to 15 percent. See, Baker, *Miranda*, 180.

267 *equally outraged*: Gallup, *The Gallup Poll, Vol. 3*, 2021.

267 *technical error*: Baker, *Miranda*, 176.

267 *equal chance with*: Lytle, *Warren Court*, 87.

267 *much less convicted*: Worsnop, "Police Reforms."

267 *Safe Streets Act*: Fred Graham, "Law: Congress Tries to Curb the Court," *NYT*, April 28, 1968.

267 *really under attack*: "Target: The Supreme Court...," *NYT*, May 15, 1968.

267-68 *most important domestic*: "63% in Gallup Poll Think Courts Are Too Lenient on Criminals," *NYT*, March 3, 1968; Louis Harris, "Public Backs Fortas Confirmation, Assails Court," *WP*, August 12, 1968.

268 *nearly tripled*: Department of Justice, Uniform Crime Reporting Statistics.

268 *railed against*: Ambrose, *Nixon*, 159.

268 *free from domestic violence*: https://www.presidency.ucsb.edu/documents/address-accepting-the-presidential-nomination-the-republican-national-convention-miami.

268 *criminal community*: Richard Nixon, *Toward Freedom From Fear*.

268 *obedience school*: R. W. Apple Jr., "Nixon Intensifies Blows at Humphrey on Ohio Train Tour," *NYT*, October 23, 1968.

269 *voters want*: Richard Reeves, "Nixon's Men Are Smart But No Swingers," *NYT*, September 29, 1968.

269 *36% of Americans*: "High Court Found in Disfavor, 3 to 2," *NYT*, July 10, 1968; "Court Poll Leans to Conservatives," *NYT*, April 19, 1970.

269 *experienced and versed*: Richard Nixon, *Toward Freedom From Fear*.

269 *never make a liberal*: Dent, *Prodigal South*, 207.

269 *our country today*: http://www.presidency.ucsb.edu/ws/index.php?pid=29570.

269 *restrictions on law enforcement*: Fadely, *Agitator Rhetorician*, 179, 181, 184-85, 188-91.

270 *tribune of the people*: http://www.shoppbs.pbs.org/wgbh/amex/wallace/filmmore/transcript/transcript1.html.

270 *crying for help*: James J. Kilpatrick, "What Makes Wallace Run?," *NR*, April 18, 1967.

270 *cities on fire*: Perlstein, *Nixonland*, 224.

270 *destroy constitutional government*: Carter, *Politics*, 217, 339.

270 *loudest applause*: Chester et al, *An American Melodrama*, 282-83.

270 *fascist state*: Homer Bigart, "3,000 Police Ring Garden As Wallace Stages a Rally," *NYT*, October 25, 1968; Carter, *Politics*, 366.

270-71 *sick Supreme Court*: Schlesinger, *History*, 3493-94.

271 *incoming president to select*: June 26, 1968 Bob Fleming memo to LBJ, LBJL WHCF-SF-AFHT B6.

271 *murder weapon*: Buchanan, *Greatest Comeback*, 276.

271 *torpedo the nomination*: Robert Semple Jr., "Nixon Pledges a Strong Campaign in the Cities," *NYT*, July 18, 1968; August 23, 1968 Peter Holmes memo to RG, Griffin-CHL B285; Dean, *Rehnquist Choice*, 4; Buchanan, *Greatest Comeback*, 277-281; Ehrlichman, *Witness to Power*, 113; Shogan, *A Question*, 9. Javits and Senator Edward Brooke of Massachusetts unsuccessfully tried to sway Nixon to publicly endorse Fortas. See, July 26, 1968 George Reedy memo to LBJ, LBJL WHCF-SF-AFHT B7; August 22, 1968

George Reedy memo to LBJ, LBJL WHCF-SF-AFHT B2; Marquis Childs, "Nixon Role Urged in the Fortas Case," *United Feature Syndicate*, September 13, 1968.

CHAPTER 13

272 *pornography issue*: August 23, 1968 Peter Holmes memo to RG, Griffin-CHL B285.

272 *this is the club*: Lyle Denniston, "Senate Uneasy After 'Punishing' Court," *WS*, October 3, 1968.

273 *case against Fortas*: Unpublished manuscript, 227, Griffin-CHL B284; November 1, 1968 Cecil memo, Griffin-CHL B418; August 11, 1969 memo to RG, Griffin-CHL B285. The date on the August 11, 1969 memo is likely wrong. Various materials in Griffin's archives point to July 19, 1968 as the correct date of the initial phone call.

273 *assistant told Graham*: Unpublished manuscript, 227-31, Griffin-CHL B284; November 1, 1968 Cecil memo, Griffin-CHL B418.

273 *senator's demands*: Unpublished manuscript, 232-33, Griffin-CHL B284; November 1, 1968 Cecil memo, Griffin-CHL B418; Jones, *The Defeat*, 235.

273 *enrolled in the class*: AFHTCH2, 1287-91, 1307-08; Marjorie Hunter, "Fortas Refuses to Appear Again in Senate Inquiry," *NYT*, September 14, 1968.

273-74 *my discretion*: AFHTCH2, 1288-89.

274 *maybe $2,000*: AFHTCH2, 1295-98.

274 *before the Court*: Murphy, *Fortas*, 507; Jones, *The Defeat*, 241-42.

274 *simply turn down*: LBJOH – Temple (Interview I, Tape 6), 1; Jones, *The Defeat*, 242-43.

274 *Why did he do it*: Shaffer, *On and Off*, 93. The episode, according to a legislative aide, turned into "another humiliating example to the Fortas camp that they were playing a game without all the cards on the table." Jones, *The Defeat*, 243.

274 *fiasco with Califano*: LBJOH – Califano (Interview LXIII), 12.

274-75 *command post*: Shogan, *A Question*, 174.

275 *to fight on*: Murphy, *Fortas*, 517-18.

275 *a final push*: July 31, 1968 WC memo to LT, LBJL WHCF-SF-AFHT B2; August 15, 1968 James Gaither letter to WC, LBJL PP WC B14; August 19, 1968 James Gaither memo to JC, LBJL WHCF-SF-AFHT B2; September 6, 1968 LT memo to LBJ, LBJL

WHCF-SF-AFHT B3; September 13, 1968 JC memo to LBJ, LBJL WHCF FG535/A B360; September 28, 1968 James Gaither memo to LT, LBJL WHCF-SF-AFHT B3; September 10, 1968 Barefoot Sanders memo to LT, LBJL WHCF-SF-AFHT B4.

275 *my liberal friends*: September 16, 1968 Paul Porter letter to John Kenneth Galbraith, LBJL PP Paul Porter B2. Joseph Rauh called Porter "paranoid" for his accusation. See, September 20, 1968 Joseph Rauh letter to Paul Porter, LBJL PP Paul Porter B2.

275 *hell-raisers*: September 12, 1968 telephone conversation No. 13413-4, LBJL.

275 *sense of outrage*: September 12, 1968 Barefoot Sanders memo to LBJ, LBJL WH-CF-SF-AFHT B3.

275 *exactly the opposite*: USSHO – Smathers, 120, 122.

275-76 *I am a follower*: February 24, 1964 Neil MacNeil memo to Parker, DCC.

276 *saintly guy*: USSHO – Smathers, 60, 89.

276 *wheeler and dealer*: Bart Barnes, "Mike Mansfield, 16-Year Leader of Senate, Dies," *WP*, October 6, 2001; USSHO – McClure, 205; "When is a Majority a Majority?" *Time*, March 20, 1964.

276 *despotic rule*: USSHO – Scott, 103; USSHO – Attig, 60; USSHO – Valeo, 232; "When is a Majority a Majority?" *Time*, March 20, 1964; David Rosenbaum, "Mike Mansfield, Longtime Leader of Senate Democrats, Dies at 98," *NYT*, October 6, 2001; Bart Barnes, "Mike Mansfield, 16-Year Leader of Senate, Dies," *WP*, October 6, 2001.

276 *Johnson over Vietnam*: "When is a Majority a Majority?" *Time*, March 20, 1964; Bart Barnes, "Mike Mansfield, 16-Year Leader of Senate, Dies," *WP*, October 6, 2001.

276 *considered a lame duck*: Lyle Denniston, "Mansfield Warns Foes on Court Fight," *WS*, June 28, 1968; Lyle Denniston, "Court Nominations Strategy Mapped by Opposing Sides," *WS*, June 29, 1968.

276-77 *during past filibusters*: June 28, 1968 Barefoot Sanders memo to LBJ, LBJL WH-CF-SF-AFHT B1; LBJOH – Temple (Interview I, Tape 6), 2; Fred Graham, "Fortas Receives Critical Setback as Dirksen Shifts," *NYT*, September 28, 1968.

277 *needed for victory*: September 30, 1968 vote count, LBJL PP Ramsey Clark B127.

277 *speeches opposing his confirmation*: September 25, 1968 RG chronology, Griffin-CHL B418; Jones, *The Defeat*, 314-15; "Defeat for Abe Fortas," *Newsweek*, October 7, 1968; Shogan, *A Question*, 181; Unpublished manuscript, 324, Griffin-CHL B284.

277 *wanted to surrender*: Jones, *The Defeat*, 316.

277 *an official vote*: December 20, 1968 WC memo to LT, LBJL WHCF-SF-AFHT B3; LBJOH – Califano (Interview LXIII), 13.

277 *Johnson repeatedly worried:* August 27, 1968 telephone conversation No. 13323, LBJL; September 12, 1968 telephone conversation No. 13413-4, LBJL. Eastland came to the same conclusion during the summer. See, December 20, 1968 WC memo to LT, LBJL WHCF-SF-AFHT B3.

277 *strung out very long:* LBJOH – Temple (Interview I, Tape 5), 42.

278 *shifted to one:* Marjorie Hunter, "Johnson Told Hope of a Fortas Victory is Fading in Senate," *NYT*, September 6, 1968.

278 *support he ought to:* September 12, 1968 telephone conversation No. 13413-4, LBJL.

278 *on September 27:* Fred Graham, "Fortas Receives Critical Setback as Dirksen Shifts," *NYT*, September 28, 1968.

278 *failed to do so:* "Concern About High Court—Why Dirksen Switched in Fortas Case," *USNWR*, October 14, 1968.

278 *Griffin turned down:* Hulsey, *Everett Dirksen*, 267; MacNeil, *Dirksen*, 335-36; Jones, *The Defeat*, 294, 297.

278 *decision to resign:* Shaffer, *On and Off*, 82.

278 *school prayer rulings:* At the height of the hearings in mid-July, the Minority Leader wrote to a friend: "I shall be glad when Chief Justice Warren leaves the Court." See, July 17, 1968 ED letter to C.H. Merideth, DCC.

279 *We Win:* October 1, 1968 vote tally, Griffin-CHL B228.

279 *lame duck charges:* Louis Harris, "Public Backs Fortas Confirmation, Assails Court," *WP*, August 12, 1968; September 10, 1968 Independent News Analyst, LBJL PP Paul Porter B4.

279 *Neither was Eastland:* LBJOH – Eastland (Interview I), 13-14.

279 *moderate from California:* October 1, 1968 telephone conversation No. 13501, LBJL; October 1, 1968 telephone conversation No. 13509, LBJL; October 2, 1968 Stewart Udall memo to LBJ, LBJL WHCF-SF-AFHT B5; October 2, 1968 Ernest Gruening memo to LBJ, LBJL WHCF FG431/J B346; December 9, 1968 Barefoot Sanders memo to LBJ, LBJL WHCF FG431/J B346; Fred Graham, "Senate Bars Move to End Filibuster by Fortas Critics," *NYT*, October 2, 1968.

279-80 *take this route:* October 3, 1968 DeVier Pierson memo to LBJ, LBJL WHCF-SF-AF-HT B3; October 5, 1968 DeVier Pierson memo to LBJ, LBJL WHCF FG431/J B346; *CQ Almanac 1960*, "Supreme Court Nominees." The resolution passed 48-37 with every Republican voting against the measure.

280 *for one another:* John MacKenzie, "Nixon and Justice Warren: rivalry to reconciliation," *WP*, July 11, 1974.

280 *happy situation for me*: December 5, 1968 telephone conversation No. 13804, LBJL.

280-81 *darkest day*: October 3, 1968 JC letter to AF, Fortas-SML B97.

281 *ruined his life*: LBJOH – LBJ (Reminiscences), 25.

CHAPTER 14

284 *source suggested*: John Kifner, "Chance Remark Led Reporter to Disclosure in Fortas Case," *NYT*, May 17, 1969.

284 *known internally*: "Coming to Life," *Newsweek*, May 19, 1969; "Reporter William Lambert Dies," *WP*, February 10, 1998; Agis Salpukas, "William Lambert, 78, Writer Who Exposed Justice Fortas," *NYT*, February 16, 1998.

284 *want to know*: John Kifner, "Chance Remark Led Reporter to Disclosure in Fortas Case," *NYT*, May 17, 1969.

285 *November 8*: James Freeman, "The World's District Attorney," *WSJ*, December 26, 2009. Morgenthau felt that Johnson had removed Katzenbach from his position as attorney general because Katzenbach was unable to stop him from indicting Wolfson.

285 *dropped the matter*: LBJOH – R. Clark (Interview V), 12-13; Kalman, *Abe Fortas*, 359-61; Murphy, *Fortas*, 546-47.

285 *$20,000 payment*: William Lambert, "The Justice… and the Stock Manipulator," *Life*, May 9, 1969; May 14, 1969 Abe Fortas letter to EW, Warren-LOC B353; John Kifner, "Chance Remark Led Reporter to Disclosure in Fortas Case," *NYT*, May 17, 1969.

285 *reporter's meddling*: "Coming to Life," *Newsweek*, May 19, 1969; Shogan, *A Question*, 225; Kalman, *Abe Fortas*, 361.

285 *had a story*: "Coming to Life," *Newsweek*, May 19, 1969; Shogan, *A Question*, 225; Kalman, *Abe Fortas*, 361.

286 *conviction to the Court*: Kalman, *Abe Fortas*, 362.

286 *starving person*: Don Oberdofer, "The Gathering of the Storm That Burst Upon Abe Fortas," *WP*, May 16, 1969.

286-87 *awaited revenge*: Murphy, *Fortas*, 550-51; Shogan, *A Question*, 225-27. Even without access to archives made available years later, Shogan provides a compelling account of the Wolfson scandal.

287 *off the Court*: Murphy, *Fortas*, 551. Ironically, Wilson quit the agency in 1971 due to his involvement in a scandal. Shogan, *A Question*, 245.

287 *play golf*: Shogan, *A Question*, 16.

288 *in my heart*: "Nixons Fete Warrens at the White House," *NYT*, April 24, 1969; April 23, 1969 Instructions for Dinner Honoring Chief Justice Earl Warren, RMNL PPF B48.

288 *ought to be off*: President's Daily Diary, April 23, 1969, RMNL; Kalman, *Abe Fortas*, 362-63.

289 *criminal prosecution*: Shogan, *A Question*, 230-33; Dean, *Rehnquist Choice*, 7-8.

289 *flip against the justice*: April 14, 1969 Will Wilson memo to FBI Director (found on the FBI's Vault web site); Ronald Ostrow & Robert Jackson, "$20,000-a-Year Lifetime Offer to Fortas Told," *LAT*, May 15, 1969; Shogan, *A Question*, 253; Murphy, *Fortas*, 559.

289 *publish his findings*: Murphy, *Fortas*, 555-56; Shogan, *A Question*, 218-20. Ramsey Clark believed that *Life* would not have run the story without the Justice Department's help. See, LBJOH – R. Clark (Interview V), 12-13.

289 *radical after all*: Ehrlichman, *Witness to Power*, 116.

290 *out of prison*: William Lambert, "The Justice . . . and the Stock Manipulator," *Life*, May 9, 1969.

290 *disgust to the press*: Lyle Denniston, "Fortas Under Fire on Wolfson Fee," *WS*, May 5, 1969; *CQ Almanac 1969*, "Justice's Resignation;" Shogan, *A Question*, 242.

290 *Thank God*: Shogan, *A Question*, 262.

290 *declined to speak*: May 29, 1969 Philip Hart letter to Paul Leidy, Hart-BHL B183.

290 *face but excrement*: May 6, 1969 Raymond O'Donnell letter to Philip Hart, Hart-BHL B183; Undated letter to Philip Hart, Hart-BHL B183.

290 *Fortas to fulfill*: "Justice Abe Fortas on the Spot," *Newsweek*, May 19, 1969; May 13, 1969 Inzer Wyatt letter to AF, Warren-LOC B353; May 13, 1969 Walter Mansfield letter to AF, Warren-LOC B353; *CQ Almanac 1969*, "Justice's Resignation."

290-91 *equally revolted*: Lyle Denniston, "Fortas Under Fire on Wolfson Fee," *WS*, May 5, 1969; May 6, 1969 Clark Clifford letter to AF, Fortas-SML B97; May 6, 1969 Patrick Buchanan memo to RN, RMNL POF:PMS B78; "Justice Abe Fortas on the Spot," *Newsweek*, May 19, 1969.

291 *his scalp*: Black & Black, *Mr. Justice and Mrs. Black*, 220.

291 *appeared on news-stands*: May 6, 1969 Patrick Buchanan memo to RN, RMNL WHCF:SF FG51 B1.

291 *ride this thing out*: "Justice Abe Fortas on the Spot," *Newsweek*, May 19, 1969.

291 *battlefield alone*: WD Travel Itinerary, Douglas-LOC B656.

291 *returning the fee*: Shogan, *A Question*, 277.

291 *grants in 1966*: February 1, 1966 Louis Wolfson letter to AF, Warren-LOC B353; Murphy, *Fortas*, 560; "Justice Abe Fortas on the Spot," *Newsweek*, May 19, 1969.

292 *having enough money*: Murphy, *Fortas*, 196.

292 *your own business*: Shogan, *A Question*, 211.

292 *kick this guy*: LBJOH – Porter (Interview I), 39.

292 *return the $20,000*: May 14, 1969 AF letter to EW, Warren-LOC B353.

292 *our own dynamite*: Bob Woodward, "Fortas Tie to Wolfson is Detailed," *WP*, January 23, 1977.

292 *actions of a guilty man*: Lyle Denniston, "Fortas Under Fire on Wolfson Fee," *WS*, May 5, 1969.

292 *expressed his sympathy*: Nixon, *Memoirs*, 420.

293 *impeachment proceedings*: "Set Fortas Study, High Court Urged," *WS*, May 8, 1969; May 6, 1969 Patrick Buchanan memo to RN, RMNL POF:PMS B78; "Justice Abe Fortas on the Spot," *Newsweek*, May 19, 1969.

293 *rebut the charge*: May 3, 1969 memo, RMNL POF:ANSS B30; May 15, 1969 Alexander Butterfield memo to Herbert Klein, RMNL WHSF:SF-CF B22.

293 *come to light*: Don Oberdofer, "The Gathering of the Storm That Burst Upon Abe Fortas," *WP*, May 16, 1969.

293 *unless Fortas resigned*: May 12, 1969 Mrs. McHale letter to EW, Warren-LOC B353; May 10, 1969 Louis Wolfson FBI transcript, EW LOC B353; "Justice Abe Fortas on the Spot," *Newsweek*, May 19, 1969; Ehrlichman, *Witness to Power*, 116. According to Bruce Allen Murphy, Wilson came up with the idea of Mitchell visiting the chief justice. See, Murphy, *Fortas*, 561. Other sources credit Nixon. See, Nixon, *Memoirs*, 420. Either way, the president endorsed the move.

293-94 *Mitchell's departure*: Shogan, *A Question*, 248-49; Newton, *Justice for All*, 503.

294 *deliver the news*: Interview with Walter E. Dellinger III.

294 *must resign immediately*: Don Oberdofer, "The Gathering of the Storm That Burst Upon Abe Fortas," *WP*, May 16, 1969; 115 *CR* 12329. Joseph Tydings privately conveyed the same message to Fortas. See, May 9, 1969 Joseph Tydings letter to AF, Fortas-SML B99.

294 *everywhere he went*: May 6, 1969 Patrick Buchanan memo to RN, RMNL WHCF:SF FG51 B1; C.K. McClatchy, "Political 'Leak' Does Harm to Court," *Sacramento Bee*, May 12, 1969; Kalman, *Abe Fortas*, 371, 375; http://historynewsnetwork.org/article/13170; "Justice Abe Fortas on the Spot," *Newsweek*, May 19, 1969.

294 *refused to yield*: Shogan, *A Question*, 254.

294-95 *good of the Court*: CUOH – Schmidt, 217; Black & Black, *Mr. Justice and Mrs. Black*, 220.

295 *review his options*: "The Fortas Verdict on Abe Fortas," *Newsweek*, May 26, 1969; Douglas, *Autobiography*, 358; Shogan, *A Question*, 256, 259.

295 *reference letters*: May 11, 1940 WD letter to Leon Green, Douglas-LOC B328; May 13, 1940 WD letter to Harry Shulman, Douglas-LOC B328; June 3, 1940, WD letter to Wilber Katz, Douglas-LOC B328; November 26, 1943 AF letter to WD, Douglas-LOC B328; June 9, 1945 WD letter to Karl Llewellyn, Douglas-LOC B328.

295 *celebrate Fortas's appointment*: October 28, 1946 AF letter to WD, Douglas-LOC B328; April 22, 1959 WD letter to AF, Douglas-LOC B328; March 23, 1964 AF letter to WD, Douglas-LOC B328; August 19, 1965 AF letter to WD, Douglas-LOC B1782; "Fortas Guests for Douglas Reception," Douglas-LOC B1768.

295 *to stay on*: Douglas, *Autobiography*, 358; Shogan, *A Question*, 256, 259.

295 *meeting with his brethren*: Bob Woodward, "Fortas Tie to Wolfson is Detailed," *WP*, January 23, 1977.

295-96 *extraneous stress*: May 14, 1969 AF letter to EW, Warren-LOC B353.

296 *facing the same fate*: Murphy, *Fortas*, 572.

CHAPTER 15

297 *quarter of a century*: Goldman, "Selecting Lower Court Federal Judges," 739.

297 *Presidents have had*: http://www.presidency.ucsb.edu/ws/index.php?pid=2063.

297 *Nixon's attention*: "What To Do About Crime in U.S.," *USNWR*, August 7, 1967; February 13, 1969 RN memo to John Mitchell, RMNL WHSF:SMOF Krogh B64; Nixon, *Memoirs*, 420.

298 *public confidence*: March 25, 1969 John Mitchell memo to H.R. Haldeman, RMNL WHSF:SMOF Haldeman Notes B294.

298 *undoing Warren's legacy*: Ehrlichman, *Witness to Power*, 114.

298 *Nixon's Fortas*: May 20, 1969 Patrick Buchanan memo to RN, RMNL POF:PMS B78; May 6, 1969 Patrick Buchanan memo to RN, RMNL WHCF:SF FG51 B1.

298 *personal friend*: May 22, 1969 Informal Meeting of the President with Members of the White House Press Corps, RMNL WHSF:SMOF Buchanan B17.

299 *acts and talks*: May 22, 1969 Bryce Harlow memo to RN, RMNL WHCF:ANF B

Warren E. Burger.

299 *this new choice*: May 20, 1969 Bryce Harlow memo to Staff Secretary, RMNL POF:PMS B78; May 22, 1969 Strom Thurmond letter to RN, RMNL WHCF:SF FG 51 B3; May 22, 1969 Bryce Harlow memo to RN, RMNL WHCF:ANF B Warren E. Burger; May 23, 1969 Quinn Tamm letter to RN, RMNL WHCF:SF FG51 B3; May 27, 1969 Herbert Klein memo to RN, RMNL WHCF:SF FG51 B3; May 28, 1969 RN letter to RR, RMNL WHCF:SF FG51 B3.

300 *lawyers in his family*: August 18, 1969 White House Press Release, RMNL WHCF:SF FG51 B3; December 19, 1960 *60 Minutes* interview with Clement Haynsworth.

300 *Nixon's criteria*: Dent, *Prodigal South*, 208.

300 *primary domestic goal*: Ehrlichman, *Witness to Power*, 115; Nixon, *Memoirs*, 424.

300 *big factor*: May 1, 1969 Harry Dent memo to RN, RMNL WHSF:SMOF Dent B2.

300 *Department of Health*: January 31, 1969 Harry Dent memo to Harry Flemming, RMNL WHSF:SMOF Dent B10; February 3, 1969 Harry Dent memo to H.R. Aldeman & John Ehrlichman, RMNL WHSF:SMOF Dent B10; February 13, 1969 H.R. Haldeman memo to Harry Dent & Bryce Harlow, RMNL WHSF:SMOF Dent B10; May 9, 1969 Harry Dent memo to Patrick Buchanan, RMNL WHSF:SMOF Dent B10; May 17, 1969 Alexander Butterfield memo to Harry Dent & Peter Flanigan, RMNL WHSF:SMOF Dent B10; May 26, 1969 Harry Dent memo to RN, RMNL WHCF:ANF B Warren E. Burger.

300 *offend the South*: February 19, 1969 Harry Dent memo to John Mitchell, RMNL WHSF:SMOF Dent B10; March 14, 1969 Harry Dent memo to Dwight Chapin, RMNL WHSF:SMOF Dent B10; Evans & Novak, *Nixon*, 145.

300-01 *vacancies on the Court*: May 21, 1969 Strom Thurmond letter to RN, RMNL WHCF:SF FG51 B1.

301 *reconsider the nomination*: John Steele, "Haynsworth v. the U.S. Senate (1969)," *Fortune*, March, 1970.

301 *achievements of the era*: "Head of the House," *Time*, March 21, 1955; J.Y. Smith & Kenneth Crawford, "George Meany, 85, Giant of U.S. Labor Movement," *WP*, January 11, 1980; https://aflcio.org/about/history/labor-history-people/george-meany.

301 *denounce the nominee*: August 20, 1969 AFL-CIO press release, Bayh-IU JC-16; August 26, 1969 AFL-CIO letter to local chapters, Bayh-IU JC-16.

302 *dubious ethics*: August 31, 1969 "ABC's Issues and Answers," RMNL PPF Ziegler B4.

302 *presiding over the case*: John Steele, "Haynsworth v. the U.S. Senate (1969)," *Fortune*, March, 1970.

302 *fallen justice*: John Steele, "Haynsworth v. the U.S. Senate (1969)," *Fortune*, March, 1970.

302 *proven on the record*: August 31, 1969 "ABC's Issues and Answers," RMNL PPF Ziegler B4.

302 *any wrongdoing*: February 28, 1964 Robert Kennedy letter to Simon Sobeloff, Bayh-IU JC-15; September 5, 1969 William Rehnquist letter to Roman Hruska, RMNL WHS-F:SMOF Ehrlichman B23; John Steele, "Haynsworth v. the U.S. Senate (1969)," *Fortune*, March, 1970.

302 *in it all the way*: John Steele, "Haynsworth v. the U.S. Senate (1969)," *Fortune*, March, 1970.

303 *around 60%*: Gallup, *The Gallup Poll, Vol. 3*, 2245.

303 *Electoral College*: John Steele, "Haynsworth v. the U.S. Senate (1969)," *Fortune*, March, 1970; Robert Sherrill, "Birch Bayh Isn't a Household Word—Yet," *NYT*, February 15, 1970.

303 *default leader*: Robert Sherrill, "Birch Bayh Isn't a Household Word—Yet," *NYT*, February 15, 1970.

303-04 *veteran of the Warren Wars*: Robert Sherrill, "Birch Bayh Isn't a Household Word—Yet," *NYT*, February 15, 1970; Indiana University (Lilly Library), *Art of Leadership*; http://www.birchbayh.com/id1.html.

304 *the wreckage*: "Senator Kennedy hurt in air crash; Bayh injured, too," *NYT*, June 20, 1964; http://thehill.com/homenews/senate/56683-bayh-remembers-1964-plane-crash.

305 *lobby the Senate*: Thomas Johnson, "NAACP Lauds its Role in Haynsworth Defeat," *NYT*, June 29, 1970.

305 *fights on the Hill*: Maltese, *Selling*, 72.

305 *involved in confirmations*: Maltese, *Selling*, 36.

305-06 *far more damning*: John Steele, "Haynsworth v. the U.S. Senate (1969)," *Fortune*, March, 1970.

306 *former law firm*: *CQ Almanac 1969*, "Senate Rejects Haynsworth Nomination."

306 *caught off-guard*: September 15, 1969 Ken Cole memo to John Ehrlichman, RMNL WHSF:SMOF Ehrlichman B23; John Steele, "Haynsworth v. the U.S. Senate (1969)," *Fortune*, March, 1970.

306 *government directory*: October 9, 1969 Robert Gray letter to RN, RMNL WHCF:SF FG51 B2.

306 *ahead of time*: May 16, 1969 Bud Krogh memo to John Ehrlichman, RMNL WHS-F:SMOF Ehrlichman B39.

306 *principle alone*: Simon, *Independent Journey*, 400.

307 *to be energized*: Maltese, *Selling*, 75.

307 *campaign donors*: October 15, 1969 Jack Gleason memo to Kevin Phillips, RMNL WHS-F:SMOF Dent B7; October 17, 1969 Harry Dent memo to Ken Belieu, RMNL WHS-F:SMOT Dent B7; October 20, 1969 Donald Johnson memo to Bryce Harlow, RMNL WHSF:SMOF Dent B8; October 21, 1969 Jack Gleason memo to Kevin Phillips, RMNL WHSF:SMOF Dent B8.

307 *for help*: October 8, 1969 Harry Dent memo to Bryce Harlow, RMNL WHSF:SMOF Dent B7; Undated Handwritten and Typed List, RMNL WHSF:SMOF Dent B8; Maltese, *Selling*, 76.

307 *made against Haynsworth*: October 8, 1969 Clark Mollenhoff memo to John Ehrlichman, RMNL WHSF:SMOF Ehrlichman B39; October 15, 1969 Roman Hruska letter to Philip Hart, Hart-BHL B183; Judge Haynsworth's Labor Record—A Rebuttal to the AFL-CIO Appraisal, Hart-BHL B183.

307 *going to understand*: John Steele, "Haynsworth v. the U.S. Senate (1969)," *Fortune*, March, 1970.

307 *be embarrassed*: Frank, *Haynsworth*, 67.

307-08 *co-equal responsibility*: October 8, 1969 Press Release, Griffin-CHL B292.

308 *major blow*: October 8, 1969 Press Release, Griffin-CHL B292; Haldeman, *Diaries*, (October 6, 1969). All of the GOP leadership within the Senate, including the new Minority Leader Hugh Scott and Margaret Chase Smith, the chair of the Republican Conference, eventually abandoned the nominee. *CQ Almanac 1969*, "Senate Rejects Haynsworth Nomination."

308 *Republican traitors*: Nixon, *Memoirs*, 421; Maltese, *Selling*, 74; Haldeman, *Diaries*, (October 6, 1969, December 4, 1969).

308 *barometer of his leadership*: Ambrose, *Nixon*, 296, 315; Ehrlichman, *Witness to Power*, 119.

308 *you can get somewhere*: October 14, 1969 Patrick Buchanan memo to RN, RMNL POF:PMS B79.

308 *twists throats*: John Steele, "Haynsworth v. the U.S. Senate (1969)," *Fortune*, March, 1970; Massaro, *Supremely*, 99.

308 *anything we've seen*: October 24, 1969 Jack Gleason memo to Harry Dent, RMNL WHS-F:SMOF Dent B8; *CQ Almanac 1969*, "Senate Rejects Haynsworth Nomination."

308 *colleagues followed suit*: John Steele, "Haynsworth v. the U.S. Senate (1969)," *Fortune*, March, 1970; Massaro, *Supremely*, 92, 102-03; Maltese, *Selling*, 78-79.

308 *echoing the mood*: September 30, 1969 Margaret Chase Smith letter to RN, RMNL WH-CF:SF FG51 B3.

309 *no Fortas affair*: Maltese, *Selling*, 81.

309 *Nixon was infuriated*: RMNOH – Price, 23; Evans & Novak, *Nixon*, 163.

309 *President in Dixie*: James Batten, "In Dixie, Nixon is Tall Cotton," *Charlotte Observer*, October 10, 1969; October 13, 1969 Harry Dent memo to RN, RMNL WHSF:SMOF Dent B1; October 23, 1969 Briefing, RMNL WHSF:SMOF Haldeman Notes B139.

309 *southern audiences*: October 8, 1969 Harry Dent memo to Bryce Harlow, RMNL WHS-F:SMOF Dent B7; October 16, 1969 Harry Dent memo to Tom Huston, RMNL WHS-F:SMOF Dent B7; October 21, 1969 RN memo to Harry Dent, RMNL WHSF:SMOF Dent B7; November 24, 1969 Harry Dent memo to RN, RMNL WHSF:SMOF Dent B7.

309 *firm commitment*: November 24, 1969 Strom Thurmond letter to RN, RMNL WH-CF:SF FG51 B2.

309 *believes in anything else*: Evans & Novak, *Nixon*, 163.

309 *further to the right*: Dent, *Prodigal South*, 210.

309 *rough confirmation*: Ehrlichman, *Witness to Power*, 125; January 19, 1970 RN Press Release, RMNL WHCF:SF FG51 B4.

309 *direction of the court*: January 20, 1970 Clarence Mitchell letter to Birch Bayh, Bayh-IU Bayh Subcommittee on Constitutional Amendments & Subcommittee on the Constitution, 1963-1980 B4; January 20, 1970 Clarence Mitchell letter to Philip Hart, Hart-BHL B190.

309-10 *constituents when necessary*: Eric Pace, "Clarence M. Mitchell is Dead; NAACP Lobbyist Till '78," *NYT*, March 20, 1984.

310 *left them exhausted*: *CQ Almanac 1970*, "Carswell Nomination to Court Rejected by Senate."

310 *committed murder*: Massaro, *Supremely*, 105. The press felt the same way. See, Ambrose, *Nixon*, 316.

310 *gripes against the judge*: January 30, 1970 Dwight Chapin memo to H.R. Haldeman, RMNL WHCF:SF FG51 B4; January 28, 1970 memo to JJ, Javits-SBU Series 3 B101.

311 *correct way of life*: January 27, 1970 American Newspaper Guild release, Bayh-IU JC-14.

311 *rights of black Americans*: "The Carswell File," *Newsweek*, March 16, 1970; January 26, 1970 Marian Edelman memo to Richard Seymour, Bayh-IU JC-26; Judge Carswell: The Candor Question, Bayh-IU JC-26; *CQ Almanac 1970*, "Carswell Nomination to Court Rejected by Senate."

311 *My God*: RMNOH – Colson, 11; Maltese, *Selling*, 14-15.

311 *level of competence*: February 18, 1970 John Griffiths et al letter to James Eastland, Bayh-IU JC-14; March 31, 1970 Jon Richardson letter to Birch Bayh, Bayh-IU JC-14; February 5, 1970 Derek Bok letter to James Eastland, Bayh-IU JC-26.

311 *in this century*: GHCCH, 242.

311-12 *distinguished Southern jurist*: March 17, 1970 Florida State University Law School professors letter to RN, Bayh-IU JC-14.

312 *our nation together*: April 1, 1970 Open letter from Boalt Law School professors, Bayh-IU JC-26; March 13, 1970 Harvard law professors letter to the members of the Senate, Bayh-IU JC-26.

312 *average of his peers*: March 5, 1970 Law Students Concerned for the Court press release, Bayh-IU JC-26; Key data for press conference, Bayh-IU JC-14; March 5, 1970 Law Students Concerned for the Court press release, Bayh-IU JC-14.

312 *legal thinkers*: March 31, 1970 Supreme Court Clerks' letter, Javits-SBU Series 3 B101.

312 *a dummy*: Ehrlichman, *Witness to Power*, 126.

312-13 *second straight defeat*: Maltese, *Selling*, 16.

313 *mediocre judges*: Jon Nordheimer, "The Carswell campaign runs into stormy weather," *NYT*, July 13, 1970.

313 *refused to back down*: Maltese, *Selling*, 16.

313 *Constitution impaired*: April 1, 1970 RN letter to William Saxbe, RMNL WHSF:SMOF Colson B43.

314 *attempted power-grab*: Ambrose, *Nixon*, 337.

314 *public policy*: 116 *CR* 10180.

314 *truly exercising*: 116 *CR* 10184.

314 *get two votes*: Small, *Nixon*, 170; Massaro, *Supremely*, 119.

314 *empowered to do*: April 7, 1970 BVW memo to JF & PJM, Bayh-IU JC-14; Scenario for tie vote on Carswell, Bayh-IU JC-14; Argument against the vice president's power to break a tie on the Carswell vote, Bayh-IU JC-14.

314 *that took place*: April 9, 1970 Statement by the president, RMNL WHSF:SMOF Colson B43.

314 *sinews of the southern strategy*: Dent, *Prodigal South*, 212.

315 *for his condition*: Powe, *Warren Court*, 205.

315 *under their skins*: March 18, 1963 FF letter to Alexander Bickel, Frankfurter-LOC R14.

315 *somebody from Mississippi*: March 3, 1970 Patrick Buchanan memo to RN, RMNL POF:PMS B80.

315 *Cletus Gaptooth*: "Why not relax and enjoy it?," *NR*, February 10, 1970.

315 *carbon copy*: April 13, 1970 RN memo to H.R. Haldeman, RMNL PPF B2.

CHAPTER 16

316 *Roman Circus*: Library of Congress Legislative Reference Service, "Role of Vice-President Designate Gerald Ford in the Attempt to Impeach Associate Supreme Court Justice William O. Douglas," GRFL VP B229.

316 *Everybody liked*: GRFOH – Griffin 2; GRFOH – Archer 3-4, 8.

317 *vote to impeach him*: April 15, 1970 House Floor Speech to Impeach Justice Douglas, GRFL GFCP:PSS D29.

317 *turn of events*: The Senate acquitted, Samuel Chase, the only justice to get impeached, in 1805.

317 *guilty by the Senate*: Final Report on H. Res. 920, 33.

317 *through the capital*: Warren Unna "Congress Greets Fortas Resignation With Relief," *WP*, May 16, 1969; May 23, 1969 John Ehrlichman memo to RN, RMNL WHCF:SF FG51 B1.

317 *third one Brennan*: Douglas, *Douglas Letters*, 391.

317 *God it will*: May 28, 1969 AF to WD, Douglas-LOC B1782.

317-18 *who must go*: June 2, 1969 "Strom Thurmond Reports to the People," Douglas-LOC B591.

318 *an active campaign*: Dean, *Rehnquist Choice*, 24-25; Ambrose, *Nixon*, 315.

318 *real trouble*: October 23, 1969 Ken Cole memo to H.R. Haldeman, RMNL WHSF:SMOF Ehrlichman B39.

318 *case against Douglas*: Murphy, *Wild Bill*, 429.

318 *we'll impeach Douglas*: Douglas, *Court Years*, 359.

318 *even more clearly*: April 17, 1970 Donald Rumsfeld memo to Ken Cole Jr., RMNL WHSF:SF-CF B22 FG51.

319 *Nixon man*: GRFOH – GRF B1 (April 24, 1992); https://www.senate.gov/artandhistory/history/common/generic/VP_Gerald_Ford.htm.

319 *Nixon's latest move*: Murphy, *Wild Bill*, 430.

319 *we were involved*: Marjorie Hunter, "Ford Asks Douglas's Ouster," *NYT*, April 16, 1970; April 24, 1970 Patrick Moynihan memo to Staff Secretary, RMNL WHSF:SF-CF B22 FG51. The fact that Moynihan wrote the memo to the "staff secretary" rather than a member of Nixon's inner circle made it likely that he inserted the memo into the record to warn against—and distance himself—from the White House's exploits.

319 *ever been divorced*: Carla Hall, "Cathy Douglas—The Woman Beside the Man," *WP*, December 9, 1979.

319 *highways of matrimony*: Simon, *Independent Journey*, 391.

319 *nobody's wife*: Murphy, *Wild Bill*, 428-29; Newman, *Hugo Black*, 476.

320 *is also revolution*: Douglas, *Points of Rebellion*, 95.

320 *hippie-yippie*: April 15, 1970 House Floor Speech to Impeach Justice Douglas, GRFL GFCP:PSS D29.

320 *with a crown*: *Evergreen*, April, 1970.

320 *Panama City*: April 15, 1970 House Floor Speech to Impeach Justice Douglas, GRFL GFCP:PSS D29.

320-21 *around their necks*: April 16, 1970 Janet Blau letter to WD, Douglas-LOC B588; April 20, 1970 Magnus Bjorndal letter to WD, Douglas-LOC B588; April 21, 1970 Donna Graham letter to WD, Douglas-LOC B588; Undated T. Klein letter to WD, Douglas-LOC B588.

321 *Americans for years*: April 15, 1970 House Floor Speech to Impeach Justice Douglas, GRFL GFCP:PSS D29.

321 *Ford convict Douglas*: April 20, 1970 Charles Keating letter to GRF, GFCP BR13.

321-22 *unsavory characters*: April 15, 1970 House Floor Speech to Impeach Justice Douglas, GRFL GFCP:PSS D29; *CQ Almanac 1970*, "Justice Douglas Impeachment."

322 *oversee the process*: *CQ Almanac 1970*, "Justice Douglas Impeachment."

322 *resolved to stay*: Douglas, *Douglas Letters*, 393.

322 *on his own*: Simon, *Independent Journey*, 399, 406-07.

322-23 *how inconsequential*: Murphy, *Wild Bill*, 436.

323 *ammunition to his detractors*: May 2, 1970 Nan Burgess memo to WD, Douglas-LOC B592; June 4, 1970 WD letter to Gerald Stern, Douglas-LOC B592; May 6, 1970 WD letter to Simon Rifkind, Douglas-LOC B591; May 19, 1970 WD letter to Owen Laster, Douglas-LOC B591; May 23, 1970 WD letter to Simon Rifkind, Douglas-LOC B592.

323 *given moment in history*: April 15, 1970 House Floor Speech to Impeach Justice Douglas, GRFL GFCP:PSS D29.

323 *constitute a crime*: Final Report on H. Res. 920, 35-39.

323-24 *concern for propriety*: "Second Interim Draft Report—Douglas" memo, GRFL GFCP BR17.

324 *justice's knowledge*: Douglas, *Douglas Letters*, 402.

324 *broken the law*: Simon, *Independent Journey*, 395, 397, 409; Douglas, *Court Years*, 366; *CQ Almanac 1970*, "Justice Douglas Impeachment."

324 *organized gambling fraternity*: Final Report on H. Res. 920, 176.

325 *dang fool speech*: Murphy, *Wild Bill*, 434-35.

CHAPTER 17

326 *fresh approach*: Ehrlichman, *Witness to Power*, 137.

326 *in the teeth*: September 29, 1971 Patrick Buchanan memo to RN, RMNL WHCF:SF FG51 B1.

326 *play catch up*: Bud Krogh to John Ehrlichman, RMNL PPF Young B17; September 24, 1971 Bud Krogh memo to John Ehrlichman, RMNL WHSF:SMOF Ehrlichman B27.

327 *fallout from Carswell*: September 23, 1971 Congressional letter to RN, RMNL WH-CF:SF FG51 B1; September 23, 1971 William Timmons letter to GRF, RMNL WH-CF:SF FG51 B1; NARA Nixon Tape No. 581-4.

327 *damn southerner*: NARA Nixon Tape No. 581-4.

327 *national stage*: NARA Nixon Tape No. 581-4. Reaching out to its allies in the Senate, the NAACP fired a preemptive strike to ground the nomination before it took hold. See, September 27, 1971 Clarence Mitchell to Philip Hart, Hart-BHL B201.

327 *another embarrassing defeat*: March 25, 1963 Richard Poff Press Release, RMNL WHS-F:SMOF Dean B61; September 28, 1971, John Dean & David Young memo to John Ehrlichman, RMNL WHSF:SMOF Dean B75; NARA Nixon Tape No. 581-4; McMahon, *Nixon's Court*, 153-54.

327 *distinguished he'll become*: NARA Nixon Tape No. 579-3.

327-28 *ambitions hurt him*: September 27, 1971 John Dean & David Young memo to John Mitchell & John Ehrlichman, RMNL WHSF:SMOF Dean B75; Dean, *Rehnquist Choice*, 119.

328 *long and divisive*: October 2, 1971 Richard Poff press release, RMNL WHSF:SMOF Dean B60. Poff joined the Virginia Supreme Court the next year.

328 *behind his withdrawal*: Dean, *Rehnquist Choice*, 121.

328 *reactionary than Wallace*: Haldeman, *Diaries*, (October 2, 1971).

328 *League of Nations*: Evans & Novak, *Nixon*, 132.

328 *fail to confirm*: William Shannon, "Mr. Nixon's Revenge," *NYT*, October 12, 1971; October 15, 1971 Charles Colson memo to John Ehrlichman, RMNL PPF Young B17.

328 *stink bomb*: Dean, *Rehnquist Choice*, 22.

329 *beat the bastards*: October 14, 1971 RN conversation with John Mitchell (American Public Media site).

329 *them a lesson*: NARA Nixon Tape No. 11-26.

329 *successful confirmation*: October 14, 1971 John Whitaker memo to John Ehrlichman, RMNL PPF Young B17.

329 *point we can*: NARA Nixon Tape No. 581-4.

329 *female justice*: Beverly Craig, "Griffin boosts Mrs. Griffiths, Judge Kennedy for high court," *Detroit News*, September 21, 1971; September 24, 1971 Grace Rice letter to RN, RMNL WHCF:SF FG51 B3; September 30, 1971 Roland Elliott memo to Ray Price, RMNL WHSF:SMOF Dean B76; RMNOH – Franklin, 22; RMNOH – King, 21; Ambrose, *Nixon*, 469.

329-30 *bag of bags*: RMNOH – Franklin, 23; RMNOH – Malek, 6; Yalof, *Pursuit of Justices*, 119.

330 *California Court of Appeal*: October 16, 1971 John Dean & David Young memo to John Mitchell & John Ehrlichman, RMNL WHSF:SMOF Dean B75.

330 *Italian-American judge*: May 20, 1969 John Whitaker memo to RN, RMNL POF:PMS B78. Anthony Colombo, the vice president of the Italian-American Civil Rights League, led a public campaign for an Italian justice. September 30, 1971 Anthony Colombo letter to RN, RMNL WHCF:SF FG51 B3.

330 *candles in their homes*: May 26, 1969 Patrick Buchanan memo to RN, RMNL PPF B2.

330 *Italian background*: September 29, 1971 Patrick Buchanan memo to RN, RMNL WHCF:SF FG51 B1.

330 *could be cultivated*: September 30, 1971 Charles Colson memo to John Ehrlichman, RMNL WHSF:SMOF Ehrlichman B27.

330 *Catholics is good*: NARA Nixon Tape No. 11-143. Nixon also looked for candidates who could check off multiple boxes. See Dean, *Rehnquist Choice*, 70, 73.

330 *after I die*: Dean, *Rehnquist Choice*, 73.

330 *placate Volpe*: NARA Nixon Tape No. 11-35; NARA Nixon Tape No. 11-40.

330 *I can't wait*: October 14, 1971 RN conversation with John Mitchell (American Public Media site).

331 *Harlan in 1954*: Yalof, *Pursuit of Justices*, 15, 42-43.

331 *earlier speculation*: Fred Graham, "Presidents asks Bar unit to check 6 for High Court," *NYT*, October 14, 1971.

331 *largely meant to appeal*: Yalof, *Pursuit of Justices*, 122.

331 *Fuck the ABA*: Reeves, *Nixon*, 383.

331 *such a bunch*: October 14, 1971 RN conversation with John Mitchell (American Public Media site).

331 *quoted obscenity*: Reeves, *Nixon*, 383.

331 *be their hero*: NARA Nixon Tape No. 11-33.

331 *frigid bitches*: NARA Nixon Tape No. 11-40.

332 *poor eyesight*: NARA Nixon Tape No. 11-133.

332 *undertake it*: NARA Nixon Tape No. 11-153.

332 *second vacancy*: Jenkins, *The Partisan*, 120.

332 *off his feet*: NARA Nixon Tape No. 11-133.

332 *searching his soul*: NARA Nixon Tape No. 11-143.

332 *later regret*: Interview with John Dean (American Public Media site); Strober, *Nixon*, 67.

332-33 *seen on the Court*: NARA Nixon Tape No. 11-143.

333 *Warren Court's achievements*: "Is Rehnquist a Counterrevolutionary?" *NR*, November 19, 1971.

333 *psychedelic tie*: Jenkins, *The Partisan*, 108.

333 *barked to Mitchell*: October 20, 1971 RN conversation with John Mitchell (American Public Media site).

333 *I'm not mediocre*: "The President's Two Nominees," *Time*, November 1, 1971.

333 *Nixon's assessment*: Dean, *Rehnquist Choice*, 156. Mitchell made a similar observation. See Dean, *Rehnquist Choice*, 139, 185.

333-34 *the finish line*: NARA Nixon Tape No. 11-133; NARA Nixon Tape No. 11-143.

334 *11-1 vote*: Kalman, *Long Reach*, 292.

334 *male candidate*: NARA Nixon Tape No. 11-131.

334 *take the rap*: NARA Nixon Tape No. 11-157.

334 *That's great*: October 20, 1971 RN conversation with John Mitchell (American Public Media site).

334 *even find him*: NARA Nixon Tape No. 11-155.

334 *out of the job*: Jenkins, *The Partisan*, 126-27; Haldeman, *Diaries*, (October 21, 1971); Interview with John Dean (American Public Media site).

334 *potential voters*: October 21, 1971 RN conversation with John Mitchell (American Public Media site).

335 *I think Plessy*: Schwartz, "Chief Justice Rehnquist," 246.

335 *Court conference*: December 8, 1971 William Rehnquist letter to James Eastland, Bayh-IU JC-28.

335 *mood for a fight*: Dean, *Rehnquist Choice*, 277-78; December 6, 1971 William Timmons memo to RN, RMNL WHCF:SF FG51 B4.

335 *given the disinterest*: December 8, 1971 Howard memo to Birch Bayh, Bayh-IU JC-17.

335 *out of town*: Willard Edwards, "How Rehnquist Filibuster Failed," *Chicago Tribune*, December 14, 1971.

Epilogue

336-37 *filibuster if necessary*: Joseph Califano Jr., "The '68 version of the Bork debate," *NYT*, September 14, 1987.

337 *case against Bork*: Joseph Biden, the future vice president who was chairman of the Judiciary Committee in 1987, read an excerpt from one of Thurmond's 1968 speeches two weeks after Bork was nominated. The particular passage he picked out highlight-

ed Thurmond's contention that the Court's outsized role in American life justified the Senate's concern for "the views of the prospective Justices." 133 *CR* 20912.

337 *precedent have prescribed*: RBCH, 921, 2831, 3693, 5517.

337 *equally correct today*: 133 *CR* 23131.

338 *Judge Bork's philosophy*: 133 *CR* 27027.

341 *sought to launch*: August 18, 1969 Finis Smith letter to Congress, Dirksen-DCC 2922.

341-42 *attend his funeral*: Stern, "Lyndon Johnson and Richard Russell," 699; Fite, "Richard B. Russell and Lyndon B. Johnson," 138.

342 *The proposal*: May 21, 1974 EW speech at Morehouse College, Warren-LOC B837; Warren, "Let's Not Weaken," 677.

342 *Tricky is perhaps*: Alden Whitman, "Alden Whitman's golden oldies," *Esquire*, April, 1975.

342-43 *Court building*: Newton, *Justice for All*, 514-15; "Warren's body to lie in repose," *WP*, July 11, 1974.

343 *the first place*: Johnson, *Vantage Point*, 543.

343 *never forget that*: September 3, 1971 LBJ letter to AF, Fortas-SML B114.

343 *is more appreciated*: December 28, 1972 LBJ letter to AF, Fortas-SML B114.

343 *He was America*: Abe Fortas, "'He was America,'" *NYT*, January 25, 1973.

344 *sister publication*: January 10, 1969 AF letter to Hedley Donovan, Fortas-SML B99.

344 *George Polk award*: Agis Salpukas, "William Lambert, 78, Writer Who Exposed Justice Fortas," *NYT*, February 16, 1998.

344 *lifetime arrangement*: March 30, 1973 Louis Wolfson letter to AF, Fortas-SML B125.

344 *Super-Chief*: July 10, 1974 Inge letter to AF, Fortas-SML B124; Fortas, "Chief Justice Warren," 406.

344 *acclaim and calumny*: Fortas, "William O. Douglas," 614.

Bibliography

Archival Collections

—Birch E. Bayh Senatorial Papers, Modern Political Papers Collection, Indiana University

—William J. Brennan Papers, Manuscript Division, Library of Congress

—Harold H. Burton Papers, Manuscript Division, Library of Congress

—Tom C. Clark Papers, Tarlton Law Library, University of Texas Law School

—Everett M. Dirksen Papers, The Dirksen Congressional Center

—Paul H. Douglas Papers, Chicago History Museum

—William O. Douglas Papers, Manuscript Division, Library of Congress

—Abe Fortas Papers, Manuscripts and Archives, Sterling Memorial Library, Yale University

—Felix Frankfurter Papers, Manuscript Division, Library of Congress

—Robert P. Griffin Papers, Clarke Historical Library, Central Michigan University

—Philip A. Hart Papers, Bentley Historical Library, University of Michigan

—Jacob K. Javits Collection, Stony Brook University

—William E. Jenner Papers, Indiana State Library

—Richard B. Russell Jr. Collection, Richard B. Russell Library for Political Research and Studies, University of Georgia

—Herman E. Talmadge Collection, Richard B. Russell Library for Political Research and Studies, University of Georgia

—Earl Warren Papers, Manuscript Division, Library of Congress

—Records of the Committee on the Senate Judiciary and Related Committees, 1816-1968, National Archives

Presidential Libraries

—Dwight D. Eisenhower Presidential Library, Abiline, Kansas

—Gerald R. Ford Presidential Library, Ann Arbor, Michigan

—Lyndon B. Johnson Presidential Library, Austin, Texas

—Richard M. Nixon Presidential Library, Yorba Linda, California

Interviews and Correspondence

Jesse H. Choper, Walter E. Dellinger III, Richard D. Friedman, Jim Newton, Lucas A. Powe Jr., Terrance Sandalow

Oral Histories

—California State Archives State Government Oral History Program, Center for California Studies, California State University, Sacramento
   Lloyd W. Lowrey, Clement Sherman Whitaker Jr.

—Clerks of Chief Justice Earl Warren, Bancroft Library, University of California, Berkeley
   Scott Bice, Donald M. Cahen, Earl C. Dudley, Dennis M. Flannery, C. Douglas Kranwinkle, Carl D. Lawson, Dallin H. Oaks, Curtis R. Reitz, Arthur I. Rosett, Benno C. Schmidt

—Columbia University Center for Oral History
   Thurgood Marshall, Benno C. Schmidt

—Earl Warren Oral History Project at the Bancroft Library, University of California, Berkeley Earl Adams, Stanley N. Barnes, Nina Warren Brien, Edmund G. Brown Sr., Herbert Brownell, Warren Burger, Edwin L. Carty, Bartley Cavanaugh, Roy P. Crocker, Thomas J. Cunningham, John Walton Dinkelspiel, McIntyre Faries, B. Joseph Feigenbaum, James C. Hagerty, Victor Hansen, Betty Foot Henderson, Frank E. Jorgensen, William F. Knowland, Thomas H. Kuchel, Wallace Lynn, William S. Mailliard, Keith McCormac, Thomas J. Mellon, Warren Olney III, Merrell F. Small, Harold Stassen, William T. Sweigert Sr., Earl Warren, Earl Warren Jr., James Warren, Robert Warren, Albert C. Wollenberg Sr.

—Gerald R. Ford Oral History Collection – Gerald R. Ford Presidential Library

Bill Archer, William Brock, John Dingell, Robert J. Dole, Robert Griffin, Lee Hamilton, Bob Michel, Leon Parma, Gail Raiman

—Lyndon B. Johnson Oral History Collection – Lyndon B. Johnson Presidential Library

Joseph A. Califano Jr., Ramsey Clark, Tom Clark, Clark M. Clifford, Warren Christopher, James O. Eastland, Abe Fortas, Arthur J. Goldberg, Robert P. Griffin, Jake Jacobsen, Jacob Javits, Lyndon B. Johnson (Reminiscences), Lyndon B. Johnson, Robert Hardesty and Jack Valenti (Special Interview), James R. Jones, Thurgood Marshall, Harry McPherson, Clarence Mitchell, Powell Moore, Matthew Nimetz, Lawrence F. O'Brien, Drew Pearson, Paul A. Porter, Larry Temple, Homer Thornberry, Earl Warren

—Princeton University Department of Rare Books and Special Collections

William O. Douglas

—Richard M. Nixon Oral History Collection – Richard M. Nixon Presidential Library

Lamar Alexander, John J. Chester, Charles Colson, John Dean, Robert J. Dole, Robert Ellsworth, Barbara Hackman Franklin, Leonard Garment, H.R. Haldeman, Tom Charles Huston, Gwendolyn B. King, Frederic Malek, Robert Odle, Raymond Price

—Richard B. Russell Library Oral History Documentary Collection, University of Georgia

Tom Johnson

—Southern Oral History Program

Strom Thurmond

—United States Senate Historical Office

Francis J. Attig, Charles D. Ferris, Carl M. Marcy, Stewart E. McClure, W. Scott McGeary, Richard W. Murphy, Jesse R. Nichols, Martin P. Paone, Floyd M. Riddick, William Ridgely, Dorothye G. Scott, Howard E. Shuman, George A. Smathers, George Tames, Francis R. Valeo, Rein J. Vander Zee

Nomination Hearings & Reports
(In Chronological Order)

Note: Other than the materials associated with Fred Vinson's nomination to become chief justice, Potter Stewart's nomination to become an associate justice, Thurgood Marshall's nomination to become an appellate judge, and Robert Bork's nomination to become an associate justice, the hearings and reports listed below were retrieved from Roy M. Mersky and J. Myron Jacobstein, Compilers. *The Supreme Court of the United States: Hearings and Reports on Successful and Unsuccessful Nominations of Supreme Court Justices by the Senate Judiciary Committee, 1916-1972.* Buffalo, NY: William S. Hein, 1975.

—Nomination of John J. Parker

Hearing Before The Subcommittee of the Committee on the Judiciary, U.S. Senate, Seventy-First Congress, Second Session, on the Confirmation of Hon. John J. Parker to be an Associate Justice of the Supreme Court of the United States, April 5, 1930, Volume 9.

—Nomination of Stanley F. Reed

Copy of the original transcript of the hearings held by the U. S. Senate Committee on the Judiciary on the nomination of Stanley F. Reed to be an Associate Justice of the U. S. Supreme Court, January 21, 1938, Volume 4.

—Nomination of Felix Frankfurter

Hearings Before a Subcommittee of the Committee on the Judiciary, U.S. Senate, Seventy-Sixth Congress, First Session, on the Nomination of Felix Frankfurter to be an Associate Justice of the Supreme Court, January 11 and 12, 1939, Volume 4.

—Nomination of William O. Douglas

Copy of the Original Transcript of the Hearings Held by the U.S. Senate Committee on the Judiciary on the Nomination of William O. Douglas to be an Associate Justice of the U.S. Supreme Court, March 24, 1939, Volume 4.

—Nomination of Frank Murphy

Copy of the Original Handwritten Minutes of the U. S. Senate Committee on the Judiciary on the Nomination of Frank Murphy to be an Associate Justice of the Supreme Court, 1939, Volume 4.

—Nomination of Harlan Stone

Copy of the original report of the proceedings of the hearing held before the Subcommittee of the U. S. Senate Committee on the Judiciary on the nomination of Harlan Stone to be an Associate Justice of the Supreme Court, June 21, 1941, Volume 4.

—Nomination of Robert H. Jackson

Hearings Before a Subcommittee of the Committee on the Judiciary, U.S. Senate, Seventy-Seventh Congress, First Session, on Nomination of Robert H. Jackson to be an Associate Justice of the Supreme Court, June 21, 23, 27, and 30, 1941, Volume 4.

—Nomination of Fred M. Vinson

Hearing Held Before Subcommittee of the Committee on the Judiciary, U.S. Senate, Nomination of Fred M. Vinson to be Chief Justice of the United States, June 14, 1946.

—Nomination of Tom C. Clark

Hearings Before the Committee on the Judiciary, U.S. Senate, Eighty-First Congress, First Session, on the Nomination of Tom C. Clark, of Texas, to be an Associate Justice of the Supreme Court of the United States, August 9, 10, and 11, 1949, Volume 5.

—Nomination of Sherman Minton

Hearing Before the Committee on the Judiciary, U.S. Senate, Eighty-First Congress, First Session, on the Nomination of Sherman Minton, of Indiana, to be Associate Justice of the Supreme Court of the United States, September 27, 1949, Volume 5.

—Nomination of Earl Warren

Copy of the Original Transcript of Hearings Held by the U.S. Senate Committee on the Judiciary on the Nomination of Earl Warren to be Chief Justice of the Supreme Court, 1954, Volume 5.

—Nomination of John Harlan

Hearings Before the Committee on the Judiciary, U.S. Senate, Eighty-Fourth Congress, First Session, on Nomination of John Marshall Harlan, of New York, to be Associate Justice of the Supreme Court of the United States, February 24 and 25, 1955, Volume 6.

—Nomination of William Brennan

Hearings Before the Committee on the Judiciary, U.S. Senate, Eighty-Fifth Congress, First Session, on Nomination of William Joseph Brennan, Junior, of New Jersey, to be Associate Justice of the Supreme Court of the United States, February 26 and 27, 1957, Volume 6.

—Nomination of Charles Whittaker

Hearing Before the Committee on the Judiciary, U.S. Senate, Eighty-Fifth Congress, First Session, on Nomination of Charles E. Whittaker, of Missouri, to be Associate Justice of the Supreme Court of the United States, March 18, 1957, Volume 6.

—Nomination of Potter Stewart

Report of Proceedings, Hearing Held Before Committee on the Judiciary, Nomination of Potter Stewart to be Associate Justice of the Supreme Court of the United States, April 9 and 14, 1959, Ward & Paul, Volumes 1 & 2.

—Report to Accompany the Nomination of Potter Stewart

Report Together With Minority Views to Accompany the Nomination of Potter Stewart, Eighty-Sixth Congress, First Session, Executive Report, No. 2, April 29, 1959, Volume 6.

—Nomination of Byron White

Hearing Before the Committee on the Judiciary, U.S. Senate, Eighty-Seventh Congress, Second Session, on Nomination of Byron R. White, of Colorado, to be Associate Justice of the Supreme Court of the United States, April 11, 1962, Volume 6.

—Nomination of Thurgood Marshall (to the Second Circuit)

Hearings held before a Subcommittee of the Committee on the Judiciary, U.S. Senate, on Nomination of Thurgood Marshall of New York to be United States Circuit Judge for the Second Circuit, May 1, July 12, August 8, 17, 20, 24, 1962.

—Nomination of Arthur Goldberg

Hearings Before the Committee on the Judiciary, U.S. Senate, Eighty-Seventh Congress, Second Session, on Nomination of Arthur J. Goldberg, of Illinois, to be Associate Justice of the Supreme Court of the United States, September 11 and 13, 1962, Volume 6.

—Nomination of Abe Fortas

Hearing Before the Committee on the Judiciary, U.S. Senate, Eighty-Ninth Congress, First Session, on Nomination of Abe Fortas, of Tennessee, to be an Associate Justice of the Supreme Court of the United States, August 5, 1965, Volume 7.

—Nomination of Thurgood Marshall

Hearings Before the Committee on the Judiciary, U.S. Senate, Ninetieth Congress, First Session, on Nomination of Thurgood Marshall, of New York, to be an Associate Justice of the Supreme Court of the United States, July 13, 14, 18, 19, and 24, 1967, Volume 7.

—Nominations of Abe Fortas and Homer Thornberry, Part 1

Hearings Before the Committee on the Judiciary, U.S. Senate, Ninetieth Congress, Second Session, on Nomination of Abe Fortas, of Tennessee, to be Chief Justice of the United States and Nomination of Homer Thornberry, of Texas, to be Associate Justice of the Supreme Court of the United States, July 11, 12, 16, 17, 18, 19, 20, 22, and 23, 1968, Volume 9A.

—Nominations of Abe Fortas and Homer Thornberry, Part 2

Hearings Before the Committee on the Judiciary, U.S. Senate, Ninetieth Congress, Second Session, on Nomination of Abe Fortas, of Tennessee, to be Chief Justice of the United

States and Nomination of Homer Thornberry, of Texas, to be Associate Justice of the Supreme Court of the United States, Part 2, September 13 and 16, 1968, Volume 9A.

—Report to Accompany the Nomination of Abe Fortas

Report Together With Individual Views to Accompany the Nomination of Abe Fortas, Ninetieth Congress, Second Session, Executive Report, No. 8, September 20, 1968, Volume 9A.

—Nomination of Warren Burger

Hearing Before the Committee on the Judiciary, U.S. Senate, Ninety-First Congress, First Session, on Nomination of Warren E. Burger, of Virginia, to be Chief Justice of the United States, June 3, 1969, Volume 7.

—Nomination of Clement Haynsworth

Hearings Before the Committee on the Judiciary, U.S. Senate, Ninety-First Congress, First Session, on Nomination of Clement F. Haynsworth, Jr., of South Carolina, to be Associate Justice of the Supreme Court of the United States, September 16, 17, 18, 19, 23, 24, 25, and 26, 1969, Volume 10.

—Report to Accompany the Nomination of Clement Haynsworth

Report Together With Individual Views to Accompany the Nomination of Clement F. Haynsworth, Jr., Executive Report, No. 91-12, Ninety-First Congress, First Session, November 12, 1969, Volume 10.

—Nomination of George Harrold Carswell

Hearings Before the Committee on the Judiciary, U.S. Senate, Ninety-First Congress, Second Session, on Nomination of George Harrold Carswell, of Florida, to be Associate Justice of the Supreme Court of the United States, January 27, 28, and 29 and February 2 and 3, 1970, Volume 11.

—Report to Accompany the Nomination of George Harrold Carswell

Report Together With Individual Views to Accompany the Nomination of George Harrold Carswell, Ninety-First Congress, Second Session, Executive Report, No. 91-14, February 27, 1970, Volume 11.

—Nomination of Harry A. Blackmun

Hearing Before the Committee on the Judiciary, U.S. Senate, Ninety-First Congress, Second Session, on Nomination of Harry A. Blackmun, of Minnesota, to be Associate Justice of the Supreme Court of the United States, April 29, 1970, Volume 8.

—Nominations of William Rehnquist and Lewis Powell

Hearings Before the Committee on the Judiciary, U.S. Senate, Ninety-Second Congress, First Session, on Nominations of William H. Rehnquist, of Arizona, and Lewis F. Powell, Jr., of Virginia, to be Associate Justices of the Supreme Court of the United States, November 3, 4, 8, 9, and 10, 1971, Volume 8.

—Report to Accompany the Nomination of William Rehnquist

Report Together With Individual Views to Accompany the Nomination of William H. Rehnquist, Ninety-Second Congress, First Session, Executive Report, No. 92-16, November 23, 1971, Volume 8.

—Nomination of Robert Bork

Hearings Before the Committee on the Judiciary, U.S. Senate, One Hundredth Congress, First Session, on the Nomination of Robert H. Bork to be Associate Justice of the Supreme Court of the United States, September 15, 16, 17, 18, 19, 21, 22, 23, 25, 28, 29, and 30, 1987 (Parts 1-5).

Other Congressional Hearings & Reports
(In Chronological Order)

—Hearings Before the Subcommittee No. 1 of the Committee on the Judiciary, House of Representatives, Eighty-Fourth Congress, First Session, on H.R. 3, April 28 – July 12, 1955.

—Hearings Before the Subcommittee No. 1 of the Committee on the Judiciary, House of Representatives, Eighty-Fourth Congress, Second Session, on H.R. 3, H.R. 10335, and H.R. 10344, April 20, 1956.

—Hearings Before the Subcommittee to Investigate the Administration of the Internal Security Act and other Internal Security Laws of the Committee on the Judiciary, U.S. Senate, Eighty-Fourth Congress, Second Session, on S. 3603 and S. 3617, May 11, 1956.

—Hearings Before a Subcommittee of the Committee on the Judiciary, U.S. Senate, Eighty-Fourth Congress, Second Session, on S. 373 and S. 3143, May 18, 1956.

—Hearings Before the Subcommittee to Investigate the Administration of the Internal Security Act and other Internal Security Laws of the Committee on the Judiciary, U.S. Senate, Eighty-Fourth Congress, Second Session, on S. 4050, S. 4051, and S. 4047, June 26-27, 1956.

—Report of the Subcommittee to Investigate the Administration of the Internal Security

Act and other Internal Security Laws of the Committee on the Judiciary, U.S. Senate, Eighty-Fourth Congress, Second Session, Report for the Year 1956, December 31, 1956.

—Hearings Before the Special Subcommittee to Study Decisions of the Supreme Court of the United States of the Committee on the Judiciary, House of Representatives, Eighty-Fifth Congress, Second Session, on the decision in the case of *Mallory vs. United States*, 354 U.S. 449, July 19 – October 28, 1957.

—Report of the Committee on the Judiciary, U.S. Senate, Eighty-Fifty Congress, First Session, Report No. 981, August 15, 1957.

—Report of the Subcommittee to Investigate the Administration of the Internal Security Act and other Internal Security Laws of the Committee on the Judiciary, U.S. Senate, Eighty-Fifth Congress, First Session, Report for the Year 1957, December 31, 1957.

—Hearings Before the Subcommittee to Investigate the Administration of the Internal Security Act and other Internal Security Laws of the Committee on the Judiciary, U.S. Senate, Eighty-Fifth Congress, Second Session, on S. 2646, February 19 – March 4, 1958.

—Hearings Before the Subcommittee on Constitutional Rights of the Committee on the Judiciary, U.S. Senate, Eighty-Fifth Congress, Second Session, on S. Res. 234, March 7-11, 1958.

—Report of the Subcommittee to Investigate the Administration of the Internal Security Act and other Internal Security Laws of the Committee on the Judiciary, U.S. Senate, Eighty-Fifty Congress, Second Session, Report No. 1477, April 28, 1958.

—Hearings Before the Committee on the Judiciary, House of Representatives, Eighty-Fifth Congress, Second Session, on H.R. 3, May 13-20, 1958.

—Report of the Committee on the Judiciary, U.S. Senate, Eighty-Fifty Congress, Second Session, Report No. 1586, May 15, 1958.

—Report Establishing Rules of Interpretation for federal courts involving the doctrine of federal preemption, Committee on the Judiciary, House of Representatives, Eighty-Fifth Congress, Second Session, Report No. 1878, June 13, 1958.

—Hearings Before the Special Subcommittee to Study Decisions of the Supreme Court of the United States of the Committee on the Judiciary, House of Representatives, July 17, 1958.

—Hearings Before the Subcommittee on Constitutional Amendments of the Committee on the Judiciary, U.S. Senate, Eighty-Ninth Congress, First Session, on S.J. Res. 2, S.J. Res. 37, S.J. Res. 38, and S.J. Res. 44, March 3 – May 21, 1965.

—Hearings Before the Select Subcommittee on Education of the Committee on Educational and labor, House of Representatives, Eighty-Ninth Congress, First Session, on H.R. 7465, September 1-14, 1965.

—Hearings Before the Subcommittee on Criminal Laws and Procedures of the Committee on the Judiciary, U.S. Senate, Eighty-Ninth Congress, Second Session, on S. 2187, S. 2188, S. 2189, S. 2190, S. 2191, and S. 2578, March 22 – May 11, 1966.

—Hearings Before the Subcommittee on Constitutional Amendments of the Committee on the Judiciary, U.S. Senate, Eighty-Ninth Congress, Second Session, on S.J. Res. 148, August 1-8, 1966.

—Hearings Before the Subcommittee on Separation of Powers of the Committee on the Judiciary, U.S. Senate, Ninetieth Congress, First Session, on S. 2307, October 30 and 31, 1967.

—Report of the National Advisory Commission on Civil Disorders, March 1, 1968.

—Final Report by the Special Subcommittee on H. Res. 920 of the Committee on the Judiciary, House of Representatives, 91st Congress, Second Session, September 17, 1970.

Document Collections

—Branyan, Robert L. and Lawrence H. Larsen. *The Eisenhower Administration, 1953-1961: A Documentary History*. Vol. II. New York: Random House, 1971.

—Carson, Clayborne et al, eds. *The Papers of Martin Luther King, Jr.* Vol. 1-7. Berkeley: University of California Press, 1992-2014.

—Holt, Daniel S., ed. *Debates on the Federal Judiciary: A Documentary History*. Vol. II. Federal Judicial Center, 2013.

—Kurland, Philip B. and Gerhard Casper, eds. *Landmark Briefs and Arguments of the Supreme Court of the United States: Constitutional Law*. Vol. 54. Washington D.C.: University Publications of America, 1975.

—Ragsdale, Bruce A., ed. *Debates on the Federal Judiciary: A Documentary History*. Vol. I. Federal Judicial Center, 2013.

—Young, Nancy Beck, ed. *Documentary History of the Dwight D. Eisenhower Presidency*. Vol. 1. LexisNexis, 2005.

Government Reports
(In Chronological Order)

—"Impeachment Move." *CQ Almanac 1953*, 9th ed., 08-311-08-312. Washington, DC: Congressional Quarterly, 1954.

—"Chief Justice Confirmation." *CQ Almanac 1954*, 10th ed., 08-399. Washington, DC: Congressional Quarterly, 1955.

—"Federal-State Powers." *CQ Almanac 1956*, 12th ed., 08-586. Washington, DC: Congressional Quarterly, 1957.

—W.R. McIntyre, "Criminal prosecution and the Supreme Court." *Editorial Research reports 1958* (Vol. I). Washington, D.C.: CQ Press.

—"Federal Preemption Doctrine." *CQ Almanac 1958*, 14th ed., 09-289-09-292. Washington, DC: Congressional Quarterly, 1959.

—"Supreme Court Powers." *CQ Almanac 1958*, 14th ed., 09-293-09-295. Washington, DC: Congressional Quarterly, 1959.

—"Mallory Rule." *CQ Almanac 1958*, 14th ed., 09-295-09-297. Washington, DC: Congressional Quarterly, 1959.

—"Federal Security Program." *CQ Almanac 1958*, 14th ed., 09-311-09-312. Washington, DC: Congressional Quarterly, 1959.

—"Supreme Court Nominees." *CQ Almanac 1960*, 16th ed., 09-264-9-265. Washington, DC: Congressional Quarterly, 1960.

—"Supreme Court Prayer Decision." *CQ Almanac 1962*, 18th ed., 05-240. Washington, DC: Congressional Quarterly, 1963.

—"Supreme Court Opens Door to Districting Litigation." *CQ Almanac 1962*, 18th ed., 11-1054. Washington, D.C.: Congressional Quarterly, 1963.

—"Court Arguments." *CQ Almanac 1962*, 18th ed., 11-1054. Washington, D.C.: Congressional Quarterly, 1963.

—"Precedents." *CQ Almanac 1962*, 18th ed., 11-1055. Washington, D.C.: Congressional Quarterly, 1963.

—"Aftermath of Decision," *CQ Almanac 1962*, 18th ed., 11-1057. Washington, D.C.: Congressional Quarterly, 1963.

—"Reapportionment Actions Follow 1962 Court Decisions." *CQ Almanac 1963*, 19th ed., 1185-86. Washington, D.C.: Congressional Quarterly, 1964.

—"Only 2% of Southern Negroes in School with Whites." *CQ Almanac 1964*, 20th ed., 380. Washington, DC: Congressional Quarterly, 1965.

—"Court Reapportionment Decree Challenged." *CQ Almanac 1964*, 20th ed., 383-90. Washington, DC: Congressional Quarterly, 1965.

—"Congress Fails to Act on School Prayer Amendments." *CQ Almanac 1964*, 20th ed., 398-404. Washington, DC: Congressional Quarterly, 1965.

—"State Apportionment Plan Loses in Senate." *CQ Almanac 1965*, 21st ed., 520-32. Washington, DC: Congressional Quarterly, 1966.

—Worsnop, R.L., "Police reforms." *Editorial research reports 1966* (Vol. II). Washington, DC: CQ Press.

—"Senate lets Reapportionment Ruling Stand." *CQ Almanac 1966*, 22nd ed., 505-11. Washington, DC: Congressional Quarterly, 1967.

—"Senate fails to Amend School Prayer Ruling." *CQ Almanac 1966*, 22nd ed., 512-16. Washington, DC: Congressional Quarterly, 1967.

—"Hearings Held on Constitutional Conventions." *CQ Almanac 1967*, 23rd ed., 08-461-08-464. Washington, DC: Congressional Quarterly, 1968.

—Gimlin, H., "Challenging of Supreme Court." *Editorial research reports 1968* (Vol. II). Washington, DC: CQ Press.

—Raymond J. Celada, "Elevation of Associate Justice to Chief Justice of the United States Supreme Court: Is Senate Confirmation Necessary?" Washington, DC: *Congressional Research Service*, June 24, 1968.

—"Attempt to Stop Fortas Debate Fails By 14-Vote Margin." *CQ Almanac 1968*, 24th ed., 17-531-17-538. Washington, DC: Congressional Quarterly, 1969.

—"Justice's Resignation First Under Impeachment Threat." *CQ Almanac 1969*, 25th ed., 136-37. Washington, DC: Congressional Quarterly, 1970.

—"'One Man, One Vote' Ruling Strengthened." *CQ Almanac 1969*, 25th ed., 152-54. Washington, D.C.: Congressional Quarterly, 1970.

—"Religion and the Schools." *CQ Almanac 1969*, 25th ed., 159. Washington, DC: Congressional Quarterly, 1970.

—"Senate Rejects Haynsworth Nomination to Court." *CQ Almanac 1969*, 25th ed., 337-49. Washington, DC: Congressional Quarterly, 1970.

—"Nixon Fills Chief Justice, Other Top Positions." *CQ Almanac 1969*, 25th ed., 1168-71. Washington, DC: Congressional Quarterly, 1970

—"Constitutional Convention." *CQ Almanac 1969*, 25th ed., 1200. Washington, DC: Congressional Quarterly, 1970.

—"Carswell Nomination to Court Rejected by Senate." *CQ Almanac 1970*, 26th ed., 05-154-05-162. Washington, DC: Congressional Quarterly, 1971.

—"Blackmun Unanimously Confirmed for Supreme Court." *CQ Almanac 1970*, 26th ed., 05-163-05-164. Washington, DC: Congressional Quarterly, 1971.

—"Justice Douglas Impeachment." *CQ Almanac 1970*, 26th ed., 05-1025-05-1027. Washington, DC: Congressional Quarterly, 1971.

—"School Prayer Amendment: House Vote Defeats Move." *CQ Almanac 1971*, 27th ed., 03-624-03-629. Washington, DC: Congressional Quarterly, 1972.

—"Constitutional Conventions." *CQ Almanac 1971*, 27th ed., 05-758-05-759. Washington, DC: Congressional Quarterly, 1972.

—"Court Nominees: Powell and Rehnquist Confirmed." *CQ Almanac 1971*, 27th ed., 05-851-05-859. Washington, DC: Congressional Quarterly, 1972.

—"School Prayer Issue Flares in Many Guises." *CQ Almanac 1984*, 40th ed., 245-47. Washington, DC: Congressional Quarterly, 1985.

—Louis Fisher, "Recess Appointments of Federal Judges." Washington, DC: *Congressional Research Service*, September 5, 2001.

—Henry Hogue, "Supreme Court Nominations Not Confirmed, 1789-2007." Washington, DC: *Congressional Research Service*, January 9, 2008.

—Richard S. Beth and Betsy Palmer, "Supreme Court Nominations: Senate Floor Procedure and Practice, 1789-2009." Washington, DC: *Congressional Research Service*, June 5, 2009.

—Denis Steven Rutkus and Maureen Bearden, "Supreme Court Nominations, 1789-2010: Actions by the Senate, the Judiciary Committee, and the President." Washington, DC: *Congressional Research Service*, August 23, 2010.

—Thomas H. Neale, "The Article V Convention for Proposing Constitutional Amendments: Historical Perspectives for Congress." Washington, DC: *Congressional Research*

Service, October 22, 2012.

—Sarah Herman Peck, "Congress's Power over Courts: Jurisdiction Stripping and the Rule of *Klein*." Washington, DC: *Congressional Research Service*, August 9, 2018.

—Richard A. Baker, "Traditions of the United States Senate" S. Pub. 110-11.

—Alexander C. Vassar (Compiler), "The Legislators of California."

Academic Journals & Law Reviews

—Abraham, Henry J. "Limiting Federal Court Jurisdiction: A 'self-inflicted wound?,'" 65 *Judicature* 179 (October, 1981).

—Aucoin, Brent J. "The Southern Manifesto and Southern Opposition to Desegregation," 55 *Arkansas Historical Quarterly* 173 (Summer, 1996).

—Barrett, John Q. (moderator). "Supreme Court Law Clerks' Recollections of *Brown v. Board of Education II*," 79 *St. John's Law Review* 823 (Fall, 2005).

—Black Jr., Charles L. "The Proposed Amendment of Article V: A Threatened Disaster," 72 *Yale Law Journal* 957 (April, 1963).

—Blaustein, Albert P. and Roy M. Mersky. "Rating Supreme Court Justices," 58 *ABA Journal* 1183 (November, 1972).

—Bone, Hugh A. "An Introduction to the Senate Policy Committees," 50 *American Political Science Review* 339 (June, 1956).

—Bonfield, Arthur Earl. "The Dirksen Amendment and the Article V Convention Process," 66 *Michigan Law Review* 949 (March, 1968).

—Buckwalter, Doyle W. "Constitutional Conventions and State Legislators," 48 *Chicago-Kent Law Review* 20 (April, 1971).

—Carson, Ralph M. "Disadvantages of a Federal Constitutional Convention," 66 *Michigan Law Review* 921 (March, 1968).

—Clark, Tom S. "The Separation of Powers, Court Curbing, and Judicial Legitimacy," 53 *American Journal of Political Science* 971 (October, 2009).

—Cohn, Roy and Thomas Bolan. "The Supreme Court and the A.B.A. Report and Resolutions," 28 *Fordham Law Review* 233 (1959).

—Dilliard, Irving. "Senator Thomas C. Hennings Jr. and the Supreme Court," 26 *Missouri*

Law Review 429 (1961).

—Dirksen, Everett M. "The Supreme Court and the People," 66 *Michigan Law Review* 837 (March, 1968).

—Dixon Jr., Robert G. "Article V: The Comatose Article of Our Living Constitution?," 66 *Michigan Law Review* 931 (March, 1968).

—Driver, Justin. "Supremacies and the Southern Manifesto," 92 *Texas Law Review* 1053 (2014).

—Elias, Elizabeth J. "Red Monday and its Aftermath: The Supreme Court's Flip-Flop Over Communism in the late 1950s," 43 *Hofstra Law Review* 207 (2014).

—Elliott, Shelden D. "Court-Curbing Proposals in Congress," 33 *Notre Dame Law Review* 597 (August, 1958).

—Emerson, Thomas I. "Malapportionment and Judicial Power: The Supreme Court's Decision in *Baker v. Carr*," 22 *Law Transition* 125 (1962-63).

—Epstein, Lee, William M. Landes, and Richard A. Posner. "How Business Fares in the Supreme Court," 97 *Minnesota Law Review* 1431 (2013).

—Epstein, Lee, Andrew D. Martin, Kevin M. Quinn, and Jeffrey A. Segal. "Ideological Drift Among Supreme Court Justices: Who, When, and How Important?," 101 *Northwestern University Law Review* 1483 (2007).

—Ervin Jr., Sam J. "Proposed Legislation to Implement the Convention Method of Amending the Constitution," 66 *Michigan Law Review* 875 (March, 1968).

—Fite, Gilbert C. "Richard B. Russell and Lyndon B. Johnson: The Story of a Strange Friendship," 83 *Missouri Historical Review* 125 (January, 1989).

—Fordham, Jefferson B. "The States in the Federal System. Vital Role or Limbo?," 49 *Virginia Law Review* 666 (May, 1963).

—Fortas, Abe. "Chief Justice Warren: The Enigma of Leadership," 84 *Yale Law Journal* 405 (1975).

—Fortas, Abe. "Thurmond Arnold and the Theatre of Law," 79 *Yale Law Journal* 988 (1970).

—Fortas, Abe. "William O. Douglas: A Eulogy," 89 *Yale Law Journal* 613 (1980).

—Frankfurter, Felix. "The Supreme Court in the Mirror of Justices," 105 *University of Pennsylvania Law Review* 781 (April, 1957).

—Friedman, Richard D. "The Transformation in Senate Response to Supreme Court Nominations: From Reconstruction to the Taft Administration and Beyond," 5 *Cardozo Law Review* 1 (1983-84).

—Frye, Brian L. "The Dialectic of Obscenity," 35 *Hamline Law Review* 229 (2012).

—Frye, Brian L. "The Fortas Film Festival," Legal Studies Research Paper Series No. 11-10.

—Goldman, Sheldon "Selecting Lower Court Federal Judges on the Basis of Their Policy Views," 56 *Drake Law Review* 729 (2008).

—Griffin, Robert P. "The Broad Role," 2 *Prospectus* 285 (April, 1969).

—Guliuzza III, Frank, Daniel J. Reagan, and David M. Barrett. "Character, Competency, And Constitutionalism: Did the Bork Nomination Represent A Fundamental Shift in Confirmation Criteria?," 75 *Marquette Law Review* 409 (1992).

—Hart, Philip A. "The Discriminating Role," 2 *Prospectus* 305 (April, 1969).

—Hustwit, William P. "From Caste to Color Blindness: James J. Kilpatrick's Segregationist Semantics," 77 *Journal of Southern History* 639 (August, 2011).

—Kagan, Elena. "Confirmation Messes, Old and New," 62 *Univ. of Chicago Law Review* 919 (Spring, 1995).

—Kauper, Paul G. "The Alternative Amendment Process: Some Observations," 66 *Michigan Law Review* 903 (March, 1968).

—Kotlowski, Dean J. "Trial By Error: Nixon, the Senate, and the Haynsworth Nomination," 26 *Presidential Studies Quarterly* 71 (Winter 1996).

—Kurland, Philip B. "The Supreme Court and its Judicial Critics," 6 *Utah Law Review* 457 (Fall, 1959).

—Kutner, Luis. "The Plot to Impeach Justice Douglas: A Look Back and a Step Forward," 24 *University of West Los Angeles Law Review* 79 (1993).

—Kyvig, David E. "Everett Dirksen's Constitutional Crusades," 95 *Journal of the Illinois State Historical Society* 68 (Spring, 2002).

—Lewis, George. "Virginia's Northern Strategy: Southern Segregationists and the Route to National Conservatism," 72 *The Journal of Southern History* 111 (February, 2006).

—Mason, Alpheus Thomas. "Pyrrhic victory: the defeat of Abe Fortas," 45 *Virginia Quarterly Review* 19 (Winter, 1969).

—Massaro, John. "LBJ and the Fortas Nomination for Chief Justice," 97 *Political Science*

Quarterly 603 (Winter, 1982-83).

—McCleskey, Clifton. "Along the Midway: Some Thoughts on Democratic Constitution-Amending," 66 *Michigan Law Review* 1001 (March, 1968).

—McKay, Robert B. "Political Thickets and Crazy Quilts: Reapportionment and Equal Protection," 61 *Michigan Law Review* 645 (February, 1963).

—McKay, Robert B. "The Supreme Court and its Lawyer Critics," 28 *Fordham Law Review* 615 (1959).

—Murphy, Walter F. and Joseph Tanenhaus. "Public Opinion and Supreme Court: The Goldwater Campaign," 32 *Public Opinion Quarterly* 31 (1968).

—Neal, Phil C. "*Baker v. Carr*: Politics in Search of Law," 1962 *Supreme Court Review* 252 (1962).

—Pepper, George Wharton. "Recent Attacks upon the Supreme Court: A Statement by Members of the Bar," 42 *American Bar Association Journal*, 1128 (December, 1956).

—Powe Jr., Lucas A. "The Senate and the Court: Questioning a Nominee," 54 *Texas Law Review* 891 (1975-76).

—Ringhand, Lori A. and Paul M. Collins Jr. "May It Please the Senate: An Empirical Analysis of the Senate Judiciary Committee Hearings of Supreme Court Nominees, 1939-2009," University of Georgia School of Law Research Papers Series No. 10-12 (July, 2010).

—Ross, William G. "The Functions, Roles, and Duties of the Senate in the Supreme Court Appointment Process," 28 *William & Mary Law Review* 633 (1986).

—Ross, William G. "Participation by the Public in the Federal Judicial Selection Process," 43 *Vanderbilt Law Review* 1 (January, 1990).

—Schwartz, Bernard. "Chief Justice Rehnquist, Justice Jackson, and the *Brown* Case," *Supreme Court Review* 245 (1988).

—Songer, Donald R. "The Relevance of Policy Values for the Confirmation of Supreme Court Nominees," 13 *Law & Society Review* 927 (Summer, 1979).

—Steamer, Robert J. "Statesmanship or Craftsmanship: Current Conflict over the Supreme Court," 11 *Western Political Quarterly* 265 (June, 1958).

—Stern, Mark. "Lyndon Johnson and Richard Russell: Institutions, Ambitions and Civil Rights," 21 *Presidential Studies Quarterly* 687 (Fall, 1991).

—Strub, Whitney. "Perversion for Profit: Citizens for Decent Literature and the Arousal of an Antiporn Public in the 1960s," 15 *Journal of the History of Sexuality* 258 (May, 2006).

—Sultan, Allen. "The Proposed Constitutional Amendments and the Oklahoma Bar," 34 *Oklahoma Bar Journal* 1535 (August, 1963).

—Swindler, William F. "The Current Challenge to Federalism: The Confederate Proposals," 52 *Georgetown Law Journal* 1 (Fall, 1963).

—Tannenbaum, Donald G. "Explaining Controversial Nominations: The Fortas Case Revisited," 17 *Presidential Studies Quarterly* 573 (Summer, 1987).

—Ulmer, S. Sidney. "The Analysis of Behavior Patterns on the United States Supreme Court," 22 *Journal of Politics* 629 (November, 1960).

—Warren, Earl. "Dedication of the New Duke Law School Building," 3 *Duke Law Journal* 386 (Summer, 1963).

—Warren, Earl. "Let's Not Weaken the Supreme Court," 60 *American Bar Association Journal* 677 (June, 1974).

—Wedeking, Justin and Dion Farganis. "Supreme Court Nominee Candor and Judiciary Committee Votes: Does Answering Questions Really Matter?" (Delivered at the American Political Science Association Conference, Washington D.C., September, 2010).

—Wilcox, Clyde. "Sources of Support for the Old Right: A Comparison of the John Birch Society and the Christian Anti-Communism Crusade," 12 *Social Science History* 429 (Winter, 1988).

Booklets and Pamphlets

—American Enterprise Institute, *A Convention to Amend the Constitution?* (1967).

—Conference of Chief Justices, *The History of the Conference of Chief Justices: In Commemoration of its 60th Anniversary* (2009).

—Equal Justice Initiative, *Lynching in America: Confronting the Legacy of Racial Terror*, 2nd Ed. (2015).

—Lilly Library (Indiana University), *The Art of Leadership: A Companion to an Exhibition from the Senatorial Papers of Birch Bayh* (2007).

Books & Chapters in Books

—Abraham, Henry J. *Justices, Presidents, and Senators: A History of the U.S. Supreme Court Appointments from Washington to Bush II*. 5th Ed. Lanham: Rowman & Littlefield, 2008.

—Ambrose, Stephen E. *Eisenhower*, Vol. I. New York: Simon & Schuster, 1983.

—Ambrose, Stephen E. *Eisenhower*, Vol. II. New York: Simon & Schuster, 1984.

—Ambrose, Stephen E. *Nixon: The Triumph of a Politician, 1962-1972*. New York: Simon & Schuster, 1989.

—Ayers, Edward L. *Vengeance & Justice: Crime and Punishment in the 19th Century American South*. New York: Oxford University Press, 1986.

—Badger, Anthony J. *New Deal/New South: An Anthony J. Badger Reader*. Fayetteville: University of Arkansas Press, 2007.

—Baker, Liva. *Miranda: Crime, Law and Politics*. New York: Atheneum, 1983.

—Ball, Howard. *Hugo L. Black: Cold Steel Warrior*. New York: Oxford University Press, 1996.

—Banner Jr., James M. *To the Hartford Convention: The Federalists and the Origins of Party Politics in Massachusetts, 1789-1815*. New York: Knopf, 1970.

—Bass, Jack and Marilyn W. Thompson. *Ol' Strom: An Unauthorized Biography of Strom Thurmond*. Marietta: Longstreet Press, 1998.

—Bass, Jack and Marilyn W. Thompson. *Strom: The Complicated Personal and Political Life of Strom Thurmond*. New York: Public Affairs, 2005.

—Belknap, Michal, ed. *American Political Trials*. Westport: Praeger, 1994.

—Beschloss, Michael R. *Reaching for Glory: Lyndon Johnson's Secret White House Tapes, 1964-1965*. New York: Touchstone, 2001.

—Bickel, Alexander M. *The Least Dangerous Branch: The Supreme Court at the Bar of Politics*. 2nd Ed. New Haven: Yale University Press, 1986.

—Binstein, Michael and Charles Bowden. *Trust Me: Charles Keating and the Missing Billions*. New York: Random House, 1993.

—Black, Conrad. *Richard M. Nixon: A Life in Full*. New York: Public Affairs, 2007.

—Black, Hugo and Elizabeth Black. *Mr. Justice and Mrs. Black*. New York: Random House, 1986.

—Blum, John Morton. *Years of Discord: American Politics and Society, 1961-1974*. New York: W.W. Norton, 1992.

—Bozell, L. Brent. *The Warren Revolution: Reflections on the Consensus Society*. New Rochelle: Arlington House, 1966.

—Branch, Taylor. *Parting the Waters: America in the King Years, 1954-63*. New York: Touchstone, 1989.

—Brune, Lester H., ed. *The Korean War: Handbook of the Literature and Research*. Westport: Greenwood Press, 1996.

—Buchanan, Patrick J. *The Greatest Comeback: How Richard Nixon Rose from Defeat to Create the New Majority*. New York: Crown, 2014.

—Burt, Robert A. *The Constitution in Conflict*. Cambridge: Belknap Press, 1992.

—Califano Jr., Joseph A., *The Triumph & Tragedy of Lyndon Johnson: The White House Years*. New York: Touchstone, 2015.

—Calluori, Joseph. "The Supreme Court Under Siege: The Battle Over Nixon's Nominees." In *Richard M. Nixon: Politician, President, Administrator*, edited by Leon Friedman and William F. Levantrosser. Westport: Greenwood Press, 1991.

—Cardozo, Benjamin N. *The Nature of the Judicial Process*. New Haven: Yale University Press, 1921.

—Caro, Robert A. *The Years of Lyndon Johnson: Master of the Senate*. New York: Vintage Books, 2003.

—Caro, Robert A. *The Years of Lyndon Johnson: The Path to Power*. New York: Vintage Books, 1990.

—Carter, Dan T. *The Politics of Rage: George Wallace, The Origins of the New Conservatism, and the Transformation of American Politics*. New York: Simon & Schuster, 1995.

—Carter, Stephen L. *The Confirmation Mess: Cleaning up the Federal Appointments Process*. New York: Basic Books, 1994.

—Chapman, Bruce K. and George F. Gilder. *The Party that Lost its Head*. New York: Knopf, 1966.

—Chester, Lewis et al. *An American Melodrama: The Presidential Campaign of 1968*. New York: Viking Press, 1969.

—Christman, Henry M., ed. *The Public Papers of Chief Justice Earl Warren*. New York:

Simon & Schuster, 1959.

—Clifford, Clark M. *Counsel to the President: A Memoir*. New York: Random House, 1991.

—Cohodas, Nadine. *Strom Thurmond and the Politics of Southern Change*. New York: Simon & Schuster, 1993.

—Courtney, Kent and Phoebe Courtney. *America's Unelected Rulers*. New Orleans: Conservative Society of America, 1962.

—Cover, Robert M. *Justice Accused: Antislavery and the Judicial Process*. New Haven: Yale University Press, 1975.

—Cowan, Geoffrey. *Let the People Rule: Theodore Roosevelt and the Birth of the Presidential Primary*. New York: W.W. Norton, 2016.

—Craven, Avery. *The Coming of the Civil War*. 2nd Ed. Chicago: University of Chicago Press, 1974.

—Crespino, Joseph. *Strom Thurmond's America*. New York: Hill & Wang, 2012.

—Currie, David P. *The Constitution in the Supreme Court: The First Hundred Years, 1789-1888*. Chicago: University of Chicago Press, 1985.

—Currie, David P. *The Constitution in the Supreme Court: The Second Century, 1888-1986*. Chicago: University of Chicago Press, 1990.

—Dallek, Robert. *Flawed Giant: Lyndon Johnson and His Times, 1961-1973*. New York: Oxford University Press, 1998.

—Dallek, Robert. *Lone Star Rising: Lyndon Johnson and His Times, 1908-1960*. New York: Oxford University Press, 1991.

—Dallek, Robert. *Lyndon B. Johnson: Portrait of a President*. New York: Oxford University Press, 2004.

—Day, John Kyle. *The Southern Manifesto: Massive Resistance and the Fight to Preserve Segregation*. Jackson: University Press of Mississippi, 2014.

—Dean, John W. *The Rehnquist Choice: The Untold Story of the Nixon Appointment that Redefined the Supreme Court*. New York: Touchstone, 2002.

—Dent, Harry S. *The Prodigal South Returns to Power*. New York: John Wiley & Sons, 1978.

—Dierenfield, Bruce J. *The Battle Over School Prayer: How Engel v. Vitale Changed America*. Lawrence: University of Kansas Press, 2007.

—Dierenfield, Bruce J. "Public Response to *Engel v. Vitale*." In *The Public Debate Over Contro-*

versial Supreme Court Decisions, Melvin I. Urofsky ed. Washington, D.C.: CQ Press, 2006.

—Dixon Jr., Robert G. *Democratic Representation: Reapportionment in Law and Politics*. New York: Oxford University Press, 1968.

—Doren, Carl Van. *The Great Rehearsal: The Story of the Making and Ratifying of the Constitution of the United States*. Alexandria: Time-Life Books, 1976.

—Douglas, William O. *The Autobiography of William O. Douglas: The Court Years, 1939-1975*. New York: Random House, 1980.

—Douglas, William O. *Points of Rebellion*. New York: Random House, 1970.

—Douglas, William and Melvin I. Urofsky, eds. *The Douglas Letters: Selections from the Private Papers of Justice William O. Douglas*. Bethesda: Adler & Adler, 1987.

—Douth, George. *Leaders in Profile: the United States Senate*. New York: Speer & Douth, 1972.

—Edsall, Thomas B. and Mary D. Edsall. *Chain Reaction: The Impact of Race, Rights, and Taxes on American Politics*. New York: W.W. Norton, 1991.

—Ehrlichman, John. *Witness to Power: The Nixon Years*. New York: Simon & Schuster, 1982.

—Eisenhower, Dwight D. *The Eisenhower Diaries*, edited by Robert H. Ferrell. New York: W.W. Norton, 1981.

—Eisenhower, Dwight D. *Mandate for Change, 1953-1956: The White House Years*. Garden City: Doubleday & Co., 1963.

—Eisenhower, Dwight D. *Waging Peace, 1956-1961: The White House Years*. Garden City: Doubleday & Co., 1965.

—Epstein, Benjamin R. and Arnold Forster. *Report on the John Birch Society, 1966*. New York: Random House, 1966.

—Evans, Rowland and Robert Novak. *Lyndon B. Johnson: The Exercise of Power*. New York: New American Library, 1966.

—Evans, Rowland and Robert Novak. *Nixon in the White House: The Frustration of Power*. New York: Random House, 1971.

—Farrand, Max. *The Framing of the Constitution of the United States*. New Haven: Yale University Press, 1913.

—Farrand, Max, ed. *The Records of the Federal Convention of 1787*. Vols. I-III. New Haven: Yale University Press, 1966.

—Feldman, Noah. *Scorpions: The Battles and Triumphs of FDR's Great Supreme Court Jus-*

tices. New York: Twelve, 2010.

—Finley, Keith M. *Delaying the Dream: Southern Senators and the Fight Against Civil Rights, 1938-1965*. Baton Rouge: LSU Press, 2008.

—Fite, Gilbert C. *Richard B. Russell, Jr., Senator from Georgia*. Chapel Hill: University of North Carolina Press, 2002.

—Foner, Eric. *Free Soil, Free Labor, Free Men: The Ideology of the Republican Party Before the Civil War*. New York: Oxford University Press, 1995.

—Foner, Eric. *Reconstruction: America's Unfinished Revolution, 1863-1877*. New York: Harper & Row, 1989.

—Frank, Jeffrey. *Ike and Dick: Portrait of a Strange Political Marriage*. New York: Simon & Schuster, 2013.

—Frank, John P. *Clement Haynsworth, the Senate and the Supreme Court*. Charlottesville: University Press of Virginia, 1991.

—Frankfurter, Felix with Joseph P. Lash, ed. *From the Diaries of Felix Frankfurter*. New York, W.W. Norton, 1975.

—Freedman, Samuel G. *The Inheritance: How Three Families and the American Political Majority Moved From Left to Right*. New York: Touchstone, 1998.

—Friedman, Lawrence M. *A History of American Law*. 2nd ed. New York: Touchstone, 1985.

—Frum, David. *How We Got Here: The 70's: The Decade that Brought You to Modern Life (For Better or Worse)*. New York: Basic, 2000.

—Galbraith, John Kenneth. *A Life in our Times*. New York: Ballantine Books, 1981.

—Gallup, George H. *The Gallup Poll: Public Opinion, 1935-1971*. Vols. 1-3. New York: Random House, 1972.

—Garrow, David J. *Bearing the Cross: Martin Luther King, Jr., and the Southern Christian Leadership Conference*. New York: William Morrow & Co., 1986.

—Garrow, David J., ed. *Martin Luther King, Jr.: Civil Rights Leader, Theologian, Orator*. Vol. 3. Brooklyn: Carlson Publishing, 1989.

—Gates, Robbins L. *The Making of Massive Resistance: Virginia's Politics of Public School Desegregation, 1954-1956*. Chapel Hill: University of North Carolina Press, 1964.

—Gillman, Howard. *The Constitution Besieged: The Rise and Demise of Lochner Era Police Powers Jurisprudence*. Durham: Duke University Press, 1995.

—Gilmore, Grant. *The Ages of American Law*. New Haven: Yale University Press, 1977.

—Ginsburg, Ruth Bader. *My Own Words*. New York: Simon & Schuster, 2016.

—Gitlin, Todd. *The Sixties: Year of Hope, Days of Rage*. New York: Bantam, 1987.

—Goldberg, Robert Alan. *Barry Goldwater*. New Haven: Yale University Press, 1995.

—Goldwater, Barry. *The Conscience of a Conservative*. Shepherdsville: Victor Publishing, 1960.

—Gore, Albert. *Let the Glory Out: My South and Its Politics*. New York: Viking Press, 1972.

—Gunther, Gerald. *Learned Hand: The Man and the Judge*. New York: Knopf, 1994.

—Haldeman, H.R. *The Haldeman Diaries: Inside the Nixon White House*. London: Endeavour Press, 2017. Kindle edition.

—Hamilton, Alexander et al. *The Federalist*. London: Everyman's Library, 1992.

—Harris, Richard. *Decision*. New York: E.P. Dutton & Co., 1971.

—Haygood, Wil. *Showdown: Thurgood Marshall and the Supreme Court Nomination that Changed America*. New York: Knopf, 2015.

—Hays, Samuel P. *The Response to Industrialism, 1885-1914*. Chicago: University of Chicago Press, 1957.

—Heath, Jim F. *Decade of Disillusionment: The Kennedy-Johnson Years*. Bloomington: Indiana University Press, 1975.

—Hoff, Joan. *Nixon Reconsidered*. New York: Basic Books, 1994.

—Hofstadter, Richard. *The Age of Reform*. New York: Vintage Books, 1955.

—Hofstadter, Richard. *The American Political Tradition and the Men Who Made It*. New York: Vintage Books, 1989.

—Holt, Michael F. *The Fate of Their Country: Politicians, Slavery Extension, and the Coming of the Civil War*. New York: Hill & Wang, 2004.

—Horwitz, Morton J. *The Transformation of American Law, 1780-1860*. New York: Oxford University Press, 1992.

—Horwitz, Morton J. *The Warren Court and the Pursuit of Justice*. New York: Hill & Wang, 1999.

—Hulsey, Byron C. *Everett Dirksen and His Presidents: How a Senate Giant Shaped American Politics*. Lawrence: University Press of Kansas, 2000.

—Hustwit, William P. *James J. Kilpatrick: Salesman for Segregation*. Chapel Hill: University of North Carolina Press, 2013.

—Hyman, Harold M. and William M. Wiecek. *Equal Justice Under Law: Constitutional Development, 1835-1875*. New York: Harper & Row, 1982.

—Hyneman, Charles S. *The Supreme Court on Trial*. New York: Atherton Press, 1963.

—Jenkins, John A. *The Partisan: The Life of William Rehnquist*. New York: Public Affairs, 2012.

—Johnson, Lyndon B. *The Vantage Point: Perspectives of the Presidency, 1963-1969*. New York: Holt, Rinehart and Winston, 1971.

—Kalman, Laura. *Abe Fortas: A Biography*. New Haven: Yale University Press, 1990.

—Kalman, Laura. *The Long Reach of the Sixties: LBJ, Nixon, and the Making of the Contemporary Supreme Court*. New York: Oxford University Press, 2017.

—Kluger, Richard. *Simple Justice: The History of Brown v. Board of Education and Black America's Struggle for Equality*. New York: Vintage, 2004.

—Leuchtenburg, William E. *The Supreme Court Reborn: The Constitutional Revolution in the Age of Roosevelt*. New York: Oxford University Press, 1995.

—Lewis, John with Michael D'Orso. *Walking with the Wind: A Memoir of the Movement*. New York: Simon & Schuster, 1998.

—Link, Arthur S. *Wilson: The Road to the White House*. Princeton: Princeton University Press, 1968.

—Lytle, Clifford. *The Warren Court and its Critics*. Tucson: University of Arizona Press, 1968.

—MacNeil, Neil. *Dirksen: Portrait of a Public Man*. New York: The World Publishing Company, 1970.

—Maltese, John A. *The Selling of Supreme Court Nominees*. Baltimore: Johns Hopkins University Press, 1995.

—Mann, Robert. *The Walls of Jericho: Lyndon Johnson, Hubert Humphrey, Richard Russell, and the Struggle for Civil Rights*. New York: Harvest Book, 1996.

—Massaro, John. *Supremely Political: The Role of Ideology and Presidential Management in Unsuccessful Supreme Court Nominations*. Albany: SUNY Press, 1990.

—Mason, Robert. *Richard Nixon and the Quest for a New Majority*. Chapel Hill: University of North Carolina Press, 2004.

—Matusow, Allen J. *The Unraveling of America: A History of Liberalism in the 1960s*. New

York: Harper Torchbooks, 1986.

—Maxwell, Angie. *The Indicted South: Public Criticism, Southern Inferiority, and the Politics of Whiteness*. Chapel Hill: University of North Carolina Press, 2014.

—Mayer, Jeremy D. *Running on Race: Racial Politics in Presidential Campaigns, 1960-2000*. New York: Random House, 2002.

—McCloskey, Robert G. *The American Supreme Court*. 2nd Ed. Chicago: University of Chicago Press, 1994.

—McCullough, David. *Truman*. New York: Simon & Schuster, 1992.

—McMahon, Kevin J. *Nixon's Court: His Challenge to Judicial Liberalism and Its Political Consequences*. Chicago: University of Chicago Press, 2011.

—McPherson, Harry. *A Political Education: A Washington Memoir*. Austin: University of Texas Press, 1995.

—Miller, Merle. *Lyndon: An Oral Biography*. New York: Ballantine Books, 1981.

—Mitau, G. Theodore. *Decade of Decision: The Supreme Court and the Constitutional Revolution, 1954-1964*. New York: Charles Scribner's Sons, 1967.

—Moore, Glen. "Richard Nixon: The Southern Strategy and the 1968 Presidential Election." In *Richard M. Nixon: Politician, President, Administrator*, edited by Leon Friedman and William F. Levantrosser. Westport: Greenwood Press, 1991.

—Mulloy, D.J. *The World of the John Birch Society: Conspiracy, Conservativism, and the Cold War*. Nashville: Vanderbilt University Press, 2014.

—Murphy, Bruce Allen. *Fortas: The Rise and Ruin of a Supreme Court Justice*. New York: William Morrow & Co., 1988.

—Murphy, Bruce Allen. *Wild Bill: The Legend and Life of William O. Douglas*. New York: Random House, 2003.

—Murphy, Reg and Hal Gulliver. *The Southern Strategy*. New York: Scribner, 1971.

—Murphy, Walter F. *Congress and the Court: A Case Study in the American Political Process*. New Orleans: Quid Pro Books, 2014. Kindle edition.

—Newman, Roger K. *Hugo Black: A Biography*. New York: Pantheon Books, 1994.

—Newton, Jim. *Justice for All: Earl Warren and the Nation he Made*. New York: Riverhead Books, 2006.

—Nixon, Richard M. *The Memoirs of Richard Nixon*. New York: Grosset & Dunlap, 1978.

—Nixon, Richard M. & Rick Perlstein, ed. *Speeches, Writings, Documents*. Princeton: Princeton University Press, 2008.

—O'Brien, David M. *Storm Center: The Supreme Court in American Politics*. New York: W.W. Norton, 1986.

—O'Neill, William L. *Coming Apart: An Informal History of America in the 1960's*. New York: Times Books, 1971.

—Pach Jr., Chester J. and Elmo Richardson. *The Presidency of Dwight D. Eisenhower*. Lawrence: University Press of Kansas, 1991.

—Parmet, Herbert S. *Richard Nixon and his America*. Boston: Little Brown, 1990.

—Perlstein, Rick. *Before the Storm: Barry Goldwater and the Unmaking of the American Consensus*. New York: Nation Books, 2009.

—Perlstein, Rick. *The Invisible Bridge: The Fall of Nixon and the Rise of Reagan*. New York: Simon & Schuster, 2014.

—Perlstein, Rick. *Nixonland: The Rise of a President and the Fracturing of America*. New York: Scribner, 2009.

—Phillips, Kevin P. *The Emerging Republican Majority*. New Rochelle: Arlington House, 1969.

—Polenberg, Richard. *One Nation Divisible: Class, Race, and Ethnicity in the United States Since 1938*. New York: Penguin Books, 1980.

—Powe Jr., Lucas A. *The Warren Court and American Politics*. Cambridge: Belknap Press, 2001.

—Pritchett, C. Herman. *Congress versus the Supreme Court, 1957-1960*. Minneapolis: University of Minnesota Press, 1961.

—Rakove, Jack N., ed. *Interpreting the Constitution: The Debate over Original Intent*. Boston: Northeastern University Press, 1990.

—Rakove, Jack N. *Original Meanings: Politics and Ideas in the Making of the Constitution*. New York: Vintage Books, 1996.

—Reeves, Richard. *President Nixon: Alone in the White House*. New York: Simon & Schuster, 2007.

—Reichley, A. James. *Conservatives in an Age of Change: The Nixon and Ford Administrations*. Washington, D.C.: Brookings Institution, 2010.

—Roberts, Gene and Hank Klibanoff. *The Race Beat: The Press, the Civil Rights Struggle, and the Awakening of a Nation*. New York: Knopf, 2006.

—Sabin, Arthur J. *In Calmer Times: The Supreme Court and Red Monday*. Philadelphia: University of Pennsylvania Press, 1999.

—Safire, William. *Before the Fall: An Inside View of the Pre-Watergate White House*. Garden City: Doubleday & Co., 1975.

—Schlesinger Jr., Arthur M., ed. *History of U.S. Political Parties*. Vol. IV. New York: Chelsea House Publishers, 1973.

—Schlesinger Jr., Arthur M. *Robert Kennedy and His Times*. Boston: Mariner Books, 2002.

—Schlesinger Jr., Arthur M. *A Thousand Days: John F. Kennedy in the White House*. Boston: Houghton Mifflin Company, 1965.

—Schoenwald, Jonathan M. *A Time for Choosing: The Rise of Modern American Conservatism*. New York: Oxford University Press, 2001.

—Schwartz, Bernard. *A History of the Supreme Court*. New York: Oxford University Press, 1993.

—Schwartz, Bernard. *Super Chief: Earl Warren and his Supreme Court—A Judicial Biography*. New York: NYU Press, 1983.

—Schwartz, Bernard with Stephan Lesher. *Inside the Warren Court*. Garden City: Doubleday & Co., 1983.

—Shaffer, Samuel. *On and Off the Floor: Thirty Years as a Correspondent on Capitol Hill*. New York: Newsweek Books, 1980.

—Shapiro, Ira. *The Last Great Senate: Courage and Statesmanship in Times of Crisis*. New York: Public Affairs, 2012.

—Shogan, Robert. *A Question of Judgment: The Fortas Case and the Struggle for the Supreme Court*. Indianapolis: Bobbs-Merrill Company, 1972.

—Short, R.J. Duke. *The Centennial Senator: True Stories of Strom Thurmond from the People Who Knew Him Best*. Columbia: University of South Carolina Press, 2008.

—Silverstein, Mark. *Judicious Choices*. New York: W.W. Norton, 1994.

—Simon, James F. *Eisenhower vs. Warren: The Battle for Civil Rights and Liberties*. New York: W.W. Norton, 2018.

—Simon, James F. *FDR and Chief Justice Hughes: The President, the Supreme Court, and the Epic Battle Over the New Deal*. New York: Simon & Schuster, 2012.

—Simon, James F. *Independent journey: the life of William O. Douglas*. New York: Harper &

Row, 1980.

—Small, Melvin. *The Presidency of Richard Nixon*. Lawrence: University of Kansas Press, 1999.

—Smith, J. Douglas. *On Democracy's Doorstep: The Inside Story of How the Supreme Court Brought "One Person, One Vote" to the United States*. New York: Hill & Wang, 2014.

—Stampp, Kenneth M. *The Era of Reconstruction: 1865-1877*. New York: Vintage Books, 1965.

—Stephenson Jr., Donald Grier. *Campaigns and the Court: The U.S. Supreme Court in Presidential Elections*. New York: Columbia University Press, 1999.

—Stern, Seth and Stephen Wermiel. *Justice Brennan: Liberal Champion*. Boston: Houghton Mifflin Harcourt, 2010.

—Strober, Gerald S. and Deborah H. *Nixon: An Oral History of his Presidency*. New York: HarperCollins, 1994.

—Strub, Whitney. *Perversion for Profit: The Politics of Pornography and the Rise of the New Right*. New York: Columbia University Press, 2010.

—Teles, Steven M. *The Rise of the Conservative Legal Movement: The Battle for Control of the Law*. Princeton: Princeton University Press, 2008.

—Thurmond, Strom. *The Faith We Have Not Kept*. San Diego: Viewpoint Books, 1968.

—Toobin, Jeffrey. *The Nine: Inside the Secret World of the Supreme Court*. New York: Doubleday, 2007.

—Toobin, Jeffrey. *The Oath: The Obama White House and the Supreme Court*. New York: Doubleday, 2012.

—Tushnet, Mark V. *Making Civil Rights Law: Thurgood Marshall and the Supreme Court, 1936-1961*. New York: Oxford University Press, 1996.

—Tushnet, Mark V., ed. *The Warren Court in Historical and Political Perspective*. Charlottesville: University Press of Virginia, 1993.

—Unger, Irwin and Debi Unger. *LBJ: A Life*. New York: Wiley & Sons, 1999.

—Warren, Earl. *The Memoirs of Chief Justice Earl Warren*. Lanham: Madison Books, 2001.

—Weaver, John D. *Warren: The Man, the Court, the Era*. London: Victor Gollancz, 1968.

—White, G. Edward. *Earl Warren: A Public Life*. New York: Oxford University Press, 1982.

—White, G. Edward. *Justice Oliver Wendell Holmes: Law and the Inner Self*. New York: Oxford University Press, 1993.

—White, Theodore H. *America in Search of Itself: The Making of the President, 1956-1980*. New York: Warner Books, 1982.

—White, Theodore H. *The Making of the President 1960*. New York: Atheneum Publishers, 1988.

—White, Theodore H. *The Making of the President 1964*. New York: Atheneum Publishers, 1965.

—White, Theodore H. *The Making of the President 1968*. New York: Atheneum Publishers, 1969.

—White, William S. *Citadel: The Story of the U.S. Senate*. New York: Harper & Brothers, 1956.

—Williams, Juan. *Thurgood Marshall: American Revolutionary*. New York: Times Books, 1998.

—Woods, Randall B. *LBJ: Architect of American Ambition*. New York: Free Press, 2006.

—Woodward, Bob and Scott Armstrong. *The Brethren: Inside the Supreme Court*. New York: Simon & Schuster, 2005.

—Woodward, C. Vann. *Origins of the New South, 1877-1913*. Baton Rouge: LSU Press, 1995.

—Yalof, David Alistair. *Pursuit of Justices: Presidential Politics and the Selection of Supreme Court Nominees*. Chicago: University of Chicago Press, 1999.

Dissertations, Research Reports & Working Papers

—Association of the Bar of the City of New York, Federal Legislation Committee, "Checks and Balances: Congressional Restriction of Federal Court Jurisdiction."

—Devins, Neal and Lawrence Baum, "Split Definitive: How Party Polarization Turned the Supreme Court into a Partisan Court," William & Mary Law School Research Paper No. 09-0276.

—Fadely, Lawrence D. *George Wallace: Agitator Rhetorician. A Rhetorical Criticism of George Corley Wallace's 1968 Presidential Campaign* (University of Pittsburgh – Pittsburgh, 1974).

—Huntington, John S. *Right-Wing Paranoid Blues: The Role of Radicalism in Modern Conservatism* (University of Houston – Houston, 2016).

—Jones, Hugh E. *The Defeat of the Nomination of Abe Fortas as Chief Justice of the United States: A Case Study in Judicial Politics* (John Hopkins University – Baltimore, 1976).

—Landes, William M. and Richard A. Posner, "Rational Judicial Behavior: A Statistical Study," John M. Olin Law & Economics Working Paper No. 404.

—Massaro, John L. *Advice and Dissent: Factors in the Senate's Refusal to Confirm Supreme Court Nominees, With Special Emphasis on the Cases of Abe Fortas, Clement F. Haynsworth Jr. and G. Harrold Carswell* (Southern Illinois University – Carbondale, 1973).

—Poder, Michael Paul. *The Senatorial Career of William E. Jenner* (University of Notre Dame – South Bend, 1976).

—Ross, Rodney Joel. *Senator William E. Jenner: A Study in Cold War Isolationism* (Pennsylvania State University – Happy Valley, 1973).

—Ross, William G., "Attacks on the Warren Court by State Officials: A Case Study of why Court-Curbing Movements Fail," (August 1, 2001). Available at SSRN: https://ssrn.com/abstract=282013.

—Wallach, Jennifer Jensen. *Remembering Jim Crow: the literary memoir as historical source material* (University of Massachusetts – Amherst, 2004).

—Westerhoff, Arjen. *Politics of Protest: Strom Thurmond and the Development of the Republican Southern Strategy, 1948-1972* (Smith College – Northampton, 1997).

INDEX